# THE FRAGILE MIDDLE CLASS

# The Fragile Middle Class

## Americans in Debt

Teresa A. Sullivan

Elizabeth Warren

Jay Lawrence Westbrook

Yale University Press   New Haven and London

Designed by James J. Johnson and set in E&F Swift type by Tseng Information Systems, Inc.
Printed in the United States of America by Vail-Ballou Press, Binghamton, New York.

*Library of Congress Cataloging-in-Publication Data*

Sullivan, Teresa A., 1949–
The fragile middle class : Americans in debt / Teresa A. Sullivan,
Elizabeth Warren, Jay Lawrence Westbrook.
     p.     cm.
  Includes bibliographical references and index.
  ISBN 0-300-07960-5 (alk. paper)

  1. Bankruptcy—United States.   2. Consumer credit—United States.
3. Finance, Personal—United States.   I. Warren, Elizabeth.
II. Westbrook, Jay Lawrence.   III. Title.
HG3766.S794   2000
332.7'5'0673—dc21                                99-41894

A catalogue record for this book is available from the British Library.

The paper in this book meets the guidelines for permanence and durability of the
Committee on Production Guidelines for Book Longevity of the Council on Library
Resources.

10 9 8 7 6 5 4 3 2 1

*In memory of our parents*

GORDON H. & MARY E. SULLIVAN

DONALD J. & PAULINE REED HERRING

JOEL & ELAINE WESTBROOK

*They taught us the middle-class values that carried them through the Great Depression and World War II to the prosperity that followed*

# Contents

**CONTENTS**

# Illustrations

ILLUSTRATIONS

# Tables

# Preface

In 1989 we published *As We Forgive Our Debtors: Bankruptcy and Consumer Credit in America* (Oxford University Press 1989; reprint, Beard Books, 1999), a study of people who filed for bankruptcy in 1981. In that book we compared how the bankruptcy process was supposed to work with how it was actually working. That project, dubbed the Consumer Bankruptcy Project, provided a great deal of information, but it also posed questions we could not adequately answer. One of the most important of those questions was why so many families were in economic trouble.

That question formed a cornerstone for the current project, Consumer Bankruptcy Project II. Conducted in 1991, this second study collected the same information from some of the case files, but it added a questionnaire for all the debtors in our sample. With the questionnaires, we were able to collect demographic data as well as information about why the respondents filed for bankruptcy. These data permit us to compare the debtors with the general population, so we could learn about the economic fractures in American society by looking at the people in bankruptcy. Our prior book was about bankruptcy and the people in bankruptcy; this book is about the middle class as viewed through the lens of bankruptcy.

Throughout the 1990s bankruptcy filings soared—and so did the stock market. The juxtaposition of prolonged economic prosperity with high rates of personal economic failure is a paradox we seek to explain. We argue that the problems that have driven the petitioners into bankruptcy are in fact widespread and indicate the fault lines that underlie the apparent economic stability of the American middle class. Many in the middle class are economically fragile, barely able to maintain their lifestyle. The bankrupt debtors represent those who have publicly announced their economic failure, but the fragility is wider and deeper than many observers of the middle class have acknowledged.

Readers of our earlier book may be disappointed to find that we do not use this volume to update our earlier findings about bankruptcy. We leave that task to articles we have written for the professional periodical literature. Our intention here is different: not to learn about bankruptcy but to discover what bankrupt debtors can tell us about the rest of society.

We are grateful to many people and institutions for their assistance in completing this book, although any opinions, conclusions, and recommendations do not necessarily reflect the views of any of those who provided funding or other support for our efforts. Our first debt is to the Education Endowment of the National Conference of Bankruptcy Judges, whose grant made possible the initial collection of data. We are also grateful for financial support and computing equipment made available by Dean Colin Driver of the University of Pennsylvania Law School, Dean Robert Clark of Harvard University Law School, and former Dean Mark G. Yudof and current Dean M. Michael Sharlot of the University of Texas School of Law. Support from Harvard was made possible by the partners of Cleary, Gottlieb, Steen, & Hamilton, who honored their founder, Leo Gottlieb, with their generous contributions for research, and particularly by Jerome Hyman, whose advocacy on behalf of legal education has been extraordinary. We received funds to pay graduate assistants through the University Research Institute at the University of Texas at Austin and the Cox & Smith, Inc., Faculty Fellowship at the University of Texas School of Law. Because Judge Arthur Moeller was himself so committed to legal scholarship in general and to empirical work in particular, we were especially pleased to receive important support from the Arthur Moeller Chair for Research in Bankruptcy and Com-</p>

mercial Law at the University of Texas School of Law. We received summer undergraduate assistance through the Research Experience for Undergraduates project, which is funded by the National Science Foundation and administered through the Population Research Center at the University of Texas at Austin. The Rockefeller Foundation provided additional research support at its Bellagio Study Center. The magnitude of these contributions reminds us that empirical research is an expensive, lengthy, and arduous undertaking. For all these contributions, we are deeply grateful and mindful that without them we would have no data to analyze.

It was necessary to mobilize a large research team to complete this project, and we were fortunate to work with wonderful people. Catherine Nicholson supervised the data collection, and no research team was ever blessed with a more capable and dedicated person. Without her remarkably hard work and extraordinary talents, this project would not have been possible. For collection of a mountain of data, we especially want to thank Judy Tumbleson of Rock Island, Illinois, who gathered data from courthouses in Illinois for both our first and our second consumer bankruptcy studies. Linda Zimmermann gathered our comparison sample from the Eastern District of Pennsylvania; we recall her cheerful efficiency with great fondness. The Honorable Samuel Bufford and the Honorable Keith Lundin provided unswerving support for our empirical undertakings. The Office of the United States Trustee and the Administrative Office of the United States Courts both provided enormous assistance that we gratefully acknowledge. A host of people in the Texas bankruptcy courts helped us gather the data there. In Pennsylvania, the Honorable Thomas C. Gibbons and the Honorable Joseph Cosetti, along with Joseph Simmons, Carol Emerich, Theodore S. Hopkins, Margaret Smith, Thomas E. Ross, Steve Goldring, Brian J. Williams, John J. Grauer, and Jean Vajda, were very helpful. In California, the Honorable Lisa Hill Fenning, the Honorable Christopher Klein, the Honorable Thomas E. Carlson, and the Honorable James W. Meyers, along with Shawnna Jarrott, Sandra Whitman, Lorraine Green, Larry Ramsey, Anthony G. Sousa, Diana Gilbertson, and Charmayne Mills, worked hard under trying conditions to help us collect useful samples. In Indiana, E. Franklin Childress and, in Texas, the Hon. Larry Kelley and William T. Neary gave us important help in our collection efforts. In Illinois, the Honorable Larry L. Lessen and the Honorable John D. Schwartz, along with Thomas J. Mackin, Harden W. Hawes, Ray Safanda, Ella J. Bright, and Randall W. Moon, assisted in our data collection efforts. In Tennessee, the Honorable George Paine II, Beth Broomfield, and Jed Weintraub offered their help cheerfully and efficiently.

Any effort to do research on a tight budget requires the special efforts of generous friends, and in that category we must include Judge Bufford's assistants, Gloria Faust, and Judge Lundin's assistants, Lisa Perlen and Anne Davis, along with Steven Reed at Stutman Treister & Glatt and Kenneth Klee, who arranged for Stutman's support in copying cases. Without their help, this project would have died in its infancy. Roy Mersky of the University of Texas Law Library procured some very expensive documents for us, and his able librarian David Gunn located elusive reports. William Draper of the University of Pennsylvania Law Library also found reams of data for us. Our thanks go also to H. Spencer Nilson at the Nilson Report for lending us 1981–82 back issues and a full set of 1991–92 and 1992–93 reports. James Watkins and Alaine Becket of Becket & Watkins kept the credit card data coming in for years. An extraordinary group of scholars led by Professor Jacob Ziegel of the University of Toronto Law Faculty exposed us to important data from Canada and elsewhere around the world in connection with a conference on consumer bankruptcy held in Toronto in August 1998. Ronald Mann provided a thoughtful review of the housing chapter, and Lynn LoPucki gave insightful (and sometimes tart) comments throughout.

Matthew Ploeger (before he became Dr. Ploeger) was the outstanding research assistant who designed our database and performed the initial analyses; we are pleased that his doctoral dissertation applied our methods to another issue in federal civil litigation. Carter Hay provided much of the library research that helped make our analysis possible. Other research assistants who ably assisted us with library research, coding, and analysis include Marie Britton, Nicola Fuentes, Melissa Tarun, and Lisa Wyatt. Jennifer Frasier, now herself a published bankruptcy empirical researcher, helped us in the early stages of this project. Grant Mallie contributed additional data analysis, and Ryan Bull and Dirk Suringa provided editorial assistance. David Johnson ably and creatively provided final help with statistics and substance. Elizabeth Guerrero spent countless hours on the final preparation of the manuscript, demonstrating unfailing good humor and supreme professionalism. At Yale University Press, we thank John Covell for his patience and enthusiasm for the project and Laura Jones Dooley for her perceptive editing.

The Honorable Barbara Sellers, a bankruptcy judge in the Southern District of Ohio, collected her own data about 1998 filings in her district and gave us permission to code and analyze the data. The Honorable Randall Newsome, a bankruptcy judge in the Northern District of California, collected data on Chapter 7 filers in 1997 and generously shared them with us. The Honorable Barry Russell, a bankruptcy judge in the Central District of California, gave us access to data he collected over the ten-year period 1975–85. The willingness of these judges to expand their workloads so that they could better understand the debtors in their districts is inspirational, and their willingness to share their work product is exemplary.

As these paragraphs indicate, we owe a great deal to many people, but our foremost debt is to the professionals of the U.S. Bankruptcy Courts, whose dedication in the face of mounting caseloads is inadequately appreciated. We are deeply grateful to all of the bankruptcy judges, their clerks, and the trustees who made our data collection possible in the sixteen districts we used for the study. Their cooperation was essential, and they were cheerful and helpful in providing us access. We must mention in particular the U.S. trustees and their staffs who distributed and collected the questionnaires that provided the heart of our data for this book. They cheerfully added to their already substantial burdens for no return except the improvement of knowledge. Without such public-spiritedness, our sort of research would not be possible.

Our families have continued to tolerate our long-distance co-authorship and our passion for empirical research. In the decade of work on Consumer Bankruptcy Project II, two of us lost our parents and all of us saw children enter college. We experienced many of the stresses reported by our respondents, including buying and selling homes, changing jobs, and handling catastrophic medical expenses. Our problems—and the problems of many readers of this book—differ from those of our respondents principally as a matter of degree, not of kind.

Chapter 1

# Americans in Financial Crisis

In the early years of the Republic's third century, America stands more economically and militarily dominant in the world than ever before. The middle class, backbone of the Republic, has experienced one of the longest runs of economic prosperity in its history. Yet in the bright blue sky there is a line of clouds. We cannot know if it is just another summer squall or a terrible storm headed our way. Prognosticators examine the entrails in their economic models while the rest of us cross our fingers. Stolid middle-class people, such as ourselves, would naturally check the house for holes in the roof and rotten floorboards. We have done just that, and in this book we report what we have found.

To many molders of opinion, the notion that the middle class could be in crisis is remote, even unrealistic. Their part of the middle class is thriving, and they point proudly to the growing ranks of young high-tech millionaires as signs of the success of the great American economic engine. The proportion of Americans living below the poverty level has also declined, suggesting that the benefits of economic expansion have been widespread. To hint at economic vulnerability seems at best naive, perhaps unpatriotic.

For other Americans, however, the 1990s were economically frustrating and confusing. The median real income recovered to its 1989 level only in 1996. For many families, income rose during the decade only because two or more earners went to work. The popular press focused on these dual-earning families who managed thirty-minute suppers, juggled chores with aplomb, and sought quality time with their children. Less often noticed was that all of this work was barely keeping the family financially afloat. In fact, some of these miracle families only *appear* to be afloat. Lurking behind the suburban house, explicit in the divorce settlement, and implicit in the pediatrician's office, is burgeoning consumer debt. The middle-class way of life can be maintained for quite a while with smoke and mirrors — and many credit cards.

In this book we examine hard data about the forces pressing on middle-class Americans. Our focus is primarily on economic effects, although social and moral factors are very much on the table as well. We do not try to resolve the debates, but we can cast some important light on them. With data drawn from federal bankruptcy courts throughout the United States, we can examine the crash victims of the American economy to better understand the financial risks all middle-class Americans face. These data permit us to quantify the stress that arises from five sources: the increased volatility of jobs and income; the explosion of consumer debt with sky-high interest rates; divorce and changing parenting patterns that are increasing the number of single-adult households; the astonishing ability to treat medical problems — at astonishing prices; and the fierce determination that Americans have to buy and retain a family home at all costs.

Our understanding of these middle-class distresses began to emerge in earlier empirical work in the bankruptcy courts. In that study, reported in a book called *As We Forgive Our Debtors: Bankruptcy and Consumer Credit in America* (1989), we found, to our surprise, that Americans in bankruptcy looked a lot like the rest of us. They were not a substratum of day laborers or housemaids but people with the characteristics of the middle class, though with lower-class incomes. Only so much could be learned from courthouse files about the middle-classness of bankrupts, however, so we undertook a second study, reported here, that added questionnaires about the personal characteristics of bankrupts, including their education levels, occupations, and other relevant data. On that basis, we report in this book that the bankrupts do represent a fair cross-section of the American middle class. On that basis, we have realized that our data from the bankruptcy courts was akin to a financial pathology of middle-class Americans. Because people's financial troubles so often arise from other sources, such as divorce or serious illness, they also reflect in part the social pathology of the great middle of American society.

Since World War II the increase in bankruptcy filings in the United States has been relentless, and recently spectacular. The increases accelerated during the 1980s and 1990s, frequently breaking records from quarter to quarter and year to year. Between 1979 and 1997 personal bankruptcy filings increased by more than 400 percent.[1] The upsurge in personal bankruptcies during the mid-1990s was especially striking because it occurred during a widespread economic recovery. Burgeoning financial collapse in the midst of prosperity is particularly poignant and deeply worrisome.

The dynamics of capitalism, combined with a thin social safety net, guarantee that some families will always fail. Without universal health insurance to protect every family from the financial ravages of illness and without higher levels of unemployment compensation to cushion the effects of a layoff, each day, in good times and in bad, some families will fall over the financial edge. And in a market that provides access to almost unlimited amounts of consumer credit, some people will accumulate a debt load that eventually takes on a life of its own—swelling on compound interest, default rates, and penalty payments until it consumes every available dollar of income and still demands more. Just as the poor will always be with us, so will the bankrupt middle class. Yet what makes the phenomenon so noteworthy in our time is that the proportion of middle-class America finding its way to the bankruptcy courts has jumped beyond any reasonable expectation (fig. 1.1).

Will Rogers said during the Great Depression that America was the first country to drive to the poorhouse in an automobile. The automobile remains a potent symbol of the economic times and our financial mores. Americans are buying larger and more luxurious cars, complete with sound systems, computer monitoring devices, and four-wheel drive. These cars, trucks, and vans are better built and

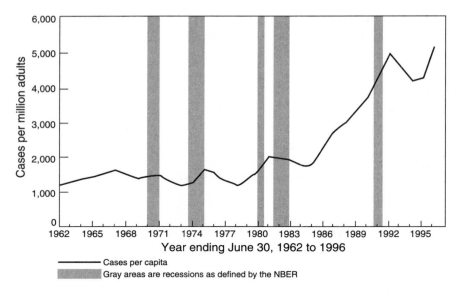

 Cases per capita
Gray areas are recessions as defined by the NBER

Fig. 1.1 Consumer bankruptcy filings, 1962–96. *Source:* Derived from "The Increase in Personal Bankruptcy and the Crisis in Consumer Credit," Hearing Before the Senate Judiciary Committee Subcommittee on Administrative Oversight and the Courts, 105th Cong., 1st sess., (1997), 39 (statement of Kim J. Kowalewski, Chief, Financial and General Macroeconomic Analysis Unit, Macroeconomic Analysis Division, Congressional Budget Office).

safer than ever before. But the breathtaking prices of these gleaming machines require most middle-class buyers to incur hefty debt, repayable over ever-longer periods at high interest rates. A single transaction encapsulates both prosperity and the risk of financial collapse.

The current prosperity is driven to a large extent by consumer debt, while inflation is largely tempered by downsizing and contract employment. Whether the combination of these factors is stable for the economy as a whole remains to be seen, but it is beyond doubt that they create instability for many American families. Even if one assumes that economic forces ultimately balance out, with new jobs and opportunities replacing old ones, transitional interruptions and reductions in income pose serious problems for families with monthly debt obligations. The combination of two elemental factors—increases in debt and uncertainty of income—contributes importantly to middle-class distress.

## AMERICANS IN FINANCIAL CRISIS

## The Bankruptcy Laboratory

In the 1980s, we undertook an empirical study of the debtors who filed for bankruptcy. That study, Phase I of the Consumer Bankruptcy Project, involved about 1,550 debtors from ten judicial districts around the country who filed for bankruptcy in 1981. We examined a systematic sample of 150 consumer bankruptcy cases filed in 1981 in each of ten federal court districts spread across three states: Illinois, Pennsylvania, and Texas. The data collected in Phase I emphasized the financial condition of the debtors, especially their debts, assets, and income. We used the detailed financial and demographic information from these bankruptcy files to draw a picture of those Americans who fell all the way into bankruptcy. We found that the bankruptcy laws served as a social safety net for middle-class people caught in financial reversal. Because of bankruptcy, people who were once solidly middle class did not lose everything and fall into the lower class. Declaring bankruptcy allowed them to shed debt, recover from pressing medical bills, and otherwise free up their income so that they could concentrate on their current bills—groceries, utilities, and medical care—as well as on their old home mortgages, car loans, and taxes. They might not keep much property after bankruptcy, years later they are likely to be still making substantial debt payments, and bankruptcy certainly did not guarantee them a job or good health. What declaring bankruptcy did for them was provide a chance—often a last chance—to retain their middle-class status. They could deal with some of the debts that threatened to move them out of their homes, take away their property, encumber their future incomes, and force them to live with a steady stream of debt collectors. They might sink lower in the middle class, but by dealing with their most overwhelming debts, they could preserve a handhold on their way down the social and economic ladder.

In the 1990s, we undertook Phase II of the Consumer Bankruptcy Project. This study, reported here, was based on a larger sample of people who filed for bankruptcy during 1991 in sixteen federal districts. Once again, the data reveal a middle-class population of bankrupts. For this project we obtained written surveys from debtors in bankruptcy and the court records for the debtors in five of the districts. As a result, we now have more nonfinancial information about these families and their financial collapse.[2] Throughout this book we look both at the court data and the survey data to explore who these people are and to outline their financial woes.

In this book we explore the persistence of the stereotype that bankruptcy is a lower-class, not a middle-class, phenomenon. We also examine the evidence that, even though some upper- and lower-class Americans may find themselves in bankruptcy court, bankruptcy is a largely middle-class phenomenon. As measured by the key nonmonetary measures we can develop—information about educational levels and occupations—the people in bankruptcy are solidly middle class. And even the monetary data, which show a substantial portion of the debtors in poverty, contain evidence of the debtors' once-middle-class financial lives: their educational attainments, their formerly higher incomes, and their substantial rates of homeownership hark back to an earlier time of more middle-class financial, as well as social, status. The middle class is, of course, a huge portion of the American population. The families in bankruptcy are a good, though not perfect, cross-section of America by age, by gender, by race, by marital status, by ethnicity, by citizenship status, by employment status. If the world were a more comfortable place for middle-class Americans, we would not be writing this book—or at least one with this title. Instead, bankruptcy would be a distant phenomenon, a last resort for the uneducated, chronically unemployed margins of society whose improvident debts outstripped their meager incomes. In short, we would write a book about *them,* not about *us.*

The debtors in our sample include accountants and computer engineers, doctors and dentists, clerks and executives, salesclerks and librarians, teachers and entrepreneurs. They are middle-class folks who are supposed to be gathering around the barbecues on the patios outside their three-bedroom, two-bath houses, not waiting to be examined under oath by their creditors in austere federal courthouses. The debtors were the first to succumb to difficulties that also face many of their fellow citizens. They are like the proverbial canaries in the mineshafts; the bankrupt debtors comprise an early warning system for all Americans. They are a silent reminder that even the most secure family may be only a job loss, a medical problem, or an out-of-control credit card away from financial catastrophe.

In Phase II of the project, we expanded our study to cases filed in 1991 in sixteen districts spread across five states: all the districts in Illinois, Pennsylvania, Texas, and California and two of the three districts in Tennessee. We thus studied the same ten districts profiled in Phase I and added six districts in two states. The five states we sampled accounted for 31 percent of all bankruptcies in the United States in 1991.[3] With 150 cases in each district, we had a sample of about 2,400 cases.

With the cooperation and help of the Office of the U.S. Trustee and the Administrative Office of the United States Courts, we asked the individuals filing for bankruptcy in these sixteen federal judicial districts to complete a questionnaire that provided information on their age, education, occupation, marital status, race or ethnicity, and citizenship.[4] When married couples filed jointly, we asked for information about both spouses. We also collected financial data from the court records for the sample of 150 debtors in five districts, one district in each of the five states. Chapter 2 gives an overall picture of the demographic, social and economic profiles of the debtors. The grittier details of the study design and a copy of the questionnaire are set forth in Appendix 1.

The final question in the survey asked debtors to explain why they had filed their bankruptcies. There we hoped to uncover more information about the factors that put people at financial risk. Some people gave only terse responses — "too much debt, too little income" — while others poured out complex stories about faithless ex-spouses and gave detailed medical histories. In the next six chapters, we develop more data both from the debtors and from a variety of other sources to explore the fractures in the middle class that they have identified.

We quote many of the debtors' explanations in the course of this book to give the reader a genuine, unfiltered glimpse at the difficulties with which these people were confronted. The debtors' names and other identifying information have been disguised to protect privacy, but their words are uncensored and uncorrected, and the financial and demographic details are accurate as the debtors reported them to us and to the courts. The debtors are not composites; they are

**AMERICANS IN FINANCIAL CRISIS**

real, live people who went through the bankruptcy system. In addition to telling their stories, we also quantify their collective responses and analyze them statistically. Again, our methods are detailed in Appendix 1.

We try to interpret these data to create a coherent picture of the stresses middle-class Americans face today. We are keenly aware of the value judgments that creep into any discussion of information about American families, particularly data dealing with such topics as debt and the failure to honor one's promises. We have given our conclusions as best we can, mostly with a focus on the economics of where the debtor is at the time of filing for bankruptcy. But in every case we have tried to expose as much of the data as possible to give anyone with another perspective the opportunity to evaluate these data critically. We also provide as much detail as we can in the recognition that some subsequent researchers will use the data to support other interpretations, even those contrary to our own. We invite their efforts, secure in the belief that by expanding the dialogue about financial failure and what it signals about the health of middle-class America, a more thoughtful and nuanced picture will emerge.

We assume that there are errors in the reported data we collected. The bankruptcy files require the debtors to record extensive information on income, assets, debts, previous trips to the bankruptcy court, current address, former addresses, ongoing payment obligations, lawyers' fees, and so on. It would be extraordinary if every dollar value, every date, every address, and every description were accurate in all respects. Families in financial crisis may not be the most careful and reliable record keepers, and the bankruptcy forms are complex and detailed. Even so, the forms are filled out in a lawyer's office, typically with the help of an attorney, paralegal, or other person familiar with gathering personal financial information. They are filed under penalty of perjury.[5] Some reported data are backed up with hard evidence. For example, many courts require that debtors include recent paystubs to verify their current incomes. The largest assets—the home and the car—typically have easily determined market values, and those listings are usually scrutinized by all the parties.[6] A trustee is assigned to review the data in each file, and the debtors must sit for examination under oath for questioning by the trustee and the creditors about the representations in the file. In addition, creditors can challenge any of the reported information at any time, challenges they have a particular interest in presenting if the debtor either understates assets or incorrectly states debts. The penalties for misrepresentation are severe: the forms are signed under a declaration warning the debtor that misreporting is perjury. A debtor who falsifies his or her financial condition is subject to losing the bankruptcy discharge and, in extreme cases, to prosecution for a bankruptcy crime. Even debtors who shade the truth may find that a court will use such lack of candor as grounds for a dismissal for filing in bad faith. In short, there are substantial reasons to support the general accuracy of the data reported in the files. Moreover, there is no reason to believe in systematic error—persistent undervaluation or overvaluation of one entry or another. Discussion in the bankruptcy community about inaccuracies in the bankruptcy files generally relates to careless—not systematic—errors.[7] Most judges and practitioners believe that the incidence of misrepresentation is more likely to occur in the areas where debtors are asked to estimate future expenses and incomes, notoriously unreliable numbers even for those in the steadiest of financial circumstances. Those data are not used in this book.

9

It is always possible that someone may have misrepresented his or her age or marital status on the questionnaire, but there is little incentive for someone to do so and the information asked is fairly straightforward. The one question that might trigger the least accurate response is the one that asks the debtor to explain why he or she filed for bankruptcy. Here the debtor may tend to give highly self-serving answers that bear little relation to what an independent financial analyst with full information of the debtor's circumstances would say.

In one sense, we can never know the reason for anyone's bankruptcy. Even if the debtors reported full information, independent analysts would see different causes. Consider the debtor who lost his job because his company cut back on staff. But the company kept some of its employees, and the debtor had failed to take additional training and didn't get moved to the more critical division of the company. The reason he didn't move was that the new job would have involved longer hours and he didn't have child care after 5:30 P.M. Was the reason for filing a layoff? Too little training? Family responsibilities? Even independent analysts might dispute the cause of economic distress. And why bankruptcy as a solution? Some people choose to lose their homes and cars rather than go to bankruptcy court. Others move off in the middle of the night, becoming economic nomads. Still others work for cash in the underground economy. And others continue the shell game of paying one creditor one month and another the next, always half a step ahead of financial collapse but never in the bankruptcy courts. When we deal with the reasons for filing, we take what the debtors say, recognizing that we are seeing their explanations, and perhaps rationalizations.

The debtors may offer the most socially acceptable versions of their reasons, but much of the information they give in their explanations for filing can be corroborated independently. When debtors describe a recent divorce and an ex-spouse's failure to pay child support, the questions about current and past marital status will offer consistent evidence of a recent breakup and the bankruptcy file may show child support owed as a source of income. The high incidence of job-related problems reported in the debtors' questionnaires is entirely consistent with our other studies, drawn entirely from court file data, which show income patterns consistent with job losses in the two years preceding the bankruptcy filing. The data are also generally consistent with some smaller, single-district studies, which we cite in our chapter on jobs. Even though we cannot verify every story or even every type of story, the debtors' descriptions of their problems are consistent with the pattern of information we can observe.

Ultimately, however, we must face the fact that we are dealing with how the people in trouble describe their own problems. Although many are full of self-loathing, others are looking for another place to lay the blame for their decline into bankruptcy. Faced with explaining either that he or she was fired for getting drunk on the job or merely that he or she lost a job, a debtor may well give the second briefer and more acceptable account. The data we have collected are not useful for assigning a carefully calibrated personal blameworthiness quotient or for evaluating debtors' morality to distinguish them from their middle-class cohorts who are not in bankruptcy. What we can document with some confidence is the mess these debtors are in. Regardless of the combination of bad judgment and bad luck that brought these families to bankruptcy court, we can verify that (1) they are in desperate financial shape and (2) they repeatedly identify similar problems to explain their circumstances.

## The Bankruptcy Process

For most individual consumers, filing for bankruptcy is a matter of collecting and reporting a great deal of financial and sometimes personal information. The process requires filing long schedules about the family's income, assets, and debts. The debt listings include home mortgages, car loans, tax debts, credit card debts, medical debts, finance company loans, and a potpourri of other debts. There are other questions about lawsuits, business activities, and previous trips to the bankruptcy courthouse. If a creditor charges the debtor with fraud or if a good deal of valuable property is involved, things can get complicated quickly, but for most people the filing is a fairly straightforward process of following the lawyer's instructions. The responses we have received make it clear that bankruptcy remains a painful and shameful experience for many people, but it is not hard to understand the major points, and the lawyer takes care of most of the details.

Most people hire a lawyer to help them through the bankruptcy process. It generally costs between $750 and $1,500. Where does someone who is stone-cold broke get that kind of money? That is the first trade secret the lawyer puts at the client's service. Sometimes the lawyer will recommend payment of fees and debts over time in a trustee-supervised plan. In other situations, the lawyer will suggest letting other bills go while the debtor gets enough cash together to pay the lawyer in advance. The lawyer then helps the debtor discharge the debts to the other creditors. Only in America would we encounter people saving up for their bankruptcies.

Bankruptcy is governed by federal law and administered in the federal courts throughout the country. Something under half of the filings are made jointly, by married couples, even though 56 percent of adults in the general population are married.[8] The other half are single filings, made by unmarried people or by one half of a married couple. The most important decision a couple or an individual debtor has to make is whether to file for a *Chapter 7* liquidation or a *Chapter 13* payout plan.

A Chapter 7 case requires the debtors to give up all their non-exempt property to a trustee for the benefit of their creditors, in exchange for which they will be *discharged* from most of their preexisting debts. Some debts will survive the bankruptcy, such as alimony and child support, taxes, and educational loans. Other debts must be paid in full or the debtor will lose the collateral that secured the loan, such as the family home or the car. Many debtors choose to keep the collateral by keeping the debt. This means that for most families who file for bankruptcy, the first postbankruptcy reality is that they will still have substantial debts to pay: the home mortgage, the home equity line of credit, the car loan, the student loans, any outstanding taxes and any alimony or child support. Bankruptcy is a "fresh start" only in a relative sense—tens of thousands of dollars of credit card debt, retail store card debts, medical debts, and other "unsecured" debts can be wiped out with a Chapter 7 filing.

The alternative to Chapter 7 is Chapter 13, a vehicle for debtors to try to repay all or some part of their debts over time under the eye of a court-appointed trustee. If the family's payment plan is approved and they make the promised repayments, they may keep all of their property and receive a discharge from the portion of their debts they did not pay. Plans typically provide for payments over three to five years.

The reality of consumer choice is often even more constrained than these two legal descriptions suggest. In Chapter 7 liquidation, most consumer debtors will have little or no property that is not already protected by state exemptions, because they have few assets of any value that are not already subject to liens and mortgages. In other words, they do not own outright much of anything valuable. They will have to give up any property that has a mortgage or a lien on it, unless they can make a deal with the lender to keep paying on the lien. Most families' remaining property usually has less resale value than state or federal law allows as the amount of exemption, and therefore they may keep it. The real objective for many debtors is keeping a house or a car or a refrigerator that is subject to a lien or mortgage. If they cannot arrive at an agreement with the lienholder, they may choose Chapter 13, where they can maintain the payments on the encumbered property and hold on to it, even over the lienholders' objections.

The usual price for a Chapter 13 payment plan is some payment to unsecured creditors as well. If Joe and Jane want to keep their car by paying off the lien on it, they may also have to pay a good part of their Visa bill over a three-to-five-year payment plan. The debtors must devote to their Chapter 13 plan all of their *disposable income,* which is defined as all the income remaining after a certain allowance is made for expenses. In reviewing a plan, courts also review home budgets and projected payments to see if the family is actually giving up all the disposable income. If they are willing to let the car go, or if they can strike a separate deal with the company holding the car lien, then a Chapter 7 plan and a quick discharge of their Master-Card balance and their other debts may seem much more attractive.[9] They will have the "fresh start" that is the traditional objective of American bankruptcy law, with their future income free of old debts.

The Chapter 7 alternative is not quite as attractive as it may seem for many debtors.[10] As we noted, debtors in Chapter 7 cannot keep property subject to a lien unless they can make a deal with the creditor who holds the lien. If the creditor takes a tough bargaining position, the debtor may be able to pay less to keep property under a Chapter 13 plan.[11] Other debtors face debts that cannot be discharged in Chapter 7, such as recent income tax liability, alimony and child support, education loans, and liability for drunken driving or deliberate injury to another. Those debtors may be able to use Chapter 13 to pay nondischargeable debts in full over time.

In either type of bankruptcy, a filing produces an *automatic stay,* a statutory injunction that immediately freezes all collection efforts and is one of the main benefits of bankruptcy for most debtors. As soon as creditors receive notice of the filing, the phone calls and collection suits must stop, bringing a blessed silence. Also under either chapter, the debtors typically go to the courthouse just once.[12] They attend a "Section 341 meeting" with a court official, where they are sworn in and the proceedings are recorded. There they are asked a set of standard questions about their financial affairs. Creditors are entitled to attend these meetings and ask questions (for example, about fraudulent purchases or hidden assets), but few bother to exercise this right. The amounts at stake in any single case are usually small, and the debtors often have no property of value.

In a Chapter 7 case, the debtors will get a discharge certificate in

13

the mail a few weeks after the 341 meeting. They will be discharged from most prebankruptcy debts, though many of them will still owe debts to creditors holding liens, because they will have entered into payment agreements with them in order to keep the house or the car or other property subject to a lien. They may also still owe alimony and support payments or other nondischargeable debts. A fair number of them will have promised to make some repayments of dischargeable debts notwithstanding their discharges. In any case, the debtors will be barred from filing for Chapter 7 again for six years.

In a Chapter 13 case, the debtors' plan will soon be approved (the lawyer is unlikely to submit a plan the judges would not approve), and they will try to continue payments as promised in the plan. The percentages of their unsecured debts that debtors promise to pay vary greatly from one part of the country to another.[13] In some parts of the country, many debtors promise to pay 100 percent of their debts, merely seeking more time to do so. In other areas, most debtors promise far smaller percentages of payment, often under 50 percent. Whatever the promise, it often goes unfulfilled. Our studies and others indicate that most Chapter 13 cases fail before all the promised payments have been made. When that happens, one of two events usually occurs. The case may be dismissed, leaving the debtors to file again or to struggle on without bankruptcy relief. Or the case may be converted into a Chapter 7 liquidation. If the debtors beat the odds over the next three to five years and complete their promised payments — as only about one out of three do — they will be discharged from almost all preexisting debts above the amount they have paid. They will still have their home mortgages, and any second or third mortgages, the alimony and child support payments, and any outstanding taxes and student loans, but they will otherwise be back to zero — owning little, but owing little.

## Bankruptcy as a Barometer of Social Change

Like studies from any good pathology lab, the data tell us what went wrong. They reveal two things about the debtors. The data are a catalogue of the financial missteps and misfortunes that brought many ordinary families to economic catastrophe. In addition, they give some basis for exploring how those cracks may be widening. As the number of people in bankruptcy climbs, the information about why they are in bankruptcy says something about where financial risk is increasing.

The data help us to understand the dramatic increases in bankruptcy over the past two decades. There were three possibilities: more people were in serious financial trouble, a larger fraction of people in serious financial trouble chose bankruptcy as a solution, or people in not-as-serious financial trouble decided on a bankruptcy escape. The data can eliminate the last; they show that from 1981 to 1991 the circumstances of those who filed bankruptcy actually worsened. On the other hand, neither these data nor other generally available data can tell us for sure which of the other two possibilities are correct. It may be that more people are in big trouble or it may be that more of those in big trouble are choosing bankruptcy as a way out. In spite of that uncertainty, these data suggest that bankruptcy is a potential indicator of social conditions. The mix of reasons that bring people to bankruptcy may change over time, reflecting the changing risks that face American families. Because there are no national studies of the reasons for bankruptcy filings from ten and twenty years ago, it is difficult to identify whether the mix of reasons for filing is changing. It is possible, however, to look at a few single-district bankruptcy studies and at economic data from outside bankruptcy courts to get some idea of which risks may be rising.

In this study, the debtors were asked to explain why they were in bankruptcy, with no limits on the number or kind of responses they could give (fig. 1.2). They told us that employment problems are at the heart of nearly two-thirds of bankruptcy filings, with other reasons spread among specific credit problems, illnesses and accidents, family troubles, housing difficulties, and a mix of additional problems.

*Income Interruptions*

Not surprisingly, anything that causes income to decline puts a family at risk for bankruptcy. Layoffs and firings create huge vulnerability. Even if the worker finds another job, a period without income may create insurmountable debts, especially if that worker was carrying substantial debt loads when unemployment hit. Job turnover, rather

15

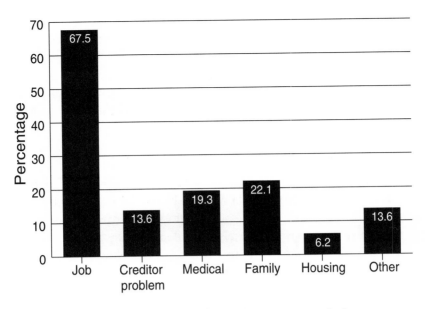

Fig. 1.2 Respondents' reasons for filing for bankruptcy. *Note:* Multiple responses were permitted.

than the actual unemployment rate, may be a better predictor for economic distress.

As dread as the word *unemployment* may be, many other income-related setbacks will also contribute to a debt-income mismatch that may lead to bankruptcy. Losing overtime hours or moving from a well-compensated executive position to a commission sales job may be enough. Employees with full benefits who become "outsourced" as contract workers with uncertain incomes and no fringe benefits may suddenly find income and debt out of balance.

Our autopsy of financial failure casts some light on the debates about the causes and cures of the pressures middle-class people are experiencing. Much of the debate, for example, has centered on the "downsizing" of corporations and the idea that long-term job security is a thing of the past. Some analysts have argued that job tenure is shrinking rapidly, while others say that it is much the same as it has always been in a country accustomed to economic change.[14] Whatever the conclusion, our data reveal that many people are finding themselves a part of the rising bankruptcy curve because they have lost their jobs, often positions they had held for some years and thought secure. Those data fit with a federal government survey of displaced workers that found that more than 30 percent of displaced, long-tenured workers had not found new employment. Of those who were working again, about 20 percent had found only part-time work or had become self-employed. This means that about 45 percent of long-tenured displaced workers had not found new full-time jobs.[15]

One aspect of the debate about job tenure—and about the export of jobs overseas—has been the claim that the recent hardships are falling most heavily on the undereducated. Even if that is true, the people we found in bankruptcy include a fair number with college degrees. In fact, the people in our sample are on the whole slightly better educated than the general population. At a minimum, therefore, a substantial group of educated people at the margins seem to be suffering job losses. That finding is consistent with the most recent figures from the Bureau of Labor Statistics and the Council of Economic Advisors, which report that in the early 1990s the risk of displacement for white-collar workers rose sharply as compared with blue-collar workers.[16]

It is further agreed that job displacement results in significant lost income for most people, even if they get another full-time job. The most recent Labor Department survey indicates that approximately eight million workers were displaced between 1995 and 1997, where "displacement" means that they lost their jobs because the plant closed or their positions were abolished. By February 1998, half were reemployed at their old salaries or better, but 25 percent remained unemployed and another 25 percent were earning 20 percent or less of their prior salaries.[17] Thus about two million workers released by one form of downsizing or another remained unemployed and another two million were working at substantially lower wages. An earlier report estimated the average loss at about 14 percent. We all appreciate that such a reduction would require a wrenching adjustment in our way of life, yet that adjustment becomes acutely difficult if the employees had already committed most of their earlier, higher disposable income to debt repayment at high interest rates. Future expenses can be slashed, albeit painfully, but existing debts cannot. Instead, debts keep climbing, often compounding at 18 percent or more. It is highly significant that a survey conducted in 1998

17

showed that almost half of the consumers who report high consumer debts relative to their incomes also reported that their incomes were "unusually low" at that time. Their incomes had recently declined, creating the classic debt-income mismatch.[18] For some, the mismatch is great enough to cause financial collapse.

### Credit Cards and Consumer Debt

The debt-income mismatch can also occur when incomes are stable but debts rise to unpayable levels. If consumers incur debt at higher levels in relation to their incomes, then they will be at greater risk for bankruptcy. The preconditions for that development are that consumers must become more willing to incur debt and the consumer credit industry must become more willing to extend it.

Stagnant incomes have affected many Americans for twenty years. Through the recessions of the early 1980s and 1990s and the recoveries in between and since, the median income of American households has remained about the same, after adjusting for inflation.[19] The increases in income since 1980 have mostly gone to the wealthiest one-fifth of the population.[20] At the same time, the willingness of consumers to borrow and of lenders to lend has increased dramatically. From 1980 to 1992, total home mortgage and consumer installment debt rose more than 400 percent in unadjusted dollars, from about $1.4 trillion to about $5.7 trillion.[21] From 1980 to 1994, total household debt had increased from 65 percent to 81 percent of total income.[22] In short, real consumer debt has risen dramatically over a long period during which real incomes for many people have stayed the same or declined. The result is exactly what a sensible observer would predict it to be: a great increase in the bankruptcy rate.

One more piece of the puzzle is interest rates. Even with stable income and debt levels, the debt burden increases when interest rates increase. Since the early 1980s, when extreme inflation led to the abolition or radical loosening of usury laws at both the state and federal levels, consumer interest has remained at historically high rates. The cost that Citibank pays its investors for the money it uses to lend out on credit cards fell by more than 50 percent (7.5 percentage points), but credit card interest rates dropped by only about 10 percent (1.7 percentage point).[23] The average 18 percent rate that consumers have

18

been paying on credit cards would have landed the credit company executives in the penitentiary twenty years ago. Today it lands the same executives in flattering profile stories in *Forbes* and *Business Week*. In 1998, an article published by the Federal Deposit Insurance Corporation identified the repeal of usury rates as the triggering event for a glut of consumer credit and the resulting rise in bankruptcy filing rates.[24] The dramatic expansion of consumer credit, and of all-purpose credit cards in particular, is largely a function of the enormous premiums permitted under current usury laws.

Because interest charges generate a continuing increase in debt, even if the consumer has stopped making any new charges because of adverse financial conditions, these high interest charges create a momentum that debt has never had before. Many creditors now impose a "default" rate of interest on the customers who fall behind, compounding the balance owed at rates of 24 percent and higher.[25] There is every reason to think that people have adjusted only slowly and imperfectly to this radical change in financial life. Furthermore, only since 1989 has ordinary consumer interest not been tax deductible, so that some people may not have fully adjusted to the ultimate, after-tax cost of these new, far-higher interest rates.

Changes in social values and behavior are both cause and effect of changes in popular culture, but popular culture is also changed deliberately by those who have something to sell, from movies to new cars to credit. Enormous amounts of talent and money fuel these efforts to change the way people perceive products and services and to generate increased demand for them. Insofar as those efforts are directed at stimulating buying by people with stagnant incomes, they must lead to increased debt and eventually to increased bankruptcy rates. Whether these efforts change moral values or simply connect with people whose values have changed for other reasons, the effect is greater financial precariousness.

*Accidents and Illnesses*

The mismatch between income and debt also occurs when debts increase unexpectedly, even if income remains the same. An uninsured medical emergency will do the trick. If more people are suffering serious medical problems, or if medical problems produce greater costs, or if fewer people have insurance to cover their medical costs, debtors will go to the bankruptcy courts in greater numbers.

Medical costs have played a prominent role in discussions of middle-class struggles, including the problem of workers' losing medical insurance when they lose their jobs. About 25 percent of long-tenured, displaced workers surveyed by the Department of Labor in 1996 remained uncovered by medical insurance, although this figure was somewhat improved over the numbers from a decade earlier.[26] The number of uninsured children in the United States continues to rise; four-fifths of these children live in homes where incomes are above the poverty level.[27] A Census Bureau study in 1995 revealed that in a three-year period, about 64 million people faced some time when they had no insurance as a backstop against medical bills, including about 9.5 million who had no insurance protection at any time during this timespan.[28]

Although our data show that medical costs contribute materially to the financial struggles of families, the medical data also show that families are vulnerable in other ways. The more serious problem for many families may be income lost due to an illness or injury. The medical problem that leads to a job problem can become an income problem that a family cannot survive. In that regard, social policies that deliberately limit disability payments to a percentage of prior income may make previously incurred debts virtually unpayable. The lower payments provide an incentive to return to work but may leave creditors holding the bag. The social safety net erected to permit families to seek medical treatment not only affects how their health care providers will be paid but may also affect all their other creditors as well.

*Divorce and Remarriage*

Changes in social mores can have profound financial effects. Divorce is a key example. In addition to its social and moral characteristics, the family is a financial unit, and the breakup of a family often creates expenses and debts quite disproportionate to the incomes available to pay them. Whenever two households suddenly must split an income that once supported only one, a financially precarious period ensues. A general increase in family instability—at a time when families are already loaded with debt—may lead to an increase in bankruptcy filings.

One in every ten adults in the population generally is currently divorced—not single, married, or widowed. Among people in bankruptcy, however, that number is two in ten—meaning that a divorced person is twice as likely to be in bankruptcy in a given year than their proportion in the population. The high proportion of divorced people in bankruptcy illustrates that the financial cost of family dissolution is often a body blow to anyone trying to re-form a new household. Both men and women flock to bankruptcy court after a divorce, although the evidence suggests that the economic straits facing women, particularly those rearing children, are even more acute than those confronting men.

*Home Mortgages*

One cause for bankruptcy filings, drowning-by-mortgage, is less obvious than the rest. Mortgages are, of course, a large and important sort of debt for most Americans, but no one ever says that buying homes causes bankruptcy. Yet people do use phrases like "house-poor" to describe a friend. In bankruptcy we find the extreme examples. The culprit once again is change. Ever since World War II, Americans have been taught that owning your own home is the ultimate investment, the ticket to long-term financial security, along with social acceptance and a nice tax deduction. Rising interest rates, stagnant incomes, and increasing housing costs (including property taxes) have made that investment a greater risk for people who can no longer be sure of their jobs. Home ownership, when combined with the need to move quickly to follow a job, second-mortgages to finance college educations and orthodontia, and stagnant or declining housing markets, can rapidly shift from the asset to the liability column in any family's balance sheet. And there has recently arisen a strong trend to use second (or third) mortgages on homes to refinance ordinary consumer debt.[29]

Homeownership is one of the most visible signs of participation in the middle class. Families in bankruptcy often want desperately to hold on to their homes, and their bankruptcy filings may be an attempt to clear out other debts so that they can pour their often-shrinking incomes into their mortgage payments. For many, hanging on to a home is no longer a matter of economic rationality; it has become a struggle to save an important part of their lives, one that a financial adviser might tell them to let go.

Home ownership problems often intersect powerfully with employment problems. The data also reveal important differences by race, suggesting that African-American and Hispanic-American homeowners may have a more tenuous grasp on their homes and may be struggling harder in bankruptcy to save them.

## Increasing Vulnerability

As American families have faced job losses and medical bills, divorces and home mortgages throughout the past decade, bankruptcy has been their safety net—much as it has throughout the past century. By themselves, the stories are interesting and the aggregated data help identify the main fault lines in the solid, reliable middle class. But the 1990s were unlike any other in the bankruptcy courts. As we noted at the beginning of this chapter, the number of families flocking to the bankruptcy courts has set new filing records. We know why the debtors are there, but the question remains: Why are so many more there now than in the early 1980s? Are the cracks in middle-class stability widening?

That question brings us to a crucial point in our findings: the central role of consumer debt in the middle-class crunch. As we noted earlier, a sharp increase in consumer debt can lead directly to a bankruptcy filing. But the proportion of people who have filed for bankruptcy because they have run up consumer debt to unmanageable levels is somewhat more modest than many might guess—perhaps about one in ten. The number is not insubstantial, but it cannot account for the threefold rise in bankruptcy filings.

Instead, consumer debt has lowered many middle-class families' threshold for financial collapse. High consumer debt loads increase families' vulnerability to every other problem—job, medical, divorce, housing—that befalls them. Six weeks of unemployment for a worker with $200 in short-term, high-interest credit card debt may be tough but manageable. That same six weeks without a paycheck is a disaster for a worker who must feed a relentless $20,000 credit card balance with interest accumulating at 18 percent and penalty fees added on at $50 a pop. Similarly, a $5,000 medical bill may be difficult but manageable for a family with no outstanding debt, but for a family already reduced to making minimum monthly payments on a debt load that matches a couple of months' income, the additional debt is unbearable. A family contemplating a marital breakup in 1970 with no outstanding debts other than a home mortgage might re-form two households, albeit at lower economic levels. That same household today, with both husband and wife already at work full-time and credit card, retail store, car loan, student loan, and other debts piled on top of a mortgage, simply cannot take on the increased expenses of two households. If unemployment, health insurance, divorce rates, and housing costs all remained steady but ordinary consumer debt burdens rose sharply, the proportion of the population filing for bankruptcy following a job loss, a medical debt, a divorce, or a move must climb. A growing consumer debt burden means a shrinking buffer against financial disaster.

At this juncture we uncover the deepest ambivalence about consumer debt and consumer bankruptcy. Our economy depends on consumer spending. Our economists take inconsistent positions about whether the spending is good or bad. They demand that people save more to increase capital investment and productivity at the same time they warn that increased consumption is essential to economic growth. In short, they want more spending and more savings. They are apparently too busy to explain how to do both of these at the same time, especially when incomes are stagnant. One thing Americans can do on the consumption side, despite their stagnant incomes, is to incur more debt. Many people have an enormous economic stake in encouraging us to do just that. No one, it seems, has an interest in providing sober reminders about the risks involved.

Adding to these general trends is the growth of a whole new segment of the consumer credit industry, one made possible by the computer and communications revolutions. The new segment is concentrated on the very consumers who were feared and avoided by credit granters just a few years ago. They are people at the margins who already have high consumer debts in relationship to their incomes. So-called subprime lending—that is, lending to people who have spotty credit histories or are awash in debt—is the most profit-

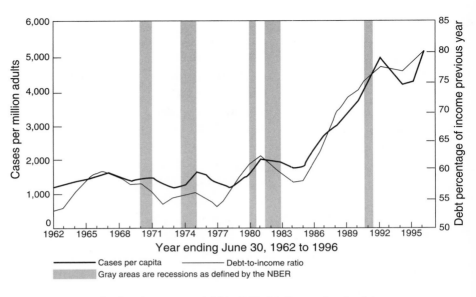

Fig. 1.3 Consumer bankruptcy cases and debt, 1962–96. *Source:* See fig. 1.1.

able, and hence the most rapidly increasing, segment of consumer lending. The fastest growing group of credit card customers are those below the poverty line,[30] and credit card issuers now actively seek those who have been through a bankruptcy and cannot return to the bankruptcy courts for six years. A new breed of credit granters has discovered that these troubled debtors have two attractive characteristics, despite their financial precariousness: they do not pay off their debts very quickly, so the interest keeps running up, and they do not argue about high interest rates. Of course, they also produce high default rates, but the wonders of modern computers enable the companies to keep close track of each individual's account, and the wonders of cheap communication enable collectors to keep in constant contact with the debtors to urge repayment and to initiate repossession or other collection activities when exhortations fail. Although this new business has proven so far to be remarkably profitable, we note that it has not yet been tested by a full-blown recession.[31] Aggressive marketing has met a seemingly endless willingness on the part of consumers to take on new debt, and Americans' debt loads since the 1980s have doubled, redoubled, and doubled again (fig. 1.3).

The overall picture that emerges in the chapters that follow, from the national data about all Americans and from the data we developed from the bankruptcy files, is of an American middle class that is taking on ever more debt even as the threats to its financial security grow more serious. Single-parent families are on the rise, medical costs and the risks of loss of insurance are increasing, housing costs are rising, and safety nets against injury at work are weakening— all at a time when job security is ever more problematic and job loss routinely leads to a sharp reduction in income. The divorce rate has stabilized but remains at historic highs. Yet the middle class continues to pile up debt, sinking the boat ever lower in the water even as the waves rise.

Aside from the substantial forces of marketing, of both things to buy and the credit to buy them with, there has clearly been a change of attitude among Americans over the past twenty years or so that permits this unprecedented accumulation of debt.[32] No doubt there are many causes, but at least one may be the difficulty of changing the direction of expectations. It is one thing to raise or lower expectations in response to the vagaries of fortune, but it is another to change the direction from up to down. In 1996 the *New York Times* ran a seven-part series on "downsizing."[33] It was filled with stories about white-collar workers and managers who had been laid off. Those stories were mostly about struggles with expectations. Typical were the Sharlows, who were steadily draining their savings, $10,000 a month, for month after month, to continue living at their previous level after the husband had lost his job as a plant manager. If it is difficult to change one's way of life after disaster has indisputably struck, how much harder is it to cut back merely at the threat? It may be nearly impossible for middle-class Americans, who inherited rising expectations, to come to grips with the reality of a world where it is distinctly possible that things may not be better next year. When there are whole industries devoted to encouraging us to "Just Do It," many may find it too easy to ignore the risk.

It is the lot of the middle class to feel vulnerable and insecure. But middle-class Americans at the beginning of the twenty-first century find themselves in a new and paradoxical situation. Like the gleaming new automobiles they buy, many things are better than they have ever been, but they cost much more and they require people to go deeper into debt to enjoy them. Never has medical care been so nearly miraculous in its achievements and never has it been so breathtakingly expensive. It was much cheaper when people died younger and faster. On a parallel track, there is far more personal freedom and far less willingness to remain in painful emotional relationships, as typified by liberalized divorce laws, but the financial penalties of breaking up are enormous. Homes are larger and filled with more gadgets than ever, but many Americans are bent or broken trying to pay for them. More and more people of a middle-class sort are living at greater risk. We have more and we risk more. The credit industry gives us ever more opportunities to pledge our future incomes at a time when the future of our incomes is less secure. In the bankruptcy courtrooms of America we explore the results.

In a larger sense, our findings show the interrelationships between bankruptcy as a financial safety net for the middle class and the other safety nets society has constructed. They also show how debt was left out of the calculations when those other safety nets were constructed. Great attention has been paid, for example, to enforcing ongoing alimony and child support obligations following divorce, but virtually no attention has been given to the obligation to pay pre-existing marital debts. Our data show that failure by one spouse to make promised payments of these debts often drives the other spouse into bankruptcy—and no doubt contributes greatly to the financial misery of single parents and children who manage to avoid bankruptcy, too. Just as with the lower payments for disability policies and programs, these provisions ignore the fact that many middle-class people enter a crisis already burdened with debt—nowadays, lots of debt.

Chapter 2

# Middle-Class and Broke
## The Demography of Bankruptcy

I was President of a Savings & Loan that failed. I have been unable to find
a permanent job for the past 2 years.
—WILLIS CREIGHTON, Houston, Texas

Willis Creighton and his wife, Sandra, filed for bankruptcy in Chapter 7. He is fifty-three years old, and she is forty-eight. He has a college
degree, and she is a high school graduate. Sandra also reports a job
disruption during the two years before they filed bankruptcy. As he
noted in his written comments, Willis is still seeking work. He explains that the failure of the thrift institution he headed also caused
his personal financial failure when he could not locate another job.
Are Willis and Sandra Creighton typical debtors? Or are they part of
a thin veneer of white-collar workers in a bankruptcy system that is
mostly a refuge for the poor?

The answer is resoundingly clear. The people who file for bankruptcy are a cross-section of society, and bankruptcy is a middle-class
phenomenon. In this chapter we shall explore who the debtors are,
how similar they are to one another, and how similar they are to
their neighbors who are not in bankruptcy. Generally speaking, the
debtors in our sample are representative of people within the United
States in terms of the demographic characteristics over which they
have no personal control: age, sex, and race. They are also similar
to their neighbors in the characteristics over which they have had
some control: immigration and naturalization, education, and occupation. One feature stands out to demarcate these debtors from their
neighbors: they are in terrible financial condition.

If the debtors are so badly off financially that they are in bankruptcy, then how can they be middle class? To answer this question requires a further examination of the contemporary American middle class and the dynamics of class formation.

## Bankruptcy and the Middle Class

The most important point to make about the American middle class is that most Americans believe that they are in it. When asked in an open-ended question to identify their class membership, nearly three-quarters of the adult population of the United States volunteer an identification with the "middle" or "average" class.[1] Although some people call themselves upper class and others call themselves working class or lower class, these identifications are numerically somewhat rare. Even in those cases, such class identifications are not always well correlated with income. As political scientists Kenneth Dolbeare and Jannette Hubbell assert, "Middle-class values are by definition those of the American mainstream."[2]

Middle-class membership is also a function of many characteristics. Although the government has defined the poverty level, no government agency defines the middle class, at least in part because class status is not a function merely of money or of other easily counted characteristics. The running joke of the television comedy *The Beverly Hillbillies* was that money did not change the social class of the newly rich Clampetts. By contrast, the genteel poor might be described by their neighbors as "classy," but the refinement is not a matter of current income.

Studies of the American population show that Americans determine class identification using many variables, including education, occupation, cultural factors, lifestyle, beliefs and feelings, and income and wealth.[3] In everyday interactions, manners, speech patterns, and dress may be the cues on which most people rely. Sociologist Michelle Lamont, in a discussion of the "Iron Law of Money" in social class identification, suggests that Americans are more sensitive to affluence as a class indicator than the French are. Yet even in her data comparing American with French respondents, 50 to 60 percent of her two American samples classified themselves as "indifferent" to affluence in determining a person's class.[4] Although money may be an important indicator, in the end most Americans consider more than money when identifying social class.

Consider, however, the special case of the bankrupt debtors who have very low incomes and negligible assets. Could any group of the middle class really be so badly off? At least one group of theorists would exclude them from the middle class by definition. To Karl Marx and subsequent neo-Marxists, money is the unique class indicator. Marx phrased class position in terms of the "access to the means of production," and neo-Marxists describe it in terms of ownership and workplace authority.[5] From the Marxist and neo-Marxist perspectives, the bankrupt debtors' precarious economic position would eliminate them from the middle class. Of course, Marxists see the middle class as doomed, eventually to disappear altogether.

Some empirical studies of bankruptcy have implicitly adopted a neo-Marxist position, eliminating debtors from the middle class by definition. Philip Shuchman writes of a group of New Jersey debtors he studied that they "were not, however, in the middle class by almost any standard, and they could pay nothing to satisfy their creditors without being pressed below poverty level. They were the near-poor — families barely getting by and always at the brink of actual poverty."[6] Yet many of his subjects were college educated — 45 percent of the black respondents had one year of college or more, as did 29 percent of white respondents, a fact he apparently considered irrelevant to social class.[7]

Bankruptcy forces us to address the ambiguities that beset American social class identification. Everyone knows people whose life-style — a visible indicator of social class — is more modest than their income would permit. The best-selling book *The Millionaire Next Door* documents a group of Americans who amass considerable wealth but live quietly. At the same time, everyone is also familiar with the impostor who conveys the impression of wealth by wearing designer clothing and driving a luxury automobile.[8] Enough of these anomalies exist to make many Americans wary of judging social class based solely on the outward show of wealth. The difficulty of determining class status by income alone is compounded by the fact that Americans are famously circumspect in discussing money. Religion, politics, and personal sexual escapades—though still not typical topics of conversation among strangers—are nevertheless more congenial subjects for most people than their finances.

This is why sociologists, like most Americans, seek alternative cues about social class. In casual conversation, cocktail-party invitees ask others what they do for a living, where they work, in which neighborhood they live, where they went to school. These socially acceptable bits of information help to locate a new acquaintance within a cognitive map of the social stratification system. It is true that education, occupation, and income tend to be correlated; that is the generalization on which everyone operates. But that generalization also recognizes that for some individuals the overlap may be imperfect. A very well respected church minister does not lose middle-class status just because his or her congregation pays a low salary. And by extension, we argue that Willis Creighton's college degree, business experience, good tennis game, and nice manners may count for more with a new acquaintance than his recent position as an unemployed, bankrupt debtor.

Willis may well prefer to think of himself as a middle-class person temporarily down on his luck. Americans resist redefining themselves in a lower class just because they have had an economic setback. Economist Milton Friedman has proposed the permanent income hypothesis. According to this hypothesis, most of us have an idea of what our long-term (permanent) income will be and we adjust our way of living (and perhaps our class identity) accordingly. A layoff or other short-term income interruption may not lead to serious cuts in expenditures, even if the expectation of better times ahead proves incorrect. Marketers have noted the tendency of downsized workers to seek to maintain their lifestyles at their current levels, adjusting as little as possible.[9] Indeed, some of our laid-off debtors may have spent themselves further into debt in an effort to maintain their middle-class way of life until they got back on their feet. It would be the greatest of ironies for them to hear that the very fact of their bankruptcy precluded their continuing membership in the middle class.

There is, however, an anxiety among the American middle class born from the reality of eroding economic security. The majority of job displacement and similar changes during the 1980s affected less-educated workers. Beginning in 1990, large-scale changes began to affect white-collar workers and especially older, college-educated men.[10] The middle class has experienced a squeeze in income that arises from several sources. Since 1969, the structure of male occupational wages has polarized and assumed the shape of an hourglass, with incomes grouped at the top and the bottom, not in the middle. One's position in the hierarchy depends on one's education.[11] The result, as we describe for San Antonio in the next chapter, has been fewer jobs in the middle for those with modest educational attainments.

While wages have polarized, income inequality has intensified. Between 1967 and 1993, the share of all income received by the highest fifth of the population increased from 43.8 percent to 48.9 percent of all income, while the shares of the remaining 80 percent of the population declined. The middle quintile of the income distribution—surely the middle of the middle class—dropped from 16.9 percent of income to 15.0 percent.[12] Real median family income peaked in 1986, then declined or plateaued until 1996, with only minor upward increments since 1996.[13]

Because the graphs of the income distribution changed little during this period, the hypothesis of a shrinking middle class seemed exaggerated. Although commentators expressed fears about what was happening to the middle class, what observers saw was that families kept spending and not much seemed to change. The reality, nevertheless, is that the American middle class is running hard to stay in place. One observer notes, "As good jobs become scarce and wages and benefits erode, workers act to forestall potential losses by working longer hours and taking second jobs, while families send more workers into the labor force."[14] Such adjustments bring additional vulnerabilities with them: if a husband cannot keep getting overtime or cannot keep a second job, or if a wife is laid off, the family will lose income and its debts may become unmanageable. Maintaining the middle-class lifestyle in the 1990s, for many families, meant moving a little closer to the edge. The declining savings rate spoke of how much closer many families had moved toward the margin. For some families, negative savings—debt—became the mechanism of adjustment.

In late 1998, for the first time since the Depression, the American people as a whole went into an overall "negative saving" rate; that is, we collectively didn't save a dime.[15]

Not much has been said so far about middle-class respectability, values, and fears. Part of being middle class in the United States is a set of attitudes and values. Among those attitudes are a strong orientation toward planning for the future, trying to control one's destiny, pulling one's weight, and respecting others who try to get ahead in the same way. The rights of property are respected. Obeying the law and getting ahead by following the rules are generally prized. There is also a well-known set of middle-class fears. Chief among them are the fear of falling from the middle class to a lower class and a fear of being squeezed between a more powerful upper class and a desperate lower class.

Bankruptcy is, in many ways, where middle-class values crash into middle-class fears. Bankrupt debtors are unlikely either to feel in charge of their destiny or to feel confident about planning their future. Discharging debts that were honestly incurred seems the antithesis of middle-class morality. Public identification as a bankrupt debtor is embarrassing at best, devastating at worst. It is certainly not respectable, not even in a country with large numbers of bankruptcies, to be bankrupt. Bankrupt debtors have told us of their efforts to conceal their bankruptcy. Arguments that the stigma attached to bankruptcy has declined are typically made by journalists who are unable to find any bankrupt debtors willing to be interviewed for the record and by prosperous economists who see bankruptcy as a great bargain.[16]

In their apparent betrayal of middle-class sensibilities, then, one could ask whether the bankrupt debtors have forfeited their right to be considered middle class. They might have attended college and they might have occupational prestige, but they are not *acting* like the middle class. They have told a court that they have debts they cannot pay, contracts they cannot honor, and obligations they cannot meet. These might be sufficient grounds, in the eyes of some critics, to bar these debtors from inclusion in the middle class.

In another interpretation, however, bankruptcy is the ultimate taking of responsibility, of squarely facing one's obligations. These debtors did not skip town or change their names. They did not burn down houses or drive cars into the river for the insurance money. Many of them indicate, in their remarks to us, that they have prioritized their financial obligations. To be sure, they acknowledge credit card debt and finance company loans, but they have more important obligations to feed and house family members now and in the future. Some see bankruptcy as a regrettable but necessary step to taking control of their out-of-control financial lives. In that sense bankruptcy becomes part of the fulfillment of a middle-class value. Some debtors may view their Chapter 13 plan as a way to meet their obligations and to learn better money management. In our surveys, nearly fifty debtors volunteered the information that bankruptcy was a last resort, filed only after all other alternatives had failed. Many say they will never let it happen again.

## The Bankruptcy Stereotype: Not the Middle Class

Presidents of savings and loans, however insecure their jobs may have been at the end of the 1980s, would generally be considered middle class.[17] And fifty-three-year-olds would usually be considered established and comfortably middle-aged. The data demonstrate that Willis and Sandra Creighton are not merely isolated examples of the middle class and middle-aged in bankruptcy. They are perhaps most remarkable for the discrepancy they juxtapose to the stereotype of the bankrupt debtor as existing far below the middle class. Perhaps the stereotype gives comfort to the middle class, but it appears to be false comfort.

Most stereotypes originate from a kernel of truth, but that kernel becomes so overwrapped with layers of myth that the stereotype often outgrows or outlives the underlying reality. Stereotypes are durable because they help people reduce their uncertainty about the world; dealing in stereotypes can save the energy required to consider complex realities. When the uncertainties involve risks that are unpleasant to contemplate, the temptation to characterize that risk in terms of stereotypes is even greater. Bankruptcy is unpleasant at best, emotionally devastating at worst. For Americans who prize economic success, bankruptcy is a notable and public failure. With personal bankruptcies at record highs, the debtors themselves are not so rare, but they are still sufficiently embarrassed that they refuse interviews and deny that they have filed for bankruptcy even in face of contradictory evidence.[18]

The persistence of a bankruptcy stigma actually fuels stereotypes because it provides an incentive to pigeonhole bankrupts as "them," not "us." The risk is farther away if those who are in trouble are a comfortable social distance from everyone else. For many years the stereotypical bankrupt debtor was believed to be a young male. One bankruptcy researcher, Robert Dolphin, Jr., described bankruptcy as "an ailment of the young man."[19] This was the mite of empirical evidence, upon which further details were layered. With greater detail, the bankrupt stereotype was eventually elaborated as a twenty-something male, a high school dropout who held an unskilled or, at best, a semiskilled job.

The bankruptcy stereotype emerged from a variety of empirical studies that were published between 1959 and 1969. Many of these studies were geographically constrained, often limited to a single district or even to one city within a district.[20] A summary portrait of bankrupt debtors that is very similar to what we have called the bankruptcy stereotype was distilled from this literature and published in 1973 in the influential Report of the Commission on the Bankruptcy Laws of the United States.[21] Careless readings of the influential multidistrict research of David Stanley and Marjorie Girth cemented the stereotype. This was ironic, because Stanley and Girth had concluded that their sample of debtors "presented a picture of neither poverty nor instability."[22]

In interviews of four hundred debtors drawn from seven districts, Stanley and Girth found that three-quarters of the debtors were male, a slight majority (51 percent) were younger than forty, and about three-quarters were married.[23] Although the debtors had completed, at the median, only 11.4 years of schooling—making them high school dropouts—Stanley and Girth were careful to note that the national median at that time was even lower, just 10.4 years of schooling. Given the norms of the day, Stanley and Girth reported that their debtors "did not come from the poorly educated groups in the population. Three-quarters of them had been to high-school—well above the 1960 average of the general population, 60 percent."[24] Three-fifths of the bankrupt debtors were blue-collar workers, with nearly half in manufacturing.[25]

MIDDLE-CLASS AND BROKE

The only way to know about bankrupt debtors is through the efforts of researchers with the time and funding to delve into the bankruptcy files or to interview debtors. Although the Administrative Office of the United States Courts routinely publishes statistics concerning the number of bankruptcy filings, the people who file the petitions have remained shadowy figures hidden behind the gross numbers. Bankruptcy petitions contain a great deal of financial information, none of which is systematically gathered and reported. The files contain little demographic data. The average credit card issuer assembles more demographic information for each card holder than is required in a bankruptcy petition. Card holders could probably tabulate their loss files to provide some excellent summary data on bankrupt debtors, but their data are proprietary and rarely shared with the public. Updates on the characteristics of bankrupt debtors have thus been anecdotal, as when an attorney describes the characteristics of his or her clientele, or sporadic, as when a researcher publishes the findings of a specific study.

Two studies appeared in the 1980s that indicated a shift in the occupations of bankrupt debtors to white-collar work, a shift that paralleled the general changes in the labor force.[26] Several studies also documented the increased filings of women in bankruptcy.[27] In spite of the more recent evidence, the well-known findings that were correct in the late 1960s underlie a stereotype that has been remarkably durable. One reason for its perseverance may be that it is comforting to assume that economic woes principally afflicted a predictable demographic group. The bankruptcy stereotype effectively eased people's worries that "there but for the grace of God go I." As the average level of schooling in the population increased and more of the labor force shifted to white-collar work, many observers remembered that the debtors were blue-collar dropouts. Fewer remembered Stanley and Girth's reminder of context: many workers in the 1960s, not just the bankrupt debtors, were both blue-collar and had not completed high school. Uncorrected, the stereotype was open to the reinterpretation that bankruptcy served not the middle class but instead the lower classes. Some observers, in fact, were dogmatic that bankruptcy filers were not middle class.[28] For this reason, it is important to examine carefully how closely the bankrupt debtors resemble a cross-section of the adult population and the further conclusion that the middle class are the major participants in the bankruptcy system.

## A Demographic Cross-Section

Willis and Sandra Creighton were hardly unique in filing for bankruptcy in 1991. In that recession year, 812,685 nonbusiness bankruptcies were filed.[29] The recession is indicated by the decline in the composite index of leading indicators from 98.4 in 1990 to 97.1 in 1991. The index rose again to 98.1 in 1992. Initial claims for unemployment insurance rose from 383,000 in 1990 to 444,000 in 1991 but declined to 412,000 in 1992. Manufacturers' new orders for consumer goods and materials declined from $1.23 billion in 1990 to $1.19 billion in 1991 and then returned to $1.23 billion in 1992. If the bankrupt debtors' households were of average size, a total of 2,584,330 debtors and their family members, or about 1 percent of the population, were affected directly by bankruptcy in 1991.[30] Many more people were affected indirectly as extended family members, neighbors, creditors, coworkers, and employers.[31] By 1996, the million mark had been passed in nonbusiness bankruptcies, and by 1997 there were 1.4 million filings.[32] Large numbers, however dramatic, display magnitude, but they tell little of the human dimension of bankruptcy. An examination of the characteristics of the individuals who filed for bankruptcy in 1991 and 1997 in this section gives some texture and meaning to the large numbers.

*Gender*

> My income changed from over 30,000 to apprx. 15,000 in 1990 due to having to somewhat involuntarily leav[e] a job. (requested to resign — sales quota did not meet new company's expectation. This occurred during a company buy out.) —MARCIA JAMES, Memphis, Tennessee

Marcia James is thirty-six years old, never married, and a high school graduate. She lost her sales job during a company buyout, and at the time that she filed Chapter 13 she was still looking for a new job. Historically, women have been less likely than men to file bankruptcy, except in joint filings by a husband and wife. The increasing participation of women in paid work and women's legally mandated access to equal credit have paralleled their increasing use of the bankruptcy courts. In our 1981 sample, 27 percent of bankruptcy petitions were men filing singly. Ten years later, men filing alone constituted virtually the same proportion of the total—26 percent. Women filing alone, however, rose from 17 percent to 30 percent of the sample total. A new form of equality had appeared—women had slightly surpassed men as single petitioners.

Over the same period, the proportion of all bankruptcy cases that had a woman petitioner—either as the single petitioner or as part of a joint filing—remained virtually constant at 73–74 percent. In our 1981 study, 56 percent of the sample were filing jointly with their husbands.[33] In the 1991 sample, only 44 percent of the sample were women who filed jointly with their husbands. Thus, although women are still involved in nearly three-fourths of all filings, they were far more likely to be in bankruptcy on their own in 1991 and far less likely to be there as part of a couple than they were a decade earlier. Meanwhile, the proportion of cases involving a male petitioner declined from 83 percent to 70 percent. 37

The reality behind these statistics is more complex than the feminization of bankruptcy. What happened is that married women joint petitioners were replaced by single-filing women in some parts of the country. Marcia James lives in the Western District of Tennessee, where single women filers are relatively most common. The national experience was not homogeneous, however, with Texas retaining significantly more joint filings than the other states. Joint filings were most numerous in Texas, where the proportion of cases that were joint filings remained consistently high from district to district.[34]

From the little that we have been able to observe, it appears that women in bankruptcy behave similarly to men. To take one example, women primary filers did not differ much from men in their chapter of filing. Women accounted for 30 percent of the sample, just about the same proportion of Chapter 7 filings (30 percent), and just a little less of the Chapter 13 filings (28 percent). Similarly, there was little difference between the women and the men in their propensity to answer the question about reasons for bankruptcy. Roughly 27 percent of those who did not give us a reason were women, and roughly 30 percent of those who did give us a reason were women. As we shall show in later chapters, however, the reasons that the women gave for their bankruptcies often differed from those given by men, with family reasons cited far more frequently by women filers.

## Age

> We married young and believed we could pay all our bills, but couldn't. In 1989 I, Michelle, had a wreck and couldn't pay for it. We would like to start over a new life. — MARK and MICHELLE GRADY, Peoria, Illinois

Mark and Michelle Grady filed in Chapter 7. They had married within two years of their bankruptcy. He is twenty-four and she is twenty-three. Neither Mark nor Michelle finished high school. Paying their bills has been complicated by Michelle's car accident and their recent work histories. Both have had recent jobs, but they are now unemployed. They are seeking the "fresh start" of Chapter 7. Given their age and level of schooling, Mark and Michelle might be examples of the 1960s bankruptcy stereotype. But they are exceptions among the 1990s bankruptcy filers. Our average filer is nearly ten years older though often no more financially secure than Mark and Michelle.

The ages of the debtors tells a great deal about where they are in life and gives clues about the constellation of financial pressures they may face. The ages of our primary filer respondents range from twenty to eighty-three, but the great majority of our debtors verge on middle age. Their median age and their mean age are both thirty-eight. Joint filers are slightly younger, with a median and mean age of thirty-six. Fifty percent of the primary filers are aged twenty-nine through forty-five; the comparable age range for the secondary filers (who are usually the wives) is twenty-eight through forty-three.[35] The debtor sample is only slightly younger than the entire population. In the United States in 1991, the median age of adults was 39.2.[36] This means that about half of the U.S. adult population was older than thirty-nine, and half was younger. By comparison, about half of the debtors were older than thirty-eight, and half were younger.

Means and medians can sometimes obscure substantial numbers of debtors who are further from the middle. In addition to twenty-somethings, such as Mark and Michelle, a substantial number of older Americans have filed for bankruptcy. In 1997, nearly one in ten of the debtors who filed for bankruptcy was fifty-five or older.[37] In later chapters we discuss how jobs, medical problems, and family issues affect the financial stability of senior citizens.

The largest story about age and bankruptcy is the story of the baby boomers. The great bulge of postwar babies born from 1946 through 1962 were aged twenty-nine through forty-five in 1991 — that is, exactly the age range spanned by half of our primary filers. Thus, not only is bankruptcy a middle-class phenomenon, but in 1991 it was a middle-aged phenomenon. As the baby boomers reach middle age, they often have not achieved the financial stability they had hoped for.[38] The rise in bankruptcy filings during the 1980s coincided with the baby boomers' reaching middle age.

The overrepresentation of the baby boom is striking. In 1991, the proportion of the population who had been born between 1946 and 1962 was 27.3 percent; if one excludes children and teenagers under age twenty-one, the baby boomers were 39.2 percent of the adult population.[39] But 55 percent of the bankrupt debtors (primary and secondary filers) were members of the baby boom. The boomers' fraction of the debtor sample was fifteen percentage points higher than their fraction of the adult population.[40]

There are good reasons to believe that workers who are in their late thirties and early forties are financially stressed. Possibly the stress was particularly acute during the tumultuous economic times of the late 1980s and the early 1990s. In their late thirties, most Americans have begun their families and face growing expenses; increasingly, however, their wages are flat or even declining in real terms.[41] When the boomers were ready to enter the labor force, their very numbers tended to depress entry-level wage rates. When they were ready to buy starter houses, their numbers pressed real estate prices up. As downsizing and recessions took their toll, one or both adults in a household might have found themselves without work. And they faced simple marketing realities: because boomers are the largest birth cohorts in the population, members of the credit industry marketed credit aggressively to them.

This is not to say that the baby boomers alone caused the increase in bankruptcy filings; after all, only half of the primary filers are in the baby boom age span. But the fact that the boomers are a large birth cohort accounts for about 14 percent of the growth in the filing rates.[42] Demographers have already demonstrated that many age-affected social phenomena have increased or decreased as the baby boomers pass through their life cycle. It seems possible that bankruptcy is to some extent age-related and that the increase in bankruptcy in the 1980s may have reflected the arrival of the baby boom in the bankruptcy-prone ages.

But it must also be noted that the boomers reached middle age amid economic jolts. Just as the boomers began to get more secure in their jobs, corporate downsizing shredded their assumptions that seniority and experience would protect them. For these reasons, we cannot be certain that we have observed a pure age effect. Instead, we might be observing a cohort effect, something unique to the baby boomers. If that is so, the boomers may always be more prone to bankruptcy than other age cohorts. It is also possible that the data reflect a period effect, the fact that the 1980s and 1990s brought unique economic stresses. If that is so, bankruptcy rates would abate if the economic stresses lessened.

Comparable information from another year helps untangle these effects to some extent (fig. 2.1). Data from a study in the Southern District of Ohio conducted in 1997 contained information on the ages of the filers. To be sure, the Ohio data may not be nationally representative. Nevertheless, the Ohio data are similar in striking ways to our 1991 data. The mean age in both samples is thirty-eight. The age distributions of the two samples do not differ statistically.[43] The 1997 debtors were still slightly younger than the adult population, in which the median age had grown to 41.9.[44] The similarity of the age distributions suggests that there is an age effect, which supports the hypotheses that there are bankruptcy-prone years. The data suggest that the bankruptcy-prone age is older than the stereotype of the young debtor.

The strong representation of the baby boom in bankruptcy continues. By 1997, the boomers were aged thirty-five to fifty-one, and they accounted for about 34.5 percent of the national population.[45] About 53.8 percent of the Ohio sample were in the baby boomer age span, a continuing overrepresentation of the age cohort. As in our sample collected six years earlier, baby boomers constituted roughly half of the debtors. The evidence is thus also strong for a cohort effect: baby boomers at two points in time have been disproportionately represented in bankruptcy. Twenty-somethings like Mark and

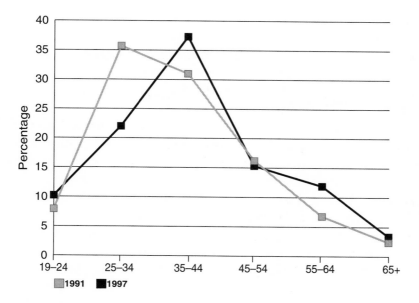

Fig. 2.1 Age of primary petitioner, 1991 and 1997. *Source:* Consumer Bankruptcy Project II, 1991; Ohio Bankruptcy Study, 1997.

Michelle are still to be found in bankruptcy, but the stereotype requires modification to include an aging cohort of baby boomers, a substantial fraction of seniors, and a median age that is only slightly below the median age of all adults.

### Race and Ethnicity

Reason for bankruptcy due to sickness in family and fell behind in payments. —JAMES and LADONNE WILLIAMS, Chicago, Illinois

James Williams is a forty-three-year-old foreman with some college education. His wife, LaDonne, is forty-two, has some college, and has worked as an office assistant, although she is not currently at work. They have experienced neither job interruptions nor marital interruptions. They list assets of $268,500 and secured debt on those assets of $208,132. They also have about $9,400 in unsecured debt, roughly $1,500 of it in credit card debt. It is reasonable to suppose that their Chapter 13 filing is motivated by concern over falling behind not just on their credit card payments but on their mortgage payment. From their earnings of about $39,000, they propose to pay 100 percent to their unsecured creditors while they recover physically from an illness and financially from the interrupted payments. There is one more fact about James and LaDonne: they indicate on their questionnaire that they are both African-American. They tell a story to which millions of Americans can relate.

The bankruptcy stereotype carries no overt color connotation with it.[46] Two hypotheses may be advanced concerning the representation of racial and ethnic minorities in bankruptcy. The first proposes that members of racial minority groups may be overrepresented in bankruptcy. The argument is that many minority group members are financially vulnerable because they are relatively recent arrivals to the middle class. Although racial segregation produced a small minority middle class,[47] the dismantling of Jim Crow laws and the advent of affirmative action promoted middle-class status for much larger numbers of African-Americans and, somewhat later, Mexican-Americans, Puerto Ricans, and Asian-Americans. As newcomers to the middle class, minority group members might be thought to be on its most fragile edge, and therefore likely users of the bankruptcy courts. We do not know if James and LaDonne Williams are the first generation in their families to own a home, but for many African-Americans, and Hispanic-Americans as well, homeownership is a dream only recently realized.[48] The Williams's dream was threatened by an illness and perhaps an insufficient cushion of savings or liquid assets. If minority group members find themselves disproportionately in precarious circumstances, then they may be forced into bankruptcy more often than majority whites. This is the overrepresentation hypothesis.

A contrary argument may also be made. As longtime outsiders to "the system," members of minority groups have had poorer access to legal assistance and limited information about how bankruptcy works. In addition, redlining and other restrictive credit practices have limited the amount of financial risk that minorities have been permitted to take.[49] Residential segregation has limited the accessibility of mortgages; credit issuers have checked zip codes before approving credit lines. As a result, minority group members have had less access to credit, lower levels of debt, and hence less need for bankruptcy. This is the underrepresentation hypothesis.

Both theses have had substantial support. The principal evidence for an underrepresentation of minority groups in bankruptcy has come from such studies as those of David Caplovitz of debtors in difficulty.[50] Caplovitz's study, conducted during 1967 in four large cities (New York City, Philadelphia, Chicago, and Detroit), showed that blacks were 65 percent of the sample of defaulting debtors but only 15 percent of a comparison sample of credit users and 18–34 percent of the populations of the cities.[51] Puerto Ricans were 7 percent of the defaulters and 2–10 percent of the urban populations.[52] Having defaulted, however, blacks were much less likely than whites to enter bankruptcy. Caplovitz reported: "In the aggregate, whites were more likely than blacks and Puerto Ricans to declare bankruptcy, 13 percent compared with 7 and 6 percent, respectively."[53]

There was some variation among cities; in Chicago, for example, 12 percent of black families in default entered bankruptcy versus 2 percent in Philadelphia. Caplovitz noted that there had been lawyer advertising in Chicago, even though at the time of his study the Supreme Court had not yet struck down the ban on lawyer advertising. These variations in relief under a federal law suggested to Caplovitz that access to bankruptcy varied. Although he did not use the phrase, his work suggested that a local legal culture affected either the access to attorneys or the nature of the advice that attorneys might provide.[54] If differential access explains intercity variations, then the Caplovitz data might also suggest that once in trouble, black debtors had less access to bankruptcy than white debtors.[55]

The Brookings Study, a multidistrict research project, offers the main support for the overrepresentation hypothesis. In their interviews conducted about two years after the bankruptcy cases had been closed during 1964, the interviewers used their own judgment to sort the respondents into ethnic or national-origin backgrounds.[56] They concluded, "The most significant result is the large disproportion of blacks—38 percent of the debtors. In the districts with substantial black populations the percentage of blacks [in bankruptcy] is high."[57] In five of the Brookings Study districts, blacks were overrepresented among the petitioners relative to their proportion of the population in the census of 1960.[58] For example, 51 percent of the interviewees in the Northern District of Illinois were black, compared with 23 percent of Chicago's population in the 1960 census.

The Brookings Study also reported on Hispanic debtors in bankruptcy. The researchers reported that in two districts Hispanic debtors were overrepresented, Southern California and the Western District of Texas. Of these districts, they wrote, "Note the large proportion of Spanish-speaking debtors in Western Texas and Southern California."[59] An accompanying table showed that 36 percent of the debtors in the Western District of Texas were Spanish-speaking, as were 13 percent of the debtors in Southern California.[60] This table, however, did not provide comparative figures for the population generally. In 1960 the approximate proportion of Spanish-surnamed population in San Antonio (in the Western District of Texas) was 50 percent, and in California it was 20 percent.[61] Thus, although the "Spanish-speaking" and Spanish-surnamed populations are not quite identical, it does not appear that there was an overrepresentation of Spanish-heritage people in these two districts. On the contrary, an observer might have expected even more filings from the Spanish-speaking population.

44     Stanley and Girth had tried to correct for the sample bias problem by comparing the proportion of blacks in their sample with the proportion of blacks in the population of large cities in the districts studied, although they omitted any similar comparisons for Hispanics.[62] The difficulty with the comparison is that bankruptcy is filed in federal courts that represent a population far larger than a single city. Illinois, for example, is divided into three federal districts. The Northern District includes Chicago, but it also includes suburban areas, smaller towns, and even some rural areas. Similarly, Texas is divided into four districts, California into four districts, Pennsylvania into three districts, and Tennessee into three districts. Although some districts are dominated by a single large city and others have no large city, each district has a mix of urban, suburban, and rural areas.

Given the difficulty of conducting a national study of bankruptcy, researchers who are constrained by both time and finances to study only a subset of all federal districts face the problem that the black population is concentrated in some jurisdictions and in some cities within those jurisdictions. The findings about African-American or Hispanic-American families in bankruptcy might be skewed higher or lower depending upon which districts are chosen for study and whether all court sites within a district are studied or only one urban location. For example, a study with data drawn only from Newark, New Jersey, is likely to find a disproportionately large number of black bankruptcy petitioners because a large proportion of the population is black, a finding that might change if debtors who filed at other courthouses in New Jersey had been included in the sample.[63] Other researchers have collected data in only a single city and drawn conclusions about the racial composition of the bankruptcy sample that are also of questionable validity.[64]

Unlike other empirical studies, we did not confine the sample to large cities. Instead, we undertook the more difficult (and much more costly) task of sampling cases from each courthouse in which they were held, both in small towns and in big cities, in the proportion in which such files were located throughout a district. This meant, for example, that we collected cases both from Chicago and from Rockford, Illinois, the repositories for bankruptcy petitions in the Northern District of Illinois. As a result, we were able to get a cross-section of everyone filing within the district. Because we also collected cases from all the districts within four states (California, Illinois, Pennsylvania, and Texas) and two of the three districts in a fifth state (Tennessee) we have a more nearly complete cross-section of all those who filed within these states.

45

Even with a more complete cross-section, however, one or more factors may confound the results. If debtors in cities file more than similar debtors in small towns and if city debtors are more often minority group members, then a bankruptcy sample would seem to overrepresent minority group members—although the determining factor might be city location rather than race.

Similarly, members of different racial groups might receive varying legal advice or be subject to different local legal cultures about bankruptcy. It is possible that the overrepresentation of African-Americans reported in the Brookings Study, for example, represents the continuation of a local legal culture and not a national phenomenon. That is, it might be the case that black debtors in Chicago have used bankruptcy as a remedy for financial problems for many years. Members of the Chicago bar serving the black community might be more likely to recommend bankruptcy than members of the bar serving other communities. Caplovitz's observation about

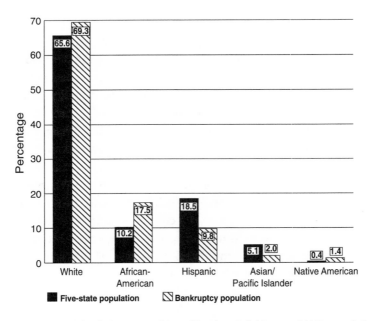

Fig. 2.2 Racial-ethnic composition of bankrupt debtors and U.S. population in five states, 1991. *Source:* Consumer Bankruptcy Project II, 1991; U.S. population calculated from *Statistical Abstract: 1996,* 34, table 35.

attorney advertising in Chicago might be relevant to understanding the legal culture of that city. These are merely conjectures that our data neither confirm nor deny, but they give some idea of the more extensive inquiry needed to understand why some differences may arise in various bankruptcy courts.

Our data, which represent a selection of all debtors in four states and debtors in two of three districts in a fifth state, are closer to those reported by the Brookings Institution study in finding an over-representation of blacks and Hispanics than they are to the Caplovitz finding of underrepresentation (fig. 2.2).[65]

African-American families are overrepresented in bankruptcy, while all other minority groups are underrepresented. African-Americans are 10.2 percent of the population of the five states we studied, but they comprise 17.5 percent of the debtors in the bankruptcy sample.

About 9.8 percent of the filers in the 1991 sample reported that they were Hispanic. We used this category to include Mexican-

**MIDDLE-CLASS AND BROKE**

Americans, Puerto Ricans, and others who reported ancestry or origin from Central or South America. In 1991, about 18.5 percent of the population of the five states from which these data were drawn was Hispanic. The proportions in the sample suggest an underrepresentation of Hispanics. In the Western District of Texas about 36 percent of the debtors are Hispanic. Interestingly, the same proportion of "Spanish-speaking" interviewees were reported for the Western District of Texas in the Brookings Study back in the 1960s.[66] Many of the metropolitan areas within the district, however, have much higher proportions of Hispanics than the district as a whole: 55.6 percent in San Antonio, 69.6 percent in El Paso, 81.9 percent in Brownsville–Harlingen, 85.2 percent in McAllen–Edinburgh–Mission, and 93.9 percent in Laredo.[67] In the Southern District of Texas, 28 percent of the debtors reported that they were Hispanic, compared with 50 percent of Corpus Christi's population and 28 percent of Houston's population.[68] The underrepresentation of Hispanic-American debtors in the sample thus does not come simply from the absence of Hispanic debtors in districts where there are small minorities of Hispanics. Instead, these data suggest that underrepresentation occurred in districts with substantial Hispanic populations. The sample districts include two southwestern states in which a large fraction of the Hispanic population resides.

Asian-American debtors were not discussed at all in Caplovitz's work or the Brookings Study. They are underrepresented in the 1991 data. Only 2 percent of the 1991 debtors—thirty-two petitioners—reported being of Asian ancestry. Of these debtors, twenty-nine lived in California and three in Texas. The Asian-American population is concentrated in California. For example, Asian-American and Pacific Islanders are about 9.2 percent of the population of Los Angeles–Anaheim–Riverside metropolitan area and 14.8 percent of the population of San Francisco–Oakland–San Jose.[69] In spite of this concentration of Asian-Americans, however, they were underrepresented in bankruptcy. The greatest concentration of Asian-American debtors was in the Northern District of California, which contains San Francisco, where 29.1 percent of the population is Asian-American or Pacific Islanders. Even there, however, only 10.9 percent of the debtors reported themselves Asian-American. Because of the differences in sampling and the gaps in the data collected earlier, it is difficult to know whether these data show a significant change in the racial and ethnic composition of bankruptcy since the 1960s.

It is possible that the overrepresentation of African-American families in bankruptcy stems from an increase in the size of the black middle class in the past decade. A larger black middle class could mean that more families were both affluent enough to acquire substantial credit and more vulnerable to the consequences of a lost job. In 1988, blacks were 6.7 percent of all professional workers and 5.6 percent of executive and managerial workers. In 1997, blacks constituted 7.8 percent of professional workers and 6.9 percent of executive and managerial workers.[70] These changes look relatively small, but because both occupational groups were growing the figures represent an additional 974,000 black professionals and managers in 1997.

It is also possible that these data signal that African-American families are more vulnerable as a group to the financial pressures that lead to bankruptcy. There are vast differences in the asset accumulation of blacks and whites even if the usual class indicators are controlled.[71] The authors of a new study of black wealth argue that the multigenerational inability of blacks to acquire wealth amounts to the "sedimentation of racial inequality."[72] Even black entrepreneurs, who were often effectively restricted to a market created by other blacks, faced limitations on their ability to accumulate assets.[73] Sociologist Troy Duster from the University of California, Berkeley, has argued: "Financially, the biggest difference between whites and blacks today is their median net worth, which is overwhelmingly attributable to the value of equity in housing stock. In 1991, the median net worth of white households ($43,279) was more than 10 times that of the median net worth of African-American households ($4,169). In contrast, while wage and salary differences between whites and blacks persist, they are relatively small. But if we look at net worth instead of salary, the differences inflate to a shocking ratio of 10 to 1."[74] For 1993, the Census Bureau reported that 12.6 percent of all households had zero or negative net worth. But almost 29 percent of black households had a zero or negative net worth, compared with 10 percent of white households.[75] The financial pressure on a growing African-American middle class may help explain the higher proportion of African-American families in bankruptcy. These data, particularly as they may have changed since the 1960s, are consistent with a story of a growing African-American middle class that is not entirely financially secure and that disproportionately finds itself at the door of the bankruptcy courthouse.

But the data show that not all minority households are similarly situated. Many Hispanic families are also newly arrived in the middle class and facing economic pressures similar to those of black families. For example, nearly 23 percent of Hispanic-origin households had a zero or negative net worth, less than black families but more than twice the rate of white families.[76] And yet, Hispanic-American families are underrepresented in our five-state study. But the data are more ambiguous than this statistic suggests. In Chapter 7 we explore the circumstances of African-American and Hispanic-American homeowners and discover that both are sharply overrepresented in bankruptcy. One possible source of variation we can explore, however, is how the black, white, Hispanic-American, or Asian-American families might differ from one another demographically. Our study permits us to examine whether subgroups in bankruptcy differ markedly. We can determine whether black families that look quite different as a group from white families are concealed by general statistics on bankruptcy.

In the national population, African-Americans and Hispanic-Americans have lower levels of education and usually hold less prestigious occupations than majority whites or Asian-Americans. This observation raises the possibility that the African-Americans and Hispanic-Americans in bankruptcy might originate from a different social class group than do other petitioners. The data, however, do not readily support this supposition. Black and Hispanic petitioners are similar to the other petitioners. Analyzing just the black and Hispanic versus Asian and white classification, the former group does not differ significantly from the latter in terms of age, education, or occupational prestige.

Some demographic differences are apparent when the racial-ethnic groups are examined separately. Among the bankrupt debtors, Hispanic petitioners are the least well educated, with 31.4 percent not having finished high school; even so, 42.1 percent of the Hispanic petitioners have attended college. The Asian-American petitioners are both the least educated (31.4 percent not having finished high school) and among the best educated (53.2 percent having attended college). The African-American petitioners are nearly as likely as the Asian-American petitioners to have attended college (52.9 percent), and they are as likely as white and Asian-American petitioners to have earned a college degree.

A more detailed examination of occupational prestige does not reveal significant differences among the racial-ethnic groups. The mean white prestige score was 40.2, compared with 39.8 for African-Americans. Hispanic-Americans were lower at 35.4, and Asian-Americans higher at 45.0. None of the differences were statistically significant.

Marital status is one variable that distinguishes racial-ethnic groups within bankruptcy. The black petitioners are significantly more likely to be single (23 percent versus 15 percent of the sample). Hispanic petitioners are significantly more likely to be married (62 percent versus 52 percent of the whole sample) and significantly less likely to be divorced (11 percent versus 22 percent of the sample).

The data presented here show a racial composition in bankruptcy that differs somewhat from that of the population generally. The data make it clear, however, that bankruptcy is not the exclusive province of any minority group. The overwhelming bulk of the debtors in bankruptcy are white—as are the overwhelming bulk of the American population. Racial divisions mirror those in the five states we sampled, with the exception of the overrepresentation of African-Americans and the underrepresentation of other groups. Nor is the bankrupt population composed of some "other" group as measured by education or occupation. The education and occupational prestige data strongly suggest that the middle class is in bankruptcy. The black middle class, much like a white, Hispanic, or Asian middle class, is at risk for financial collapse—only more so.

## Citizenship

Unable to raise equity financing for business on account of recession and because of the Iraq war in 1990–1991.—MEHDI HOSSEINI, Los Angeles

Mehdi Hosseini is a naturalized citizen, aged fifty-two and divorced. He holds an advanced degree. He also reported a recent income interruption, and it is unclear from his questionnaire whether he currently had a job or was searching for one. It appears that he owned a business that ran into trouble during the recession of 1990–91, a recession that struck California with particular intensity. We cannot tell the nature of his business or why the Gulf War might have affected it, but one speculation is that his business relied on business relationships in a Middle Eastern country. Mehdi reports assets worth only $10,000 and secured debt of only $3,000. Of his total debt 98 percent is unsecured ($316,000), but less than 2 percent ($5,200) is due to credit card debt. Although we cannot be certain, it seems likely that many of his debts were incurred for his business.

Immigrants are represented in bankruptcy in the same proportions that they are in the population. In the 1990 census, about 8 percent of the population was foreign-born. In our five-state study, the proportion of primary filers who were foreign-born was only marginally higher: 9 percent. Six percent of the filers were naturalized citizens and only 3 percent were resident aliens. The immigrant debtors are also concentrated in California, the state that is far and away the most favored destination of recent immigrants.[77] Relative to the population of these districts, the foreign-born are not disproportionately represented. In California's Central District, which includes Los Angeles, 22.3 percent of the primary petitioners are foreign-born, 9.2 percent of whom are resident aliens. In the Northern District, where San Francisco is located, 18.9 percent of the sample are foreign-born persons, 10.5 percent of them still resident aliens. The population of these two districts, which comprise twenty-two counties, was 24.6 percent foreign-born according to the 1990 census.[78]

Most immigrants come to the United States in the hope of economic success and, eventually, at least middle-class status. For some immigrants who reached these shores, the American dream has not yet materialized, and bankruptcy is one way to deal with their financial failure. Their representation seems consistent with their proportion in the population.

*Education*

> Despite having completed medical school and started a residency training program in psychiatry, my current first-year salary as a resident is not sufficient to meet my total financial obligation. I had received assistance from my parents for several years, but with my mother's untimely ill-

ness, this assistance is no longer available. In addition I must meet certain obligations here to be paid by my mother (e.g. automobile payment of $284/mo).

I realize that my income potential is tremendous, and look forward to an increased income in the coming years. The average yearly income for practicing psychiatrists is $120,000. I know that such an income is more than sufficient to meet all financial obligations, yet realistically that income figure is some five years in the future. I must meet current obligations (including child support payments) now, and petition only for sufficient time to allow my income to equal ordinary expenditures.

—MICHAEL REED, M.D., Nashville, Tennessee

Michael Reed is a psychiatrist. At the time of his Chapter 7 filing, he could not make ends meet on his salary as a resident, and the help he had received from his parents had ended because of his mother's illness. At age thirty-two, he has child support payments and car payments. With debts of $181,000 and an income of only $24,000, he understands his income potential and asks "only for sufficient time to allow my income to equal ordinary expenditures." Michael owes $152,000 in unsecured debt, of which credit cards account for $22,000. His assets are worth around $19,000—possibly his car and a few household possessions. He does not own a home. It is possible that much of his remaining debt represents loans undertaken to help pay for his extensive schooling, which will not be discharged in his bankruptcy. His medical training did not prepare him to cure his own financial ills.

Education is one of the foundation stones of the American middle class because of its relation to eventual income and to lifestyle. America is not alone in associating higher education with higher class standing. One of Professor Higgins's challenges in the transformation of Eliza Doolittle was to overcome her lack of a fine English education—for it was in those vaunted classrooms that a young lady learned to pronounce "the rain in Spain" in the absence of a scheming tutor. What distinguishes American education from that of many other nations is its extreme democracy, not only in making public education widely available through twelfth grade, but also in making higher education more widely available. Part of the citizen's democratic heritage in the United States is the ability to seek more educa-

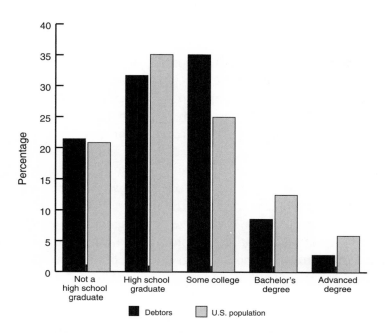

Fig. 2.3 Completed education of bankrupt debtors and U.S. population, 1990–91.
*Source:* Consumer Bankruptcy Project II, 1991; data for U.S. population aged 18 and
older in 1990 calculated from *Statistical Abstract: 1993*, 154, table 234.

tion, and an education has historically been one of the most important means of access to the middle class. Higher education remains
expensive, both in terms of time and money, but it is also a means by
which to overcome possible handicaps of birth and class.

Moreover, the better-paying jobs within the economy usually require extensive schooling, including advanced degrees. American colleges and universities are the gatekeepers of access to professional
jobs, for which licensure is dependent upon graduation from an ac-
credited school. One test of the proposition that the bankrupt sample
is middle class should be a level of education that is at least equivalent to that of their fellow citizens.

In contrast with the bankruptcy stereotype, which characterized
the bankrupt debtors as less educated and often as high school dropouts, the debtors in our five-state study were somewhat better educated than the adult population (fig. 2.3).[79] In 1991, 36 percent of the
population were high school graduates with no further formal education, compared with 31.7 percent of the primary filers. The primary

**MIDDLE-CLASS AND BROKE**

filers were nearly one-third again as likely as the national sample to have completed one to three years of college, with 35.1 percent of the primary filers versus 25 percent of the population having attended college one to three years but without receiving a bachelor's degree.

Compared with the national population, however, the debtors were less likely to have earned their degrees. About 12.5 percent of the national population but only 8.6 percent of the primary filers had earned a bachelor's degree. Advanced degree holders such as Michael were least likely to be in the sample; not quite 3 percent of the primary filers held advanced degrees, compared with 5.9 percent of the national population. Aggregating the figures, 11.4 percent of the primary filers had one or more college degrees, compared with 18.4 percent of the national population holding one or more degrees.

The modal (most frequently occurring) category of education for both primary and secondary filers was some college—one to three years of college, but without a degree. Almost one-half of the primary filers, 47 percent, had schooling beyond high school, a higher proportion than the 43.4 percent of the national population who had some education beyond high school. Thus, the primary petitioners were more likely than the general population to have gotten some higher education but less likely to have achieved a degree.

Among married couples filing jointly, there was also a second debtor of whom we could ask questions about education. Nearly 96 percent of the secondary filers are women, the wives of the primary filers; in the remaining 4 percent of joint petitions, the wife was listed as the primary filer and the husband as the secondary filer. These spouses are slightly less well educated than the primary filers. More than a thousand of these secondary filers reported their education to us, and the distribution of their schooling is very similar to that of the primary filers (the index of dissimilarity is 9.2, indicating that fewer than 10 percent of the secondary filers would have to change their education to have the same distribution as the primary filers). The principal difference is that the secondary filers are more likely than the primary filers to be high school graduates (38 percent versus 32 percent) and less likely to have attended college (31 percent versus 35 percent). Only 8 percent of the secondary filers have a college degree.

If we compare the secondary filers with all married adult women, we find that those in bankruptcy have achieved lower levels of education than other wives. Roughly one-sixth of adult women (16.7 percent) have not completed high school and another 36 percent are high school graduates. About 23 percent of married women generally have at least a bachelor's degree.[80] The secondary filers are much less likely to have attended college and also much less likely to have finished a degree.

The primary filers thus look very similar to the rest of the country in terms of education, and the secondary filers are about as likely to be high school graduates but much less likely to have college degrees. Nothing in these data suggests that the debtors are not middle class, but the relative absence of college degrees may indicate that they are in the center of the class distribution and not in the upper reaches where Michael Reed's education may put him.

The educational background of the primary debtors differs significantly among the states.[81] Both in California and in Texas, the debtors are more likely to have attended college, with over 55 percent of the California debtors and 56 percent of the Texas debtors having at least some college. More than 15 percent of the debtors in the two Sun Belt states had earned at least one college degree. By contrast, in both Pennsylvania and Tennessee, more than 18 percent of the debtors had attended school for fewer than eleven years. Pennsylvania debtors were the least well educated members of the sample, but even so, more than three-quarters of the Pennsylvania debtors were at least high school graduates, with more than a third of them having attended at least some college.[82]

If our data are characteristic of the national bankruptcy population, roughly 100,400 college graduates and 134,700 high-school dropouts filed for bankruptcy in 1991.[83] In between, we would find more than 500,000 debtors who were high school graduates, including many who have attended at least some college. Based on their educations alone, we would judge the great majority of the bankrupt debtors to be solid members of the middle class.

*Occupation*

Bad investment. I started a small dress shop. My partner stole most of the money I had put in the store and left. I had to close the shop and I

could not pay the bills, for the shop or my bills—I got sick and had to
have surgery. Then I had a car reak.—MILLIE BROWN, Dallas, Texas

Millie Brown is a fifty-two-year-old divorced high school graduate. She is filing alone in Chapter 13 after the failure of her small
dress shop. She attributes her business failure to theft by her partner,
but her life got worse because she needed an operation and had an
automobile accident.

Millie's story is familiar. For many Americans, running a small
business is the dream of a lifetime. Working for themselves, and not
for a boss, can be enormously satisfying. Just knowing that Millie is a
small business proprietor tells us something about the risks she must
have taken to make the business work. At least one contemporary
theorist has argued that risk-taking is becoming the defining characteristic distinguishing social classes.[84] For risk-takers like Millie—
for whom the risk failed—there is small comfort in knowing that
sociologists consider her to be solidly middle class.

What one does for a living is a critical indicator of both eventual
income and lifestyle. Even though technology has made some new
occupations unfamiliar to us, occupation remains a touchstone for
social class. Occupation is such a key indicator of identity for Americans that many Americans continue to identify themselves by occupation even after they have retired or are temporarily unemployed.[85]
It is a key indicator for many reasons deep in our national charac-
ter. The upper class might be known, as Thorstein Veblen claimed,
for how they spent their leisure—the leisure itself being a sign of
their status. But for the great bulk of Americans, it is how they spend
their working hours that often defines not only them but their non-
working spouses and even their dependent children.[86] As for their
adult children, Americans often answer the question "What is Stanley
doing now?" with an account of his job.

Americans have a pretty good idea of the relative prestige of different occupations. Sociologists have developed prestige scales through
a series of studies that began shortly after World War II and asked
a cross-section of people to rank-order the prestige of various occupations. These scales have been replicated on numerous occasions
within the United States and in a number of foreign countries. The
rankings of the occupations are remarkably stable. Prestige scores,

moreover, correlate fairly highly with income of the occupations and with the typical education level of the workers who pursue those occupations. We were able to develop and analyze prestige scores for debtors in the Western District of Texas, the Northern District of Illinois, and the Middle District of Tennessee because we had copies of the schedules they filed with the court, which indicated their occupations.[87] For these districts, the mean and median prestige score for primary filers was 39 points and for secondary filers it was 37 points. These numbers are higher than the mean score of 37 and the median of 36 we reported for the primary filers in the 1981 sample.[88] More tellingly, they are quite similar to the national mean of 40.7 and the national median of 40 for the United States in 1990.[89]

To put the prestige scoring instrument in some perspective, the scale runs from a low of 9 (bootblack) to a high of 82 (physician). Some of the debtors who are quoted in this chapter would easily fit into the upper half of the scale. The highest score in the sample was 82 for physicians such as Michael Reed. Willis Creighton rated a 72 when he was a bank officer. Another score of 72 was recorded for an electrical engineer in the sample. Others are closer to the middle of the prestige distribution. James Miller, the foreman, has a score of 45; his wife LaDonne's former position as an office assistant would receive a 36. Millie Brown's position as the proprietor of a small store carries a prestige score of 47. Marcia James, the former saleswoman, would have a score of 40 for that job. The lowest score in the sample, 16, was recorded for a laundress. There were two modal scores—that is, the scores that occurred most often—at 47 and 36. Nearly 9 percent of the sample had a score of 47, which is associated with such jobs as technician, flight engineer, insurance agent, broker, underwriter, and tool programmer. Another 9 percent had a score of 36, the score for secretaries and nurses' aides.

Half of the occupational prestige scores lay between 31 and 48.[90] Some examples of occupations around the mean value of 40 include sales representatives in wholesale trade (40), library attendants (41), payroll clerks (41), and cabinetmakers (39). More than a fourth of the sample had prestige scores higher than 48. Some typical occupations with scores at this level include purchasing agents (48), bookkeepers (48), insurance adjusters (48), examiners (48), investigators (48), and metal job and die setters (48).

The close parallel between the occupational prestige scores of the bankruptcy sample and of Americans generally is even more remarkable when the data from the next chapter are explored. In that chapter, in which we focus on the role of job problems in causing bankruptcy filings, we examine evidence that many of the debtors in bankruptcy have suffered downward shifts in their employment status. Managers who became salespeople and professional workers who cannot find similar opportunities are among the debtors explaining their bankruptcies in terms of problems with their jobs. If the debtors in bankruptcy have suffered declining occupational status, as the data suggest, then the suggestion that these debtors are—or, at least at one point were—the professional equivalents of those not in bankruptcy is strongly reinforced.

Another indication of the occupational status of the debtors in bankruptcy is the likelihood that they will work for themselves. In our 1981 study, one-fifth of the debtors were or had been entrepreneurs, and they accounted for half of the scheduled unsecured debt.[91] It appears that in 1991 many of the debtors were also self-employed. The self-employed, whether they owned a farm or a small shop, have historically been regarded as the part of the backbone of the middle class. In 1981, we were able to determine that about 10 percent of the petitioners filing for personal bankruptcy were self-employed. In 1991, we collected the data somewhat differently and determined that once again at least 10 percent were self-employed. Ambiguities in the responses of the debtors made it impossible to determine whether another 10 percent of the debtors were self-employed, which means that the actual total of self-employed debtors in 1991 may have been as high as 20 percent.[92] In 1981, the 10 percent who were self-employed were matched by another 10 percent of the sample that had been self-employed before the filing but by the time of the bankruptcy were either working for someone else or identified themselves as unemployed. Although we are unable to capture the number of formerly self-employed from the 1991 data because of reporting differences, using the 1981 data as a guide, we estimate that in 1991 about 20 percent of the nonbusiness consumer bankruptcy cases might be, like Millie Brown, casualties of an entrepreneurial failure.

These data suggest that the increase in bankruptcy filings between 1981 and 1991 did not come about from drawing more unskilled and low-level workers into the bankruptcy courts. Rather, it was workers in the middle of the prestige distribution who were filing for bankruptcy in such large numbers. In 1991, it appears, even though three times as many persons were filing for bankruptcy as had filed in 1981, the occupational status of those people was approximately the same or maybe just a bit higher than in 1981. Although bankruptcy in the 1990s involved many more people, it involved many more of the same kinds of people as in the 1980s.

### Really a Cross-Section?

To renew the question with which we began this chapter, are these debtors a cross-section of the American population? To a large extent the answer must be "yes." Men and women are about equally represented in the sample. The debtors are about as middle-aged as a true cross-section of the population, although the baby boomers are somewhat overrepresented. Given the districts and states we studied, whites, Hispanic-Americans, and Asian-Americans are somewhat underrepresented and African-Americans are somewhat overrepresented relative to the states in which they reside. Immigrants are present in rough proportion to their presence in the population. Bankrupt debtors are somewhat more likely than other Americans to have attended college but less likely to have completed the requirements for a degree. The occupational prestige of the debtors' jobs is close to that of workers generally, although there is a greater representation of entrepreneurs among the debtors. Judged by these data, debtors in bankruptcy are a demographic cross-section of America.

How then are the debtors different? Financially, they look very different from other Americans.

## A Financial Portrait

The financial portrait of the debtors in bankruptcy comes from coding data from bankruptcy petitions that we collected from five districts, one in each of the five sampled states. In addition, we have financial data collected by Judge Barbara Sellers in 1997 in the Southern District of Ohio using similar reporting techniques. The bankruptcy petitions provide the court (under penalty of perjury) with

**Table 2.1** Annual household income by state (1989) and by bankruptcy sample (1991) in five states (in 1989 dollars with means and medians also reported in 1997 dollars)

| | Texas | | California | | Pennsylvania | | Illinois | | Tennessee | |
|---|---|---|---|---|---|---|---|---|---|---|
| | State | Sample | State | Sample | State | Sample | State | Sample | State | Sample |
| <$5,000 | 8.17 | 4.6 | 3.9 | 10.6 | 5.4 | 9.7 | 6.1 | 3.4 | 8.8 | 7.1 |
| $5,000–9,999 | 9.57 | 7.9 | 7.6 | 13.6 | 10.1 | 16.7 | 8.1 | 11.5 | 11.2 | 14.2 |
| $10,000–14,999 | 9.82 | 22.5 | 7.4 | 27.3 | 9.2 | 25.0 | 7.9 | 25.7 | 10.5 | 25.5 |
| $15,000–24,999 | 18.76 | 35.1 | 15.2 | 25.8 | 18.2 | 35.4 | 16.2 | 34.5 | 19.8 | 29.8 |
| $25,000–34,999 | 15.76 | 20.5 | 14.7 | 9.1 | 16.6 | 9.0 | 15.5 | 14.2 | 16.4 | 16.3 |
| $35,000–49,999 | 16.55 | 7.3 | 18.2 | 13.6 | 18.4 | 3.5 | 19.1 | 8.1 | 16.2 | 5.0 |
| $50,000–74,999 | 13.34 | 1.3 | 18.4 | 0.0 | 14.1 | 0.7 | 16.7 | 2.0 | 11.4 | 1.4 |
| $75,000–99,999 | 4.32 | 0.0 | 7.6 | 0.0 | 4.3 | 0.0 | 5.6 | 0.7 | 3.0 | 0.7 |
| $100,000< | 3.71 | 0.7 | 7.1 | 0.0 | 3.6 | 0.0 | 4.9 | 0.0 | 2.6 | 0.0 |
| Median | $27,016 | 19,173 | 35,748 | 14,530 | 29,069 | 14,512 | 32,252 | 16,857 | 24,807 | 15,686 |
| Mean | 35,618 | 20,845 | 46,247 | 17,778 | 36,684 | 15,985 | 40,885 | 19,981 | 31,864 | 18,031 |
| Median ($ 1997) | 34,968 | 24,817 | 46,271 | 18,807 | 37,626 | 18,784 | 41,746 | 21,819 | 32,109 | 20,303 |
| Mean ($ 1997) | 46,102 | 26,981 | 59,860 | 23,011 | 47,482 | 20,690 | 52,920 | 25,863 | 41,243 | 23,339 |
| N | 6,079,341 | 151 | 10,399,700 | 66 | 4,492,958 | 144 | 4,197,720 | 148 | 1,853,515 | 141 |
| Missing | — | 3 | — | 85 | — | 1 | — | 4 | — | 2 |

*Source:* Consumer Bankruptcy Project II, 1991; 1990 Census Volumes: California CP-2-6, 176, table 42; Illinois CP-2-15, 126, table 42; Pennsylvania CP-2-40, 237, table 42; Tennessee CP-2-44, 48, table 42; Texas CP-2-45, 167, table 42.

*Note:* To obtain the median and mean in 1997 dollars, the 1989 figures were multiplied by 1.2943548. This factor was calculated from the Consumer Price Index.

information on the income, assets, and debts of the petitioners. In the following sections, we investigate each of these financial variables separately. Collectively, these data reveal a group of debtors in serious financial difficulties.

## Income

As a group, the 1991 bankruptcy filers are in terrible financial shape. Median family income for the five-district group of debtors was $17,964, compared with the national median family income in 1991 of $36,404.[93] The median is the number that divides the distribution in half, so half of all the debtors earned less than $17,964, and half of the U.S. population earned less than $36,404. The median income for the 1991 debtors in bankruptcy was almost exactly half the median income for Americans generally. The 1991 debtors are concentrated in the lower half of the national income distribution. In 1997, the Ohio debtors' median income was $18,756, compared with the 1997 national median of $42,300.[94] The 1997 data show debtors who have fallen even further behind: their median income was only 44 percent of the national median, concentrating them even lower on the income distribution scale.

We compared the incomes of our sample with the mean and median household income in their states (table 2.1).[95] Regardless of the state in which they have filed, the debtors bear a striking resemblance to one another. In 1989 dollars, their median incomes range from a low of $14,512 in Pennsylvania to a high of $19,173 in Texas, a range of $4,661. The mean incomes range from $15,985 in Pennsylvania to $20,845 in Texas, a range of $4,860. In each state more than half the debtors are concentrated in the income range from $10,000–$24,999 compared with the national median of $36,404. The ends of the distributions vary somewhat from state to state: about 10 percent of California's and Pennsylvania's debtors are in the very lowest category, less than $5,000,[96] and 2 percent of Illinois debtors are over $50,000. The conclusion, however, is that these distributions look quite similar regardless of state. Whether from the East Coast or the West Coast, the Midwest or the Midsouth, the debtors are concentrated well below the U.S. median income.

The distributions of household incomes make it clear that the

**MIDDLE-CLASS AND BROKE**

average household in each state is better off than the average debtor household in the same state. More than 50 percent of the debtors are concentrated in the income ranges $15,000–24,999, whereas about 50 percent of the general population are concentrated in the ranges $25,000–74,999.[97]

In each state, the debtors look poorer than their neighbors at the time the sample was drawn. The debtors' median income in California is a mere 41 percent of the state median. The median of the best-off debtors—those in Texas—is only 71 percent of the state median income. In Pennsylvania, the debtors' median is 50 percent of the state median; in Illinois, it is 52 percent; in Tennessee, 63 percent. By contrast, the general population is much more likely to be found in the high-income brackets. At the upper regions of the scale, incomes over $75,000, there are virtually no bankrupt debtors. Outside bankruptcy, people with incomes over $75,000 are 15 percent of all California households, 8–11 percent of households in Texas, Pennsylvania, and Illinois, and more than 5 percent of the households in Tennessee.

In California people with very low income (less than $5,000) are overrepresented in bankruptcy. In Tennessee people with low income are in the bankruptcy sample and in the general population in roughly similar proportions. The striking question is why so few low-income people in Texas, Pennsylvania, and Illinois are represented in the bankruptcy sample. In Texas, for example, 8 percent of the households report incomes below $5,000, twice as high as the 4 percent of Texas bankrupt debtors with incomes so low. In Illinois, 6 percent of all households are in the lowest income category, twice as high as the 3 percent of the bankrupt debtors in the same category. One interpretation might be that bankruptcy is underused in these states and that poorer people are denied access to the bankruptcy court simply because they cannot afford it.[98] But the high proportions of debtors with above-poverty incomes, and particularly those for whom there may once have been substantially higher take-home pay, suggests that bankruptcy is a function not only of low income but also of high debt. Households with very low incomes over a long period may not have had the same opportunities to incur much debt; households that currently have low incomes but once had higher incomes may also have incurred higher debts when their incomes would support it.

Many of the debtors are, at least at the time of their petition, poverty-stricken by the government standards. The poverty level income estimated by the government for 1991 was $13,924.[99] In 1991, 12.8 percent of American families lived below the poverty level.[100] Among the populations of the five sample states, the poverty rate ranged from a low of 11.1 percent in Pennsylvania to a high of 18.1 percent in Texas.[101] In the sample, however, a full 32.4 percent of the debtors fell below the poverty rate, more than two and a half times the national average.

That a third of the debtors are in poverty, however, does not mean that they are necessarily among the chronically poor, although some might be. In a society in which income is volatile, there is substantial movement into and out of poverty. Between 1990 and 1991 alone, for example, 2.9 percent of nonpoor people in the United States fell into poverty.[102] Another 21.2 percent who had been poor in 1990 escaped poverty in 1991. Half of all poverty spells in the United States last less than four months; only 13 percent last for more than two years. The bankruptcy data are a snapshot at one point in time. They reveal a group of debtors with very low incomes at the time of filing, but these low incomes often reflect neither their long-term earnings history nor their long-term earnings potential. As we demonstrate in the next chapter, many debtors suffered a recent fall in income that precipitated, or at least accompanied, their fall into bankruptcy.

## Income and Education

One truism of American economic life is that earnings tend to rise with education.[103] A population with very low income, such as the bankrupt debtors, may simply lack the skills to compete in American economic life at the beginning of the twenty-first century. But the data we have presented show that these debtors are about as well educated as the rest of the population. It is important to examine their earnings in relation to their schooling to be certain that the very low earnings of one poorly educated group has skewed the group averages.

It turns out that at every level of schooling, the bankrupt debtors

**Table 2.2**  Mean earnings by educational level, U.S. population and bankrupt debtors from five districts, 1991 (in 1991 and 1997 dollars)

| Educational level | U.S. population | | Bankrupt debtors | | Ratio of population to debtors |
|---|---|---|---|---|---|
| | 1991 | 1997 | 1991 | 1997 | |
| High school graduate | 18,261 | 21,519 | 17,697 | 20,854 | 1.03 |
| Some college | 20,551 | 24,218 | 18,000 | 21,211 | 1.14 |
| Bachelor's degree | 31,323 | 36,911 | 22,790 | 26,856 | 1.37 |
| Advanced degree | 48,652 | 57,332 | 25,344 | 29,866 | 1.92 |

*Source:* U.S. Census data from http://www.census.gov/population/socdemo/education/ext-table19.txt (July 4, 1996), derived from *Current Population Survey,* and based on individual incomes.
*Note:* The 1991 figures were inflated to 1997 constant dollars by multiplying by 1.1784141 (derived from the Consumer Price Index).

are doing much worse financially than other Americans at the same educational level (table 2.2). Near parity is found only for those who graduate from high school. For every dollar earned by a bankrupt debtor who was a high school graduate, a high school graduate in the general population earned $1.03. At every subsequent level the gap increases. People who have some college education earned on average $1.14 for every dollar that the debtors with some college earned. Among degree holders, the contrast is even more stark. In general, bachelor's degree holders earned $1.37 for every dollar earned by their bankrupt counterparts, and the advanced degree holders earned $1.92 for every dollar their bankrupt counterparts earned. The total dollar gap among the advanced degree holders in and out of bankruptcy is more than $23,000.

The low earnings of the bankrupt debtors are not due to low levels of education. Rather, their low earnings occur in spite of their educational levels. Moreover, the bankrupt debtors with the most education show the greatest relative disadvantage in their earnings. At every level of education, the bankrupt debtors were worse off.

In tables 2.3 and 2.4 we recapitulate the data on income and add data for assets, total debt, secured debt, and unsecured debt for the debtors in the five districts from five states, with a comparison to the ten districts in three states that we studied in 1981 and to the Ohio district for which we have 1997 data.[104] As we have seen, the 1991 debtors are worse off than the rest of the nation. To this we add the gloomy news that the 1991 debtors are even worse off than

**Table 2.3** Distribution of income, assets, and debts for bankruptcy petitioners in 1981, 1991, and 1997 (in 1991 dollars)

| 1981 | Income | Total assets | Total debt | Secured debt | Unsecured debt |
|---|---|---|---|---|---|
| Mean | 23,643 | 43,984 | 57,835 | 34,514 | 23,222 |
| s.d. | 14,398 | 59,985 | 82,133 | 57,785 | 46,850 |
| 25th percentile | 14,156 | 4,476 | 14,604 | 3,896 | 5,733 |
| Median | 22,436 | 21,014 | 31,399 | 14,386 | 10,566 |
| 75th percentile | 31,958 | 66,427 | 66,647 | 45,640 | 20,880 |
| N | 1,289 | 1,490 | 1,496 | 1,501 | 1,495 |
| Missing | 213 | 12 | 6 | 1 | 7 |

| 1991 | Income | Total assets | Total debt | Secured debt | Unsecured debt |
|---|---|---|---|---|---|
| Mean | 20,305 | 38,478 | 55,293 | 32,519 | 22,588 |
| s.d. | 12,183 | 57,290 | 77,674 | 60,514 | 41,124 |
| 25th percentile | 12,000 | 3,160 | 15,187 | 449 | 6,966 |
| Median | 17,952 | 12,650 | 29,527 | 9,775 | 12,838 |
| 75th percentile | 26,400 | 57,585 | 65,522 | 45,300 | 22,856 |
| N | 641 | 681 | 684 | 687 | 687 |
| Missing | 95 | 55 | 52 | 49 | 49 |

| 1997 | Income | | Total debt | Secured debt | Unsecured debt |
|---|---|---|---|---|---|
| Mean | 16,675 | — | 52,061 | 25,118 | 25,070 |
| s.d. | 8,899 | — | 54,506 | 37,248 | 31,938 |
| 25th percentile | 10,249 | — | 20,633 | 2,392 | 10,500 |
| Median | 15,924 | — | 34,775 | 10,430 | 16,568 |
| 75th percentile | 21,860 | — | 66,587 | 35,255 | 26,649 |
| N | 100 | — | 100 | 100 | 100 |
| Missing | 0 | — | 0 | 0 | 0 |

| t-tests of statistical significance | Income | Total assets | Total debt | Secured debt | Unsecured debt |
|---|---|---|---|---|---|
| 1981 v. 1991 | 5.04*** | 2.01* | 0.68 | 0.74 | 0.31 |
| 1981 v. 1997 | 4.77*** | | 0.70 | 1.61 | 0.39 |
| 1991 v. 1997 | 2.87** | | 0.41 | 1.19 | 0.58 |

*p < .05; **p < .01; ***p < .001

*Source:* Consumer Bankruptcy Project I, 1981; Consumer Bankruptcy Project II, 1991; Ohio Bankruptcy Study, 1997.
*Note:* Cases with extreme values on assets, total debt, or income are removed. Outliers removed are beyond the cutoff points used in *As We Forgive Our Debtors* adjusted to constant dollars using the Consumer Price Indexes. The 1981 figures were adjusted to 1991 and 1997 dollars by multiplying by a factor of 1.4983498 and 1.7656766, respectively. The 1991 figures were adjusted to 1997 dollars by multiplying by a factor of 1.1784141 (derived from the CPI). The 1997 figures were adjusted to 1991 dollars by multiplying by a factor of 0.8485981.

**Table 2.4**  Distribution of income, assets, and debts for bankruptcy petitioners in 1981, 1991, and 1997 (in 1997 dollars)

| 1981 | Income | Total assets | Total debt | Secured debt | Unsecured debt |
|---|---|---|---|---|---|
| Mean | 27,861 | 51,831 | 68,154 | 40,671 | 27,365 |
| s.d. | 16,966 | 70,687 | 96,786 | 68,094 | 55,209 |
| 25th percentile | 16,681 | 5,275 | 17,210 | 4,591 | 6,755 |
| Median | 26,439 | 24,764 | 37,002 | 16,952 | 12,452 |
| 75th percentile | 37,660 | 78,279 | 78,538 | 53,783 | 24,605 |
| N | 1,289 | 1,490 | 1,496 | 1,501 | 1,495 |
| Missing | 213 | 12 | 6 | 1 | 7 |

| 1991 | Income | Total assets | Total debt | Secured debt | Unsecured debt |
|---|---|---|---|---|---|
| Mean | 23,927 | 45,344 | 65,158 | 38,320 | 26,618 |
| s.d. | 14,357 | 67,512 | 91,533 | 71,310 | 48,461 |
| 25th percentile | 14,141 | 3,724 | 17,897 | 529 | 8,208 |
| Median | 21,155 | 14,907 | 34,795 | 11,519 | 15,128 |
| 75th percentile | 31,110 | 67,859 | 77,212 | 53,382 | 26,934 |
| N | 641 | 681 | 684 | 687 | 687 |
| Missing | 95 | 55 | 52 | 49 | 49 |

| 1997 | Income | Total assets | Total debt | Secured debt | Unsecured debt |
|---|---|---|---|---|---|
| Mean | 19,641 | — | 61,320 | 29,586 | 29,529 |
| s.d. | 10,482 | — | 64,201 | 43,872 | 37,618 |
| 25th percentile | 12,072 | — | 24,303 | 2,818 | 12,368 |
| Median | 18,756 | — | 40,960 | 12,285 | 19,515 |
| 75th percentile | 25,748 | — | 78,431 | 41,525 | 31,389 |
| N | 100 | — | 100 | 100 | 100 |
| Missing | 0 | — | 0 | 0 | 0 |

*Source:* Consumer Bankruptcy Project I, 1991; Consumer Bankruptcy Project II, 1991; Ohio Bankruptcy Study, 1997.

*Note:* Cases with extreme values on assets, total debt, or income are removed. Outliers removed are beyond the cutoff points used in *As We Forgive Our Debtors* adjusted to constant dollars using the Consumer Price Indexes. The 1981 figures were adjusted to 1991 and 1997 dollars by multiplying by a factor of 1.4983498 and 1.7656766, respectively. The 1991 figures were adjusted to 1997 dollars by multiplying by a factor of 1.1784141 (derived from the CPI). The 1997 figures were adjusted to 1991 dollars by multiplying by a factor of 0.8485981.

the debtors in 1981, with a significantly lower mean income (adjusting for inflation). Moreover, the Ohio debtors in 1997 were worse off than the 1991 debtors. The drops in income from 1981 to 1991 and from 1991 to 1997 are statistically significant. The rise in consumer bankruptcy filings has not drawn in more high rollers with higher incomes. Instead, it has drawn in even more people with even lower incomes.[105]

A significant portion of the debtors in bankruptcy are in genuine financial collapse. They have a median income that is only half the national median, and nearly one-third are below the poverty level at the time of filing. Another 57 percent of the sample is sandwiched between the poverty level and the median income, leaving a bare 10 percent above the median income for the nation. Financially, the debtors resemble one another much more than they resemble their neighbors in their home states. Their incomes are concentrated around the median of $17,964. Relatively few are among the very low income category (less than $5,000), but even fewer are to be found with incomes above $75,000. These differences cannot be attributed to poor educations, because at every level of education the debtors have lower earnings than similarly situated members of the general population. Perhaps most surprisingly, the incomes of these debtors are significantly lower than the incomes of the debtors we studied at the beginning of the 1980s, and the Ohio data suggest that incomes continued to drop during the 1990s.

The low incomes of the debtors in bankruptcy were confirmed in a careful multidistrict study of debtors who filed in 1995. Marianne Culhane and Michaela White examined more than a thousand debtors who filed for Chapter 7 in seven districts to determine whether these debtors had any "excess" income to pay their creditors.[106] They used a series of complex financial tests laid out in a 1998 proposal to amend the Bankruptcy Code. The proposal required that bankrupt debtors be limited to a tight budget already used as the basis for certain Internal Revenue Service negotiations and that the debtors give all their remaining income to repay their debts, saving just $50 per month for additional expenses.[107] The researchers concluded that even if they made a series of optimistic assumptions about the debtors' future incomes, the calculation of their present debts, and the computation of the expenses of the bankruptcy pro-

67

cess, only about 3 percent of the debtors could pay even 20 percent of their outstanding debts (excluding interest) and have $50 left over. The data strongly suggest that at least 97 percent of the debtors can barely meet their day-to-day expenses, making debt repayment far outside their reach.

*Assets*

Assets are a measure of wealth that complement the discussion of income. For a complete financial portrait, it is important to know not only whether the debtors have a current source of income but also whether they have tangible valuables or financial resources available to them or to their creditors. Schedules disclosing the type and value of assets are filed with the bankruptcy court under penalty of perjury. In addition, the Bankruptcy Code specifically forbids hiding assets. The code provides grounds for denying discharge and even for prosecution for criminal fraud if debtors conceal assets.[108] A court-appointed bankruptcy trustee scrutinizes the list of assets for obvious reasons: in a Chapter 7 proceeding, nonexempt assets may be sold and the proceeds paid pro rata to the creditors. In a Chapter 13 filing, debtors may keep all their assets, but they still must disclose them and their value to the court because asset values determine the baseline payouts required in Chapter 13 plans.

Compared with all Americans, the debtors in bankruptcy have little wealth. The median asset value among the debtors was $12,655 (in 1991 dollars), a level significantly lower than in 1981. (No 1997 asset values were available for comparison.) This 1991 asset value represents only about one-third of the median asset value of all Americans, which was $36,288. The most common asset owned by American families is a car; 84.4 percent of all families reported owning a vehicle in 1993.[109] Used vehicles are relatively inexpensive, accounting for only 3.6 percent of family assets. Yet as commonplace as automobiles are, even the value of the automobiles owned by most Americans represented more assets than many debtors in bankruptcy could muster. The median value of the vehicles owned by Americans in 1991 was $5,221. By contrast, the lowest quartile of debtor sample reported only $3,155 in total assets of every kind.

The second most common asset for all families, but the most important in terms of value, is a home. In 1991, 64.7 percent of Americans owned a residence.[110] The principal residence of American families constitutes about one-third of their total asset value. In 1991, their median home equity was $40,486.[111] Extrapolating from the one-third figure for home values would suggest an approximate median asset value for all American homeowners of about $121,457. But even the debtors who are homeowners do not match the asset value of other American homeowners: their median asset value is only $61,426. Thus the bankrupt debtors who own the most, the homeowners, still own much less in assets than their counterparts in the general population. And, of course, many of these assets are encumbered by liens, which means their real wealth is far lower.

With few assets relative to other Americans, and significantly lower asset value than bankruptcy filers in 1981, the debtors in our sample are not well off by any financial measure.

*Debts*

Total debt for the 1991 debtors (in 1997 dollars) was a whopping $65,158 at the mean, but only $37,002 at the median. There is a large standard deviation, an indication that the debt distribution is skewed by a few debtors with extremely large debts.[112] Even at the first quartile, however, debtors reported $17,897 in debt, an amount of debt that is alarmingly close to the median income for the sample. As high as this debt is, the 1981 and 1991 debt levels are comparable. Compared with the 1981 debtors, the 1991 debtors have about the same level of debt, but with much less income and significantly fewer assets. By 1997 the mean debt level had dropped insignificantly in the Ohio sample to $61,320, while the median debt level had risen to $40,960.

Two pieces of debt that we identified separately are secured debt —that is, debt for which there is some collateral for the creditor to seize—and unsecured debt. Home mortgages are a good example of secured debt, as are car loans. Most credit card debt is unsecured. It is useful to separate the two kinds of debt because they are treated differently in bankruptcy and because the practical effects of the debts are different. Most Americans expect their home mortgages to be long-term commitments, and they understand that their car may be repossessed if they miss a car payment. Short-term, high-interest debt may not be part of a family's long-range budget. Once incurred, it can be difficult to repay. Short-term unsecured debt often carries a huge annual percentage rate; interest mounts quickly and minimum monthly payments may do little to pay down the balance. The 1981, 1991, and 1997 figures for secured and unsecured debt do not differ significantly. In 1991, at the mean, the debtors owe $38,320 in secured debt with a median $11,519 in secured debt (1997 dollars). These are debts for which the debtors may end up losing their homes or their cars if they cannot pay off the debts in full.

The short-term debt figures are lower at the mean, $26,618, but much higher at the median, $15,128. Half of the sample owes more than $15,128 in short-term debt alone. The mean is pulled higher by a few debtors who, like Mehdi Hosseini, the failed businessman, have extremely high unsecured debt levels.

*Debt-Income Ratios*

A more meaningful way to review the debt figures is to look at them in relation to income. How much debt a family can safely carry is in part a function of how much income the family takes in. A debt of $20,000 might overwhelm Jim, who earns an income of $10,000; his debt-income ratio would be 2.0. But the same $20,000 debt might be steep but manageable for Jane with an annual income of $110,000. Jane's debt-income ratio would be 0.18, indicating that she owed more than two months' income. We calculated debt-income ratios for the individuals in the 1981, 1991, and 1997 samples (table 2.5). The mean debt-income ratios for all types of debt range from 2.51 in 1991 to 3.20 in 1981. These are stunning figures. They can be interpreted as indicating that at the mean, debtors owe from two and a half to more than three years of income just to repay their debts (and with no other expenses during those many months, even for eating and paying rent). At the median, debtors owe seventeen to thirty months' income to pay their debts. Because of large standard deviations, these ratios do not differ significantly.

As striking as these figures are, however, they describe an aggregate and not any single debtor family. Take the case of James Williams, the foreman from Chicago. With earnings of $39,000, he and

**Table 2.5**  Total debt-income ratio and total nonmortgage debt-income ratio, 1981, 1991, 1997

| Total debt-income ratio | 1981 | 1991 | 1997 | Total nonmortgage debt-income ratio | 1981 | 1991 | 1997 |
|---|---|---|---|---|---|---|---|
| Mean | 3.20 | 2.51 | 2.76 | Mean | 1.88 | 1.48 | 1.87 |
| s.d. | 10.45 | 3.03 | 2.05 | s.d. | 7.24 | 1.94 | 1.66 |
| 25th percentile | 0.70 | 0.93 | 1.19 | 25th percentile | 0.47 | 0.57 | 0.79 |
| Median | 1.41 | 1.68 | 2.44 | Median | 0.75 | 0.96 | 1.54 |
| 75th percentile | 2.60 | 2.98 | 3.68 | 75th percentile | 1.39 | 1.67 | 2.22 |
| N | 1,241 | 609 | 94 | N | 1,238 | 524 | 34 |
| Missing | 214 | 127 | 6 | Missing | 264 | 212 | 66 |
| t-values | | | | t-values | | | |
| 1981 v. 1991 | 1.597 | | | 1981 v. 1991 | 1.246 | | |
| 1981 v. 1997 | 0.407 | | | 1981 v. 1997 | 0.008 | | |
| 1991 v. 1997 | 0.773 | | | 1991 v. 1997 | 1.145 | | |

*Source:* Consumer Bankruptcy Project, Phase I, 1981; Consumer Bankruptcy Project, Phase II, 1991; Ohio Bankruptcy Study, 1997.

his wife are not only well above the median income for the debtors, they are well above the median for the national population. Yet with total debts of $217,000, the Williams family, with a whopping 5.6 debt-income ratio, is also well above the median. The family would have to dedicate more than five and a half years of their income to repay their creditors—exclusive of interest charges. Businessman Mehdi Hosseini, with more than $315,000 in unsecured debt alone, has a debt-income ratio of 13.13. If he devoted every dollar of his $24,000 income to his creditors from 1991 forward (and could somehow otherwise be fed and sheltered) it would be February 2004 before all of his creditors had been paid. If the interest were still accumulating, it is conceivable that he could never escape debt.

If the home mortgage debt is removed for homeowners in the sample, the debt-income ratio changes significantly (see bottom panel of table 2.8). To be sure, the homeowner cannot avoid paying the debt (except by losing the home), but removing the long-term debt gives a better picture of the immediate problem that the debtors face. The short-term debt is due quickly, often without a specific payoff schedule. More important from a financial health standpoint, the short-term debt often carries a much higher interest rate.

In 1991 a debtor at the mean had a nonmortgage debt-income

ratio of 1.48, indicating that the average debtor owed eighteen months' income in short-term debt such as credit cards. At the median, the figure was 0.96, or almost a year's income. Again, these ratios are lower but still do not differ significantly from the figures calculated in 1981 nor in 1997. They do, however, indicate a substantial debt burden for the bankruptcy petitioners. Given the high interest rates that often accompany unsecured debts, it is likely that many of these debtors could literally never keep up with the interest accumulating on their debts.

*Net Worth*

Net worth gives a composite financial picture for a household. Although accountants would insist on more nuances, net worth is basically the value of assets minus the value of debts. Net worth may be either positive or negative, depending on the relative size of debts and incomes. The mean net worth of the bankrupt debtors is −$16,819, and their median net worth is −$10,542.[113] Given their debt burden, it is hardly surprising that the debtors' net worths are negative, with their debts considerably greater than their assets.

Net worth has the advantage of providing another way to compare the bankrupt debtors with the national population. Data from the 1991 portion of the Survey of Income and Program Participation have been analyzed to compute average net worth figures for the population. The median net worth for Americans generally in 1991 was $36,190, a convenient multiple of the −$6,819 figure for the debtors.[114] Only 12.6 percent of the total United States population had a net worth of zero or negative value, compared with nearly all of the bankrupt debtors. Even the lowest income quintile of American households had a net worth of $5,000, putting the debtors at the very bottom of the American wealth distribution.

A review of the financial data indicates few bright spots for the bankruptcy petitioners. Perhaps they never had high incomes, or perhaps they had higher incomes before downsizing or a medical problem forced them from their job. By the time of their bankruptcy filings, their incomes are low. With low incomes and negligible assets, they face extraordinarily high debts. Compared with the rest of the American population, they earn less and own less than might other-

72

wise be expected. They owe far more than most Americans in both short-term and total debt. As a result, their net worth is nearly always accompanied by a minus sign.

The data we have reviewed here show a group of Americans drawn from five varied regions of the United States and yet remarkably similar to one another and to other Americans in many ways: gender, age, race, nativity, education, and occupation. The people in the sample resemble one another—but differ from other Americans—in two important respects: they earn much less and they owe much more. The average debtor owes more than two and a half years' income in debts of all types. Their educations and occupations place them in the middle class, but their incomes and net worth put them at the bottom of the class structure.

Where do they belong in the great and shifting American class scene? Toward the middle with their home-owning neighbors, classmates, and office colleagues? Or at the bottom with the homeless, the indigent, and the welfare recipients, some of whom actually have a larger net worth than the bankrupt debtors?[115] And how shall we decide where they fit?

The claim that these debtors are not really middle class is at one level a form of denial, linked to a belief that they could have controlled the situation if only they had tried. The debtors in our sample experienced a series of random shocks and structural shifts: an earthquake in California, Operation Desert Storm in Texas military towns, corporate downsizing, and a sea change in family structure. Most of these changes were beyond their control. Without doubt the debtors also made mistakes, misjudged situations, or perhaps even sought to take unfair advantage of others. As far as we can determine from what they have said about their backgrounds, these debtors come from the middle class. We believe that their bankruptcies show not that they have left the middle class but that they are in bankruptcy to hang on to their fragile position in the middle class.

No one plans to go bankrupt. The belief that our lives can be completely planned and that we can assert control over all that touches us is false. This dream is never completely realized, and that is why the fears of the middle class so closely mirror their aspirations. Our lives are far more complicated. In spite of our best intentions, our liability insurance, our exercise regimes, and our low-fat diets, we all face risk. None of us can adequately buffer our lives from our milieu, our mistakes, and simple bad luck. Some of us are prudent and plan more carefully than others—but sometimes these people are the ones who seem to be most sorely tested.

Some of the debtors were not prepared for the unexpected and costly event. Michael Reed could not anticipate his mother's illness, and Mehdi Hosseini could not plan for the Gulf War. Perhaps Willis Creighton should have seen the savings and loan debacle bearing down, but he didn't—or at least not soon enough to save his skin. Some of the debtors probably made mistakes. Millie Brown should never have trusted her partner. Marcia James's job did not survive a company buyout, but perhaps she was not such a good saleswoman anyway. Michelle and Mark Grady should have stayed in school and postponed their wedding. And James and LaDonne Williams experienced enough bad luck for themselves and everyone else. We can label such bankrupt debtors as lower class *because* they declared bankruptcy, but that does not change the reality that something similar could happen to the most stolidly middle class of any of us.

In what follows we detail what happened to their jobs, their families, their homes, their credit, and their health. What our data suggest, but cannot quantify, is how much more of the middle class is near the fragile edge of economic failure.

Chapter 3

# Unemployed or Underemployed

I lost my job in Dec. 1990. I have not been able to get a job with similar pay.

—JEANNE SALEM, dry cleaning clerk, San Antonio, Texas

San Antonio is a flourishing metropolitan area of over one million people located at the confluence of the southwestern migration of American citizens with the northward migration of Mexican nationals. A sunny, cosmopolitan city, the tenth largest in the United States, it is home to a flourishing tourist industry, five military installations, and civic monuments to professional sports and commerce that dwarf its historical claim to fame, the Alamo.

San Antonio is a good place to begin exploring the relation between jobs and the severe financial distress that may lead to bankruptcy. For one thing, it lies in one of the federal judicial districts (Western Texas) that was included in earlier studies so that we have data from more than one point in time. For another, the changes in its economy over the past two decades illustrate developments that we believe are important to understanding the fault lines in middle-class America. Our data suggest that job-related income interruption is by far the most important cause of severe financial distress for middle-class Americans.

Job-related financial stress is implicated in over two-thirds of the bankruptcies we studied. Although layoffs are a major factor, middle-class people can find themselves in serious trouble even if they have a job because the job may change and both income and benefits may erode. If there is a single, dominant crack in middle-class security, it is the fissure related to jobs and the changing structure of employment. The structure of employment risk we have found tracks the evolution of the work force in San Antonio and throughout the country. These factors continued to operate throughout the 1990s, fueling a record number of bankruptcies even amid record low unemployment.

San Antonio never appears on the lists of cities with high unemployment rates, but a quiet transformation of the 1980s changed San Antonio with results familiar to residents of the rust belt, the Pacific coast, or New England: the job mix changed. For the sake of simplicity, we might classify jobs as requiring either high or low skills from the worker, and as providing either high or low pay in return. There are then four possible categories: high skill–high wage, high skill–low wage, low skill–high wage, and low skill–low wage. During the 1980s, the proportion of San Antonio jobs that fell within each quadrant of this categorization shifted.

Some good jobs came to San Antonio, providing high pay for high skills. These good new jobs overwhelmingly employed skilled service professionals, people with college educations and often advanced degrees. Between 1980 and 1990, San Antonio added 23,678 high skill–high wage jobs, a little over half of them in medical and dental services and laboratories, and nearly 17 percent each in education, law, and management services.[1]

But many of San Antonio's new jobs were less attractive. San Antonio gained even more new jobs—26,552—in the low skill–low wage sector. Although these jobs were also service jobs, they required little in the way of formal credentials. Over half were in eating and drinking establishments, with food stores, hotels, and amusement services accounting for the remainder. Such jobs keep the worker out of the unemployment line, but they typically offer low pay. They are more likely to be part-time or seasonal, and they rarely provide fringe benefits. Chances for promotion and greater job security are slim. Even so, where such jobs are plentiful, few people are likely to be looking for work, because these jobs are readily available to anyone who can run a cash register or wipe a table.

Academics call this phenomenon job polarization: the loss of middle-range jobs, leaving only the extremes of high skills and wages and low skills and wages. San Antonio lost nearly 9,000 low skill–high wage jobs in textiles, food, transportation and equipment, and electrical manufacturing. Another 5,600 jobs disappeared in construction and railroads. With relatively low levels of schooling, many workers who were displaced from these jobs had few options in the new high skill–high wage sector. Their principal option was to seek jobs in the growing low skill–low wage sector, with a resulting loss of income, benefits, and job security. Workers just entering the labor market found that there were few low-skill jobs with high wages open to them. The sea change in employment is captured in one statistic: for every four low skill–low wage or high skill–high wage jobs San Antonio gained, a low skill–high wage job was lost, most of them jobs in manufacturing. The polarization of income follows close onto the polarization of jobs.

Jeanne Salem, whose answer to the bankruptcy questionnaire opens this chapter, tells us only that she attributes her bankruptcy to her lost job. We do not know if she was a factory worker in food processing or in electrical assembly, industries in which San Antonio lost jobs. We do know that the dry cleaning establishment where she works is a good example of a service industry in which many new jobs have been developed. In 1990, the average hourly earnings in laundry, cleaning, and garment services was $6.82, for a full-time, full-year annual income of about $13,600.[2] Jeanne's job may be a little better than average for the industry, because she reports an annual income of $15,396. Average earnings in the United States in 1991 for full-time, year-round female workers were $23,778; that is 54 percent greater than Jeanne's earnings.[3] Jeanne notes that she earned more at her previous job.

One block from the Alamo is the beige limestone courthouse that is home to the U.S. Bankruptcy Court for the Western District of Texas. A geographically vast district that stretches from Waco in the north to the Rio Grande in the south and hundreds of miles west to El Paso, the Western District of Texas has been studied in four consumer bankruptcy studies: the Brookings Study, the Purdue Study, and our two studies. Like the rest of the country, the bankruptcy rate in this district has risen dramatically. In 1980 the filing rate in Western Texas for Chapters 7 and 13 was 0.76 per thousand adults; by 1990 the figure had risen to 2.50 per thousand, more than a threefold increase.[4]

The Western District of Texas is similar to other districts in this study because jobs are an important reason the debtors gave in 1991

77

for their decision to file for bankruptcy. Sixty-eight percent of the filers from the Western District of Texas reported a job problem, exactly the same proportion as all the filers in our study. These data, along with other indicators we developed from our questionnaire, help us sketch out the magnitude of employment issues as shocks to the middle class. Probably no other issue is so critical to the middle class as the maintenance of a steady income through steady work, and no indicator of fragility is so persuasive as the evidence of job instability. Many of the findings we present here confirm the popular intuition that jobs are crucial to financial health.

## Identifying Job Troubles

Just how significant job problems are for bankruptcy filers can be determined in at least two ways. One is to ask people in bankruptcy systematically about their work histories. The second is to ask them why they filed for bankruptcy and to count how often someone gave a job-related reason. We used both approaches with a surprising result: when we totaled the systematic answers and analyzed the free responses, more than two out of every three bankruptcy filers (68 percent) reported a job problem (fig. 3.1).

Unemployment has long been the most direct measure of job difficulty, and we sought to identify it by asking several different questions. We asked each person in our sample, including both husbands and wives in the case of joint filings, whether they were currently seeking work. The question we used is approximately the same as that used by the Bureau of Labor Statistics to measure unemployment: "If not currently holding a job, did this person actively SEEK work during the past four weeks?" The precoded possible answers were "Yes, sought work," "No," and "Has a job now." By using the government's question for measuring unemployment, we sought to maximize the comparability of our data with data for the overall U.S. population.

We also asked each person if he or she had experienced an interruption of work-related income for at least two weeks during the preceding two years. The possible answers were "Yes," "No," and "Not employed during this time." This question is not asked by government interviewers, and it is open to somewhat more interpretation.

**UNEMPLOYED OR UNDEREMPLOYED**

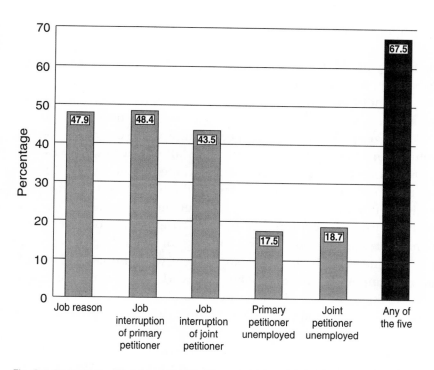

Fig. 3.1 Proportion of bankrupt debtors reporting job problems by source of report, 1991. *Note:* Multiple responses were permitted; the combined column omits cases with missing values on all indicators (N=21).

A worker might have left work voluntarily for a number of reasons. Alternatively, the worker might have experienced short-term layoffs or job searches. Regardless of the reason for the work interruption, the answer to this question is a useful indicator of financial stress because of the importance of work-related income to the finances of nearly all families.

Finally, in our open-ended question about the reasons for bankruptcy, our respondents could write any reasons they wished to explain their bankruptcy filings. We coded up to five reasons from each response in the order in which the respondent mentioned them. Bankruptcy filers could list multiple work-related problems, such as a cutback in hours followed months later by a layoff. Through this combination of open and closed questioning, we developed a more comprehensive view of the job problems of the debtors.

**UNEMPLOYED OR UNDEREMPLOYED**

Unemployment

Unemployment is the most severe of the job problems that show up in bankruptcy. A total of 490 respondents in our sample reported that they did not have a job and were actively seeking work, which is the government's definition of unemployment. This number included 332 primary petitioners, either people filing alone or one spouse of a couple, and 158 joint petitioners, nearly all of whom were wives. As a proportion of all the valid responses, these numbers yield 17.9 percent unemployment, more than two and a half times the prevailing national rate in 1991 of 6.7 percent.[5] But the government's statistic excludes from its denominator any adult over the age of sixteen who is neither working nor actively looking for work. Such people are not considered to be in the labor force. If we eliminate the people in our sample who are not looking for work and who do not have a job—making our statistic directly comparable to the government's—the unemployment rate among bankrupts rises to 21.4 percent, more than three times the national rate.[6]

In our first study of consumer debtors who filed for bankruptcy in 1981, we did not survey the debtors directly. When we examined their court files to try to determine unemployment rates, all we had were the debtors' responses to a question about their occupations at the time of filing.[7] Even among those who are unemployed, some will list the occupation they held when they were employed rather than identifying themselves as unemployed. Nonetheless, from the answers to that question, which almost certainly undercounted the number of unemployed debtors, we found that between 7 percent and 17 percent of them were unemployed at filing. Interpreting ambiguous responses to a question not directed specifically at unemployment, we estimated that perhaps 14 percent of the debtors were unemployed, compared with a prevailing national rate of 7.6 percent.[8] In Judge Sellers's 1997 study in Ohio, the cases indicated an unemployment rate of about 20.5 percent,[9] a rate about four times the rate of unemployment in Ohio in that year.[10] These data show a remarkably consistent pattern of the unemployment rate in bankruptcy as a multiple of the unemployment rate in the general population. This finding persists over a period of sixteen years and in good times as well as bad. Without claiming an undue precision for these numbers, we can

**UNEMPLOYED OR UNDEREMPLOYED**

nevertheless assert that the unemployed are substantially overrepresented among bankrupt debtors.

For most workers whose work contracts exclude golden parachutes and hefty severance payments, unemployment is financially devastating. By itself, unemployment is a major contributor to the woes of the people in bankruptcy. The double-digit unemployment rates of the magnitude found in our bankruptcy sample are usually reported only for groups of workers believed to be extremely marginal to the labor force—teen-aged males (19.8 percent), black single mothers (13.9 percent), and high school dropouts (11 percent).[11] Such high rates of joblessness are not supposed to be found among the middle-aged and the middle class who comprise the bankruptcy sample.

## Job Interruption

Even if a debtor finds a new job, the job interruption itself often leads to bankruptcy. The unemployed debtors at the time of filing are in the minority among those who identify a job-related problem. For most debtors, a previous period of unemployment put them in financial trouble. By the time of filing, the debtor was back at work but was facing bills that could not be paid. In some cases, the bills were run up while everyone was fully employed. Or bills that seemed reasonable on an income of $60,000 became insurmountable on a new income of $26,000. In other cases, bills may have been run up during a period of unemployment because a laid-off worker used credit cards to supplement meager unemployment insurance and savings.[12] Once the worker is back on the job, the day of reckoning may come: there is not enough income to cover the outstanding bills—ever. In any case, more than three-quarters of the people filing for bankruptcy are currently working, but their earlier job problems may lead them to bankruptcy to stabilize themselves economically.

An astonishing 48 percent of the first respondents reported that they had had an interruption in their job-related income (see fig. 3.1). Among the spouses in the joint petitions, 44 percent reported that they had had an income interruption. Of the couples who reported any income interruption, 40 percent reported that *both* the husband and the wife had suffered a job interruption. As serious as open unemployment seems to have been among the debtors, the incidence of job interruption was twice as grave.

From the wording of the question we asked, we can be certain only that there was at least one interruption per worker, but some debtors indicated in their written responses that a single earner had experienced multiple interruptions. Although we have no comparable national data on income interruption, it seems likely that the loss of an earner's income for at least two weeks could create serious difficulties for many families, and the loss of two earners' income, even at different times, could be devastating. The systematic questions on current unemployment and past income interruptions reveal a picture of debtors in highly unstable work situations. The tie between job loss and economic failure is unmistakable.

### Job-Related Reasons for Bankruptcy

In contrast to the specific questions on unemployment and job interruption, our third source of data on job-related problems comes from our open-ended question about the reasons for a debtor's bankruptcy. We asked respondents to explain in their own words why they filed for bankruptcy. Almost one-half (48 percent) of the sample who reported any reason gave a job-related reason for filing. More than half of these, and therefore more than a fourth (27.5 percent) of the sample, were like Jeanne Salem in identifying *only* a work-related reason for their bankruptcy.

The job-related reasons were general in coverage. Although unemployment rates vary around the country, job troubles affected bankrupt respondents everywhere. From one-third to a majority of the debtors in each district identified work problems as the reason for bankruptcy.[13]

The written responses of the debtors can be summarized into several patterns through which work was tied to economic downfall. The first pattern was the one experienced by Jeanne Salem: simple job loss. For many workers, job loss results in weeks of unemployment while they seek new work. Some bankrupt debtors report owning businesses that have failed. Others report working for firms that have failed or closed. Some of them saw their jobs exported overseas, whereas others saw their jobs disappear in a merger. Sometimes these changes result in unemployment for a time.

For other debtors, the result is job skidding or job erosion, two patterns that cost both job quality and income. Besides job loss, Jeanne Salem also illustrates job skidding because her new job as a dry-cleaning clerk did not pay as well as her previous job. Sometimes the job skidding leads only to part-time work. But the job skidder is in a better position than the job loser, because the skidder finds some kind of new job, albeit with lower wages, benefits, and seniority. The third pattern is job erosion, which happens when the working conditions for a job change, so that even with the same job and the same employer, and no period of unemployment, take-home pay declines or hours of work decrease. With job erosion, there is at least the stability of having the same job, but it is accompanied by the disquieting reality that the job no longer provides as well. The open-ended responses to our question enable us to see beyond the gross statistics on unemployment to various other forms of job-related income reduction. The reports from our sample reveal several patterns.

## The Layoff

> On Oct. 1, 1990—the City of San Antonio—because of budget cuts eliminated my job.—JOHN WHITE, San Antonio, Texas

Income interruptions were most common from layoffs and subsequent unemployment. One quarter of our sample (511 responses, 25.4 percent) cited the layoff of the primary petitioner, and 6.5 percent (130 people) reported the layoff of a spouse as the event that caused their bankruptcy filing. John White attributes his bankruptcy to losing his job in public administration. John is sixty-one and now reports his occupation as retired, but he also says that he is looking for work. He is married and has some college background. John filed Chapter 13 with debts of $23,700 and an income of $18,000. He and his wife do not own a home. They list no credit card debt and no tax debt.

John White can tell you the exact day on which he lost his job. Social psychologists have learned that most people remember key dates that are linked to important events in their lives. For example, most Americans who were old enough at the time to keep up with the news can identify what they were doing on December 7, 1941, or November 22, 1963. John White can probably tell you what the weather was like in San Antonio on October 1, 1990. He probably remembers how he felt cleaning out his desk and how he and his co-workers said good-bye. Americans identify so much with their work that a job loss is an occasion for grieving, a critical life event for which the date, the weather, and the circumstances remain etched in memory. Our respondents' specificity about when they lost their jobs is a reminder of how memorable these events must have been. By contrast, their accounts of divorce and illness are often far less specific.[14]

Millions of Americans have a date such as John White's to remember. The 1980s were a decade of pink slips—and not just for blue-collar workers. Between 1984 and 1986, 600,000 mid- and upper-level executives lost their jobs. Between 1987 and 1990 alone, 1,987,553 separations were documented as a result of mass layoffs. Data from forty-five states for 1990 indicated that 2,605 establishments had 3,078 "layoff events" that resulted in the separation of 586,690 workers.[15] These "layoff events" were not the traditional idling of production workers for model changeovers or plant remodeling. They were permanent job losses that affected previously secure jobs.

During the 1990s the pink slips continued but in different industries and with lower-level white-collar jobs. The government reports data on "displaced workers," defined as workers aged twenty and older who have worked for at least three years for their employer and who have lost their job because the plant or company closed down, the work was slack, or the position or shift was abolished. (The last phenomenon is now known as downsizing.) In 1992 there were 5.6 million displaced workers, of whom a little more than half (52.1 percent) lost their jobs through plant shutdowns and about a sixth (16.3 percent) lost their jobs through downsizing at companies that remained open for business. Two years later another 4.5 million workers were displaced, this time 28 percent of them through downsizing.[16] And between January 1995 and December 1997, 3.6 million workers were displaced.[17] In addition, an uncounted number of families lost their livelihood when the small businesses they were running failed.[18]

UNEMPLOYED OR UNDEREMPLOYED

Through the 1980s the industry most affected by restructuring, "right-sizing," or downsizing was manufacturing. The figures for plant shutdowns reflect this, with more than half of the displaced workers losing jobs as their workplaces closed. During the 1990s, however, the service industries began to replicate the pattern. Layoffs reached new highs in wholesale and retail trade, then in professional services, finance, insurance, and real estate.[19]

During the 1980s elimination of job positions or elimination of shifts of work became a more important source of displacement. Increasingly these layoffs are permanent. In the recession ending in 1992, 85 percent of job losers did not expect recall to their jobs, compared with 56 percent in the four prior recessions.[20] Job displacement is no longer a temporary phenomenon requiring workers to ride out a recession. It has begun to be a part of a constant rolling readjustment of the economy.

As industry after industry has undergone restructuring, layoffs have struck even prosperous companies seeking to position themselves more favorably by cutting labor costs. No longer a management response to a pressing financial exigency, these layoffs followed decisions by executives that their companies were too fat and needed to become "lean and mean." Profits were high, but they could be higher, and job cuts were one way to improve profitability. When there was a financial crisis, job cuts have been a first response, with results that are sometimes draconian. For example, following "Black Monday" (October 19, 1987) on the stock exchanges, Wall Street brokerages laid off thousands of managers.[21]

Interestingly, the willingness to lay off more workers has become a sign of managerial ability. In the first two months of 1994, 144,000 jobs were lost in staff cutbacks, a process that is now termed "job shedding."[22] One observer comments that "job shedding has become fashionable—the mark of a good manager."[23] Middle managers continue to be targets for job shedding, but other white-collar occupations are also feeling the pressure. The threat of layoffs has become a staple for cartoonists who depict the modern work force, from Doonesbury to Dilbert. Even comic career woman Cathy was downsized from her office job to become a home-based freelancer.

From the late 1980s to the late 1990s layoffs spread from the blue-collar jobs in shutdowns of manufacturing plants to the shedding of white-collar jobs in services, even high-paid services. In the process, layoffs became commonplace for the middle class. Unlike previous decades, job loss did not signal a more general economic crisis. Indeed, productivity increased and many industries became more competitive nationally and internationally. The remaining workers were stressed by the additional work they had to undertake, although most workplaces ran reasonably smoothly with the addition of occasional temporary workers.[24] But the workers who were laid off, often unexpectedly, discovered for themselves a crack in the middle class. Their lost income during their job search widened the fissure.

Francis Socorro, a forty-one-year-old Pennsylvanian of Italian extraction, knows firsthand about intermittent layoffs and plant closings. He is a high school graduate and is currently separated from his wife. He reports that he is actively seeking work. One imagines that Francis is rather methodical from his careful listing of the reasons for bankruptcy:

1. Being laid off from U.S. Steel off and on the last couple of years and then the shutdown of the mill this year (1991)
2. Being separated and not having wife's income partially hurt
3. Not being able to find a decent full-time job since lay-off
4. Waiting for paperwork to be completed through the PA displaced worker program so that I may go to school.

Francis may have tried a number of things to maintain his income. He has experienced several temporary layoffs, but because the last one involved a plant closing, his prospects for rehiring are nil. Steel was one of those industries that underwent a major restructuring during this period, with many plants closing. The old industrial areas of the Northeast and Middle Atlantic states were often the sites of technologically obsolete factories. In addition, steel was under tremendous competition from foreign producers. As a result of the economic pressures on the industry, between 1983 and 1994 employment in blast furnaces and basic steel products declined by 102,000 workers for an annual decline of 3.2 percent.[25]

Francis qualified as a displaced worker. He is unable to find a full-time job, and he is seeking approval for additional schooling to improve his marketability. As Francis's account shows, even his efforts to improve his situation through retraining may end up being part

**UNEMPLOYED OR UNDEREMPLOYED**

of his immediate economic problem. His marriage has deteriorated, although we can only speculate about the relation between the economic uncertainty and his separation. As a result of the separation, Francis no longer has his wife's income as a cushion.

In both 1991 and 1981, the years in which we conducted our studies, the nation was in a mild recession. The seasonally adjusted annual unemployment rate for the nation in 1991 was 6.7 percent, and the rates for the states in our sample varied around that average.[26] These recessions were not uniform in their severity. In 1981 the areas hardest hit were the rust belt in the Northeast and the Midwest, but in the mid-1980s recession hit the oil patch and by the early 1990s the West Coast was in recession. Peace and the concomitant decline in military spending hit California hard; the unemployment rate there for 1991 was 7.5 percent. Illinois was slightly lower at 7.1 percent, and Tennessee and Texas each had unemployment rates of 6.6 percent. Francis's home state, Pennsylvania, had a relatively high unemployment rate of 6.9 percent.[27]

The 1991 data were collected during a time of rising unemployment. In 1990 the national unemployment rate had been 5.5 percent; by 1992 it would be 7.4 percent. It was in this context that a presidential candidate could say, "It's the economy, stupid," and gain the attention of the electorate. According to a national study, in January 1990 only 3 percent of all people said that they lived in a household where someone was receiving unemployment compensation. By the time our study ended, in January 1992, the proportion had risen to 5 percent.[28] Keith Burns, a thirty-eight-year-old married college graduate had been unemployed for more than eighteen months at the time of his bankruptcy filing. He writes: "I believe the reason for my bankruptcy is due to loss of my job as an insurance underwriter in June, 1989—and the inability to acquire a full-time job since, particularly in my field."

Finally, there is the double-whammy: the unemployment of both spouses. Carlos and Carmelita Cardenas, two naturalized citizens who live in Austin, Texas, filed for bankruptcy in Chapter 7. When asked the reason for their bankruptcy, they wrote: "unemployment both husband and wife." Both Carlos and Carmelita have less than an eighth-grade education. Although they both list their current occupation as unemployed, it seems that life was once good for the Cardenas family. They own a home worth $38,000 for which they report no mortgage.[29] They report no credit card debt. Their debts are not overwhelming at $9,400, but about half of this is tax debt and the Internal Revenue Service may be relentless. The remainder of their debt is unsecured. Carlos and Carmelita are now separated, perhaps contemplating divorce. Finding a job might not save their marriage, but the continued unemployment is surely a devastating strain.

Even with unemployment compensation, a program that covers only about one in four of the unemployed, the loss of a job and the subsequent job search usually involve a substantial reduction in a family's available income. For the workers who are covered, payments expire after a period, usually twenty-six weeks. Workers with short job tenure, part-time workers, and workers in some industries are not covered.[30] In recessionary times, bankruptcy can serve as one cushion for laid-off workers with debts that remain and income that shrinks. And even in times of prosperity, the individuals who lose their jobs may find that previously manageable levels of debt spiral out of control.

## The Job Skid

When a spell of unemployment ends, the results may not be completely satisfactory. It may be hard for workers to find comparable jobs, especially when there are many other job seekers. As Marta Rodríguez wrote on her questionnaire: "husband lost job of 8 years and had to take another job and start over again in terms of income." Marta is thirty-two, José is thirty-three, and both are native-born and high school graduates. Their annual income is $17,280. Marta has also had a job interruption. Although both are working now, Marta describes a job skid for José as the cause of their bankruptcy. They own a small home worth $28,000, and all but $1,500 of their debt is secured debt. Marta and José did not run up credit card debts or spend profligately, but the loss of income has nevertheless left them in financial trouble.

Kathleen Newman popularized the term "skidding" in the late 1980s to describe unemployed managers whom she studied who had eventually found employment, but with reduced responsibilities and salaries.[31] Through detailed interviews she charted the economic decline of managers who had been laid off and explored how they adjusted to their changed circumstances. Newman discovered that although these were people who had high-level job skills and advanced educations that should have made them very marketable, they were not quickly back at work. Many upper-level white-collar workers feared that taking a lower-level job would stigmatize them as being incapable of tackling greater responsibilities. The laid-off managers hesitated to take available jobs for fear that they would never again be considered for a managerial position. Wives who had previously been homemakers sometimes became the breadwinners, hoping by their participation in the labor force to delay their husbands' skid down the job ladder.[32]

As expensive as the job skid is likely to be, delaying the job skid by temporizing and continuing an unrealistic job search is even more costly. Newman's study suggests that the displaced executives are encouraged to keep on trying for another top post, to keep sending out résumés and not to give up, because both they and their job counselors have adopted the belief that motivation (rather than labor demand) is all that matters in the job market. She never mentions bankruptcy as an explicit option taken by her subjects, but it is likely that the lengthy job searches she documents stretched family finances far beyond what savings and unemployment compensation could cover. Some of our respondents filed for bankruptcy because the job skid cost them so much income. Others may be there because of the expenses they continued to incur while postponing the inevitable and taking a lower-level job.[33]

There are no completely comparable national data on the job skid, only occasional studies from the Bureau of Labor Statistics (BLS) on job displacement. The BLS studied displaced workers who had been at work for at least three years before their layoff between 1990 and 1992. When displaced workers were interviewed in 1992, only about a fourth of the displaced workers were working at full-time wage and salary jobs paying as much or more than they had earned at their lost job. The remainder appeared to be headed for a job skid. One-third had not yet been reemployed, so they were still counted among the unemployed. About one-quarter had found new full-time wage and salary jobs, but at lower pay levels than previously.[34]

Job skidding has proven to be very costly. The BLS study determined that men who lost full-time employment and then found another full-time job saw their average weekly earnings drop from $529 to $423 in their new jobs. For women, the comparable decline was from $397 to $305.[35] For both men and women, then, the job slide on average translated into a loss of more than 20 percent of their income—for those fortunate enough to find full-time jobs. The remaining displaced workers found new jobs working part-time, were unpaid family workers, or had become self-employed—usually suffering a much greater decline in income, along with lost benefits and decreased economic stability.[36]

Corinna Duben's story is a typical example of job skidding, except that she lost even more income than the 20 percent median reported in the government survey. Corinna is a forty-six-year-old divorced college graduate, and her story sounds familiar from the results of the displaced worker survey: "Loss of income in January 1990; inability to find full time work until the end of October 1990 and income from that position at less than half of my former position."

Her counterpart, Willis Jelison, lost 44 percent of his earnings. Willis is a thirty-two-year-old man who entered bankruptcy with his wife, Anne, aged thirty-three. Both are high school graduates, and both are working. Willis writes, "I lost my job with Rock Ridge Cable TV at which I was making $12.65 per hr and got highered at a job which only paid $7.00 per hr. I could not keep up with present bills due to lack of funds."

One study has concluded that the magnitude of the earnings loss is far greater than earlier analyses had determined. As much as three years before the actual separation, the employing firms had presaged the eventual displacement with reduced overtime, wage cuts, and temporary layoffs. The actual losses, then, were not reflected merely in the immediately pre- and postdisplacement comparisons, but involved lower-than-projected earnings even before the final job loss. The average discounted value of the earnings losses from three to six years before separation amounted to $50,000 per worker.[37] This finding implies that by the time workers move to new, lower-paying jobs, many have already undergone a long period of job erosion followed by a period of job loss.

## The Partially Employed

In spite of the difficult stories told by Corinna and Willis, some people would consider them fortunate. After all, they found full-time jobs, while many others are still looking for full-time work. Juan Vargas works part-time in community service work. His sixty-two-year-old wife is a homemaker. Although his debts are only about $5,500, with no credit card debt, his income is only $11,700. At one time the Vargas family did well enough to purchase a home, now valued at $43,000 for which they report no mortgage.[38] He writes: "I have been employed only part-time with no guarantee or fixed hours for the past two years or more—therefore, I wasn't able to make my payments and am falling behind."

Juan and others who are partially employed, even if they are seeking work, are not counted in the official unemployment rate. A person can be counted as unemployed officially only if he or she did not work even one hour for pay or profit in the preceding week. Thus, in the extreme case, someone who worked from 9 to 10 on Monday morning and then looked for work the rest of the week would be counted as employed, not unemployed. In fact, this type of job-seeking is invisible in government statistics.[39]

Census Bureau data indicated that a job change between 1990 and 1992 was more likely to result in a downgrade to part-time work than to be an upgrade to full-time work. Between 1990 and 1992, the period of our study, 13 percent of the men who had been full-time workers and who were then unemployed for at least one month returned to work as part-time workers. For women, the proportion jumped to 18 percent.[40]

The increase in temporary workers and of workers who are on short-term contracts suggests that there may be many more partially employed workers in the future.[41] Juan, who works with no guarantee and no fixed hours, may be typical of the worker who is able to find work but who has no permanent work relationship with an employer. In 1995 the Bureau of Labor Statistics began to study contingent workers, those holding jobs that are not expected to last.[42] A total of 5.6 million workers held a contingent job under the government's broadest estimate. The contingent workers were younger and more likely to be female; 43 percent were part-time workers.

A variety of work arrangements qualify for the label "contingent." About 6.7 percent of the labor force were independent contractors who might also be freelance workers or consultants. This group was more likely to consist of middle-aged men. Of all the contingent workers, this group was most likely to be satisfied with their work arrangements. Some of the consultants may be able to command substantial fees and therefore be satisfied, although the group of "consultants" also includes many contingent workers looking for contract jobs. Another 1.6 percent of the labor force were on-call workers, who reported to work whenever they were notified. Another 1 percent of the labor force were temporary agency workers, and a final 0.6 percent were provided by contract firms. The majority of the contingent workers, according to the survey, would have preferred a full-time job.[43]

Many of our respondents also wanted a full-time job but could not find one. Some of them worked desperately to put together enough part-time jobs to make ends meet. The champion in the multiple part-time job category is Lena Arthur, a forty-three-year-old divorced woman with some college. She carefully explains the reason for her bankruptcy as follows:

> Indebtedness occurred because of the following:
>
> a. Single parent, one dependent, for 16 years
> b. Cost of living versus income increases
> c. Lack of fulltime work—worked 5 parttime jobs to meet rent, utilities, phone, food & insurance.

Even five part-time jobs were, in the end, insufficient to keep Lena out of bankruptcy.

### The Job Erosion Pattern

The eroded job may once have been a good job, but the working conditions gradually deteriorated. The debtors described several types of eroded jobs. August Rencher, a thirty-nine-year-old with some college and a wife, Tina, who is a homemaker, reports: "At beginning of 1990 employer gave many wage earners a 40% pay cut after exhausting savings, we started to fall behind on payments to the point that we had to file Chapter 13." August's job erosion took the form of a substantial pay cut. He and Tina own a fully mortgaged home worth $72,000; they owe a total of $91,000, with no credit card debt, but their earnings are now about $29,000. At the time of the pay cut, August and Tina had savings, but these savings have also been depleted. At 60 percent of his former salary, he and his wife cannot make their payments. They are attempting to develop a plan in Chapter 13 to repay their creditors.

John Seymour's job erosion took the form of a demotion and a pay cut at the car dealership where he works. "I lost a management position with my employer. I went from sales manager to salesperson which reduced my income in half—this change was also due to poor management conditions." It is not clear what the poor management conditions were at the car dealership. Perhaps John was not working out as a manager, or perhaps the dealership was losing business through the fault of someone higher up. Whatever the poor management conditions were, John has a home worth $169,000 with only $6,000 in equity. Besides the whopping mortgage, he and his wife, Clarice, who is a homemaker, owe more than $34,000 in credit card debt and now have a family income of about $50,000. They have filed in Chapter 7 to deal with a total debt burden of more than $323,000.

John and Clarice have a lot of debt, but perhaps it was not so daunting when they had an income in six figures. Now, even though John has stayed with the same employer, his demotion from manager to salesperson has put his salary back in five figures. At $50,000, John's salary is still well above the American median income of $32,780 for Americans generally in 1991 and at the top end of the bankruptcy sample. Even so, it is not the salary he had when he was approved for that large mortgage. And the downward adjustment is proving rocky.

No national statistics are available on the number of jobs that have been eroded either directly through a direct pay cut or indirectly through a demotion. Job erosion is difficult to assess in terms of its national significance, but such cuts are an important problem for the debtors in bankruptcy. In our sample, 4.5 percent of respondents reported a lower-paying job or a pay cut for the primary petitioner, with 0.6 percent reporting such a cut for their spouse. Commissions were reduced for another 0.8 percent of the sample. If our sample could be extrapolated to the nation generally, that would mean forty-seven thousand bankruptcies a year from job erosion alone. Furthermore, given that more than 5 percent of our sample cited job erosion as a reason for bankruptcy in response to an open-ended question, we almost certainly would have identified a good deal more of it if we had asked a specific question about pay cuts and reduced hours.

The national data suggest that job erosion continues in the midst of prosperity. The process of job erosion may take the form of partial layoffs, so that workers have fewer hours on the job, which is one form of erosion for which we do have some information. The federal government does report on the number of workers who are involuntarily part-time "for economic reasons." This language refers to workers whose part-time status is due to economic circumstances beyond their control, including slack work, equipment failures, materials shortages, and so on. Even in January 1998, when unemployment was generally very low, more than 4.1 million workers, or about 3 percent of the labor force, were working part-time for economic reasons. Of this number, 1.4 million had been able to find only part-time work, while the remainder were full-time workers reduced to part-time work at the time they were surveyed.[44]

The erosion in total hours of work is financially disruptive. Erosion—whether it is from overtime to full-time, from full-time to part-time, or from a higher salary to a lower one for the same hours—translates into lower income for the debtors. In 1995 the median hourly earnings of part-time workers were $5.86, versus $9.14 for full-time workers.[45] In some companies, the cut from full-time to part-time status may also mean the loss of important fringe benefits, of which health insurance is probably the most important. With their reduced wages, the new part-time workers may not be able to afford continued insurance payments, or the company may not cover part-timers. The national data indicate that only 12 percent of part-time workers were covered for pension plans and 19 percent had group health plan coverage.[46] This compares with 49.5 percent coverage and 62.6 percent coverage, respectively, for full-time workers.

This sort of job erosion—fewer hours of work—was reported by even more of our respondents than reduced pay. Overall, 5.6 percent of our respondents reported reduced hours as a reason for their bankruptcies. Some of these were likely people reduced to part-time work, like 3 percent of the national work force, but our term is somewhat more inclusive than the government's comparative figure, because a respondent could be classified into this category for reporting that he or she had lost overtime or lost a second job—that is, this could be a full-time worker who was normally working a longer schedule. Julie Keys, a forty-eight-year-old divorced woman with ten years of schooling, reported as the reason for her bankruptcy "a definite decrease in weekly hours. Used to work a lot of hours, 50 to 75 hours per week. Regular work week is 40 hours. For the past year my hours were cut drastically. Work never picked up again."

Jobs may erode for the self-employed because of poor economic conditions. Bart Sager is a twenty-six-year-old, never-married high school graduate who was in the construction business for himself. He is now seeking work with an employer, but there is no work available either as employer or independent contractor. As Bart wrote on his questionnaire: "I'm in the construction business and the past year has been very slow with work and the jobs I did get was only because I had to bid the job low to make sure I had the job. With that it lowered my income which in turn put me in a bad position financially and when September came, I had no work at all. Through September, October, November, December, and January I continued to seek for work with other contractors and companies, but everyone else was in the same work shortage."

95

Bart's account would have been familiar to James Gearny, who identifies himself as of Irish ancestry, is married, aged forty-five, and a high school graduate. James says: "In April 1989 I started my own heating and air conditioning service company. At first it went well but do to a mild summer and winter in 1989 accompanied with a housing start slow down, business took a down turn in 1990. In fact there were periods of weeks sometimes with no income. As of January 28 I started working for Cooley Express Couriers and am still employed by them."

As Bart's account shows, what begins as job erosion may eventually slide into complete unemployment. James's case shows that the self-employed in name may in fact be without income for weeks at a time. His case is happier because he has now been employed, whereas Bart is still looking. Small business failure such as James has experienced has been implicated in the rising rate of residential home mortgage foreclosure rates.[47]

A third story shows how job erosion may occur even with the same employer. Doug Zallek is forty-seven, married, and holds a bachelor's degree. He writes: "The company I work for was purchased by another. My salary was reduced by $60,000. At the time I had purchased a home and my wife was pregnant." Job erosion is an important problem for the debtors because both they and their creditors entered the credit relationship expecting that a certain level of earnings would continue into the future. Doug Zallek took out his home mortgage in good faith and reported a salary that was eventually $60,000 more per year than he earned. With neither Doug nor his creditors able to anticipate the deterioration of earnings, even on an actuarial basis, job erosion became a precipitating event in his decision to file bankruptcy. Recent government data, including information about the substantial numbers of involuntarily part-time workers, suggest that job erosion is a continuing phenomenon.

## The Job Loss Cascade

Jobs are so important to the well-being and identity of the American middle class that a job loss may trigger other unhappy events. The accounts of several of the debtors show how a job problem can stimulate other problems, especially family disruption. The loss of a job often precipitates a series of events, one of which may be bankruptcy but many of which are unpleasant. We call this the job loss cascade. Herb and Ann May, who live in San Antonio, describe such a cascade of troubles. Concerning the reasons for their bankruptcy, Herb wrote: "Company Ann worked for went bankrupt and suddenly without prior notice had no job. Sudden drop of $1500 month net put us behind. Then Ann had to have surgery—after surgery the insurance company said they would not pay for it. Another financial struggle. This was the only alternative left." Herb is forty-five, has some college education, and he is a sales representative. Ann, forty-one, also has some college and worked as a bookkeeper until her company went bankrupt. The employer's bankruptcy led to her job loss and perhaps to the loss of health insurance to cover the surgery. Herb reports that she is looking for work. The Mays report an annual income of $38,000 and total debts of $35,300, of which $17,000 is owed on credit cards.

This account by Ann's husband also reveals a chain of causation of the sort that our respondents sometimes reported.

The loss of a job initiates a vulnerability to many unpleasant consequences, some of them costly. Increased symptoms of both mental and physical distress are common; substance abuse, child and spouse abuse, marital difficulties, and educational problems for children are documented sequels of layoffs.[48] The loss of fringe benefits hits many families hard. More than four million workers who left their jobs during 1990–92 also lost employer-sponsored health insurance.[49] We cannot be certain that Ann's difficulties with the health insurance company resulted from the loss of her job-related benefits, but at least some Americans suffer from the double-whammy of the job loss and the reduction or loss of their medical benefits.[50]

## How Demographic Backgrounds Intersect with Work Histories

In their own words, our respondents identify job loss as an important cause of their financial distress. By analyzing their demographic backgrounds from their questionnaires, we can draw a profile of the respondents most affected by job problems. In general, the people who are least likely to be in bankruptcy at all are the very people most likely to report a job-related problem for their bankruptcy.

Married debtors were significantly more likely than nonmarried debtors to report a job problem.[51] A full three-quarters of married people, versus one-half of widowed petitioners, reported a job problem. As we saw in the previous chapter, the proportion of single-filing women in bankruptcy has grown as the proportion of married women has decreased in our sample. In Chapter 6, on divorce, we indicate the disproportionate numbers of all bankrupt debtors who are divorced, separated, or never married. Marriage may well have some insurance effect against bankruptcy. The possibility of two earners, the pressure toward stability represented by children, and the general psychological and health benefits of marriage may give married people added financial stability. And yet, these data suggest that even the most stable married couple may not be able to forestall economic disaster after a layoff or job erosion.

Degree-holders are underrepresented in bankruptcy, as we noted in Chapter 2. This is perhaps not surprising, because education has long been thought of as a hedge against job loss. Better educated workers could capture more stable jobs and be less likely to endure the vagaries of plant cutbacks and seasonal readjustments. But the bankruptcy sample showed that education had no relation to job interruptions, which were prevalent at every level of schooling.[52] Even the possession of advanced degrees provided no sure protection against job loss, with about 55 percent of those holding advanced degrees reporting periods without work. The bankruptcy data suggest that by the 1990s, everyone has become at risk for a job problem.

Notwithstanding the ubiquity of job interruptions reported among the debtors in bankruptcy, those with higher education were more likely to blame a job dislocation as the source of their financial collapse. Among debtors holding advanced degrees, 63.3 percent gave a job-related reason for their bankruptcy, about 8 percentage points higher than those who had actually experienced a job interruption. Overall, there was a significant relation between giving a job-related reason and having more formal education. The degree-holders who are underrepresented are in bankruptcy largely because of job problems.

It may be that job erosion and job skidding, without income interruption, are more important aspects of employment-related income loss for these upscale debtors. Thomas Moore has noted that downsizing especially affected the prospects for upward mobility among the college educated.[53] Both less educated and better educated people may be experiencing job problems, but those problems may more frequently involve a period of unemployment for those with less education. It is also possible that these better educated workers feel, as Moore suggests, that the implicit contract that once guaranteed the security of managerial and professional employees is being rewritten, and the terms of the new contract have heightened career anxieties.[54] The better educated may thus report their job problems more readily because job issues are especially salient to them in framing their economic failure.[55]

Race and age do not appear to be related to job problems as strongly as marital status and education are. All racial groups are equally likely to say that they are currently seeking work, although whites are disproportionately likely to frame their explanations in terms of a job-related reason. All age groups reported job problems. At least 65 percent of every age group reported a job problem, with 73 percent of those aged nineteen to twenty-four giving a job reason. The only exception was the very oldest filers, who reported fewer job problems — presumably because of the higher incidence of retirement. Even among the filers aged sixty-five and older, however, 41 percent reported a job problem.[56] These data strongly suggest that the elderly are supplementing their retirement years by working and that the loss of a job is devastating.

If bankruptcy is indeed a middle-class phenomenon, then our data may reveal problems that government statistics obscure. National patterns of unemployment show disproportionately high unemployment among the young, minorities, and the poorly educated. These figures may, however, have effectively concealed the job problems that occur among the middle-aged, majority group members, middle-class minorities, and the well educated who have nevertheless encountered the pink slip or the reduced pay in a job they continue to hold. These data remind us that workers who do not fit the gross statistical profiles may nevertheless be hard hit in an economy engaged in constant restructuring. For the same reason, these data may help us explain why there are record bankruptcies at a time of low unemployment.

## Job Restructuring and Bankruptcy

To many observers, a restructuring of the American economy is essential to maintain international competitiveness. The dislocations of layoffs, unemployment, and income interruption are to be expected in this process. But for the people who experience the stresses and strains of the restructuring directly, it can be a wrenching experience.

Calvin Granger is a sixty-two-year-old man with a bachelor's degree. He is married. He explains his bankruptcy filing:

> A job loss in the last quarter of 1987 extended through 1988. To meet bills, taxes, mortgage payments, etc., I had to use my savings and finally my retirement account. Although several thousand resumes were sent out between 11/87 and 12/88 no placement resulted in my line of work, namely technical writing. I decided to start up my own business of repairing and restoring Volvo automobiles, since I had a

99

background as a mechanic, and had been involved with Volvos for over 20 years. To start up the repair business, I needed equipment beyond what I owned at the time. My funds were almost depleted, so I resorted to the use of credit cards to purchase the tolls and equipment necessary. The business built nicely, starting 1/1/90 and the cash flow was sufficient to meet all my bills. When the current recession hit, business slowed down, as it did with many of the small businesses I dealt with, and I could no longer meet all my monthly commitments.

Kevin Watson tells a similar story. He is forty-eight years old and also holds a bachelor's degree. His wife, Judy, is a forty-eight-year-old high school graduate. Both are employed. He writes: "This bankruptcy has resulted from a prolonged period of time in which I was unemployed/underemployed. This period began with an elimination of my position at UniSys Corporation 4/89. Although I did consulting during the remainder of 1989 and was able to keep my bills current, 1990 saw my salary drop from $75,000 to $11,000 and resulted in all my bills escalating."

In both this and the preceding chapter we have alluded to the growing inequality and polarization of American family incomes. Many analysts see income polarization as a direct outcome of job polarization.[57] The job changes we described in San Antonio occurred throughout the nation, with the elimination of large numbers of middle-level jobs. Some of the jobs lost were the good manufacturing jobs, "good" because they paid relatively high wages although the skill requirements were not high. The position eliminated at UniSys is a good example of a lost job that not only paid well but probably provided substantial fringe benefits. As manufacturing jobs were exported or simply eliminated, equally good jobs have been hard to find.[58]

Other jobs lost were middle-management jobs and professional jobs that were replaced, outsourced, or contracted back to the previous incumbents, but without fringe benefits or job security. Some of the job-losers could find new jobs, often with the kind of skidding we have described, but rarely at the same levels they had previously enjoyed.[59] Others billed themselves as "consultants" but received only a fraction of their former incomes. Kevin is a good example of such job skidding. Still others struck out for themselves, as in the case of

Calvin, the technical writer-turned-mechanic, only to discover how volatile conditions can be for small business owners.

Increasing bankruptcy filings in the midst of prosperity may indicate that bankruptcy serves those who have been most surprised by hardship: middle-class people who have never been out of work and do not expect to be. Anyone who expects job security is more likely to incur debts closer to the edge of income. Everything is fine until an employment change reduces that income. Then debts that seemed reasonable cannot be repaid. It appears from our data that many workers who might otherwise have been fairly well off were caught unaware when they encountered job difficulties.

One indication of the surprise element of job loss is that of all the reasons for bankruptcy, only job-related reasons correlate with the dollar value of assets.[60] This correlation is positive and highly significant; that is, a debtor with a high level of assets was significantly more likely to indicate a job-related reason for bankruptcy, and a debtor who gave a job-related reason was significantly more likely to have accumulated assets. In particular, homeowners were significantly more likely than renters to give job-related reasons for their bankruptcy.[61] Because most people are able to accumulate assets only by virtue of ready cash or credit-worthiness, these debtors who had accumulated assets were likely to have had substantial employment. For those who had already developed some stake in the American dream, the loss of the dream was especially difficult.

## The Paradox of Bankruptcy amid Prosperity

That people who lose their jobs may end up in bankruptcy seems plausible, especially given the conditions during the recession of 1991. Anyone can understand why bankruptcy rates would be high during a recession. But why are bankruptcy rates high during a time of prosperity? How are we to explain the continuation of very high levels of bankruptcy—over 1.35 million in 1998—with the minimal inflation and low unemployment rates of 1998? Is it possible that by 1998 the bankruptcy filing rates somehow became disconnected from work-related hardship and emerged from a different set of causes?

The data Judge Sellers collected in Ohio in 1997 offer strong support for the continuing significance of work interruptions in bankruptcy. The year 1997 opened with a national unemployment rate of 5.3 percent and closed with an unemployment rate of 4.7 percent, both rates that would classify the year as a very good one for workers.[62] Ohio shared in the general prosperity, with comparable unemployment figures: a rate of 5 percent in February 1997 and a rate of only 4.4 percent by December 1997.[63] The unemployment rates in cities in southern Ohio were a little higher: 6.4 percent in Cincinnati, 5.1 percent in Dayton–Springfield, and 7.2 percent in Youngstown–Warren.[64]

In the bankruptcy data from Ohio, a large fraction of the sample had had some kind of employment problem. Of the cases for which a valid reason was coded, 27.1 percent cited a job-related reason for their bankruptcy. This figure is almost surely an underestimate, because Judge Sellers did not have the benefit of questionnaire data. Instead she had to find evidence of job loss from the court papers alone rather than from interviewing the debtors.[65]

Judge Sellers also recorded the length of time in years that the petitioners had been employed, a datum that is routinely collected in the court filings. If a score of zero years could be taken to mean current unemployment or very recent employment of less than a year's duration, then the cases with a reported job tenure of zero would produce an estimated unemployment rate of 20.5 percent. This figure differs little from the 21.4 percent we reported in our debtors' sample in the recessionary year of 1991. It appears that even in the nonrecession year of 1997, when unemployment was generally low, the bankrupt debtors appeared much more likely than the rest of Ohio's population to be unemployed.

Another source of evidence suggests the continuing significance of job problems as a leading cause of bankruptcy. In 1997 the Institute for Survey Research conducted the Panel Study of Income Dynamics (PSID), which asked the members of its sample whether they had ever declared bankruptcy and if so, the reason for the bankruptcy (from a precoded list). As a national representative sample, the PSID should include at least some people who declared bankruptcy, although some would have declared bankruptcy many years ago and others more recently.[66] The study could be thought of as a chronicle of the stock of all the bankrupt debtors in the population regardless of the year of filing. In spite of significant problems with the data, it

UNEMPLOYED OR UNDEREMPLOYED

is interesting that 23 percent of those who acknowledged having declared bankruptcy also explained that the reason was loss of job.[67] A full 21 percent gave job loss as the first reason. The only reason with more answers given was the generic reason that debts were too high.

In the PSID sample, job loss was a major cause for bankruptcy regardless of when the respondents had filed. For filers before 1970, 23 percent reported a job loss. For the 1970s, 25 percent reported a job loss. For the 1980s, 22.8 percent reported a job loss. And for those who reported filing in the 1990s— more than half of those who admitted a bankruptcy—19 percent reported a job loss as the first reason for bankruptcy.

The Ohio data point to the significance of job loss in times of prosperity. Our sample data point to the significance of job problems in times of recession. The PSID data indicate the long-term importance of job loss across the cycles of the economy, good times and bad. The data from our studies in 1981 and 1991 and the Ohio data from 1997 all suggest a pattern of unemployment at two to three times the rate in the general population in good times and bad over sixteen years. The numbers suggest that even when the unemployment rate is low, there are important pockets of people out of work and for whom a loss of income is a seriously destabilizing financial event.

Beyond that conclusion, however, it is worth considering why the official unemployment rate is so low. As workers are outsourced or develop new statuses as independent contractors, freelancers, and contingent workers, they are classified among the employed even though their work situations may remain highly precarious. A few indicators gleaned from government data suggest that job instability persists in other forms. In 1997, although unemployment was low, there were 8.5 million independent contractors, nearly 2 million "on-call" workers, 1.3 million workers in temporary help agencies, and 809,000 people working in contract firms.[68] In early 1998, 4 million part-time workers were part-time involuntarily. Almost half a million self-employed workers wanted to work full-time but were working only part-time. Another 1.2 million workers were on temporary layoff, and half a million had completed temporary jobs and were looking for other positions. There were still 1.5 million who had lost permanent jobs. The rate of multiple job holding was ticking upward.[69]

Nor have the rounds of layoffs stopped, despite low unemployment and governmental budget surpluses. For many years employers wouldn't schedule layoffs in December because of the upcoming holidays. But December 1998 brought headlines of layoffs throughout the nation: 48,000 jobs lost at Boeing, 9,000 eliminated through the merger of Exxon and Mobil, 5,500 lost from Deutsche Bank's acquisition of Bankers Trust, 4,100 cut at Johnson & Johnson.[70] Kellogg announced intentions to lay off 21 percent of the salaried work force at its Michigan headquarters. Even Fargo, North Dakota, with a population of 160,000, saw 25 workers laid off at Case Corporation and 283 jobs eliminated when Federal Beef Processors closed its plant.[71] What was the result of these layoff announcements, according to broadcaster Elizabeth Farnsworth of *The NewsHour with Jim Lehrer?* The stock market went up.

Layoffs have become so commonplace that Americans seem used to them. The outcry has died down, but the consequences remain serious. In Rochester, New York, Kodak has cut 30,000 jobs since the 1980s and 6,300 since 1997, and Xerox has cut 3,000 jobs since 1994. Rochester outplacement firms find that about one-third of their clients fail to match their previous salaries.[72] In central Indiana more than three dozen companies had layoffs in 1998. Thomson Consumer Electronics closed its Bloomington, Indiana, plant to move to Mexico. Of its idled 1,100 workers, only 100 of them have been able to match their previous salary.[73]

Why no outcry? The low unemployment rate is surely one reason. Other jobs are available. In Fargo, for example, where the unemployment rate dropped below 1 percent, other companies advertised for job applications from the laid-off Federal Beef Processors employees. But a concentration on the unemployment rate may overlook other problems. As the Rochester and Indianapolis accounts suggest, job skidding and job erosion may be the alternatives to unemployment. Many middle-class Americans find their salaries lower than they once were. Their jobs have slipped, their pay has slipped, their hours have slipped, so they find themselves unable to pay the debts they have accumulated in a society increasingly hooked on consumer credit. These phenomena are not inconsistent with prosperity. They actually seem to be part of it insofar as the restructuring of employment is creating prosperity and increasing the distance between winners and losers.

UNEMPLOYED OR UNDEREMPLOYED

As these workers patch together job contracts and part-time work, there will be times when the jobs do not come through and the money does not stretch far enough. The problems these individuals face will not cancel out the rosy macroeconomic picture: companies will be lean and mean, and labor costs may fall. Profits, productivity, and competitiveness may rise. The paradox of prosperity and bankruptcy may be our future.

The paradox of rising bankruptcy during prosperity is not such a puzzle when rapid job changes are taken into account. Prosperity itself is often measured by a low unemployment rate, the much heralded mark of a boom economy. This measuring stick assumes that unemployment is the only economic malady. But the unemployment rate ignores the workers whose response to a layoff is eventually to slide down the job ladder, as debtor Jeanne Salem did, or to report a premature retirement, as debtor John White did. The unemployment rate also ignores the laid-off workers who swelled the ranks of the self-employed, taking themselves off the unemployment rolls but not enjoying the stability or income of an earlier job. Moreover, the failures of small businesses leave many families without their main source of income, but the owner-operators are listed among the "business closings" rather than the unemployed.[74] The jobless rate also ignores job skidding and job erosion. Even very low unemployment rates can hide a variety of financial ills that plague the fragile middle class.

The jobs data are overwhelming: by every measure, the debtors in bankruptcy are there as a result of trouble at work. For some, it is unemployment. For others, they are now at work, but a period of unemployment put them in a financial hole from which they cannot escape. For still others — perhaps the largest group — the reduced circumstances of their employment have left them in financial collapse. They are back at work at jobs that pay less, offer fewer benefits, and give them less security. Altogether more than two-thirds of the debtors who filed for bankruptcy identified a work-related problem.

The lesson that emerges from each of these patterns is that job interruption or job loss, with subsequent unemployment or underemployment, are major threats to the middle class. A few members of the middle class may win the lottery, and a few others may eventually own a string of rental houses and live off the rents. But for most Americans, keeping a good job is the key to getting into or staying in the middle class. The people who have publicly declared themselves as economic failures—those in the bankruptcy courts—are also examples of how many of the middle class are one pink slip away from the downward spiral.

In one sense, the finding that the single biggest crack in the economic security of the middle class is job-related should come as no surprise. Most middle-class families live off their incomes, not their investments or inheritances. When they lose those incomes, they are in trouble. Nonetheless, the scope of the job problem is somewhat jarring. The PSID data hint that job loss is an issue of long standing for bankrupt debtors. If the Ohio data are representative of the country generally, the job problem also remains current and immediate. If the 1991 data were applicable across the country in 1998, about a million families were filing for bankruptcy as a way of dealing with their job problems.

Bankruptcy is a handhold for middle-class debtors on the way down. These families have suffered economic dislocation, but the ones that file bankruptcy have not given up. They have not uprooted their families and drifted from town to town in search of work. They have not gone to the underground economy, working for cash and staying off the books. Instead, these are middle-class people who are fighting to stay where they are, trying to find a way to cope with their declining economic fortunes. Most have come to realize that their incomes will never be what they once were. As their comments show, they realize they can live on $30,000 or $20,000 or even $10,000. But they cannot do that and meet the obligations they ran up while they were making much more. When put to a choice between paying credit card debt and mortgage debt, between dealing with a dunning notice from Sears and putting groceries on the table, they will go to the bankruptcy courts, declare themselves failures, and save their future incomes for the mortgage and the groceries.

The greater flexibility of an increasingly market-driven economy, especially on a global scale, means that employment is necessarily more uncertain for a larger group of people. Anxieties about work that used to be limited to less-skilled or less-educated workers are now distributed more evenly up the economic ladder. When a job disappears or becomes a contract or temporary relationship, when pay is reduced or overtime eliminated, previous debts are mismatched with current income. As job insecurity mounts higher in the middle class, the middle-class remedy of bankruptcy becomes more widely used, creating the paradox of record bankruptcies at a time of record low employment. These developments have been reported mostly anecdotally or through episodic studies. Government statistics, regularly collected and reported, are not yet designed to reveal them, so that the pluses and minuses of global competitiveness are not so obvious. The data from the bankruptcy courts supplies some of the missing evidence about a wide crack in middle-class security and how families are trying to cope.

Chapter 4

# Credit Cards

Credit cards got out of hand. Was borrowing from one to pay other, before I knew it they were more than I could pay. Bankruptcy was my only
way to get back on my feet.
—SUZANNE VANKELL, Galveston, Texas

There were no breathless stories on the evening news or even dry
but carefully detailed reports in the *Wall Street Journal*, yet 1995 was a
landmark year in the long history of buying and selling. In 1995, for
the first time ever, Americans reached into their pockets and pulled
out little plastic cards more than they pulled out cash. Plastic outstripped coins and folding money as the payment of choice for consumer transactions.[1] In this chapter we explore how those credit card
debts—a $60 charge for new shoes for the kids and a $26 charge for
pizza and sodas—have forged another crack in the financial security
of middle-class Americans and increased Americans' vulnerability to
every other problem that comes their way.

As the third millennium begins, middle-class America is awash
in plastic payment cards. By 1996 consumers used credit cards to
purchase an estimated *one trillion dollars'* worth of goods and services
in a single year.[2] In circulation to make those purchases are 1.3 billion cards—more than a dozen credit cards for each household in
the country.[3] Industry analysts predict that credit card purchases will
more than double during the next decade, while both cash and check
purchases will lose market share as a means of payment.[4]

This chapter is not an essay about the morality of buying too many
things on credit. Nor is it about the morality of knowingly marketing
lines of credit to debtors who cannot possibly afford to pay. Instead,

we focus on the risk that accompanies every credit card purchase. Every buyer, by committing to spend part of tomorrow's income, has taken on a little extra risk that if something goes wrong, the buyer will be in a suddenly unmanageable position. At the same time, every creditor has joined in the gamble about the buyer's future.

## The Development of a Credit Society

Consumer credit has been around since the early twentieth century. In 1910 (four years before the establishment of the Federal Reserve system), Sears, Roebuck and Company was lending working people money so that they could buy the goods Sears had to sell.[5] The company's first application asked, "How long at your present address?" and "How many cows do you milk?" Sears, and then other retailers, gave consumers the credit that banks would not give them.[6] These early credit cards, often called merchant cards or retail cards, were issued by the same companies that sold the goods. In 1949 the Diner's Club card was born, marketed as a way for the executive on the go (and often on a corporate expense account) to keep a record of expenses and make a single payment each month for travel and entertainment.[7] In 1958 American Express and Carte Blanche joined the fray. The so-called T & E cards were not originally all-purpose cards, but over time their focus changed to all-purpose use.

In the mid-1960s the MasterCard and Visa systems were established, and banks issued all-purpose credit cards bearing their logos.[8] Within a decade, MasterCard and Visa had established a network by which millions of people could make billions of purchases. American Express responded to the bank card challenge, expanding both its customer recruitment and its merchant base.[9] In 1986 Sears entered the all-purpose card market with its Discover card. By the 1990s the all-purpose card gained dominance over traditional store cards, making it possible for millions of cardholders to charge anything from their dental fillings to their parking tickets.[10]

By the end of the 1990s the credit card had become firmly woven into the texture of American consumer life.[11] It is very difficult to rent a car from Avis, reserve a room at a Holiday Inn, or order a pair of hiking boots from L. L. Bean without one. Credit cards provide security; no cardholder fears being caught without enough cash to meet an emergency, even late at night or far from home. Cards offer safety for travelers or shoppers who no longer need to carry large amounts of cash that can be stolen or lost. Credit cards offer convenience; a cardholder's single payment can handle a number of purchases. Credit cards provide record keeping for tax purposes, receipts for expense account reimbursements, leverage for resolving disputes with merchants, and a way to pay for an unbelievable bargain on a four-karat cubic zirconium on the Home Shopping Network. Credit cards offer consumers a wide array of advantages over other systems of payment.

Credit card debt has become as much a part of American life as has the credit card itself. People who would never have considered going to a finance company to borrow $5,000 to buy odds and ends will run up a credit card bill to $5,000 in charges of $25 and $50. Of the three-quarters of all households that have at least one credit card, three out of four of them also carry credit card debt from month to month.[12] This means that the bill payers in half of *all* households (sweeping the card carriers and the non-card carriers in together) get up from the kitchen table after paying the bills each month, carrying over one or more credit card balances to the next month.

As the 1990s drew to a close, American households carried an estimated $500 billion in outstanding credit card debt, more than double the amount of credit card debt due at the beginning of the decade.[13] Government researchers estimate that the fifty million families making regular payments carry an outstanding balance on a bank card that amounts to about $1,500 a family, although with the addition of retail credit, other researchers place the number much higher.[14] With average interest rates pegged at 18.72 percent on the outstanding bank card debt, the typical household paid about $281 — the cost of a new twenty-five-inch color television set—in interest payments on MasterCard and Visa bills in 1997 alone.[15]

The debtors who carry these credit card burdens generally are neither poor nor rich; they are middle-class, middle-income Americans. The proportion of households reporting consumer debt increases as income rises, peaking in the $50,000–$100,000 annual income range, then declining as incomes rise further.[16] Credit card debt follows the same pattern, available to about one-quarter of the debtors with incomes below $10,000 but owed by nearly three-quarters of the debtors with incomes in the $50,000–100,000 range.[17] Access to credit is more sharply restricted for the poor, who have low incomes and few assets. Fewer than half of households with incomes below $10,000 had any consumer debt, compared with more than nine-tenths of those with incomes above $50,000.[18] These data suggest that consumer debt—the short-term, high-interest debt that is largely credit cards—is concentrated among middle-income families.[19]

For middle-class Americans, credit cards are a way of life. Just as fewer and fewer people recall a time without phones or even without answering machines, fewer Americans remember a time when it was hard to pay with plastic. Increasingly, however, they do not pay—they finance. Quietly, without much fanfare, Americans have taken to buying school shoes and pizza with debt—and paying for those items over months or even years.

## How to Go Bankrupt with Credit Cards

In some households the monthly credit card balance is out of control. Some credit card holders in trouble have steady jobs and generally good payment records, but they have used their credit cards to take on more and more debt, finally borrowing from one card to pay another, until they have no hope of recovering their financial stability. We call them the sliders. For others, the path to ruin is slightly different. They have heavy credit card debts, but they are managing—managing right up until something goes wrong. A bump in the financial road—a layoff, the loss of overtime, a car accident—takes them over the edge. They move from barely able to pay to unable to pay. We call them the crashers. These two groups, the sliders and the crashers, find themselves with credit card bills they cannot possibly pay.

In addition to sliders and crashers, our data also show how small business owners and those who let third parties use (or abuse) their credit can end up in bankruptcy. These four patterns add up to trouble with plastic.

### The Sliders

Many people slide into debt, falling a little farther behind on their cards every month until bankruptcy is the only way out. Industry analysts estimate that using a typical minimum credit card pay-down rate, it would take thirty-four years to pay off a $2,500 loan, and total payments would exceed 300 percent of the original principal.[20] With minimum monthly payments and 18 percent interest, most families will only fall further behind.

Betina Darvilian typifies the debtors who slide into financial disaster a little at a time, charge after charge. Betina is a single woman living in Encino, California. She is forty-two, has never been married, and is a citizen by naturalization. She was steadily employed and working when she filed for bankruptcy. Betina describes rather modest circumstances, living in an apartment and owning household goods valued at $500. Her clothes are valued at $1,500. She has a five-year-old Oldsmobile worth $2,500. Her only other asset of any value is a piano she bought about two years before filing, for which she still owes $1,170.

All of Betina's remaining debts are on credit cards. She owes $42,620 in outstanding charges. She was careful to list each creditor and to specify each credit card debt, so that it is possible to identify both the bank card debt and the retail credit card debt she owes. Betina lists eight all-purpose cards (Bank of America, American Express, Choice, Citibank, First Card, Household Card, Imperial Savings, and NCNB National Bank) on which she owes a total of $38,150. She has five more retailer's cards (Nordstrom's, Saks, TWA Getaway, I. Magnin, and Bullock's) on which she owes another $4,150. She has one gasoline card (Chevron) with an outstanding balance of $300. If the list of cards seems breathtaking, it may be worth noting that Betina has only two more cards than the average number of cards per household in circulation at the time; it is her outstanding balance that is unusual.

Betina gives the most generic description of her problem: "Accumulation of too much debt." Her description is accurate, but the debts that sunk her were not the modest loans for the car and the piano. It was the $42,620 in credit card debt that bankrupted Betina. In her careful detailing of her debts, Betina notes when she applied for each credit card. She got her first cards six years before she filed, a retail card from Bullock's Department Store and an all-purpose card from Household Card Services. Over the next three years, she picked up twelve more cards. She had held all her cards at least two years before her bankruptcy filing. None of her creditors had taken any legal steps to collect from Betina before she filed for bankruptcy, and they raised no objections in her bankruptcy case.

When she filed for Chapter 7, Betina discharged all this debt in full. If she planned to keep her car and her piano, she would have to continue those payments, but her property and her income were otherwise unrestricted. She would not have much, but shedding $42,620 in debt—and the accompanying interest payments and monthly bills—improved her financial life substantially. If, however, Betina had tried to pay without filing bankruptcy, she would have faced average prevailing interest rates of 18.43 percent on her credit card debt—if she had no late payments or default rates of interest.[21] Regular interest payments would have been almost $8,000 a year. Her file does not list her income, but if it was $13,530 (in 1991 dollars), she would have had the median income for unmarried women in our sample. If Betina wanted to pay off her debt in five years, it would require $1,099 per month, or 97 percent of her pre-tax income. If she paid $667 a month—just about half of her pre-tax income— she would have to pay for more than twenty-two years to pay in full. Living on the remaining $5,500 for a year in Encino, California, would put her at one-fourth of the per capita personal income for the Los Angeles metropolitan area in 1991.[22]

*The Crashers*

Although some of those who file for bankruptcy see credit cards as the direct cause of their downfall, others were managing their credit card debt—even if just barely. Then something else went wrong, and they found themselves overwhelmed with debt that they had no hope of managing.

The Barres, a couple in their early thirties, live in a Pittsburgh suburb. They explain: "We got ourselves way over our heads with credit cards and other debts. Then my husband was unemployed and we were not able to keep up with payments. We also have no means of making a settlement." Wilner Barre has a twelfth-grade education, but he never got his high school diploma. The Barres described how they ended up in bankruptcy court. Wilner had been out of work before the bankruptcy filing, and he was still unemployed at the time they appeared in court. Beverly Barre, who has a high school diploma, has been steadily employed, but her income alone did not leave them enough to make those low, minimum monthly payments. They filed for Chapter 7 not because they got in too deep with credit card debt but because they were in too deep to deal with credit card debt *and* Wilner's job loss. Without Wilner's layoff, they might have been among the half of all American households who routinely carry credit card debt. Their debt load was higher than average, but they had already managed it for years. Without the credit card debt, they might have survived the unemployment. Beverly's check and unemployment insurance covered a bare minimum for living expenses. It wouldn't have been comfortable, but they might have gotten by. The difficulty was that their reduced income could not cover their living expenses and maintain their credit card payments, too.

About 60 percent of the bankrupt debtors who list bank card debt (such as Visa and MasterCard bills) have experienced a job interruption during the two years before filings—layoffs, firings, strikes, cutbacks, companies that folded. The rate of job interruption for the debtors with credit card debt is the same as that for all other debtors in bankruptcy.[23] Perhaps the surprise in the data should be that only 60 percent of all the debtors who experienced a job interruption listed any bank card debt. This means that 40 percent either did not incur credit card debts before or while they were unemployed or were able to pay them off before the filing—or they just didn't list their credit card debts.

The tangle between credit card debt and unemployment may run another way as well. Some debtors may have had more modest—or even no—credit card debts before they lost their jobs, but they may have used credit cards to supplement their sharply lowered incomes. The recently unemployed, hopeful that they will be back at work in a matter of days or weeks, may not be prepared to tell the children there will be no new soccer shoes this season or no back-to-school clothes. They may not have made the switch from buying books to checking them out from the library. A credit card permits them to, as economists describe it, smooth out their incomes over time—spending tomorrow's income when today's income falls short. If they are back at work quickly, the plan works. But if they are out of work longer than they expected or they return to a job at a lower income, they may learn that the purchases they financed when their incomes were low will sink them even after they are back among the fully employed. Credit card companies make no move to remedy this situation. They do not inquire about a debtor's changing circumstances. Even when the cards are up for renewal, so long as the debtor is current on any minimum monthly payments, the lines of credit—$2,500 here, $5,000 there, $25,000 on another card—are available even if the income that supported those lines has vanished.

In fact, when a debtor demonstrates warning signs of the inability to make payments, such as exceeding a credit limit, the credit doors stay open. Stranger still, they often open wider. Many credit card issuers respond to a customer who is exceeding his or her credit limit by charging a fee—and raising the credit limit.[24] The practice of charging default rates of interest, which often run into the 20 and 30 percent range, makes customers who give the clearest sign of trouble—missing payments—among the most profitable for the issuers.[25] If current creditors limit credit when the customer stops paying, they can be replaced quickly by handfuls of offers for new cards that arrive with each day's mail.

## The Business Owners

The need for credit to finance a small business and the drain that interest payments can put on a small business are the twin components of a harsh financial reality facing most entrepreneurs. Credit can be hard to come by for a fledgling enterprise. Start-up money is tough to get, and money to bail the business out in a crisis is even harder to find. And yet, if the owner can't put goods on the shelf or pay the utility bills or have the materials needed to do the work, the business is finished. To stave off that day of collapse, some entrepreneurs turn to credit cards.

In the 1981 Consumer Bankruptcy Project we made the unexpected finding that a substantial proportion of the debtors in bankruptcy were not people working for wages. Instead, as we have noted in Chapter 2, about 20 percent were either self-employed at the time of filing or had been self-employed before they filed for bankruptcy.[26] Self-employment rates in the country were about 7.3 percent at the time the bankruptcy data were drawn, which meant that entrepreneurs were nearly three times more likely to end up in personal bankruptcy than were their wage-earning counterparts.

A distinctive feature of bankrupt entrepreneurs was that they carry extraordinarily high debt levels, with particularly high levels of unsecured debt. Although the entrepreneurs comprised 20 percent of the bankruptcy sample, for example, they accounted for more than half of all the listed unsecured debt.[27] The typical failed entrepreneur owed four times as much unsecured debt as his or her bankrupt wage-earning counterpart (mean debt of $67,290 for the self-employed versus $17,362 for salaried workers in 1997 dollars).[28] Worst of all, the entrepreneur carried a much higher debt load on an income that was statistically indistinguishable from that of a bankrupt wage earner. The data suggest that credit cards can be a significant portion of that debt load.

Stan Ekland lives in northern California. He is forty-one, and he has some college education. He writes: "I started in business d.b.a. Stan Ekland Cabinetry six years ago Aug. 15, 1985 with nothing but my hand tools and no capitalization. As time elapsed I gradually acquired basic woodworking machinery and when times of no work and no money came I drew on my credit and was able to make payments until I married and subsequently had a child in April of 1990. At that time it became obvious that I couldn't make the credit card payments any longer so I sought protection from my creditors." Stan is married, but he filed for Chapter 7 alone. Because his credit cards were issued before he was married, the companies probably had never asked his wife to agree to joint liability for the cards. Whether he was dealing with debts he incurred alone before he was married or charges put on his cards after marriage, if his wife had not applied for the cards and had not used them, she was not legally responsible for paying those bills. Because he filed alone, which means that she would still be responsible for any joint debts, it is probably a good assumption that their joint debts were manageable. Stan kept his business, kept his family solvent, and discharged his separate credit card debts through bankruptcy.

Stan wasn't alone in using cash advances from his MasterCard and Visa to finance his business. A poll of two thousand companies conducted in the same year these data were collected revealed that 30 percent of the businesses interviewed were relying on personal credit

116

cards.[29] By 1998 an Arthur Anderson study reported that 47 percent of small businesses used credit cards to finance their operations in the previous year, compared with 45 percent who used bank loans.[30] Why did they use high-interest credit cards for business financing? How could they anticipate making a profit after they paid 18 percent or more for their financing? Owners explained that they couldn't get bank lines of credit or other, less expensive loans. Besides, as one owner explained, "It is still very easy to get access to credit cards, with no application or approval necessary. An average consumer could acquire between $50,000 and $90,000 worth of credit if he wanted to."[31]

Small businesses may be using credit cards to see them through troubled times, but someday the bills come due. When they do, as one industry commentator says, "It's a killer."[32] The high interest rates that accompany credit card debt make it very likely that any entrepreneur who is using plastic to replace or supplement commercial financing for a business is doing so because he or she has no choice. Credit cards are the most expensive form of debt available, and few entrepreneurs would use them if they had other means of financing their businesses. In effect, these data suggest that Visa and Master-Card are likely becoming lenders of last resort, providing credit to businesses so shaky that no bank or credit association will lend to them.

There is strong evidence that card issuers know cards are being used in this way. When asked to comment about the survey showing that 30 percent of small businesses are using credit cards to finance their operations, Visa International executive vice president Richard Hagadorn replied that his company is "essentially indifferent to how or when" a customer uses the cards.[33] He announced that Visa had stepped up efforts to market corporate cards directly to small businesses.[34] American Express identifies 1.5 million small business accounts among its portfolio.[35] Fair Issaac and Company has developed new software so that credit issuers can send preapproved credit through the mail directly to small businesses, just as they already send preapproved credit cards to every business owner.[36] The *Nilson Report* on credit cards confirms that several card issuers are competing for small business debt. The targeted users are "proprietors of small businesses . . . particularly start-up companies that are too new to qualify for business loans."[37]

117

One last risk that is special to credit cards is worth noting because of how often it is mentioned in the debtors' explanations of their difficulties. These debtors stated that their troubles with credit card debt started not because of their own overspending relative to their incomes but because they were liable for someone else's use of their cards. Many told tales of deceit and disappointment that left them with little choice but to file for bankruptcy.

Mary Jeanette Hakins was separated from her husband about three years before her bankruptcy filing and divorced sometime later. She lives alone now in southern Illinois, where she holds a steady job. She is forty-nine years old and a high school graduate. She explains what happened (although we have changed the identities): "All credit cards since 1988 (Aug) has been in the possession of Gary W. Hakins. I had no knowledge of what was purchased or balances due. I did not consent to any of the purchases. He has been living with his girl friend since 2/89—at 422 E. Camino." Mary Jeanette seems as angry about Gary and his girlfriend as she is about her credit cards. Perhaps by giving his address, she hopes that someone in the legal system will do a little justice and call Gary to account. The problem that pushed Mary Jeanette into bankruptcy, however, is that even if Gary isn't called to account, she will be.

Fred Wilbur tells the same tale, but with the genders reversed. Fred describes himself as separated, but judging from his comments, he may have just stopped off in the bankruptcy court on the way to the divorce court. Fred is a naturalized citizen, forty-six, and a high school graduate. He is unemployed, but that isn't how he frames his financial problems. His problem, as he sees it, comes from the risk involved when he gave someone else access to his credit cards: "Letting an irresponsible woman have credit cards." Fred filed for Chapter 7 in Memphis, Tennessee, all alone. The fact that he is still legally married may make Fred liable for certain financial obligations for support, and a court may impose set amounts that Fred must pay. In some circumstances, one spouse may also be charged directly by creditors for certain "necessaries" supplied to the other spouse for maintenance. State law determines the scope of such obligations. There is wide disparity among the various states and sometimes even among judges

118

within a state. Fred is not automatically liable on all the credit cards held by his wife. For him to be legally responsible for a credit card debt, he must agree to be bound by signing a joint credit application, and he can terminate his agreement for any future charges whenever he chooses. Similarly, if Fred wants to discharge his liability on his credit cards, he can do so.[38] If his wife wants to deal with the credit card debts after Fred's bankruptcy, they will be hers exclusively—and she could pay them or file her own bankruptcy.

Other debtors tell of friends, ex-spouses, children, and parents who used the debtors' credit cards and left the debtors holding the bag. Those caught in a marital split often found that they did not cancel their credit cards quickly enough, and they faced huge bills for which they were responsible after the ex-spouse was long gone. These debtors might assert that without credit cards they would not have needed to file for bankruptcy. Perhaps so and perhaps not. They may have also had a number of other financial problems to resolve. Whether the credit cards were the only problem or one of several, however, their stories are a reminder that credit cards can be dangerous—a weapon in the hands of a vindictive ex-spouse or a high-risk gamble in the hands of some other loving but irresponsible family member. To be sure, the debtor could have canceled the cards, but for some, by the time they knew they had been duped, it was too late. The bills went elsewhere, the debtor forgot about the card or didn't know it was missing, and the first sign of trouble is the call from a collection agency.

Anything anyone owns can be carted off, stolen, or appropriated, especially by someone else who lives in the home. People with family problems often have long and painful stories to tell about cars that have been wrecked and money that has disappeared in the course of a family upheaval. But credit cards are unique. The debts can continue piling up long after the little plastic card has left the debtor's hands.

## Charging into Bankruptcy

The ubiquity of the credit card among the middle class may obscure the problems that the cards can engender. All-purpose credit card debt is the most frequently listed debt in the bankruptcy files. In our 1981 study measuring only bank card (such as Visa and Master-

Card) and other all-purpose debt (such as American Express), which we lump in with the bank card debt, nearly 60 percent of all the debtors list some all-purpose credit card debt.[39] This is true whether debtors explain that they are filing for bankruptcy because of medical problems, job loss, business failure, or any other reason.

*Measurement Problems with Credit Card Debt*

All-purpose card debt substantially understates the magnitude of the credit card problem.[40] When retail credit card debt is added to the bank card total, the debt attributable to credit cards is even greater. Data from our 1991 study suggest that perhaps 88 percent of the debtors in bankruptcy may have credit card debt of some kind.[41] An independent study by the National Consumer Law Center confirms this estimate. Researchers examined a sample of Massachusetts debtors' files in detail in 1991, the same year as our second study. They also identified debt they classified as credit card debt in the files of 88 percent of the debtors they studied.[42] A newer study based on data collected in 1997 by Judge Barbara Sellers in Ohio also includes all kinds of credit card debt, both bank cards and retail store cards. Those data show that about 83 percent of the debtors had some credit card debt.[43] In a single-district study of Chapter 7 debtors also in 1997 in the District of Northern California, Judge Randall Newsome found that 95 percent of the debtors had credit card debt of some kind.[44] If these data are accurate and representative of debtors filing in other parts of the country, then between eight and nine out of every ten bankrupt debtors list credit card debt when they file.[45]

Even when both the retail cards and bank cards are combined, the debt figures are likely understated because some debtors do not list their credit card debt in hopes of paying off that debt and keeping the card.[46] Perhaps they cannot imagine a future without plastic. Like the alcoholic who takes a bottle to the rehab center just in case things get rough, some debtors go to bankruptcy court reserving one or two credit cards in their hip pockets—just in case things get too tough.[47]

Such underreporting masks the difficulties the debtors will have when they emerge from bankruptcy. Unlisted debt is not discharged and must be paid in full. Of course, it seems reasonable to assume that debtors would protect only their cards with low outstanding balances, so the understatement of debt might be minimal. On the other hand, the need to retain credit cards is not an entirely rational process—as proven by the practitioners in the field who stress how often they encounter debtors willing to flout the explicit provisions of the law in order to conceal their credit card charges.[48]

The possibilities of underreporting do nothing to diminish the underlying truth: bankrupt debtors did what most other Americans did—they carried credit balances on their charge cards. They did it more often than Americans generally, which suggests that credit card use makes anyone more vulnerable to bankruptcy. But the fact of carrying a credit balance alone did not create their problems. Not everyone with a credit card balance is headed for bankruptcy. It is the size of their credit card debts that distinguishes the debtors in real trouble.

*How Much Credit Card Debt?*

We have summarized the results of several studies of bankrupt debtors (table 4.1). Although the data are not entirely comparable, the various reports provide a picture of the role of credit card debt in the bankruptcies of American families.[49] The comparison between the 1981 and 1991 data give an idea of how the amount of bank card debt, even when corrected for inflation, has been increasing for bankrupt debtors. Although the 1981 debt is substantial, in 1991 the mean bank card debt is more than $11,529, with the median debt somewhat lower at $6,913.[50] The 1997 data from Ohio show that when all credit card debt is counted, retail and bank cards, the debt load rises further.[51] At the mean, the Ohio debtors owed $14,260, while at the median they owed $9,345, on all their credit cards combined.[52] Even when we correct for inflation, credit card debt burdens for bankrupt debtors are substantial and have been climbing.

The rise of credit card debt in 1997 may be even sharper than the Ohio data suggest. In the single-district California study the median credit card debt was $21,785 and the mean was a whopping $28,955. Because the California data included only Chapter 7 debtors, the sample is not directly comparable to the other three studies, which are drawn from all consumer debtors in both Chapter 7 and Chap-

**Table 4.1**  Credit card debt listed in bankruptcy, 1981, 1991, 1997 (in 1997 dollars)

| 1981 (Visa, MasterCard, American Express, and Discover cards only) | | 1991 (Visa, MasterCard, American Express, and Discover cards only) | |
|---|---|---|---|
| Mean | 3,635 | Mean | 11,529 |
| s.d. | 3,828 | s.d. | 15,553 |
| 25th percentile | 1,401 | 25th percentile | 3,057 |
| median | 2,649 | median | 6,913 |
| 75th percentile | 4,423 | 75th percentile | 14,485 |
| valid cases | 588 | valid cases | 400 |
| **1997** (all credit card debt) | | t-values | |
| Mean | 14,260 | 1981 v. 1991 | 11.80*** |
| s.d. | 17,395 | 1981 v. 1997 | 12.82*** |
| 25th percentile | 4,371 | 1991 v. 1997 | 1.43 ns |
| median | 9,345 | | |
| 75th percentile | 16,047 | *p < .05; **p < .01; ***p < .001 | |
| valid cases | 83 | | |

*Source:* Consumer Bankruptcy Project I, 1981; Consumer Bankruptcy Project II, 1991; Ohio Bankruptcy Study, 1997.

ter 13. Nonetheless, the California data may indicate a staggering rise in credit card burdens for the debtors in bankruptcy.[53]

Comparable national data give some idea about how the bankrupt debtors compare with other credit card holders. As we noted earlier, among the half of all American households that carried outstanding balances on any kind of credit card, the total debt burden was $1,500 at the median.[54] The most comparable data are those from Ohio, which report the same aggregation of credit card debt. Those data suggest that in a straight comparison of debt holders to debt holders in and out of bankruptcy, the debtors in bankruptcy, at the median, were carrying card debts more than six times higher than other card holders.[55]

The prevalence of credit-card debt among the bankrupt debtors was remarkable. Of one hundred debtors in the Ohio sample, eighty-three had some credit card debt. Of those, nearly half (47 percent) listed credit card debt in excess of $10,000. The concentration of high levels of debt among relatively few debtors is also worthy of note.

**CREDIT CARDS**

Nearly 20 percent of the debtors listed credit card debt in excess of $20,000. Even in the relatively small sample of Ohio debtors, five debtors had credit card debts in excess of $50,000, and one debtor who surely won the prize for the hottest cards in the district listed $91,430 in ordinary credit card debt.[56] The top twelve debtors collectively owed nearly half of all the credit card debt listed in the Ohio sample. In other words, when some debtors get into trouble with their credit cards, they get into a lot of trouble.[57]

*The Growing Impact of Credit Card Bills*

Americans' use of credit cards grows every year. Just when we decide that surely no one needs another card, the credit card companies report yet more cards in circulation. In the fifteen years from 1980 to 1995, the amount of revolving credit outstanding jumped sevenfold.[58] By the early 1990s, with credit card debt at historic highs, economists speculated that Americans could tolerate no more credit card debt. But since 1993 the growth of credit card loans has been faster than any other type of consumer loan. Credit card debt doubled in just four years: the amount of credit card debt outstanding at the end of 1997 was $422 billion, twice as much as the amount in 1993.[59] Both the number of cards and the median balance on each card jumped dramatically.[60] With three and a half billion credit card solicitations mailed out during 1998, it seems a safe bet to predict that there will be even more debt in the next few years.[61]

At the same time, all consumer debt, including all other types of loans except mortgages and home equity loans, jumped as well, although more modestly. From 1980 to 1996 the debt outstanding on credit cards plus car loans, credit union loans, finance company loans, and other open-end and closed-end credit more than tripled, but the rate of growth on all consumer debt was less than half the rate on credit card debt.[62]

The bankrupt debtors were the leading edge of the larger American trend to more debt. As we reported in the early 1980s (see table 4.1), the evidence is that debtors who found themselves in bankruptcy carried bank credit card debt of $3,635 at the mean and $2,649 at the median in 1997 dollars.[63] Ten years later, bankrupt debtors reported bank card debt of $11,529 at the mean and $6,913 at the median in

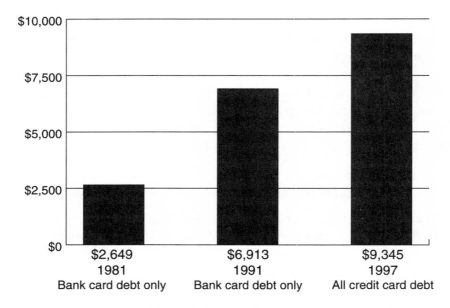

| | | |
|---|---|---|
| $2,649 | $6,913 | $9,345 |
| 1981 | 1991 | 1997 |
| Bank card debt only | Bank card debt only | All credit card debt |

Fig. 4.1 Median credit card debt listed in bankruptcy, 1981, 1991, and 1997. *Note:* All numbers are reported in 1997 dollars. *Source:* Consumer Bankruptcy Project II, 1991; Ohio Bankruptcy Study, 1997.

1997 dollars, a sharp rise in per family debt. Even when the numbers are adjusted for inflation, as these are, the amount of credit card debt carried by bankrupt debtors more than doubled at the median and tripled at the mean (fig. 4.1).[64]

The impact of credit card debt comes into stark relief when consumer debt is compared with income. In 1995, among Americans generally, people who had some credit card debt committed, at the median, $4.72 out of every $100 of their pre-tax incomes to their credit card debt.[65] This is a substantial fraction of total income for all Americans, who must stretch that $100 to cover all family expenses. Yet the debtors in bankruptcy demonstrate just how out of hand credit card debt has become.

To do this analysis, we matched credit card debts with incomes for each person in our five-district subsample (table 4.2). A debt to income ratio of 1.00 indicates that the debtor owes one year's income in credit card debts; a debt to income ratio of 0.25 indicates that the debtor owes three months' income in credit card debts. All other outstanding debts, such as home mortgage debts, car loans, educational

**CREDIT CARDS**

**Table 4.2**  Ratio of consumer credit card debt to income

| 1981 (Visa, MasterCard, American Express, and Discover cards only) | | 1991 (Visa, MasterCard, American Express, and Discover cards only) | |
|---|---|---|---|
| Mean | .177 | Mean | .531 |
| s.d. | .458 | s.d. | .775 |
| 25th percentile | .047 | 25th percentile | .122 |
| median | .088 | median | .310 |
| 75th percentile | .179 | 75th percentile | .645 |
| valid cases | 482 | valid cases | 351 |
| **1997** (all credit card debt) | | t-values | |
| Mean | .767 | 1981 v. 1991 | 8.25*** |
| s.d. | 1.154 | 1981 v. 1997 | 7.98*** |
| 25th percentile | .167 | 1991 v. 1997 | 2.19* |
| median | .469 | | |
| 75th percentile | .874 | *p < .05; **p < .01; ***p < .001 | |
| valid cases | 77 | | |

*Source:* Consumer Bankruptcy Project I, 1981; Consumer Bankruptcy Project II, 1991; Ohio Bankruptcy Study, 1997.

loans, and so on, have been deleted from this analysis to focus exclusively on the impact of credit card debt. The Visa study did not provide enough data to make a similar debtor-by-debtor analysis, but other aspects of their data suggest that an analysis based on their data would be comparable.[66]

Here, too, the data show a rising credit card debt load over time. These data also demonstrate that by 1991 the average debtor in bankruptcy who owed some credit card debt would have had to commit nearly half a year's take-home pay to satisfy the principal on those credit card bills.[67] For the debtors in the middle of the 1997 Ohio sample, outstanding credit card debt represented $46.90 of every $100 of take-home pay.[68] At the mean, the bankrupt debtors had committed an astonishing $77 of every $100 of income to credit card debt.

Of all the indicia of rapidly increasing credit card debt, none is more astonishing or more significant than the increased credit card debt as a fraction of the income available to pay it. Bankrupt debtors with some credit card debt listed, at the mean, about six weeks' income in bank credit card debts in our 1981 study. Ten years later, they

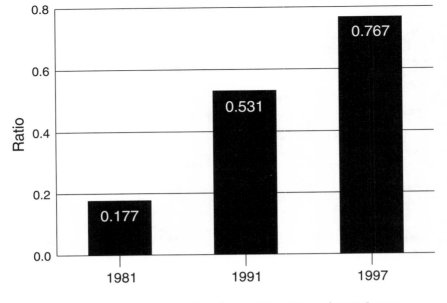

Fig. 4.2 Ratio of mean credit card debt to income, 1981, 1991, and 1997. *Source:* Consumer Bankruptcy Project I, 1981; Consumer Bankruptcy Project II, 1991; Ohio Bankruptcy Study, 1997.

listed six months' worth of income in those same credit card debts. Six years after that, they listed a total credit card debt that exceeded nine months of income.

A glance at housing data brings the magnitude of this debt burden into perspective. Home owners in the United States spend, on average, about $18 of every $100 of take-home pay for principal, interest, taxes, and insurance for their mortgage payments.[69] According to one Census Bureau study, a family spending more than $25–28 of each $100 of take-home pay on house payments is deemed "house poor."[70] Such precarious housing arrangements represent less than 10 percent of all homeowners. By committing $47 of each $100 of income to their credit cards, the median debtors in bankruptcy owe nearly triple a year's worth of average house payments on their credit card bills alone.[71] At the mean, of course, with debtors committing $87 of each $100 of income to credit cards, the numbers are worse.

Could these debtors buckle down and repay? Maybe, but the harsh facts of compounded interest work against them. If the debtors had

**CREDIT CARDS**

the average prevailing interest rate on those cards (18.72 percent), interest alone would have consumed more than one month's income each year. If the debtors with median credit card debt had given every twelfth paycheck to their credit card companies, they still would not quite cover their outstanding interest. Most families could not survive if every twelfth paycheck were taken away—leaving nothing that month for food, rent, car payments, gasoline, insurance, doctor bills, or anything else. Without bankruptcy, these families would simply owe more and more every month, with debt steadily mounting and no hope of recovering financial stability.

Among these debtors carrying credit card debts that absorb a huge fraction of their incomes are Lynn and Yvonne Pluncket, an African-American couple from West Los Angeles. He is thirty-two and a high school graduate, and she is twenty-nine and has been to college but did not graduate. Lynn is a security officer at a hospital in nearby Culver City, and Yvonne works as an operator for the telephone company in Gardena. She has had her job for two and a half years, and he has had his for two years. Both had jobs at the time they filed, but both had experienced periods of unemployment within the two years before filing. Lynn's monthly take-home pay is $1,090 and Yvonne's is $1,309, giving them an annual combined after-tax income of $28,788—well above the bankruptcy median annual income of $18,000. They pay $400 rent each month, and their other expenses run about $1,100 monthly. When they filed, they had $157 in their checking account, $15 in a savings account, and $150 in a money market account. Their previous year's tax refund for $488 had not yet arrived.

The Pluckets owed $9,195 on a five-year-old Toyota and $4,750 on a four-year-old Mazda. They also owed Levitz Furniture $1,720 for a sofa and dining room furniture. They owed Sears $1,300 for a dryer, a video camera, and a typewriter. These items were not on their Sears charge card. Instead, the Pluckets used separate payment contracts that permitted Sears to repossess the items if they failed to pay. The Pluckets owed the Internal Revenue Service $1,350 and the state of California $800. The remainder of their listed debt is $30,321—all on credit cards. They have nine all-purpose cards, three retail merchant's cards, and two gasoline cards. Their brief explanation of why they got into so much trouble: "Failure to budget. Strike, unemployment." When Lynn and Yvonne filed for bankruptcy, they were back up to full salary, but they were facing credit card debts that exceeded a year's pay for the two of them. Yearly interest payments alone on their credit card debt would have been $5,588—if they could have paid it off immediately and not faced any penalties or compound interest charges.[72] They would have needed to devote every penny of their take-home pay for two months a year just to make the interest payments on their credit cards.

Credit card debt has risen across the nation, and the number of debtors and the amount of their debt have risen in step. No matter how the data are sliced, one fact is unmistakable: credit card debts are a bigger burden for Americans now than they were in the early 1980s when industry analysts said Americans already had too much consumer debt.

*Risk: Growth and Constancy*

128    In the midst of extraordinary growth in credit card debt, there is one surprising constant: the total debt burden and ratio of total debt to income among bankrupt debtors remains remarkably steady. From 1981 through 1991 through 1997, available data show about the same "tipping point," that is, the point where debts are so large that people file for bankruptcy. Overall, the bankruptcy data show no change—no growth and no reduction—in total debt loads during the years 1981–97. When debt is reported in constant dollars, there is no significant difference in the amount of debt reported in 1981 and 1997 among the bankrupt debtors.[73]

Nor have the proportional debt loads increased. When debt is reported as a fraction of income, the sixteen-year comparisons remain the same. In 1981 debtors carried short-term debt that was, at the mean, equal to just over twice their annual income and, at the median, just under a year's annual income.[74] In 1991 and 1997 the numbers were not statistically significantly different.[75]

This is not some unusual statistical paradox. The evidence suggests that people tend to declare bankruptcy when the ratio of short-term debt to income approaches 1.5. The 1981, 1991, and 1997 bankruptcy data, when combined, show a remarkably constant drowning point for consumer debtors.[76]

Where the impact of greater credit card debt shows up is in the increase in bankruptcy filings. The problem is not that debtors are in worse trouble when they file; it is that more debtors are in similar trouble. Bankruptcy filings are climbing in pace with the increase in consumer debt generally and with credit card debt in particular. In 1981 the Administrative Office of the United States Courts reported 312,914 nonbusiness bankruptcy filings.[77] Ten years later that same office reported 811,206 nonbusiness filings.[78] By 1999 nonbusiness filings had climbed to 1,378,071.[79] Filings over this eighteen-year period increased more than fourfold while the ratio of debts to income for the debtors themselves remained constant. More people are accumulating enough debt or losing enough income to reach the "tipping point" of bankruptcy.

Debtors have taken on higher and higher consumer debt relative to their incomes, and they have fallen in greater numbers into bankruptcy. As the fastest growing proportion of consumer debt, credit card debt has led the way to bankruptcy for an increasing number of Americans.[80] The chief of the Financial and General Macroeconomic Analysis Unit of the Congressional Budget Office, Kim Kowalewski, has examined the long-term trends in bankruptcy and consumer debt ratios. From the early 1960s through the late 1990s, the consumer bankruptcy filing rates are not explained by recessions, inflation, or unemployment. Instead, consumer debt explains bankruptcy.[81] Bankruptcy filing rates and consumer debt to income ratios rise and fall together over time.[82] In 1997 testimony to a subcommittee of the U.S. Senate, the Congressional Budget Office produced the chart reproduced below (fig. 4.3). Economist Lawrence Ausubel, business historians David Moss and Gibbs Johnson, and Federal Deposit Insurance Corporation analyst Diane Ellis all attribute the sharp rise in consumer debt—and the corresponding rise in consumer bankruptcy—to lowered credit standards, with credit card issuers aggressively pursuing families already carrying extraordinary debt burdens on incomes too low to make more than minimum repayments.[83] The extraordinary profitability of consumer debt repaid over time has attracted lenders to the increasingly high-risk–high-profit business of consumer lending in a saturated market, making the link between the rise in credit card debt and the rise in consumer bankruptcy unmistakable.[84]

129

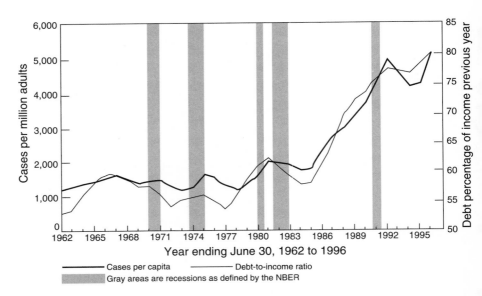

Fig. 4.3 Consumer bankruptcy cases and debt-income ratio, 1962–96. *Source:* See fig. 1.1.

The effects of credit card debt are felt in another way that is not obvious in these data. Of course, the increase in consumer debt is not the same as the increase in credit card debt. Two things have happened at the same time: consumer debt has risen dramatically and a dramatically greater proportion of consumer debt is now by way of credit cards. These facts reflect two important shifts that reinforce each other: credit cards make it far easier to incur consumer debt by encouraging a-little-at-a-time borrowing and too-little-at-a-time repayment, and credit card issuers have made consumer debt vastly more available than other forms of consumer credit in the past with aggressive solicitation and preapproved credit. The consequence? The increase in credit card use is a major cause of the increase in consumer debt.

The bankruptcy data reflect this shift. Although the proportion of unsecured debt for each family remains about the same as the debtors file for bankruptcy, the proportion of debt that is credit card debt has grown (table 4.3). Debtors in bankruptcy list two kinds of debt: secured debt and unsecured debt. A home mortgage or a car loan or a furniture loan typically is secured debt, while nearly all other

**CREDIT CARDS**

**Table 4.3**  Credit card debt as a fraction of unsecured debt, 1981, 1991, 1997

| 1981 (Visa, MasterCard, American Express, and Discover cards only) | | 1991 (Visa, MasterCard, American Express, and Discover cards only) | |
|---|---|---|---|
| Mean | .210 | Mean | .426 |
| s.d. | .183 | s.d. | .290 |
| 25th percentile | .067 | 25th percentile | .175 |
| median | .159 | median | .379 |
| 75th percentile | .303 | 75th percentile | .649 |
| valid cases | 588 | valid cases | 398 |
| **1997** (all credit card debt) | | t-values | |
| Mean | .497 | 1981 v. 1991 | 14.33*** |
| s.d. | .322 | 1981 v. 1997 | 11.93*** |
| 25th percentile | .188 | 1991 v. 1997 | 1.99* |
| median | .503 | | |
| 75th percentile | .791 | *p < .05; **p < .01; ***p < .001 | |
| valid cases | 83 | | |

*Source:* Consumer Bankruptcy Project I, 1981; Consumer Bankruptcy Project II, 1991; Ohio Bankruptcy Study, 1997.

debt is unsecured. Among the kinds of debt listed as "unsecured" on a debtor's schedules are educational loans, alimony, child support, most taxes, many finance company loans, cash advances from banks, lawsuits from car accidents, medical bills, dental bills, veterinary bills, most home repairs (but not a major renovation that resulted in a second mortgage), claims from the government for overpayment of benefits, and, of course, credit cards. Although only about $16 of every $100 of unsecured debt was bank card debt in 1981, ten years later that same debt accounted for $38 of every $100 of unsecured debt. The 1997 data suggest that about $50 of each $100 of unsecured debt is credit card debt.[85] When these data are combined with the Congressional Budget Office's findings on the rising debt loads per household, they suggest not simply that families are substituting credit card debt for other kinds of debt but that they are using credit cards to acquire more debt than ever before—debt that leads an increasing number of people to the bankruptcy courthouse.

The purveyors of credit card debt predict its continuing rise.

Double-digit increases in credit card debts in the mid-1990s portend continued growth even as growing numbers of debtors choke on unmanageable debt loads.[86] It would seem likely that more middle-class Americans—perhaps joined by some new recruits from among the poorest citizens—will find themselves in financial trouble.

### The Debtors' Testimony

Credit card problems are clearly implicated in many of the debtors' stories. Some debtors came directly to the point: they said they could not manage their credit cards. When we asked them why they filed for bankruptcy, about 5.4 percent of the sample specifically identified credit card debt as a reason for filing bankruptcy. The overwhelming majority of these people identify their own follies in dealing with credit cards.

Caroline Shick explains how she used her cards and how, over time, she lost control of them. Caroline lives in Fortuna, a small town on the northern California coast. She is forty-two years old, has been divorced for a few years, and has children to raise. She has a high school diploma and a steady job. She explains how she ended up in bankruptcy: "Single parent—no child support used credit cards to help support, etc.—everything just gets away from you before you realize your far far in debt." Caroline filed a Chapter 7, discharging all her credit card debts.

Many debtors offered no details. They cut to the heart of their problems. Why did you file for bankruptcy? "Credit cards." "Over use of credit cards." "Bank credit cards." That only about 5.4 percent of the debtors explain their financial troubles as credit card problems seems somewhat surprising; given the size of their credit card debts, we expected a much larger fraction of debtors to identify credit cards as the reason for filing. But the questionnaire permitted debtors to frame their responses however they wanted.[87] Although not all debtors specifically mentioned credit cards, many discussed their huge debt levels in general terms.[88] They explained that their debts had overwhelmed them. They filed because there was "not enough income to pay my debts now," or "I can't afford to pay my bills or rent all at the same time." [89] Nearly half of the debtors—48.6 percent—explained that they were filing for bankruptcy because their debts had grown so large they had no hope of paying them off. In fact, Betina Darvilian, who owed $42,620 in credit card debts, described her problems only as "accumulation of too much debt." The details of her file make it a fair inference that she was referring to credit card debt. But because she discussed debt only generally, she escaped the strict coding guidelines and did not join the 5.4 percent of debtors who mentioned a specific credit card problem.

It is possible to explore the bankruptcy files directly and to make an independent judgment of what seems to be the debtor's problem. When Judge Sellers did that with her bankruptcy cases in the Southern District of Ohio, she concluded that credit card debts were the reason for filing in about 24 percent of the cases. By her categorization, this was the most frequent reason for all bankruptcy filings. Another observer might characterize each debtor's problems somewhat differently, but a single, consistent observer adds unique perspective. Judge Sellers's data suggest that credit card debt plays a direct, observable role in the financial collapse of a large fraction of debtors.

133

## My Fault, Your Fault

The debtors who identified their problems with credit cards were a self-critical group. Some debtors explained that they were young and foolish, and others identified with care when they began to use credit cards—in college, early in a marriage, when a new baby arrived. Most described their failings as personal. One debtor labeled himself "very stupid," and others used the epithets "stupid," "foolish" and "careless." Several referred to their "poor judgment" and "mismanagement." Some debtors talked about not fully appreciating the implications of high interest rates, and others spoke of "not knowing about credit" or "not know money." A number described their "poor money management" or how they "mishandled finances." One divorced woman explains: "I was given credit for the first time in my life & I didn't know how to handle the credit. I wanted to give my son a better life."

These debtors knew that credit card debt was avoidable. They trapped themselves in a snare that they understood fully only after irretrievable financial collapse. Other debtors saw their credit card debts as the sources of their problems, but they were unwilling to shoulder the emotional burden of their staggering debt loads by themselves. They attributed plenty of blame to the card issuers as well.

Jason White was only twenty-five when he filed for bankruptcy. He had completed some college and had never been married. He had been out of work for a couple of months the year before he filed, but by the time of the filing, he was employed full-time. Jason lives in Santa Ana, California, where he filed his bankruptcy petition. Jason split the blame for his financial collapse between greedy credit card issuers and his own bad luck: "Over zealous recruitment by credit card companies to provide me with their cards and services coupled with a two month unemployed period in late 1990."

"Credit cards are to easy to obtain and use," observed one bankrupt debtor. Others lamented the widespread availability of "preapproved credit cards." Another debtor blamed his own mishandling of finances, but he noted that no matter how much trouble he was in, he "kept getting new credit cards and using them." These debtors raise the issue of accessibility. By itself accessibility does not cause crushing debt burdens. No credit card issuer forced a credit card on a consumer. But accessibility may be a factor in growing debt burdens—and growing financial failures.

## The Expanding House of Cards

How easy are credit cards to obtain? Aside from the anecdotes that regularly dot the filler sections of the local newspapers about a cat or a dog that received a preapproved credit card, anyone who picks up the daily mail knows that credit cards are readily available.[90] In 1980 credit card industry experts estimated that the retail credit card market was 84.7 percent saturated, while the bank card market was not far behind at 80.5 percent.[91] Four out of five of the people with reasonable incomes and reasonable credit histories already had as many credit cards as they wanted or needed, said the experts. During the following decade, however, the number of cards in circulation nearly doubled from 116 million to 226 million.[92] Nor does the growth show any sign of abating; there are now well over a billion cards in circulation. The amount of credit card debt outstanding at the end of 1997 was $422 billion, twice as much as the amount in 1993.[93]

The credit card industry did not grow by being cautious about distributing credit cards. It grew because it solicited a broad range of debtors, and when they didn't take cards the first time or the second time they were offered, the companies sent mailings ten, eleven, and twelve times. So saturated is the market with credit cards that the typical credit card issuer spends about $100 in solicitation costs to acquire each new cardholder.[94] From 1994 through 1996 credit card issuers sent out more than two and a half billion card solicitations each year.[95] They followed up in 1997 with three billion solicitations.[96] More than forty-one invitations went out each year to *every* American household. Based on estimates by industry analysts George Salem and Aaron Clark, those offers add up to about $243,000 of credit per household per year from mail solicitations alone.[97] At this rate, in the years 1995–98 alone, the credit card companies would have offered about a million dollars of credit to every household in the United States.

Why have credit card issuers expanded so rapidly? The reason, says the Federal Deposit Insurance Corporation, is the deregulation of consumer interest rates that has made credit card lending more than twice as profitable as all other bank lending.[98] Independent economists attribute the explosion in credit card marketing and in credit card debt outstanding to a credit industry intent on capturing the high profits of credit card lending even if it means significantly lowering credit standards.[99]

Interest drives profitability. The plain fact is that interest payments account for more than 80 percent of the profits of credit card issuers, with the remaining 20 percent coming from annual fees, late fees, over-limit fees, and merchant fees.[100] The enormous profits available from people who charge up to the limits and pay only the minimum each month have made delinquent card holders who pay high interest the most valued customers in the business. "Subprime lending," granting credit specifically to people who are living on the edge, is a large new niche in the credit business, and one much ap-

135

plauded on Wall Street.[101] Like junk bonds, subprime debt pays such high returns that big profits still remain even after the defaults and bankruptcies are subtracted.

During the same period in which credit card growth has been so spectacular, other areas of traditional banking and finance have declined in profitability.[102] The dramatic changes in the financial marketplace have greatly reduced the role of traditional lenders in the corporate-loan market, for example, with more and more corporations borrowing directly in public markets. As corporate lending has been squeezed, consumer lending has opened up profit opportunities that bankers twenty years ago never dreamed could be possible.

The marketing and ready availability of ready credit card debt, especially for marginal borrowers, undoubtedly contributes to the growth in use—and increase in defaults. Few forms of debt can be so easily acquired as credit card debt. There are no serious talks with a bank president or careful reviews of outstanding debts and assets before undertaking a credit card obligation. If the weak and the foolish are not tempted by easy credit, they will not amass enough to drown in it. This is not to say that credit should not be available but to recognize that availability has a cost for those who are slow to understand the risks of carrying monthly payments and the powerful effects of minimum monthly payments and 18 percent interest rates compounded daily.

The credit card companies hope to expand credit card debt even further.[103] Although our data show who is most likely today to incur credit card debt—middle-aged, middle-income folks—the credit card companies have undertaken a plan to change all that. Their most aggressive targeting is aimed at the only group left that is not already inundated with plastic: the poor. In a marketing push that they euphemistically refer to as the "democratization of credit," credit card lenders have pressed their credit cards on people they shunned only a few years ago. Such "democratization" means that more poor people will be able to spend their way into middle-class consumption at 18 percent interest.

The results of the industry's extraordinary marketing efforts have paid off. Credit card usage has grown fastest in recent years among debtors with the lowest incomes.[104] Since the early 1990s, Americans with incomes below the poverty level nearly doubled their credit card usage, and those in the $10,000–25,000 income bracket come in a close second in the rise in debt.[105] The result is not surprising: 27 percent of the under-$10,000 families have consumer debt that is more than 40 percent of their income, and nearly one in ten has at least one debt that is more than sixty days past due.[106]

More recently, credit card companies have launched aggressive solicitation campaigns aimed at young people, especially the college students likely to occupy a future position in the middle class. Inserts in college bookstore shopping bags routinely offer a credit card with no need for a parent's signature, no need for a credit history, and no need for an annual income. Industry analysts note that direct solicitations of both college and high school students have intensified,[107] so that an estimated 69 percent of all college students now have at least one card[108] — and 20 percent have four or more.[109] Adding to the credit card solicitations on campus touting free T-shirts and key chains with university logos, a college freshman can now expect as many as fifteen preapproved credit card applications in the mail, suggesting that debt levels among 18-to-22-year-olds may be on the rise.[110]

The practices show that credit card companies increasingly fail to ask for vital information, such as employment and income, even at the start of the credit relationship.[111] Preapproved credit card solicitations flood debtors, with more than three billion mailings in 1997 alone.[112] Such cards are issued based on other information, such as zip codes or appearance on a catalog database or mailing list. Because few credit issuers inquire closely about credit-worthiness, an unemployed person or someone already drowning in debt can maintain a substantial lifestyle for a while just by opening the mail.

Consumers can now use credit cards to see them through a time of crisis for which public assistance is unavailable or inadequate. If they survive, as most do, they will pay high interest rates, but they will eventually get back on their feet. If they do not, they can nonetheless consume the goods and services they need and shuck the credit balances when the debt scheme eventually collapses. If they have managed to find a job by the time of collapse, as most of the debtors who file for bankruptcy have done, they can resume their lives living off their incomes without worrying about their old unsecured debts. What might have been provided by a more munificent system of unemployment insurance or more generous medical insurance is now provided by MasterCard and Visa.

This result may be the ultimate market-based social welfare program. Of course, for debtors who must deal with unpaid creditors, file for bankruptcy, lose all their property in excess of stated exemption levels, open their financial and personal lives to examination by a court-appointed trustee, and list the fact of their bankruptcies on every credit form and job application they fill out for ten years, it may not seem quite so attractive as standing in line in the unemployment office or applying for a medical aid supplement. And yet, credit cards allow relatively better-off consumers to maintain more generous consumption than any publicly sponsored social program is likely to permit. Those who lived with higher incomes before their times of trouble are likely to have greater access to credit even as their incomes cease. And for those who make it, 18 percent interest may seem modest to maintain a family and minimize the disruptions that accompany an income interruption or a serious medical problem.

Their creditors might shudder at the notion of supplying welfare to their unemployed and overwhelmed customers. Nonetheless, they rake in profits from the paying customers that more than offset the losses from the nonpayers, keeping their credit card businesses the most profitable form of lending in America. Moral ambiguity and financial ambiguity intertwine throughout these stories.

Credit cards are everywhere in America. The little plastic cards are carried by people in big cities and tiny villages, people who live on small farms and people in sprawling metropolitan areas. They are used to buy cheese steaks and to pay college tuition, to get cash and to make charitable donations. The cards and the people who carry them and the merchants who accept them are part of virtually every consumer transaction. Credit cards are tightly woven into the economic fabric of American life.

For many, credit cards are merely a convenience. For some, they are a source of worry, a problem that surfaces and recedes. For a few, they pave the road to economic destruction. Some decent, hardworking people with sober habits and modest incomes, seemed changed by a handful of plastic. They slide into $30,000, $40,000, and $50,000 of credit card debt. Interest on their credit card debts alone can eat up two or three months' income. Once these card holders find themselves in this position, their only way back to financial stability is to file for bankruptcy. The bankruptcy files tell of those who slid too far to recover without help.

For others, credit cards are part of a larger, more complex economic picture that involves risk. These people suffer more by crashing than by sliding. The bills they ran up on their cards kept them a little nearer to the edge of disaster, but they avoided falling over. For years, they managed to pay everything, even if they failed to build a safety net. If everything worked perfectly, they could — and did — pay. But for some of these people, not everything worked perfectly. They got sick, their overtime hours were cut back, a spouse was laid off, they took in their sister's children, they were transferred to a distant town, or something else happened that strained the family budget. The "something else" may have been enough to cause a financial disaster by itself. Or the "something else" may have been the sort of thing that many people weather but those already staggering under a load of debt could not. For these people, credit card debt was a way of gambling that it would all hold together. The bankruptcy files tell of those who lost the gamble.

Banks and retailers dropped plastic into the hands of millions of Americans who had never considered paying with anything other than cash or checks. In just two decades, they doubled and doubled and doubled again the number of cards carried by millions of shoppers who had just one or two charge accounts at their favorite stores. At the same time, the bank card issuers aggressively marketed their credit card systems to merchants, sweeping hundreds of thousands of small stores, national chains, and specialty outlets into a worldwide credit card system.

It is interesting to read the debtors' comments and to note how willingly they accept blame for what has happened. A few want to point the finger of responsibility elsewhere, but more seem full of self-loathing and humiliation in recognition of what their spending habits have brought them to. Perhaps this is only the contrition that often accompanies punishment, quickly to be forgotten when the next round of credit cards arrive in the mail. Or perhaps this is the deeper humiliation of having gotten caught, of living in a world in which so many others seem to play a juggling game from one paycheck to the next and failing where others succeeded.

If the data from the 1997 Ohio sample are good estimates for all the debtors nationally who filed for bankruptcy in 1998, the latest year for complete data, more than half a million people filed for bankruptcy owing credit card debts that exceeded half a year's income.[113] Unless these families could figure out how to take every sixth paycheck to make nothing but interest payments on their credit cards, they were falling further and further behind every day until they filed for bankruptcy. It is not hard to see why some people decide that they will never get themselves straightened out financially without declaring bankruptcy.

Like the jobs data, the credit card data show the vulnerability of the middle class after a decade of unmatched prosperity. For some Americans, credit card debt is just one more landmine—an opportunity to court financial disaster. Some people cannot manage credit, and its ready availability puts them at risk for a heady ride of consumer consumption followed by mounting bills and financial juggling that eventually comes tumbling down. The availability of consumer debt has forged a crack in middle-class economic stability.

The crack, relatively narrow in the early 1980s, has been widening at an alarming pace. Credit card debt burdens have grown at the same time that jobs have become less secure. Any family facing the unemployment of a principal wage earner is at risk for serious financial trouble, but the family whose income has sharply declined has a much better chance of survival if it begins the period of unemployment with no consumer debt. For the family stretched to the limit to make it from payday to payday, even a short period of unemployment means catastrophe. The same point can be repeated with families jarred by medical problems and divorce: every economic problem is worse when a family is loaded with high-interest consumer debt. The riskiness of every bad thing that can happen increases with every dollar of credit card debt a family carries from month to month. The data reported in this chapter show middle-class Americans taking on more credit card debt—and more risk—than ever before. And they show the consequences: more than a million families are headed to the bankruptcy courthouse each year.

CREDIT CARDS

Chapter 5

# Sickness and Injury

> Wife died of cancer. Left $65,000 in medical bills after insurance.
> —STANLEY ELICKSEN, Webster, Texas

> Was working as asst. mine foreman when I had an accident on the job
> and all my bills were based on my income before the accident. I am not
> able to return to work by the Doctor's report.
> —JEROME JENKINS, Scotrun, Pennsylvania

Medical science has flowered beyond the wildest dreams of earlier generations, yet sickness and injury remain a major threat to the economic health of every middle-class family. The two components of that threat—either of which can plunge a family from comfortable circumstances to financial collapse in a matter of months—are the spiraling cost of medical care and the loss of income because of accident, illness, or disability.

The first element—cost—has preoccupied policymakers and the media. Medical costs have burgeoned, especially in the past decade, at the same time that job security, including medical insurance benefits, has declined. A diagnosis of a malignancy or a sudden crash at an intersection can leave a family economically devastated by the costs of medical care. In one year, over nine million families spent more than 20 percent of their annual incomes on medical care.[1] These blows were by no means limited to the poor. Among the mostly higher income households that itemized their deductions on their federal income tax returns for 1991, more than five million families claimed deductions for extraordinary medical expenses.[2]

The second threat to the economic lives of middle-class Americans—the loss of income that arises from illness and accidents—has received less public discussion in recent years, yet millions of Americans lose their jobs as a result of disability or lose substantial income during their recovery from an illness or accident. More than six hundred million workdays are lost annually for those reasons.[3] Our data suggest that the loss of income and employment is even more devastating financially than the direct cost of medical care.

In combination, medical costs and lost income are frequently lethal to the financial survival of previously secure members of the American middle class.[4] If the debtors in our sample are representative of the entire country, medical problems were an important part of more than a quarter of a million bankruptcies in 1998. Approximately one household in five in our sample listed a medically related problem as a reason for their bankruptcy filing, making it the third most common reason listed, after job loss and family problems. Although more recent data from a 1997 study in Ohio yield a similar result,[5] we have some evidence that these problems may have increased during the past decade. That increase may explain in part the dramatic rise in bankruptcies in recent years.

142

Among the families in bankruptcy who reported medical problems as reasons for their failures, about 60 percent (11.4 percent of the sample) cite the income effects of illness or injury. They identified injury or illness as causing lost time from work, reduction in hours worked, and demotion and job termination. The results are smaller incomes and financial collapse. Taking consumer bankruptcy as the pathology of middle-class finance, the lack of income support during illness or after injury, and the lack of rehabilitation and retraining after recovery, may be even more important causes of financial distress than specific medical costs.

The costs of medical treatment and the loss of income following illness or injury together threaten a double whammy for middle-class Americans. Jerold Lee Mumford, a 66-year-old widower from San Felipe, California, may have summed up the interrelated causes for bankruptcy as succinctly and completely as any of the debtors: "Bad planning, bad decisions, bad luck, bad health."

Our report on the impact of medical problems begins with an overview of debtors' responses, followed by a discussion of the two major medical causes of bankruptcy: medical costs and loss of jobs and income. We also look at the differing effects these problems might have on different types of people, including women, minorities, and the aged.

## Overview of Debtors' Responses

In gathering our data, we did not ask debtors specifically about medical factors in their bankruptcy. Our information comes from their responses to our open-ended question about why they became bankrupt. As we have noted in other chapters, the very fact that these responses were spontaneous reactions to an unstructured question reinforces their importance. If we had asked debtors if they had difficulties with medical bills or with lost income because of medical problems, a higher proportion of the sample would undoubtedly have been tagged with a medical problem. Instead, we limited our analysis to those who see themselves as overwhelmed by a medical problem while excluding those who added medical bills and lost time from work to a long litany of financial woes.

Every story has its own twists, but several files made clear the trap- 143
door nature of a serious medical problem. Frank Anderson filled out the bankruptcy forms for himself and his wife, Dolores. Frank is in his mid-fifties, but it was Dolores who, in her early forties, had the serious medical problem. Frank explained that they filed for bankruptcy because "my wife had a heart attack which led to a quadruple bypass and she is unable to return to work." Frank was also out of work for a while when Dolores was ill, although he was back at work as a cook in a restaurant by the time he filed for bankruptcy, with an annual take-home pay of $13,400. Their files demonstrate how seriously the medical debts set them back. They owed $2,886 on their seven-year-old Dodge Ares. The car was valued at $1,400, but they planned to repay the loan in full—which was twice the value of the car—so that they could keep their transportation. Their other debts totaled $23,093 to the county hospital, attorneys for the hospital, collection agencies for medical suppliers, emergency medical services, and clinics. The Andersons had borrowed another $5,000 from a finance company, but the files do not explain how the money was spent.

The Andersons do not list a single credit card or a debt for the purchase of clothes, furniture, or vacations. We can tell from their list of assets—$10 cash, $1,600 in household goods and clothing, $50 in jewelry, and $25 in fishing equipment—that they did not have much left by the time they filed for bankruptcy. Although bankruptcy stopped collection activities against the Andersons, their proposed budget did not suggest a bright future. Without Dolores's salary, they would be relegated to an apartment that rented for $300, $245 for utilities, $200 for food, $30 for clothing, and $90 for transportation. Perhaps the most optimistic estimate in their budget is the low figure they put on all future medical costs—$25 monthly for check-ups, tests, medicine, and anything else that Dolores or Frank might need. There is no indication that they will have any medical insurance, so their financial plan may simply have been to stay healthy.

Overall, almost 20 percent of the debtors in our bankruptcy sample cited medical reasons for their bankruptcies. Their explanations of medical problems could be divided into five categories. Two explanations related specifically to medical costs: medical debts and medical insurance problems. Two focused on the job and income effects of illness, injury, or disability, classified further as the lost income of the first-listed petitioner, or of the second petitioner in joint cases (a husband or wife), and the lost income of the other members of the petitioners' families. The final, miscellaneous category encompassed general medical problems that the debtors did not specify (fig. 5.1).

Judge Barry Russell, who serves as a bankruptcy judge in Los Angeles, has kept track of the reasons for bankruptcy filings in his court. He has calculated that 25–30 percent of the debtors in his court from 1975 to 1985 were there because of medical problems, including both medical expenses and loss of work owing to medical causes. Whereas we found that medically related loss of work produced about two-thirds of the bankruptcies with medical causes, Judge Russell found medical expenses and medically related loss of work to be roughly equal causes in his court.

We allocated responses to the medical category very conservatively. In addition to the obviously medical responses of the debtors, some debtors cited the birth of a baby, while others listed the support of an extended family member or friend. We did not classify these responses as "medical," although some might see a pregnancy and the consequent job loss as a medical problem, and the "support" responses undoubtedly included the care of some individuals who were infirm or otherwise in need of care for medical reasons.

**SICKNESS AND INJURY**

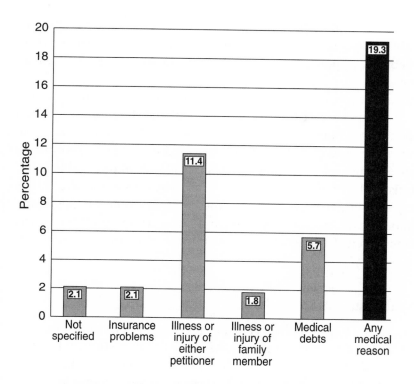

Fig. 5.1 Medical reasons mentioned by bankrupt debtors, 1991. *Note:* Multiple responses were permitted. *Source:* Consumer Bankruptcy Project II, 1991.

A number of the responses that we listed under "birth of a baby" and "care of a family member" may have been connected with financial distress through medical cost or the effects of caring for others who were sick or incapacitated. For example, cost was implicated when the baby or the family member needed expensive treatment, while in another case the need for nursing care for a family member would be cited to explain why a petitioner could not work. The most poignant example was a California couple who explained, "We had to file because of a medical problem with our child and her cancer problems—and the cost to us—and she died on 7–15–91." We included that case as clearly medical because the debtors identified a medical problem, but many other similar listings were not sufficiently clear regarding medical causes to be listed in the medical category. Nearly 10 percent of the debtors listed general family support and care rea-

**SICKNESS AND INJURY**

sons as their explanation for financial collapse, but finer gradations and direct links to medical problems could not be constructed from the debtors' responses, so they were not included under "medical reasons."[6]

If we had counted as medical cases those debtors listing the subsets "pregnancy" or "care of a family member," the total proportion would rise to about 25 percent of all debtors. Under this more inclusive definition of "medical problems," the estimated number of families filing for bankruptcy in 1998 for reasons of unpayable medical bills and lost time from work would have been about 250,000. By any estimate, the strict requirements we imposed on classifying a response as a medical problem understate the magnitude of the problem, even if the extent of that understatement is not entirely clear.

Medical Costs

Medical costs have been the central preoccupation of recent debates about health care in the United States.[7] The litany of stunning facts is now familiar. Medical costs from 1950 to 1990 increased almost tenfold, *after* adjusting for inflation.[8] Since the 1950s, American expenditures for health care have gone from about 5 percent of national income to over 13 percent.[9]

Although much of the health care bill is paid by "third-party" payers, such as insurance companies or Medicare–Medicaid, a large portion remains payable by each of us personally, even if we are insured. For some families, if their costs are low or their incomes are high, the amount left over after third-party payment can be handled in a single payment. But for many others, the high *cost* of medical care translates directly into the high *debt* to meet those costs.

Although little study has been devoted to medical *debt*, as opposed to medical cost, the available evidence suggests that medical debt is a serious problem for many Americans. Even in the late 1970s, a major survey of American consumers reported that medical debt was an important part of the debt picture. They reported that the number-one reason for taking out personal loans other than for durable goods was to pay medical costs.[10] Those consumers reported that the loans they took for medical reasons constituted more than a quarter of the loans taken for any specified purpose. Medical debts generally were by far the most important single type of debt reported.[11]

The limited information available for more recent periods suggests that medical debts continue to be a major financial factor for many Americans.[12] The Federal Reserve Bank reports that in 1989, for example, 3.5 percent of second mortgage loans—relatively long-term loans secured by the debtors' homes—were taken out to pay medical bills.[13] The data are spotty, but they point toward medical debt as a key factor in the financial collapse of many families.

*The Role of Insurance*

The importance of medical debts in the lives of so many Americans should come as no surprise when so many people face rising medical costs without the buffer of health insurance. In the great health care debates of recent years, one item of contention has been the number of uninsured Americans. One major variable that produces different figures from different sources is based on the shifting definitions used in the studies. Who are the "uninsured"? Are they people who have no coverage at any point in a year? People who have no coverage for at least eleven months of the year? People who have no coverage for at least one month of the year? Different definitions yield different estimates of the number of uninsured Americans.

In 1987 the Public Health Service compiled the most specific and detailed study conducted in many years. In its report, the National Medical Expenditure Study, the service concluded that more than twenty-four million people had no health insurance at any time during the year. More than twenty-three million were covered for only part of the year, yielding a total of forty-eight million people without insurance for at least part of the year.[14] By this reckoning, 10.2 percent of Americans had no health insurance during 1987, and another 9.7 percent were without health insurance for at least part of the year.[15]

Based on the annual Survey of Income and Program Participation, the Census Bureau reports even more Americans with gaps in their insurance coverage during 1991. The bureau reports the part-year uninsured total for 1991 as fifty-one million, higher than the Public Health Service figure for 1987, but it identifies a substantially lower

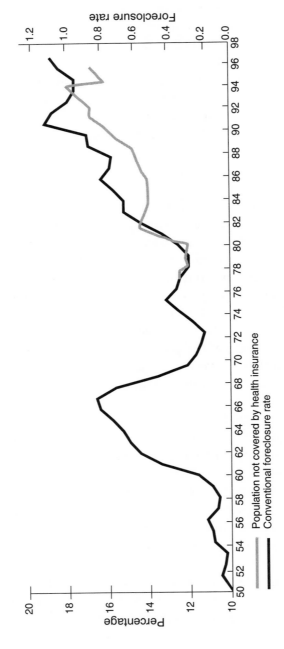

Fig. 5.2 Percentage of population not covered by health insurance, 1950–98. *Source:* Peter J. Elmer and Steven A. Seelig, "The Rising Long-Term Trend of Single-Family Mortgage Foreclosure Rates," FDIC Working Paper 98-2 (1996), 6.

figure for people uninsured all year.[16] The Census Bureau says that about seventeen million people had no insurance throughout 1991. The multiple reports from a single agency in a single year also act as a caution against inferring trends over time; the differences among the reports may reflect alternative definitions and survey techniques rather than changes over time in insurance coverage.[17] In spite of some confusion, however, it appears that by 1996 at least forty million people were uninsured at some point during the year.[18] For our purposes, it is enough to note the general agreement that somewhere between thirty and fifty million Americans are without health insurance during any given year.[19] This figure represents between 11 percent and 19 percent of the U.S. population of 263 million.

Another perspective on insurance coverage emerges from an examination of the data over a somewhat longer period. One of the Census Bureau studies includes data that cover about two-and-a-half years from 1991 through mid-1993. During that time, 4 percent of Americans had no health insurance for the entire period. In addition to this core of long-term uninsured, an additional 26 percent of Americans had no insurance coverage for at least one month.[20] This meant that about seventy-nine million people faced some time when they had no insurance as a backstop against medical bills, including about ten million who had no insurance protection at any time during a period of nearly three years.

It also appears that the ranks of the uninsured are growing steadily.[21] In 1998, the Census Bureau published a study focusing on health insurance coverage for children. It concluded: "The number of American children without health coverage rose from 8.2 million to 10.6 million from 1987 to 1996, overall a period of relative prosperity. . . . The proportion of uncovered children rose as well, from 12.9 percent to 14.8 percent of the under-18 population. . . . By number, the largest group of children are not poor, as four-fifths are above the poverty level." [22] The recent decline in insurance for children probably reflects the decline in coverage for families generally.

Finally, figures from the National Center for Health Statistics give an idea of the long-term trend in health insurance coverage in the United States (fig 5.2).[23] This is a negative report of the portion of the population without health insurance beginning in 1950. The uninsured percentage peaked in the mid-1960s, then dropped to an all-

149

time low in the early 1970s, and has risen fairly steadily ever since, so that by 1996 more people were uninsured than in the 1960s.

Because most health insurance in the United States is provided by employers, we have to look first at the workplace to discover why its coverage is shrinking. We find that the explanation for declining insurance is not merely unemployment or even a shift to lower-benefit jobs. The reduction in employer-provided insurance is found across all industries and job classifications.[24] Even among the insured, as many as 29 million Americans who have some health insurance may be seriously underinsured.[25] The primary explanation may be simple: carrying health insurance is an expensive benefit for employers.[26] In 1995 employers paid $1.06 per worker-hour for health insurance. This figure varied, of course, from 28 cents for part-time workers to $1.40 for full-time workers, and from $1.58 in manufacturing to 90 cents in service production. Union workers were the big winners, at $2.09.[27] These figures have risen greatly in the past two decades, and after a pause, they are on the rise again.[28]

150 The high numbers of uninsured Americans, combined with estimates of underinsurance, suggest that a large proportion of the population is at risk for financial failure. Many will survive their periods without insurance with little more than missing a few check-ups or paying for some prescriptions over time. But if a serious medical event occurs—an accident or an illness that involves a hospital stay or extended outpatient treatments—there is no financial backstop. The uninsured play a game of roulette, hoping to survive without insurance and facing financial catastrophe if they lose.

*Medical Costs and Bankruptcy*

Medical costs and medical debt have been a major financial problem for decades. A large number of Americans at any given moment are exposed to financial disaster from illness or injury because they lack health insurance. One might simply assume that medical debt would have been seen as a major cause of financial crisis and bankruptcy. On the whole, however, the relationship between medical debt and financial collapse has remained ambiguous and confused. The important Brookings Institution study from the 1960s lumped medical problems with family difficulties, finding that together they were an important factor in the reasons families file for bankruptcy.[29] Two small studies conducted by physicians found that medical debts were not important in personal bankruptcies: medical debts were reported in many bankruptcies, but they were not an important factor in most.[30] Several larger studies conducted in the 1970s and 1980s by Philip Shuchman reported similar findings,[31] as did the study that we conducted based on cases filed in the early 1980s.[32] On the other hand, Shuchman suggested that because medical debt is an unanticipated burden, it may trigger a financial crisis for some number of debtors in bankruptcy even though its proportion of their debts is not that great.[33]

Susan Kovac's study of bankrupt debtors in the Eastern District of Tennessee in the mid-1980s etched a somewhat different picture. In the Tennessee study, medical debt was the most important cause of bankruptcy.[34] Kovac also focused on medical debt listed in the bankruptcy schedules, but she found medical debt far more frequently and in far larger amounts and percentages than earlier studies had reported.[35] For example, earlier studies found medical debt at 6–10 percent of unsecured debt,[36] whereas the Tennessee study put it at 42 percent. Similarly, prior studies found medical debt to be about 10–15 percent of annual income on average, whereas Kovac's study estimated medical debts at 85 percent of income.[37]

Kovac offers several suggestions to explain the difference in the Tennessee results.[38] The most obvious explanation is that her sample is not a cross-section of all consumer bankruptcy filers even in Tennessee, much less for the United States. Instead, it is drawn from the very poorest debtors. Kovac studied only debtors considered "judgment-proof," by which she meant debtors whose wages were so low that they were protected by law from garnishment (seizure) of their wages.[39] It seems plausible that these debtors, the poorest slice of the bankruptcy population, might have a higher percentage of medical debt for two reasons: even modest amounts of medical debt would be unmanageable for people living in such straitened circumstances, and their proportion of medical debt would have been high relative to other debts precisely because they are unlikely to have been able to get much trade credit of the usual sort. We suggested in our 1980s study that the very poor do not use bankruptcy in large numbers because they are not apt to get enough credit to make debt the major problem in their lives,[40] although we recognize that their access to credit is now changing.[41] It is a reasonable hypothesis that many of the judgment-proof debtors in Kovac's study were people who would never have had the sort of debts that require bankruptcy help had they not taken ill or been injured. For many of these very poor debtors, it may be that, ironically, only health care providers would give them credit and therefore only ill health could create enough debts to drive them into bankruptcy.

More recently, Ian Domowitz has argued that uninsured medical debt is the largest single contributor at the margin to bankruptcy filings. Households with medical debt in excess of their income are twenty-eight times more likely to file for bankruptcy than are other households.[42] Of course, the fact that large medical debts are likely to lead to bankruptcy does not demonstrate that many families in bankruptcy are there because they have large medical debts. Although medical debt is an important factor pushing some families into bankruptcy, it remains unclear how many bankruptcies are linked to unpaid medical debts. By the time a family files for bankruptcy, much medical debt is no longer clearly identifiable.

### Identifying Medical Debt

We cannot make direct comparisons between our present study and those earlier studies, including our earlier works, because we cannot isolate specific medical debt in the current study. That is, even in the five districts from which we have obtained detailed financial information, we did not separately tabulate medical debt as we did home mortgages and credit card debt. In the 1990s medical debt simply became too hard to identify. For some debtors, such as the Andersons, whose story was described earlier in this chapter, medical debt is easily identified as the debtors tried to pay their health care providers over time. With a $20,000 debt to their hospital and a who's who among medical providers of doctors, emergency medical services, clinics, and medical supply companies, the source of their debt was not hard to pinpoint. But for many families, a serious medical problem will not result in bills that can be easily identified as medical in origin. Even the Andersons had a single nonmedical debt for $5,000 to a finance company. That $5,000 may have been used to pay doctors and hospitals, but nothing in the files explains where the money went. We would have to classify the debt as "general" even though every penny might have been used to pay doctors and hospitals, sharply understating actual medical debt.

Many providers now require payment at the time of service, so that many patients put their medical bills on an all-purpose credit card. As a result, a listing for credit card debt today may conceal ambulance costs, physicians' bills, pharmaceuticals, home health care costs, medical appliance and equipment fees, and hospital charges. Nor will a home equity line of credit or a finance company loan on a bankruptcy schedule show a connection to earlier, substantial medical debts. This problem was undoubtedly present to some extent in earlier studies, including our own, leading to an underestimation of the significance of medical debt in bankruptcy filings.

The discovery of medical debt as a cause of bankruptcy has likely proven elusive for other reasons. In addition to the problem of identification, where medical debt is camouflaged within another category, especially the ubiquitous credit cards category,[43] it is possible that medical debt, like the "last credit card,"[44] is often omitted from the debt schedules. Some families may be worried that a failure to pay their doctors or clinics may result in the loss of future services.[45] Others may be so grateful for help that they are determined to pay regardless of the dischargeability of their debts. Still others may want to save face, hoping that their health care providers will not learn of their bankruptcy filing. Medical providers may be acquainted with the debtors—unlike the faceless banks and finance companies who solicit their business—and this may cause families in bankruptcy to fail to list at least some of these providers even though these are the very debts pushing them into financial collapse.

Although some debtors may not list their health care providers in their bankruptcy schedules because of their personal relationships with their creditors, other debtors may find health care providers to be their most aggressive creditors. Medical debt could be a frequent trigger for bankruptcy even when it is not the largest debt. Aggressive collection activity by hospitals and doctors may drive debtors with medical problems into bankruptcy when their counterparts with credit card or other debt might survive outside bankruptcy. If hospitals and doctors are quicker to sue for their money and to seek

153

collection through wage garnishment and otherwise, then medical debts might provide a greater incentive for seeking bankruptcy protection than their relative size on the debtors' schedules would suggest.

Many collection specialists assert that doctors are particularly quick to turn bills over to lawyers or bill collectors. It would be understandable if they did, because doctors appear to lose much more from unpaid bills than do hospitals. It should be understood that these losses are over and above "indigent care," where a doctor or hospital understands from the start that free, charity care is being provided.[46] A great deal of charity care is being provided, but the debts and losses discussed in this section are "uncollected bills" for which payment was expected at the time the services were provided. One New England study showed doctors writing off more than $23,000 each, in addition to indigent care provided for free. This is a substantial sum for anyone, but the $23,000 write-off occurred in an area where average physician annual income before write-offs was about $70,000.[47] Many of us would get testy about people costing us a third of our yearly income.

Kovac's study in Tennessee produced some evidence that medical providers are aggressive collectors. She supplemented her interviews with debtors with evidence in the debtors' schedules that medical creditors "were by far the most aggressive in their collection efforts."[48] This conclusion was based on the greater proportion of lawsuits filed by health care providers. Another piece of evidence supports that conclusion. In our study of more than fifteen hundred cases from ten districts in 1981, we found that people with medical debts had significantly more lawsuits filed against them than did other bankrupt debtors who did not list such debts.[49] Although we did not have data identifying what type of creditor filed what lawsuit, our finding is consistent with the idea that medical providers, or some of them, may be more aggressive in collection efforts and may therefore trigger more bankruptcies.

Anecdotes do not prove the point, but they do put flesh on it. One Central Illinois couple, Jerry and Doreen Ellinger, squarely nailed the lawsuits filed by their medical creditors as the cause of their bankruptcy: "We have a son with allergies and asthma who has been in the doctor's office and the hospital several times. We were making monthly payments on the resulting bills, but the hospital and clinic decided that it was not enough even though it was what they had agreed to earlier. They turned the bills over to the Credit Bureau of [town omitted] which wanted us to pay $100 a month. We told them we couldn't afford to pay that much so they decided to file suit against us. They left us no choice but to file for bankruptcy." The Ellingers are high school graduates with steady jobs, but they had no insurance coverage at work to cushion the blow. Bankruptcy schedules for couples like the Ellingers would show some medical debt, but they would also show high credit card debt, high home equity lines of credit, and debts to finance companies. A lawsuit judgment might or might not reveal the debt's origin as a medical bill. In short, an analysis of outstanding debts listed in the bankruptcy schedules cannot give a full picture of the impact of high medical bills on middle-class families.

We have no listings of medical debts in the 1990s studies; we do, however, have data unique to any of the larger studies since the 1960s: our compilation of the debtors' explanations of the causes of their bankruptcies. By asking debtors directly why they had filed for bankruptcy, they could sort out their credit card and finance company bills and explain when medical debts were the source of their problems.

*What the Debtors Report*

Based on our earlier study, we did not expect to find that medical debt and medical costs were significant causes of bankruptcy, but the debtors' responses identified medical expenses as among the most important reasons for serious financial distress. Of our sample of debtors, 7 percent specifically reported medical debt or the loss of medical insurance as a major cause of their bankruptcy.[50] If that percentage could be extrapolated to the nation as a whole, more than fifty thousand bankruptcies a year would be attributable directly to the burden of unpaid medical bills.[51]

These findings, it seems to us, cut through a good deal of the ambiguity and confusion in earlier studies to demonstrate that medical care is a devastating problem for a number of Americans caught in the middle between affluence (and the ability to pay their medical bills) and poverty (and access to such government programs as Medicaid). Of course, the size of that gap varies. As Susan Kovac's study demonstrated, access to government assistance for medical care is sharply limited even among the poor in some states, making medical problems a risk for a larger pool of families.[52] And even moderately affluent families can be wiped out by major medical bills.

Betty Lee Halmer's story, though less typical in one sense, reflects many others in our files in the richness of the narrative a debtor could scrawl in a few minutes on a court bench before being called up to answer a trustee's questions. It also reveals one reason studies of bankruptcy can underestimate the impact of medical debt. Betty Lee is a Los Angeles woman with a college education and a job and a large credit card debt (more than $13,000). Her bankruptcy schedules show no medical debt. A study that looked at the classification of debts she lists would never peg her as a medical-problem debtor. But Betty Lee told us: "When I converted to another religion, I had to start tithing. I moved in with my folks and was still okay, but when a medical situation came up that required a payment outside of my medical coverage of about $300 a month for about 1½ years, that put me over the edge and I filed for bankruptcy." Aside from the interesting impact of religion on her financial life, it is noteworthy that the hole in her budget created by her medical problems ended up as big credit card charges.

Medical costs, and the lack of medical insurance, may be a more important cause of middle-class financial disaster than had previously been thought. A variety of factors may conspire to hide this reality from empirical researchers, but a more focused and intensive analysis, combining the study of files with questionnaires or interviews, may make it possible to quantify the effects more clearly. In particular, it may be possible to discover if it is true that medical creditors are both more willing to extend credit to bad-risk debtors and more aggressive in using collection agencies and legal action to collect those bills. At a minimum, our data suggest that medical debts represent a significant fault line for today's middle class.

Many of the complications and ambiguities of this area of life are captured in the story told by the Sanchez family, a California couple who listed their ethnicity as "Spanish." Both had some college and both have steady jobs. But they decided to file Chapter 7 bankruptcy in anticipation of huge debts arising from elective surgery: "We need to have $11,800 for the end of this year, for an operation called tubal ligation reversal, because when our second daughter born by a cesarean operation, I, Maria Sanchez, got my tubes cut. We need to have another baby because our second daughter died (crib dead) and since then we can not put together our lives." This file raises more questions than it answers. Could the Sanchezes not get loans or direct medical credit without stripping away their existing debts in bankruptcy? Will they be able to get medical credit so soon after discharging their obligations in Chapter 7? Were they badly advised by their bankruptcy lawyer? If they could have gotten the operation on credit, should they have waited until they had run up those medical charges and then filed for bankruptcy, because bankruptcy can discharge only debts already incurred, not those coming up in the future? If they waited to file and then discharged the surgeon's fee without paying, how would the surgeon have felt about that? In the final analysis, what does it mean that Maria is attempting to have another baby when she and her husband cannot afford the operation? In the midst of medical crises, moral dilemmas can pile up even faster than debt.

## Disability and Lost Income

Although the bankruptcy questionnaires show that medical costs are a major component of middle-class financial distress, medically related unemployment—temporary or long-term—creates an even more important financial risk. Almost 60 percent of the debtors who report medical problems as causes of their bankruptcies cite the direct effects of the medical problem in lost jobs or lost time on the job. Most often those effects have been monetarized in the form of lost income and thus have led to bankruptcy. Of the 19 percent of the responding debtors who mentioned medical reasons for bankruptcy, more than half also mentioned job reasons.[53] About one in every ten debtors explains the reasons for bankruptcy as a combination of medical problems and time lost from work (fig. 5.3). Again, if these numbers could be generalized to the 1997 bankruptcy filings, more than 130,000 families would have filed for bankruptcy because of a medical problem resulting in a job loss or interruption.

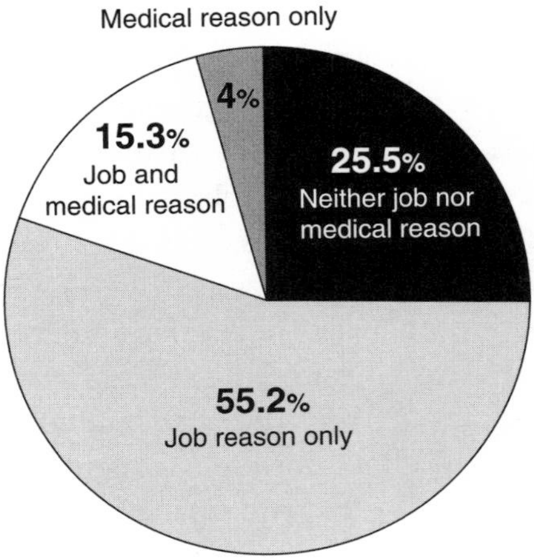

Fig. 5.3 The medical–job problem overlap in reasons for filing for bankruptcy, 1991. *Source:* Consumer Bankruptcy Project II, 1991.

Our inference that loss of income contributes to those bankruptcies arising from medical causes is supported by evidence from Canada and Australia. Both of these countries have comprehensive medical care systems that make it unlikely that medical costs or debts per se will cause many bankruptcies.[54] Thus, when recent studies report that medical problems cause about 7 percent of bankruptcies in each of those countries, the cause is very likely loss of work and income as the result of medical problems.[55]

We discussed the problem of job loss in general in an earlier chapter, but income interruption and job loss as a function of illness or injury are different. A recent intense focus on job loss arising from downsizing of the workforce, shifting manufacturing overseas, outsourcing work to independent contractors, and other such causes has obscured the enormous impact of sickness and injury in producing lost jobs and lost income.

In general, the collective response to income and job loss from illness and injury falls into three categories: worker's compensation for job-related injuries; sick pay and disability for income loss; and rehabilitation and retraining for job loss and loss of specific capacities. Although we do not attempt to discuss these three large subjects at length here, it is important to understand that these are the three social safety nets through which a large number of the debtors in our sample have fallen, only to be caught in the bankruptcy net, one of the lowest and stiffest.

People seem to end up in severe financial trouble after an enforced medical layoff for two reasons. First, many people are not rehabilitated because of shortfalls in rehab program support. Those people never return to the income stream they counted on when they incurred the debts. Second, U.S. compensation systems are specifically designed to avoid supporting people at their prior levels of income. Even most of those who are successfully rehabilitated will never regain the income they lost during the period of disability and rehabilitation, because the programs are explicitly and deliberately targeted at a level of income during the rehabilitation period that is lower than the one previously enjoyed. Therefore, they may never catch up. Debts incurred before the disability may be difficult or impossible to repay.

More than six hundred million workdays a year are estimated to be lost because of illness and injury.[56] In general, the three systems designed for income maintenance and return to work are deliberately tied together to ensure that workers can rarely receive their previous incomes until they return to work.[57] Because many of our debtors were hurt on the job, the worker's compensation system may have a good deal to do with whether they can avoid bankruptcy. The worker's compensation income limit is about 80 percent of preinjury income,[58] and compensation benefits are currently undergoing reduction in state after state around the country.[59] Most other disability programs are designed to limit income to not more than 60 percent of prior levels. As to nonwork-related disability, only about half of the private industry work force has long-term disability insurance.[60] The Social Security Disability Insurance benefit is limited to those with a complete disability. Payments average only $587 a month.[61]

These various payments may or may not be adequate to support the injured employee and the employee's family, but they are almost certainly too small in many cases to sustain payments on substantial credit obligations incurred at a time when the employee was enjoying full employment and full compensation. The family gets hit with a double whammy. Debts that were just manageable on a full salary fall into arrears as interest and penalties mount while the family tries to survive on a suddenly lower disability paycheck. If the family uses credit during the period of disability to make ends meet and to live at their pre-injury levels, the family goes further into debt. In a short time, the debt may be beyond control.

Of course, it is quite plausible to argue that disability and compensation insurance are designed to meet irreducible current expenses and that a government program should not be paying prior creditors or new debt picked up while the worker was disabled. But if full income supplementation is not provided, it should not be surprising that many debtors will be forced to seek bankruptcy protection. If a person's income is just enough to survive currently, then it may not be possible to pay prior debts, even though those debts may have seemed reasonable in amount before illness or injury led to lost income or even a loss of employment. In that case, the debtors may survive, but only at the cost of falling into bankruptcy and perhaps out of the middle class.

Following disabling sickness or injury, the American system for returning people to the workplace rests primarily on vocational rehabilitation. There is virtually universal agreement that such programs return far more money to society than they cost.[62] There is also nearly universal agreement that there are not nearly enough programs to meet the need.[63] Although the focus in the literature has been almost entirely on employer and government savings, returning an employee to something like previous earning levels could significantly increase repayments to creditors and reduce bankruptcy rates. There is no evidence than any policymaker has ever considered that aspect of vocational rehabilitation. There is thus no reason to suppose that a change in policy is likely and that rehabilitation programs will be refocused toward a goal of restoration of someone's prior rate of earnings. Absent such a program, bankruptcy will inevitably be the method by which unpayable prior commitments will be resolved.

Given the structure of income and rehabilitation programs for the ill and injured, it is not surprising that a number of these people were swamped by debt and became part of our bankruptcy sample. Job-related reasons were the most common reasons for bankruptcy given in this study. More than 20 percent of those who had job problems also mentioned medical problems.[64] Those who had a job-related reason for bankruptcy were significantly more likely to have a medical reason as well.

The intersection between the two types of problems is revealed when we look at the detail of the debtors' responses. The connection is demonstrated in two ways. The first is that debtors who listed a medical reason for bankruptcy in response to our open-ended question about the cause of their bankruptcies were disproportionately those who also reported having suffered a job interruption. Of those who gave a medical response specifically related to illness, injury, or disability of the debtor, two-thirds also listed a job reason for filing.

The connection is made even clearer in the joint cases, in which the medical problems and the job losses line up together: the spouse who was disabled is usually the one that is shown with a job loss. The data confirm a direct link between illness and job interruption because the illness of the primary petitioner is significantly linked to the job interruption of that petitioner, whereas in cases where the joint petitioner (almost always the wife) is listed as ill or hurt, job interruption is often listed for her. Over 70 percent of those listing an illness for the first petitioner (husband) also reported a job interruption for the husband. The same thing was true for a wife's illness, with 75 percent of those indicating a medical reason for the wife reporting a job interruption for her. In every respect, there is a strong relation in these data between loss of health and loss of income.

Strengthening the connection between illness and job loss is the fact that medical problems and job loss are often listed together as the reasons for bankruptcy. Again the connection is clearer in the joint husband-wife cases, in which half of those reporting the husband's illness as a reason for bankruptcy also report his job loss as a reason. Almost half of those listing the wife's illness also list her job loss as a cause of their bankruptcy. It seems clear that job loss and income loss from illness and injury are major causes of the financial disasters that lead to bankruptcy.

The debtors explain that their problems came from both illness and injury. Job-related injury permeates their comments. Memphis Morgan is a black Texan with a bachelor's degree. At thirty-five, she is a solid, dues-paying member of the middle class, with a house, a low mortgage, and a $30,000 annual income many other divorced women would envy. She is also up to her ears in unsecured debt, enough to consume ten months of her income if she could ignore the interest that was undoubtedly being added every month. Why? "Work injury is the #1 factor in my bankruptcy." She doesn't list another reason, nor does she describe the holes in the various safety nets that let her fall all the way into bankruptcy court.

Simple, devastating disease is also a common report. John and Helen Torville, who live in a suburb just outside Pittsburgh, were both in their mid-thirties, with some college under their belts and getting by okay, when Helen lost her job and John developed multiple sclerosis. John reported that they filed for bankruptcy after "the disease slowed me to the point I am unable to work." Helen is looking for another job, but they evidently decided that she was not likely to make enough to pay the past bills plus whatever medical bills John might incur in the future.

An interruption in income does not have to last long to tip over a precarious bark. Darren and Sissy Dombrowski, a young couple in downstate Illinois, found themselves in bankruptcy after Darren suffered an injury that put him out of work for just six weeks. Back at work by the time of the filing, Darren explained their problem quite simply: "we just couldn't catch up." Of course, no one should be that close to the edge financially, but at age twenty-eight you haven't had much time to fill the reserve tank.

There are three tasks society might address from a financial perspective when someone has been ill or injured, once medical treatment has been provided. They are to support the person, to return the person to productive life, and to deal with the person's predisability financial obligations. In effect, the three safety-net systems described earlier—worker's compensation, disability payments, and vocational rehabilitation—are designed to deal with the first two of these tasks. If we do not provide income supplementation at the same level and a person cannot or does not return to the same level of income production, however, we have effectively decided that bankruptcy may be the solution for the third task.

As these examples suggest, there is enormous variety in the debtors' medical histories, but the constant theme of their comments is income loss and often job loss. What these data from the bank-

162

ruptcy courts reveal is that middle-class people face a substantial risk that sickness or injury will result in financial disaster if they have accumulated significant debts, the repayment of which rests on the assumption of an income uninterrupted by sickness or injury. With disability income support intentionally set at less than two-thirds of prior income, savings and insurance may be consumed by continuing expenses, leaving nothing to make the minimum monthly payments on credit cards, mortgages, and car loans incurred in healthier times. Even after rehabilitation, there is no guarantee of a return to the full income production once enjoyed and therefore often little chance of paying prior debts in full or of enjoying the lifestyle that predated the crash or the diagnosis.

## Medical Risks for Everyone

Whether or not universal health coverage is a good idea, there can be no question that medical problems and medical costs are a universal problem. Insofar as medical problems produce financial disaster, our data suggest that disaster can befall any of us.

Medical problems in our sample were spread throughout the country, without significant differences among districts.[65] Although there were a substantial number of African-Americans, Hispanic-Americans, and noncitizens in our sample, there was no significant difference in their reports of medical reasons for their bankruptcies as compared with the rest of the sample.[66] In order to make a useful comparison between the debtors in bankruptcy and the population generally, we looked at out-of-pocket medical costs rather than total medical costs per capita, because out-of-pocket costs reflect the amounts being paid by or billed to the patients themselves and not to their insurance providers or to the government. Those being charged substantial amounts separate from their third-party payments are those who may end in bankruptcy court. Viewed in this light, the lack of difference by ethnicity was not surprising, because outside of bankruptcy blacks and whites report similar instances of large out-of-pocket expenditures, whereas Hispanic families report somewhat fewer instances.[67]

We were more surprised to find no difference in medical debts by gender.[68] In the population generally, households headed by females more often report large percentage expenditures (over 10 percent annually) for health care, so it is somewhat surprising not to see a significant gender difference in our figures. Furthermore, our earlier work and other previous studies have suggested that single women may be carrying a relatively greater burden of medical expense and medical debt.[69] It is possible that single women are carrying relatively more medical burdens for themselves and their children and that those debts are an important feature of their financial failures, yet some of them describe their reasons for filing bankruptcy in terms of divorce or the failure of an ex-spouse to provide promised support. We know, for example, that divorced women are more likely to list the divorce as the reason for their financial failure than are divorced men.[70] Without a systematic question about the debtor's medical debts, we cannot be sure whether single women are carrying relatively similar medical burdens as single men and married couples or whether they are describing their problems somewhat differently.

164

There is also no significant difference between the debtors who listed medical reasons for bankruptcy and the rest of the sample as measured by income or debt-income ratios.[71] Given the staggering expenditures as a percentage of income that are generated for so many families by medical crises, one might have thought that these families would have disproportionate levels of debt.[72] Instead, one finds here, as elsewhere, a remarkable homogeneity in the debt-income ratios of those who reach the point of filing for bankruptcy. Whether the source of a family's financial trouble is medical problems, job loss, divorce, or some other problem, only when the typical family reaches a certain imbalance between debts and incomes does it conclude that it cannot recover financially without bankruptcy. Medical crises may be different only in that they can generate a financial crisis faster than other causes.

The only respect in which there is great variation in reporting medical reasons for bankruptcy among our debtors is not surprising: medical reasons become more important as the debtors become older. One might have thought that government programs would have leveled that playing field a bit, but the field still tilts. There is a close relation between age and medical reasons for bankruptcy (fig. 5.4). The slope of the graph in figure 5.4 after age thirty-five shows

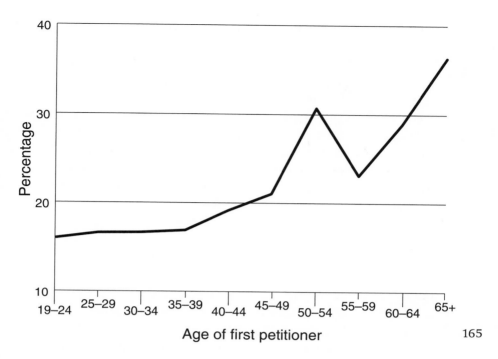

Fig. 5.4 Bankrupt debtors who cite a medical reason for bankruptcy by age group, 1991. *Source:* Consumer Bankruptcy Project II, 1991.

the closeness of the relationship. It is especially striking that those over sixty-five and presumably eligible for Medicare still have medical reasons for bankruptcy and that there are even more of them proportionately than those a few years younger.[73] Americans aged sixty-five and older are nearly twice as likely as younger Americans to identify a medical problem as the reason for filing.

The high incidence of medically related bankruptcies for debtors in their early fifties is also striking. This may be a group that is particularly vulnerable to medical problems that lead to financial collapse. In terms of medical bills, this is the sandwich generation. In their fifties, they face rising medical needs. At the same time, some are still responsible for children and young adult family members who do not have separate insurance, and some will try to supplement the medical expenditures of their elderly parents as they learn that Medicare provides incomplete coverage. As they age and their children become more independent and their parents die, the pressure from medically related bills for others declines, only to rise again as they hit their later years and their own highest medical expenditures.

People in their fifties may be vulnerable in yet another way. They are too young to have Medicare but just the right age to be downsized or otherwise lose their health insurance. The connection between medical problems and jobs in bankruptcy may run another way: those who lose their jobs are more likely to discover that any serious illness or accident will sink them financially. As people age, they may be more vulnerable to both the threat of job loss and the possibility of financial collapse if they have any health problems.

## The Widening Crack

There is some reason to think that medical problems may have become a more important part of middle-class financial crisis in the 1980s, although the lack of data for earlier years makes it difficult to be certain. In our earlier work, we reported that medical debt was often part of the financial troubles of bankrupt debtors but that in relatively few cases were medical debts sufficiently high, or a sufficiently great percentage of overall debt, to seem likely to have been the reason for the bankruptcy. As we have seen, however, a number of factors may have masked the role of medical debt in that study and in other studies as well.

Local court rules required debtors in one district in 1981 to list reasons for their bankruptcies. The debtors in the Western District of Texas, which includes San Antonio and El Paso, were required to file a form that asked an open-ended question like the one in our present study, "Why did you file for bankruptcy?" We captured those answers in our 1981 study and discovered that only 8 percent of the debtors listed a medically related problem as the reason for their filing. In 1991, when the questionnaires permitted us to gather this information in all sixteen districts, the percentage of debtors reporting medical causes for their bankruptcies was more than twice that high.

The obvious question is whether Western Texas was representative at the time of our first survey in 1981. As it turns out, among the districts in our 1991 study, Western Texas was the second-lowest district with regard to the percentage of debtors reporting medical causes for bankruptcy. It may thus have also been at the low end in reporting medical reasons for bankruptcy in 1981. Without more complete historical information, we cannot tell. For that reason, we should not overstate the strength of the inference from these figures that there has been an increase in medical causes for bankruptcy. And yet, the report of medical causes for bankruptcy in Western Texas itself rose sharply, from 8 percent in 1981 to 14 percent in 1991. This is a 75 percent increase. Even if this single district is atypical, with medical problems posing a less significant threat for its citizens, the rise in a decade is remarkable. These data suggest that the crack in middle-class stability that begins with medical problems may be widening.

The data also support an alternative explanation, albeit a speculative one. If the information from Western Texas was generally representative of debtors across the country in the early 1980s, then the combined data from the 1960s, the 1980s, and the 1990s would suggest a trough in the importance of medical problems in causing financial collapse. The Brookings Institute found in the 1960s that *combined* medical and family problems were a precipitating cause of bankruptcy for 28 percent of the debtors,[74] and our 1991 data demonstrate that medical debt *alone* was a significant reason for bankruptcy filings for 21 percent of the debtors and that combined medical and family reasons accounted for 36.8 percent of the debtors.

The multiyear data suggest the possibility of a double-humped curve. That is, medical problems may have been more dominant in the mid-1960s, before the adoption of Medicare and Medicaid as part of the Great Society legislation. These safety nets may have reduced the impact of medical problems by the early 1980s, only to see them rise again with the dramatic increase in medical costs. This hypothesis is consistent with the data on the rise in the number of uninsured Americans in the 1960s, the decline in the 1970s, and the subsequent rise during the 1980s and 1990s (see fig. 5.2).[75] In any case, whether medical problems as a cause of bankruptcy were unusually low in the 1980s or not, the proportion of debtors pushed into bankruptcy by the financial consequences of medical problems was unmistakable in the 1990s.

167

The statistics and the debtors' accounts of the effects of illness and injury sketch a picture of a substantial and perhaps increasing burden of medical costs, medical debts, and income loss leading to bankruptcy. The most profound implication, however, may have arisen after our debtors turned in our questionnaires and left the bankruptcy court. That is the postbankruptcy effect of failure to pay medical bills.

Middle-class families who have filed bankruptcy and do not have company insurance coverage may find themselves facing demands for advance payments for medical treatment, or they may be relegated, like the poor, to emergency rooms and clinics for primary health care—if they can qualify for treatment there. Most hospitals are reluctant to grant credit to uninsured patients, leaving such patients to a distinct minority of hospitals that provide most of the uncompensated care to the indigent.[76] Doctors who have suffered serious losses by way of unpaid bills may not be eager to continue rendering medical services after a patient's bankruptcy.[77]

Even more troubling is the likelihood that doctors willing to give those services will find it increasingly difficult to do so because they will be part of managed-care plans that do not allow uncompensated, uninsured services to be rendered.[78] The experience with such plans has been too short to permit prediction, but in the past physicians relied on "cost-shifting" to cover uncompensated care. In years past, all the paying patients paid a bit more to cover the treatment of the ones who were broke.[79] The procedure was informal and somewhat haphazard, but many patients received free treatment. Whether such informal risk-spreading can continue in an environment of carefully calibrated cost-containment is not at all clear. In any case, even if this kind of care is available, the evidence suggests that it may not be very satisfactory.[80]

Even the care available to the poor may not be easily obtained by people struggling to stay in the middle class. As we noted earlier, the mean income for debtors filing for bankruptcy was about $20,400. That income would have been far too high to qualify for Medicaid in our five study states in 1991. Much of the eligibility for Medicaid, the federal medical program for the poor, overlaps Aid to Fami-

168

lies with Dependent Children (AFDC) welfare eligibility. Aside from other requirements, in 1991 the AFDC income cutoff went from a high of $1,161 per month in California (about $14,000 annually) to a low of $396 per month in Texas (about $4,800 annually).[81] The "medically needy" program is sometimes more generous. It permits Medicaid coverage once a person's monthly income minus that person's monthly medical expenditures—that is, a person's net post-medical-cost income—falls below a set amount. That amount in 1991 for a family of four ranged from $1,100 per month in California to $301 in Texas.[82] Few people who qualified for Medicaid on either standard could call themselves middle class any more, at least financially. Only time will reveal the further effects of the deep cuts in welfare programs now being undertaken.

The families who emerge from bankruptcy may find that they fall into a newly created health care gap—they face a more regulated health care market that demands either public or private payment, their incomes are too high to qualify them for indigent care, and they have little insurance and insufficient assets to pay for care themselves. Middle-class people, particularly those who have been in financial trouble, may find themselves left with the lowest level of medical care: a particularly dismaying fall in their standard of living and one that ordinary economic indicators may not reveal.

A 1988 survey revealed that 7.5 percent of Americans—about eighteen million people—reported not getting needed medical care for financial reasons, whereas only 1 percent of Canadians made the same report.[83] Whatever the virtues or drawbacks of the Canadian system of health care as compared with the U.S. system, this report dramatically illustrates the impact of financial considerations in staying healthy and in getting well.

Throughout this book we talk of the bankruptcy system as a social safety net for middle-class Americans hit with financial troubles. The safety net lets them remain middle class—albeit in more straitened circumstances than they originally faced. It is clear that many lawyers see it just that way. A few years ago, the television news program *Sixty Minutes* reported on a family with a hemophiliac child, Michael, who had become infected with AIDS in the era of a tainted blood supply in the United States. Although the family had some insurance coverage

169

from work, their medical costs exceeded $250,000 per year—far more than their insurance would cover. Both husband and wife worked, but they were falling farther and farther behind in their medical bills. As they cast about for a way to deal with their mounting debts, they consulted an attorney about personal bankruptcy. Their attorney advised them: "Wait until Michael dies, so you can discharge *all* the bills in your bankruptcy."[84] Knowing that they would have only one opportunity in six years to discharge their debts, their lawyer was recommending that they keep in mind that they had not yet finished incurring debts on Michael's behalf. They needed to save their bankruptcy opportunity.

Not many families face the same kind of crushing debts as Michael's family, yet the Andersons, whose story began this chapter, serve as a reminder that $25,000 of uninsured medical debt can sink a family—especially if those debts are coupled with a loss of future income. The cold numbers in the bankruptcy files, and the reports of the bankrupt families who answered our questionnaire, depict a middle-class nightmare. One or both breadwinners is struck down by illness or an accident, or a child or parent requires expensive treatment and constant nursing. Either way, income drops suddenly, and insurance coverage may be lost, just as medical bills mount at the startling rate required by the great engine of modern medical technology. The resulting charges may be unpayable, and even more often, the family may never be able to return to prior levels of income or even to catch up from weeks or months of income deprivation.

Bankruptcy serves as a social safety net, but as Michael's family and the Andersons illustrate, the net is not a comfortable one. Without bankruptcy, these families could work forever and never repay their debts. Large bills and reduced incomes create a mismatch that can be resolved only if the families can discharge some of the debt. Our files show that only a few days of medical care may be enough to sink a middle-class family. For a family with an asthmatic child or a breadwinner with a heart condition, the trip to the bankruptcy courts does not end their worries. They still face an uncertain future. Bankruptcy may discharge the debts, but it neither replaces the insurance coverage nor persuades hospitals and doctors to continue medical care.

As we noted earlier, nine million American families in a late 1980s

170

survey were paying more than 20 percent of their incomes in medical costs. A more recent report suggests that more than 20 percent of the total health care bill in the United States is still ponied up by individuals.[85] One in five of those who declare themselves financial failures identified illness and accidents as the reasons for their filings. These data demonstrate that millions of families live just one serious illness or one substantial accident away from financial disaster. In the midst of affluent modern America, a family can still be struck down overnight.

171

Chapter 6

# Divorce

Due to separation in upcoming divorce, bills are too much to pay and also care for 3 kids on my income.
—MARY JO HENKEL, Peoria, Illinois

My ex-wife made many charges while we were married. She received most assets and I do not have the income to pay these debts off and still live a normal life style.
—KEVIN GILLIAN, New Braunfels, Texas

It may not be true, as young lovers sometimes assert, that two can live as cheaply as one. But it is certainly true, and former lovers will attest, that two households can never be run as cheaply as one. Mary Jo is running a household with one adult's earnings where once she had two. Kevin is still trying to pay off the debts from his former household arrangement. Divorce, whatever emotional and social havoc it may wreak, is often a financial wreck. Some of the economic debris washes ashore in the bankruptcy courts, as it has for Mary Jo and Kevin.

No change in the lives and fortunes of the middle class over the past twenty-five years has been more important than the dramatic shift in the laws and mores concerning sex and marriage. No-fault divorce has gone from a radical notion to an almost universal enactment, ruining the quickie-divorce industry in Nevada and some of the nicer Caribbean destinations. Cohabitation without marriage has been transformed from covert and unrespectable to common and unremarkable.[1] These changes have created new categories of problems, from the trivia of party etiquette to the profoundly troubling impact of single parenthood. A by-product of these changes has been increased financial stress on middle-class America.

Marriage is an institution with many facets: social, emotional, physical, spiritual. It is also a very important financial institution. Other things being equal, sociologists report that married people enjoy greater economic stability than divorced or single people.[2] Indeed, marriage has been described as "a kind of long-term 'co-insurance' pact between spouses that buffers them against the stresses of life."[3] The growth of divorce and the decline of marriage have now left a number of middle-class people struggling financially. It is hard enough for two people to deal with the rising cost of living, to cope with illnesses, to worry over the possibilities of layoffs and reduced income, and to raise children. When an adult has to confront these difficulties alone, it is much harder. The difficulties are even greater if a lifestyle, including financial commitments, has been created together by two people who are now apart.

Both marital problems and financial difficulties may arise from the same sources of trouble. Once financial and marital problems have developed, they are likely to reinforce each other. The interaction is often fatal both to the marriage and to the balance sheet. Kevin thought that his ex-wife spent too much, and this no doubt became one of the issues that their marriage could not survive. Mary Jo's divorce has increased whatever financial pressures she felt during her marriage. One result is that the bankruptcy courts record an extensive financial pathology of the American marriage. We found ex-wives in bankruptcy because husbands failed to pay child support, a possibility for Mary Jo, and we found ex-husbands in bankruptcy because they were forced to pay child support. We found both men and women, like Kevin, arguing that they were dragged into bankruptcy by the financial irresponsibility of spouses and cohabitees. Financial trouble often snowballs in marriage, with dropping incomes and rising debts leading to divorce and divorce exacerbating the financial trouble.

It has been a durable finding among bankruptcy scholars that divorce is closely tied to bankruptcy.[4] Our sample of debtors bears this out, while also providing nuance and a chance for deeper analysis. One key finding is that the debtors are much more likely to be divorced than people in general. Another less intuitive finding is that the debtors in bankruptcy are much less likely to be remarried than other divorced people, confirming that remarriage is the postdivorce key to financial rehabilitation, especially for women. We had thought that remaining single—that is, having never married—might also characterize bankrupt debtors, but we were wrong. It is the trilogy of marriage, divorce, and no remarriage that appears to correlate with financial ruin.

### The Costs of the Divorce Revolution

The national change in marriage and divorce patterns, with declining marriage rates and high divorce rates, has been blamed on a number of social factors ranging from the declining influence of religion to the selfishness of the baby boomers. Lawyers may always be accused of overemphasizing the importance of formal laws, but other professionals have also speculated that the most important single cause of these changes has been the adoption of no-fault divorce laws. In a period of less than a decade, from 1969 to 1977, the number of states with no-fault divorce went from zero to forty-seven—from its first adoption in California to its enactment in forty-six other states.[5] These changes in divorce laws prompted an outpouring of commentary, but for many years few discussions of this social and legal juggernaut even mentioned the financial consequences of the divorce revolution.[6]

Of course, questions about the financial impact of no-fault divorce eventually emerged. Many researchers have explored the economic consequences of divorce. Despite considerable controversy and disagreement, almost all the studies agree on two points: divorce leads to a sharp drop in income for women, and women are much worse off financially than men after divorce. There is also reason to think that well-off women fall further following divorce than less-affluent women, even though in absolute terms the former are better off both before and after divorce.[7]

Popular consciousness awoke to the economic consequences of divorce in 1985 with the publication of Lenore Weitzman's book *The Divorce Revolution*.[8] Basing her arguments on data from the 1970s, Weitzman asserted that women's postdivorce incomes plummeted to as little as one-third of their predivorce level, while men's incomes greatly increased.[9] Weitzman's book has had an enormous impact on Americans' general understanding of the financial consequences of divorce and has generated a great deal of additional research, both critical and supportive.[10] Although many disagree on the particulars, the studies agree that divorce reduces postdivorce income, especially for women.[11] The decline measured in these studies was around 20 percent for women and a third of that for men.[12] Weitzman's book and a number of subsequent commentaries have urged that the criteria for awarding alimony and child support be changed drastically in favor of divorced women, especially when they are custodial parents.[13]

Because most of these studies are based on divorces in the 1970s, these data might be discounted as outdated. Changed expectations and the huge increase in women in the workforce may be leaving wives less dependent on their spouses and readier to fend for themselves after divorce. Pamela Smock designed her recent study with precisely that hypothesis in mind. To everyone's surprise, she found that a 1970s cohort of divorced women and a 1980s cohort suffered about the same economic difficulties, including sharp drops in income.[14] Notwithstanding women's gains in the workforce, the data demonstrate that economic hardships following divorce continue to fall disproportionally on women.

## Divorce Law and Bankruptcy Law

Marriage and divorce are legal institutions regulated almost entirely by state law. But federal bankruptcy law radically alters all the financial obligations created by state law. For this reason, the postdivorce, postbankruptcy circumstances of divorced people and their children result from the interaction of state and federal law.

Mary Jo, with whom we opened this chapter, is separated from her spouse and planning a divorce in addition to her bankruptcy. In general, with numerous qualifications and variations, state law will require payment for her three children in the form of child support. In many states, the law may also provide for payments for the ex-spouse in the form of alimony. Mary Jo alludes to paying the bills with only her own income. It might be that after her divorce, she will receive some payments from her ex-spouse. The court may order continuing support obligations, sometimes tied to specific financial obligations such as future orthodontia or upcoming college tuitions.

The divorce process also divides the property the couple has jointly accumulated during the marriage and allocates responsibility for paying the debts jointly incurred during the marriage. A final decree of divorce may be accompanied by a complex reordering of the financial lives of the couple, perhaps granting the house to one, a car to each, and splitting the furniture and whatever remains in the checking account. Although public consciousness of it is much less acute, the court decree will also allocate the debts: the mortgage, the car loans, the credit card balances, the finance company loans, outstanding medical bills, the home equity line of credit, and so on. Kevin complains that his ex-wife got the assets and he got the debts. There might be more than one side to this story, but divorce does allocate both property and debts in some fashion.

176 Not surprisingly, in the divorce courts the allocation of property, debts, and support are interrelated. A court may award a home to the wife who has custody of the children, order the soon-to-be-ex-husband to continue making mortgage payments and to pay off the credit cards, and then reduce child support payments because a large portion of their living expenses have been covered. The judge presiding over a divorce must be satisfied that an equitable distribution of both assets and debts has been accomplished.

Kevin has filed for bankruptcy after his divorce. This filing carries the potential for federal law to dramatically affect the obligations that were fixed by the state divorce decree. Kevin and his ex-wife remain divorced and custody of any children remains undisturbed by the bankruptcy filing, but the financial relationship between Kevin and his ex may change radically.

Legislators have sought to have the Bankruptcy Code provide special protection for the family creditor by leaving intact the support and alimony obligations. Support obligations have received special treatment since the early twentieth century, and the code was amended in 1994 to expand that protection. The debtor in serious financial trouble may discharge nearly every other kind of creditor, but certain family obligations are unshakable. If these obligations were discharged, some legislators fear that more families would become charges of the state, increasing the welfare rolls and harming the innocent children. Perhaps the special hostilities that run among estranged family members have guided Congress as well; bankruptcy is not designed to be a way for angry fathers or disappearing mothers to evade financial responsibility. Bankruptcy is about discharge of debt and financial rebirth, but not at the expense of families left behind.

Debts such as alimony and child support obligations would ordinarily be dischargeable in bankruptcy, except that the bankruptcy laws have specific provisions to make such debts nondischargeable.[15] Alimony and child support would also be subject to the generally applicable automatic stay that stops all creditors' collection efforts the instant a bankruptcy petition is filed. Once again, however, the Bankruptcy Code makes specific exceptions so that enforcement can be pressed notwithstanding the bankruptcy filing.[16] On the other hand, enforcement of support and alimony obligations becomes more limited when an ex-spouse declares bankruptcy. If an ex-husband has filed in Chapter 7, an ex-wife may be temporarily halted from collecting from assets of the newly formed bankruptcy estate. She may not seize the ex-husband's property or garnish money in his checking account, for example, but she will receive a priority repayment from the bankruptcy trustee. She may also collect from his postbankruptcy income. If the ex-husband has filed in Chapter 13, the ex-wife can collect only through his plan, waiting for a check from the ex-husband's bankruptcy trustee.[17]

Bankruptcy laws offer special protection to children and ex-spouses because they are unlike most other unsecured creditors, such as credit card issuers or finance companies. Children and ex-spouses cannot charge higher interest rates to cover their bankruptcy losses. They cannot decide to stop doing business with someone to control their credit risks. They cannot spread their risks by taking on hundreds of fathers or husbands, so that they are able to withstand the impact of having one of them file for bankruptcy. The special protection for alimony and child support is solidly entrenched in bankruptcy policy and reflected in the statutes.

Of course, as with many protective policies, the glass that is half-full for one party is half-empty for the other. To the extent that the party obligated to pay support believes that an excessive payment obligation is the root cause of imminent financial catastrophe, bankruptcy provides only limited help. The only benefit bankruptcy law allows to the ex-spouse with support obligation is the chance to discharge all other kinds of debt. The effect can be to clear the decks for the spouse who has the obligation to pay, eliminating all the other preexisting demands on income. Whether this provides sufficient relief to restore a debtor to some semblance of financial stability varies from case to case.

Notwithstanding the protected status of alimony and child support payments, the family may still suffer a sharp blow when an ex-family member files for bankruptcy. State judges presiding over divorces determine payment obligations in tandem, considering both future support and the allocation of responsibility for past bills. Bankruptcy courts, by contrast, look only at the situation of the individual petitioner. Perhaps the state court set support obligations at a lower level because a former husband or ex-wife had agreed to repay joint debts. If the former husband is ordered to repay the joint debts, for example, but he discharges those joint obligations in a post-divorce bankruptcy, the wife remains legally responsible for the debts—and in a more precarious financial condition. Thus, a wife with custody of the children who believed the ex-husband would be paying off the outstanding credit card bills may suddenly find that she is responsible for another $18,000 in debts that she never budgeted. This might be the fate in store for Kevin's ex-wife. (Kevin's side of the story, to be sure, is that she ran up the debts with little help from him and that she ought to pay them off on her own.)

The situation in which Kevin finds himself has been the subject of frequent disputes. Until a few years ago, federal law was sketchy about whether a bankruptcy petitioner could discharge the responsibility to repay debts incurred before a divorce. The legal issue was whether a debtor such as Kevin had to pay the debts specified in his divorce decree after filing bankruptcy. Ex-spouses would fight their way through bankruptcy courts, increasing both their attorneys' fees and their own bile as they argued over the status of bills the debtor-spouse was supposed to pay. In the process, it was common for the bankruptcy of the first ex-spouse to trigger bankruptcy filing for the second.

The law was in this uncertain state when Kevin and the other debtors in our sample filed in 1991. In 1994, in response to a crescendo of complaints about the effects of bankruptcy on divorced women and their children, Congress passed substantial reforms designed to improve the legal position of spouses and children in bankruptcy. Unfortunately, the new amendments are not a model of clarity.[18]

One provision the amendments address directly is the problem of predivorce debts. The amendments make it more difficult for ex-spouses such as Kevin to discharge predivorce debts they were ordered to pay by the divorce court. A new provision makes such debts nondischargeable *if* the bankrupt spouse can afford to pay them while supporting any new family *and* the court finds that the benefit to the nonbankrupt spouse from payment of these debts outweighs the hardship imposed on the bankrupt spouse and new family.[19]

Presumably the result of this provision will be that more spouses who have agreed to pay marital debts following divorce will be told that bankruptcy does not offer a way out. Of course, that conclusion depends upon the court's finding no serious hardship in most cases, which is not a foregone conclusion. This is, after all, a bankrupt population. Kevin's current income is $20,160, and his assets are worth only $1,865. He reports unsecured debt of $34,600, nearly $31,000 of it credit card debt. Given the miserable financial position of many of these bankrupt ex-spouses, hardship may be relatively easy to prove. A legal declaration that the joint marital debts are still the responsibility of the ex-spouse may be more likely under the new statute, but a declaration is not the same as a repayment. If he filed today, Kevin might leave bankruptcy still owing his marital debts. But if Kevin simply does not pay the joint marital debts, whether he is in bankruptcy or not, the creditor is legally free to collect from his ex-wife, the divorce decree notwithstanding. If the creditor finds it cheaper or easier to pursue the former Mrs. Gillian, she will have to pay—or initiate her own bankruptcy filing.

As we noted earlier, continuing alimony and child support obligations cannot be discharged. The 1994 amendments further protect these debts by making repayment of old alimony and support obligations a priority ahead of most other unsecured debts.[20] This means that unpaid alimony and support must be paid from assets in a Chapter 7 bankruptcy before taxes, credit cards, medical debts, and almost every other kind of unsecured debt are paid. In Chapter 13, the alimony and child support debts must be paid in full.[21]

Once again, the protection offered may look better on paper than it does in reality. Although empirical data are scarce, it appears that in most Chapter 7 cases there are not enough assets to pay much to *any* unsecured creditors, so in those cases the new provision gives the ex-spouse and children first crack at an empty box.[22] In Chapter 13 filings, the new priority for these family obligations should have more impact, but it does not offer any guarantees. Ex-spouses who owe past-due child support and alimony may simply file for Chapter 7 instead, so the protection offered may be illusory.

In short, the reforms enhance the collection rights of those relying on alimony and support, but they cannot alter the economic realities of divorce: too many obligations balanced against too little income. Much folk wisdom is based on the theme of the inability to take value when none exists (squeezing blood from turnips, for example). The bankruptcy laws deal concurrently with those who need much and those who have little to give. The statute cannot guarantee a happy ending to that story for anyone concerned.

Notwithstanding the protected status of family obligations in bankruptcy, the economic realities facing the parties suggest that both ex-spouses are at greater risk for financial failure following a divorce. The bankruptcy data confirm this suspicion. Whether they are the mothers who cannot collect support for their children or the fathers who claim to be unable to make their support payments, the bankruptcy courts are filled with people trapped in the financial aftermath of family breakups.

## Married, Single, Widowed, Separated, and Divorced

The breakfast tables of middle America are changing. Who is eating with whom—if there are two people there at all—has been changing for forty years. Marriage rates in the United States have fallen every decade since the 1950s.[23] At the same time, divorce rates have soared in the last forty years.[24] Cohabitation rates have climbed steadily.[25] In addition, the number of unwed parents has climbed dramatically.[26]

One major result of these trends is that in 1990 there were ten million families with children with no fathers living with them.[27]

Adults who live alone or with minor children are economically vulnerable. Earlier studies offer indirect evidence of the economic vulnerability of being single. In our study of debtors who filed for bankruptcy in 1981, about 17 percent were women filing alone and 26 percent were men filing alone.[28] By 1991 our data show that 28 percent of those filing for bankruptcy were women filing alone and 28 percent were men filing alone. We observe parenthetically that women have achieved parity in one economic measure: they now file for bankruptcy at the same rates as their male counterparts. Without questionnaire data, earlier studies could give only a glimpse of the effects of single life and divorce, sorting debtors who filed jointly from those filing alone.[29] A person need not be single to file bankruptcy alone, and in the 1981 study we searched the files for evidence that single filers were married.[30] To understand better the relation between family status and economic vulnerability, we needed data focusing specifically on marriage and divorce. Our 1991 questionnaire asked three questions directly related to marital status, marital disruption, and the relation between marital circumstances and bankruptcy.[31] On the front of the questionnaire each debtor was asked to list current marital status: married, separated, divorced, widowed, or never married. A second question asked if the debtor had experienced a change in marital status during the two years before bankruptcy.[32] Joint cases, available only to married couples, received double treatment: the questionnaire asked for a response from each of the two debtors. Finally, our open-ended question about the reasons for bankruptcy yielded a number of responses in which debtors cited martial discord, along with other family problems, as reasons for their financial distress.

The debtors themselves often identify marital disruption as an important part of their financial collapse. In the open-ended questions asking why people filed for bankruptcy, more than 15 percent of the debtors specifically identified marital disruption as a source of their financial troubles.[33] Only job loss and medical problems were cited more often by the debtors as the cause of their financial collapse.[34] In fact, if other family problems — such as an unexpected child or caring for a family member—were added to the divorce category, almost one-quarter of the debtors cited family problems as a cause of their bankruptcy.[35]

Notwithstanding the variety of explanations of family disarray and financial collapse, one explanation overwhelmed all others: marital discord. More than two-thirds of those reporting a family problem—and more than 15 percent of the debtors—described their financial collapse as directly related to the breakup of a marriage.[36] Jeanette Rae Rookham is typical of the debtors explaining the relation between marital breakup and financial collapse. She tells her story without embellishments: "Due to the dissolution of my marriage and the fact that I am responsible for my two young children, getting on top of my financial situation has been very difficult. When the marriage ended I had no job and before separation was being supported by ex-husband. Since then I've been working hard trying to support my family." She hopes that in Chapter 7 she can wipe the slate clean and start over with her children.

The debtors' stories are a reminder of the complexities that can be obscured even with survey techniques. Although many debtors report themselves as married, and thus boost the proportion of "married" in the sample, they explain that they are married at the time of the bankruptcy filing only because the bankruptcy court is faster than the divorce court. Mary Jo Henkel, with whom we opened this chapter, is a good example; she lists herself as "married." Debtors in this group check "married," but they write about impending separations and divorces that will become final as soon as there is enough money for a deposit on an apartment or when the papers are signed. Some of the debtors in our sample separated and moved back together, surviving the emotional consequences of marital breakup but still facing the economic ones. Others are single, but they report the loss of a live-in roommate who had shared the expenses for many years. Without a dozen more systematic questions we could not capture this fringe of marital problems that do not show up in the quantitative data, but the stories indicate that we may systematically underestimate the financial consequences of the breakup of households.

The overall effects of family dissolution are clear not merely from the debtors' stated reasons for their bankruptcies but from the hard demographic data we obtained. There is a key difference between

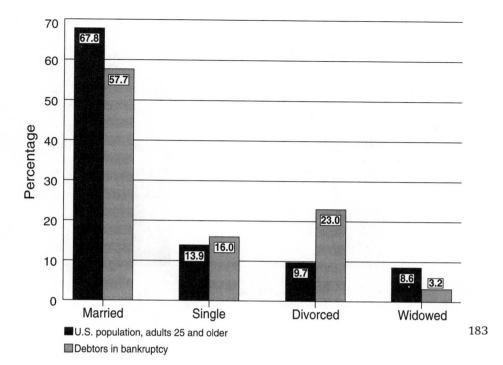

Fig. 6.1 Marital status of bankrupt debtors and U.S. population, 1991. *Source: Statistical Abstract: 1992,* 43, table 48.

bankrupt debtors in bankruptcy and Americans generally: the bankrupt debtors are less likely to be married (fig. 6.1).[37] With an adjustment to reflect the age bias in our sample of bankrupts (fewer young adults), 68 percent of American men and women twenty-five and older in 1991 were married, as compared with just 62 percent in our bankruptcy sample.[38]

But it is the change in economic status—particularly the downward change—that presents the particular opportunities for economic disaster we study here. The debtors are not only less frequently married but more often divorced than average Americans. About 23 percent of the bankruptcy sample was divorced, compared with about 10 percent of the general population in 1991.[39] Another 8 percent in the bankruptcy sample were separated, so that a total of more than 30 percent were either currently divorced or separated when they filed for bankruptcy.[40] These data demonstrate that divorced

**DIVORCE**

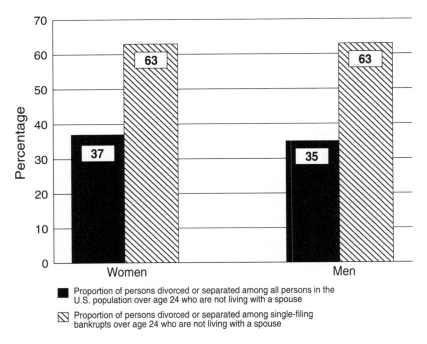

Fig. 6.2 Divorce and separation among persons living without a spouse, 1991. *Source: Statistical Abstract: 1992*, 46, table 55.

people are twice as likely to find themselves in bankruptcy than any other group. The robustness of the finding is supported by similar results recently reported in Canada.[41]

The sample of debtors in bankruptcy reflects the financial strains imposed on average Americans by marital instability. We can focus more clearly on the effects of divorce, rather than the effects of non-marriage, by looking at single people in the population generally and single people in bankruptcy (fig. 6.2). In 1991, among Americans generally who were not living with a spouse, more than one-third were currently divorced or separated. The figure for men and women was about the same, around 37 percent. Among the people in bankruptcy, the proportion who are divorced or separated is truly astonishing. About 63 percent of the unmarried debtors are divorced or separated. This demonstrates once again that the proportion of divorced and separated people in the bankruptcy sample outstrips that in the population generally, vividly illustrating that divorced people

**DIVORCE**

are much more financially vulnerable than their single or widowed counterparts.[42]

The debtors' reports of the reasons for their bankruptcies strongly suggest a disparate impact on women. Women are significantly more likely to cite divorce as the *cause* of their bankruptcies.[43] In particular, among debtors who report a divorce or separation within two years of bankruptcy, 52 percent of the women list that marital discord as a cause of their bankruptcies, while only 31 percent of the men do so.[44]

The effects of divorce appear to continue long after the divorce has occurred. By combining information from three questions on the questionnaire, we could form some idea of the long-lasting effects of divorce. We knew the debtor's marital status, we knew whether the debtor had changed marital status within the preceding two years, and we knew the reason that the debtor gave for the bankruptcy. An analysis of the data indicates that both men and women suffer long-term effects from divorce, but in different ways.

There were 384 debtors who were divorced or separated at the time of the survey but who reported no change in marital status during the past two years. We could consider them the "long-term divorced." The majority (58 percent) of the long-term divorced were women. By and large, the long-term divorced give reasons other than divorce for their bankruptcy, but 18 percent of them still point to the divorce as the reason for the bankruptcy. Interestingly, among the long-term divorced debtors, the men and women flip-flopped in giving divorce as a cause. Although women cited divorce far more often in the short-term, it was men, by 23 percent to 14 percent, who pointed to divorce as a cause of bankruptcy when the divorce was more than two years old.[45] For some ex-husbands, who were still not remarried, the financial repercussions of a divorce that had occurred more than two years previously were still being felt.

A different conclusion stems from examining the reasons for bankruptcy more broadly. Many of the people who get a divorce subsequently remarry, but the preceding analysis was limited only to those who were still divorced or separated. This time, we ignored the current marital status of the debtors—they could be divorced, married, or in some other status—but continued to limit the analysis to those who reported no marital change within the past two years. And we broadened the reasons for the bankruptcy to include family problems that were not separately coded, divorce, single parenting, and the expenses of maintaining two households or family separation. There were now 163 respondents, or 8 percent of the sample, who identified a family problem as the reason for the bankruptcy. Women were three times more likely than men to identify this broader family problem as the reason for their bankruptcy. Almost 15 percent of the women but only 5 percent of the men gave one of these family reasons for the bankruptcy.[46]

One conclusion from this pair of analyses is that although both men and women suffer the long-term financial consequences of the divorce, they frame the problem somewhat differently. For example, women are more likely to define the issue in terms of their current role as a single parent than in terms of the divorce that has made them a single parent. Men, however, and especially men who have not remarried, are more likely to identify the divorce event itself as the cause of the bankruptcy.[47] Both are identifying the aftermath of a family breakup.

186    The focus on family dissolution sharpens with the finding that it is the divorced, not the always single, that swell the ranks of bankrupt debtors. In the adult population, about 14 percent of Americans generally have never married (see fig. 6.1). In the bankruptcy sample, about 12.5 percent have never married. Notwithstanding the presumed superiority of the married unit, single people seem to survive economic bumps in about their proportions in the population. It is the fact of marriage and divorce—combining households, then separating them—that promotes financial instability.[48]

Divorce and bankruptcy seem to be tied to each other, twin catastrophes visited on middle-class families. One financially healthy household may subdivide into two financially unhealthy homes. The resulting sudden drop in disposable income per household is a classic prescription for the bankruptcy of at least one.

The difficulties of collecting alimony and child support—mirrored by the trouble in paying it—also make the once-married more vulnerable to financial troubles. For some people the bills run up during the marriage turn out to sink one or both of the postdivorce households.

DIVORCE

The drop in income experienced just after divorce is only one indication of the relative economic differences between married and divorced people. The relative financial vulnerability among divorced people is evident in the data on remarriage.

Most divorced people remarry.[49] In a study conducted by Greg Duncan and Saul Hoffman, 68 percent of the men and 49 percent of the women remarried within five years.[50] Recent studies have demonstrated that the most crucial factor in the financial recovery of a divorced woman is remarriage. Remarriage largely eliminates the financial shock of divorce for women. After five years, remarried women return to the financial position they enjoyed before divorce.[51] Duncan and Hoffman found that even in the first year after divorce, remarried women had 80 percent of their former incomes, whereas not-remarried women had only 70 percent. Smock found more dramatic differences. Just one year after a divorce, the incomes of not-remarried women were less than 40 percent of their predivorce incomes, whereas the incomes of remarried women exceeded prior levels by more than 10 percent.[52] Most women who do not remarry remain mired in financial circumstances well below those they had enjoyed before they divorced. Smock's findings are particularly significant because they included younger women who married and divorced in the 1980s.

The studies provide little information about the relative change in men's economic circumstances brought about by remarriage. But the data available about the changed circumstances of women are persuasive. The research consistently shows that divorce has a devastating effect on women's economic circumstances and that remarriage is usually the key to their return to a prior level of affluence. Failure to remarry has enormous financial significance, because remarriage is the key to financial recovery after divorce, especially for women.[53] The presence of two adults in the household may be the critical contribution to solvency. Even if one member of the couple is a homemaker, the joint value of their market and nonmarket work makes them more likely to stay afloat financially.

Our data suggest that those who remain unmarried following di-

187

vorce are at greater risk for financial collapse. Duncan and Hoffman found that one-third to one-half of divorced Americans, men and women, remarry within three years. Our bankruptcy questions used a two-year interval rather than three. Among the debtors divorced more than two years before their bankruptcies, only 15 percent had remarried, so that 85 percent were still unmarried at least two years (and often more) after divorce.[54] The debtors in bankruptcy are disproportionately those who lose the remarriage sweepstakes.[55]

The bankruptcy data portray the worst case of the results of divorce: those who experienced financial failure. Comparing the marital status of the bankrupt debtors with the general population, it appears that remaining married is some safeguard against economic ruin. Those who remain single following divorce are at risk of financial failure, and for the women the risk is especially acute.

## Alimony and Child Support

188    The simple division of assets and increase of expenses that create economic strains for the newly divorced is supposed to be remedied by court-ordered support. The party with the higher income, so the theory goes, shares that income in sufficient quantity to assist in the support of two households. Surely there are few places in law where the theory is so distantly separated from the reality.

In 1990, according to the U.S. Commission on Interstate Child Support, courts awarded support to only 58 percent of the women living with children apart from the children's father.[56] Still fewer women actually received support. Another study estimates that only 45 percent of the separated or divorced women with children are actually getting support and that only 29 percent receive all the support that was ordered.[57]

Lenore Weitzman asserts that the financial problems facing women stem from inadequate support awards as well as nonpayment.[58] She claims that the courts focus on the amount that the father can afford, rather than on the amount that the wife and children need. Weitzman found that the courts usually award no more than a third of the husband's income in support, although the wife and children are typically a three-person household. The court effectively awards two-thirds of the income to one person of the four who formerly constituted the family.

One Connecticut study supports Weitzman's conclusions. The study was based on the "levels" of income established by the Department of Labor. The department has constructed three budget levels: low, moderate, and liberal. The Connecticut study compared the awards to mother and children with the father's level of income, and it found that although support rises with the father's income, it is usually a level below it. If, for example, the father's income is at a moderate level, as defined by the Department of Labor, then the study found that the level of support produced a low-income budget. If the father's income is at the liberal budget level, the study found a moderate budget for the ex-wife and children.[59] A third study suggests that divorced women may receive even less than these two studies suggest: only one-third of all divorced women were receiving support. The support they received amounted to only 10 percent of their income.[60]

For those ex-spouses — usually women — who are counting on support payments to provide a standard of living similar to their pre-divorce circumstances, reality is harsh. The data suggest that support awards are often too small, too infrequent, and too often ignored to provide any steady assurance of financial stability.

## Support Payments: Can't Get Them

We did not ask about the number of dependents living with the debtors, but a Canadian survey is suggestive. It found that half of the "unmarried" women (including never-married, separated, divorced, and widowed) in bankruptcy had dependents under age twenty-one.[61] Of the 15 percent of debtors in our sample who report that marital troubles were a cause of their bankruptcy, most just cite divorce or separation in general. This group represents all ethnic groups and comes from every region of the country. A young Pennsylvania woman, divorced and left with a child at twenty-three, cites "difficulties as a result of divorce and raising a child and self on one income." A woman from Tennessee says simply, "My husband divorced me and I was unable to pay my monthly bills." Because the questions were open-ended, we have no systematic way to see how often lack of support is the specific cause of the debtors' problems.

Even so, when debtors get specific, many frame their problems in terms of lack of support. Marty deGroot is typical. She is forty-six and starting over after a divorce. She lives in Encino, California. She explains the reason for her bankruptcy: "My reason for my chapter 13 was my divorce. My ex-husband left with the responsibility of my two teenage kids. . . . He also refused to pay child support and spouse support." Marty is not without resources. She has some college education and a steady job. Interestingly, her hope for the future includes a upcoming court hearing where she plans to ask the judge to force her ex-husband to pay up.

Michelle Conners lives in Upper Darby, Pennsylvania. She is luckier than many divorced women because she is young (thirty), she has a steady job, and she has a home. And yet, two years after her separation she is not remarried, and she is making only $22,000 a year. The files report her as a homeowner, but she claims to have no equity built up in the house. Because there is no report of a default, she is probably making her mortgage payments on time. Michelle's problem is that she cannot maintain all her monthly living expenses and deal with her growing debts. Her nonmortgage debts amount to ten months' of her gross income. One large part of what she owes is a big balance on her 1989 Camaro, which was stolen the preceding year, apparently with no insurance to cover the theft. Michelle traces her financial troubles straight to her ex: "I am raising our 2 children on my own with little financial help from their father." She discharges her debts on the car and credit cards in Chapter 7. After bankruptcy, she will continue to support herself and the children on her $22,000 salary.

Ex-husbands and fathers are not the only ones who duck their financial obligations to families they have left behind. Wives and mothers can be equally irresponsible. Twenty-five-year-old Tom Froks, who lives in San Diego, was awarded custody of his child. His family's financial trouble came in part because of reduced hours and lower earnings at work, but Tom and his son also got nothing from the boy's mother: "Single father, no money from the mother. Was only working part time. But have full time job now." Tom has filed for Chapter 13 to repay some of his outstanding debts. He felt strongly enough about his ex-wife's neglect that he listed it as the number one reason for his bankruptcy filing.

The loss of child support may affect even those debtors who have remarried. Frederick Potts is forty-two and living in Springfield, Illinois. He is on his second marriage, as is his new wife. He begins the explanation of his Chapter 7 with the following: "Divorce then—remarried—Loss of wife's child support." His new spouse has not joined in the bankruptcy. Although until recently he was out of a job, he does not see that as the source of their problems. He blames his bankruptcy on his second wife's ex-husband for failing to pay up to support the kids she brought into their new marriage.

The stories vary, but for many debtors in the bankruptcy courts, the inability to collect from an errant ex-spouse court-ordered alimony and child support has left them without financial options.

## Support Payments: Can't Make Them

If the absence of child support is a major factor in the financial agony following divorce for many women, enforcement of child support is an important financial travail for many men. That side of the coin has received little attention in the academic literature, or even in the media, but it is another major theme in our files.

Although most of the academic literature focuses on the courts' failure to order child support or a spouse's failure to pay, many of our debtors are men citing child support as the reason for their bankruptcy. Because alimony and child support cannot be discharged in bankruptcy, these men are not escaping their ongoing support obligations by filing under the Bankruptcy Code.[62] In effect, they are claiming that, unlike many other men, they *are* paying their required support and therefore cannot meet other debts. Typical was the comment of Tony Dembroski, "I was unable to meet the demands of my creditors and have enough money to support myself and pay the ordered child support."

In general, alimony and child support enjoy a favored enforcement status in most states. Although imprisonment for most kinds of debts was ended in most parts of the United States by the early 1800s, nonpayment of support obligations can still lead to jail. In addition, a support order may often be enforced by a wage garnishment, which is seizure of a portion of a person's paycheck directly from the employer. Garnishment is one of the few effective ways to collect a debt from the average working person, since most people have few assets worth seizing and many of those assets, such as clothing and household goods, are exempt from seizure under state law. Wage garnishment is also potentially devastating, taking away someone's livelihood at the source, so that state and federal laws heavily regulate the process and limit the amount. Because of the hardships it imposes, there are significant restrictions on the amount of income that may be seized in wage garnishments, and some states prohibit them outright. But the restrictions make an exception for support orders, permitting larger and more aggressive garnishments against nonpaying ex-spouses than any other kind of wage action. Some of the debtors in this sample specifically mentioned a garnishment action to enforce a support order as the precipitating cause of bankruptcy. An ex-husband from Riverside, California, was one of a number who reported "child support garnishing of wages" as the precipitating cause of his bankruptcy.[63]

A support obligation can be particularly worrisome for some people because the amount is never firmly fixed. If circumstances change either for the household receiving support or for the one paying it, the court may revisit its initial order and change the amount due. Forty-year-old Stan Trout and his wife, June, filed for bankruptcy in El Paso, Texas. Stan has a bachelor's degree, and June has some college but no diploma. Although June is not working, Stan has had a steady job for years. He identifies his one problem as his former marriage—and the support payments he could not make: "Increase in child support to 7,000 a year plus threat of collect of back child support. I began paying support on my own." Stan does not explain why he and the state domestic relations judge apparently had such different views of what he could afford. The state court judge obviously thought Stan could have paid all along and indeed could afford to pay more from now on, along with the arrears of past unpaid support. Stan and June found the prospect so daunting that they filed for bankruptcy.

We would like to know many other things about a case like Stan and June's (Are there children in the second marriage? Is June choosing to stay home and not work?), but the most important point is that Stan's child support payments will not go away because of bankruptcy. All of it, the arrearages and the new, higher payments for the future, will still be there when Stan and June emerge from the bankruptcy court. Even while they are in bankruptcy, Stan must make the current support payments or face jail time. The effect of bankruptcy here is to discharge their other debts. In effect, bankruptcy acts for this middle-class family as a method of clearing the decks of all other obligations, leaving enough (one hopes) for payment of the obligation that combines the highest moral commitment with the most potent legal enforcement.

The debtors tell their stories in many ways, but the theme is much like that of the preceding section: too little income to support two households. Whether the problem is not receiving the support that is needed or not making the payments that are scheduled, the people in the bankruptcy files are living testaments to the difficulties of creating two households where there once had been only one.

## Predivorce Debts

A divorce decree usually allocates between the spouses responsibility for paying predivorce debts, but ordering a spouse to pay predivorce debts is not the same as getting those debts paid. Although there has been much discussion in the scholarly literature of the difficulty of enforcing court-ordered support, there has been virtually no discussion of enforcement of court decrees that require a spouse to pay debts remaining from the marriage. Payment of such debts is often accounted for in the overall settlement between the parties, but there has been no systematic study of the extent to which such agreements are honored.

The reports of the debtors in our bankruptcy sample indicate that predivorce debts create another layer of postdivorce problems. The obligation to pay these debts often represents a severe strain for the primarily responsible spouse. Nonpayment of joint debts by one spouse often contributes to the financial stress of the other spouse.

Melanie Hart is a Chicago woman who was divorced at age forty. Since her divorce, she has worked sporadically, mostly on commission, and her income has declined. Melanie's struggle has been uphill from the moment of her divorce because her husband, Gregory, went into bankruptcy before the divorce was completed, leaving her with all the family's bills. By the time of bankruptcy, she faced almost $50,000 in short-term unsecured debt on top of her $78,000 mortgage. Half of the unsecured debt was credit cards, because, "After a year of struggling to keep up the payments on my own, I took cash advances on some of the credit cards to meet the monthly payments." After two years of robbing Peter to pay Paul, Melanie followed her ex-husband into the bankruptcy court.

The women in our sample repeat what a Pennsylvania woman said: "After my divorce, my ex-husband did not pay the bills he agreed to pay in our divorce decree." Another explained, "Pending divorce proceeding, entering work force and not having sufficient income to pay for debts incurred during marriage."

The lament over predivorce debts is not limited to women. Richard Fine, thirty-six, lives in Philadelphia. Even though he has some college education, he earned only $7,000 in income during the year before his bankruptcy. His divorce left him with no home and only $800 in assets. He blames his bankruptcy on his ex-wife's failure to pay the bills she agreed to cover during the divorce. Buddy Wallace, a Nashville, Tennessee, man in a similar position, had a double complaint: not only did his ex take off, leaving him with the bills for a new car, but the darned car was always in the shop. He didn't say if she had promised to fix it.

From a legal perspective, predivorce debts enjoy a protected status second only to the protection for alimony. The law, particularly as it was amended in 1994, makes these debts difficult to discharge. But their legal status is often not at issue. If the ex-spouse is not paying — or cannot pay — a determination that the debts are nondischargeable is cold comfort in the face of creditors demanding payment from the spouse left behind.

## Financial Strain, Emotional Strain

Financial trouble is the result of divorce, but it may also be the cause. Duncan and Hoffman, for example, point out that couples who divorce have average predivorce income levels substantially lower than those of couples who do not divorce.[64] In other words, people who divorce are less affluent than couples who stay married.

Neither their study nor other studies of predivorce incomes consider why couples who divorce are less affluent overall than those who do not divorce. One way of rephrasing the issue, although it is not really an explanation, is that people in lower income brackets are more likely to divorce. The explanation may lie in the fact that economic stresses lead to marital stresses. It is plausible that the persistent financial strain facing people at lower income levels increases the likelihood of divorce. It may be, however, that drops in income are particularly associated with marital stress. Perhaps economic declines—layoffs, declining incomes, and increasing bills—breed marital unhappiness. A steady state of little money may not contribute to marital disruptions so much as sharp drops, uncertainties, and sudden reversals.[65]

Which comes first, the bankruptcy or the divorce? David Caplovitz found that with increased financial strain, 14 percent of families reported that their marriage was worse.[66] Caplovitz also found that 34 percent of families with debt problems reported increased quarreling.[67] We hypothesize that the same economic difficulties that lead to bankruptcy are likely to lead to divorce, so that by the time of divorce couples who have broken up may have lower incomes than equivalent couples who stay together, precisely because their economic difficulties lead to a breakup. Of course, that breakup in turn creates still greater economic difficulty because living separately is much more expensive than living together. The snowball effect of economic trouble leading to, and then exacerbated by, divorce drives many debtors into the bankruptcy courts. But the issue of which comes first, the bankruptcy or the divorce, may be a matter merely of legal logistics.

The financial troubles preceding a bankruptcy and a divorce are as varied as the peculiarities of any unhappy situation. But the patterns are not hard to see: couples face increasing financial pressure when their incomes and debts swing out of balance. That can happen when either income or debt changes.

A decline in income often makes debts that seemed reasonable at an earlier time unpayable later on. Toby Klein, a thirty-six-year-old woman from Midland, Texas, explains her bankruptcy filing: "Ex-husband at time of marriage lost job. Just before that a custom house was bought and sold at a loss. Divorce took place and ex-husband filed bankruptcy. Then I felt a need to." Toby has been through some important changes just before filing: divorce, losing a home. She has a steady job that pays $31,500 a year, but her secured debts are $22,572 and her unsecured debts are another $44,658—more than Toby can ever pay on her income alone. For Toby and her ex-husband, two incomes and a custom-built house may have made for a comfortable life just a few years ago. But after her ex lost his job, they sold the house, and they struggled with other debts beyond their ability to pay, they found themselves in the divorce court, with each then making separate stops in the bankruptcy court.

Of course, financial collapse may come another way: incomes may stay steady but debts may rise, creating similar financial pressures. Lynda Ryerson explains the reason for her bankruptcy filing: "Misuse of credit cards by ex-husband—used for investments in his account (stocks). Divorce settlement left me with ½ bills of which I did not incur." Like Toby, Lynda is recently divorced. Evidently the bills piled in during the last years of their marriage. Whether it was her husband's irresponsibility that drove them apart or the pressing bills that resulted, probably neither could say. But at thirty-five, Lynda saw divorce and then bankruptcy as the only way to start over.

Perhaps the stresses of financial problems and the distractions of personal problems are so intertwined that any effort to sort them out is bound to fail. The bankruptcy files are full of comments about "fighting" and "trying" and "giving up." We were struck by the comments of Juan and Maria DeJesus, who described a very uncertain time as they filed for bankruptcy: "We had a lot of family and personal problems that just started getting out of hand. Stop carring about our assets and each other. But were trying to resolve our marrage and assets." They described themselves as "married," and evidently hoped their bankruptcy would help them stay that way.

More and more middle-class people lack the stability, financial as well as emotional, that comes from family life. Marital breakup and financial difficulty are mutual causes and effects. They interact in a dynamic of heartbreak and financial collapse. Not surprisingly, therefore, the bankrupt debtors are very much more likely to have been divorced or separated than most people are, and they are much less likely to remarry promptly.

**DIVORCE**

Although financial difficulty is almost inevitable in divorce or separation, research in recent years has suggested that our laws are inadequately drawn to protect women and children from the effects of divorce. Recent studies reinforce these conclusions, showing that women are disproportionately disadvantaged by divorce and more likely to be driven into bankruptcy as a result of it. Since our study was done, Congress has amended the Bankruptcy Code in a variety of ways that may protect spouses, especially custodial spouses who are usually women, from some of the legal consequences of bankruptcy.

It is always a mistake, however, to think that the law can fix everything. Among other things, the comments in our files about child support bankrupting fathers remind us of the grim economic realities: some people have taken on financial obligations they cannot afford. The ex-husbands and fathers who show up in bankruptcy court are a reminder that marital dissolution puts families at risk—not just rich daddies who do not want to pay.

In no way have the lives of middle-class people changed more quickly or completely than in marital and parental relationships. Although we lack comparative data from earlier times, it seems very likely that some significant portion of the tremendous increase in bankruptcy in the past fifteen years has been a function of increased family instability. The pain and perils of family breakup, and the new risks of nontraditional relationships, represent an enormous social change. This change has been accompanied by few adjustments in the social safety net and little help to steady the families that re-form following a marital breakup. Perhaps that is why so many find themselves in bankruptcy court, trying to make their own solutions to an impossible financial situation.

The data on divorce and financial collapse, divorce and incomes, divorce and collection of support, and divorce and predivorce debts paint a stark statistical picture of economic vulnerability associated with family breakup. Ultimately, however, these data are simply stories about people making painful readjustments. These are not stories about people who cannot live on $25,000 a year so much as they are stories about how hard it is to readjust from supporting a household on $40,000 to supporting it on much less. In some cases, the data suggest that no matter how quickly a person tries to adjust, bills incurred in better days will sink them financially. In other cases,

**DIVORCE**

people may have been slow to understand the financial implications of their dissolutions. They may not have moved quickly enough to find jobs, put the kids in cheaper day care, stop the orthodontia and piano lessons, and cut up the credit cards. They may have thought of themselves as people who lived a certain way. Only over time did they come to understand they could no longer afford to live as they once did.

The data on bankruptcy and divorce suggest that people need all their planning skills, all their financial acumen, and all their wits about them at precisely the time they are at an emotional low tide. They need to make wise decisions quickly when they are distracted by a thousand other thoughts unrelated to their financial circumstances. The bankruptcy courts are filled with people who are adjusting slowly and painfully.

198

# Chapter 7

# Housing

To keep our home is the main reason for filing bankruptcy. I have tried all other means.

—DWAYNE and SHAWNA LARUE, Nashville, Tennessee

In a book about financial failure, a chapter on "homeowners" seems out of place. Job loss is bad, and health problems are worse. Overwhelming credit card debt is a well-recognized risk, and family dissolution is an almost universally unhappy event. But in this litany of woe, homeownership stands out. Homeownership is supposed to be good news.

Homeownership is the status to which most Americans aspire. To nearly everyone, a home is an asset. With the exception of the bleary-eyed homeowner standing knee-deep in a flooded basement at 2:00 A.M., homeownership is nearly always treated as desirable—symbolizing wealth and status throughout the society.[1] Homeowners are widely regarded as the backbone of the large and stable group that will mow lawns, support local schools, worship regularly, pick up litter, obey traffic laws, and perform the thousand acts of responsibility that weld a community together.

By the time they reach their fifties, 90 percent of Americans own their own homes.[2] Government analysts, economists, and census bureau officials worriedly track whether each succeeding generation is finding its way into homeownership as its parents did, implicitly assuming that once people have made it, policymakers can shift their concern elsewhere. But those who work with assets and debt see a darker underside of homeownership: the struggle to keep a home in the face of economic upheaval.

For most middle-class Americans, homes are and will remain the family's most valuable asset, a financial shelter as well as a physical one. But the bankruptcy files show a persistent subgroup of Americans slipping through a slender but devastating crack in middle-class stability. For these homeowners, the home itself may be the debtors' financial ruin, with its relentless demands for mortgage payments, maintenance, and taxes. For some, the refusal to abandon a home that is no longer affordable brings them to collapse.

A look at the homeowners in bankruptcy is a hard look at the clash between hope and reality. Precisely because homeownership is about status, about participation in a community, about school districts and opportunities for children, about family memories and continuity, about emotional as well as financial security, homeowners do not make decisions based entirely on economic criteria. The homeowners in bankruptcy are often those debtors who cannot bear to give up the ground they have gained. And in their desperate struggle to hang on, they fall deeper and deeper into financial ruin. These data show that the home is a matter both of heart and of hard financial truth—and a significant part of the story of middle-class vulnerability.

## A Helping Hand

To help Americans achieve homeownership has been one of the most persistent, well-supported domestic policy goals of all levels of government for more than fifty years. Federal income tax laws, state property tax laws, the Federal Home Loan Bank, the Federal Housing Administration, slum clearance projects, construction subsidies for low-income housing, the Community Reinvestment Act, Veteran's Administration loan guarantee programs, mortgage securitization programs, Fannie Mae and Freddie Mac, urban homestead laws, and financial institution regulations are among the many government programs designed in part to get more Americans into their own homes. During the 1980s, the federal government alone pumped more than a billion dollars each year into programs to help Americans buy homes, while states added substantial sums of their own.[3]

In the aggregate, these programs have been wildly successful. Nearly two-thirds of all Americans—64.2 percent—live in homes they own.[4] A higher proportion of Americans live in their own homes than do the citizens of many parts of the industrialized world, including parts of Western Europe, Russia, China, and Japan.[5] From the Great Depression, when homeownership rates fell to 44 percent, until the 1980s, when nearly two of every three families lived in their own homes, the trend toward homeownership was consistently upward.[6] Housing affordability has also improved; on average, homes are now more affordable as a percentage of income than a decade ago.[7]

Not only have Americans bought their own homes over the past decades, but the homes they bought have gotten better.[8] During the 1980s, newly built housing units were 21 percent larger than in the preceding decade.[9] The fraction of the population living in homes of at least seven rooms rose, while those living in homes with only two rooms was cut in half.[10] By 1990, nearly 90 percent of homeowners lived in detached, single-family homes.[11]

Census data show that once Americans become homeowners, they tend to remain homeowners throughout their active lives.[12] American homeownership is a cumulative phenomenon, as a growing number of people attain homeownership status over time. As we noted above, by their fifties and sixties, nearly 90 percent of Americans live in their own homes.[13] Only late in life, when some elderly Americans opt for apartments, for institutional living, or for moving in with other family members is there any significant shift away from homeownership to some other housing status.[14]

Homeownership is, in some sense, the ultimate symbol of middle-class security. Homeowners, on average, have substantially higher incomes and more substantial assets than renters.[15] Homeowners are slightly older as a group than renters,[16] and they tend to move less frequently.[17] They are more immune to the pressures of inflation and recession, and according to researcher David Caplovitz, they are less likely to feel mental stress, unhappiness, or marital strain.[18] They are the most solid and financially secure portion of the middle class.

Concern over the ability of newcomers to enter the housing market is the dominant concern of housing policy, and it frames the dominant social and economic issues in one direction. Housing policymakers concentrate on increasing the opportunities for Americans to become homeowners. They worry, quite appropriately, over the homeless who are unable to obtain shelter. Policymakers also express concern over shifts in data suggesting that homeownership may be moving out of the reach of some groups.[19] The implicit assumption of most housing research is that once a person can purchase a home, that person is safely ensconced in the financially secure middle class.[20] After that, it is mostly a question of whether to paint the living room eggshell white or to build a deck this summer.

By all accounts, a book about the fractures in the solid financial stability of the middle class should not have a chapter on homeownership. It should simply note in passing that homeowners are safely ensconced in the middle class; those subject to serious economic risk are renters. But the bankruptcy data show that homeowners are not insulated from the economic catastrophes that strike the middle class. Indeed, the data suggest that homeownership itself may be part of the problem, the cement life raft that causes some Americans in financial difficulty to drown in their debts.

202

## Homeowners Entering Bankruptcy

Homeowners enter bankruptcy in significant numbers. About half of all the debtors in our five-state bankruptcy subsample owned their own homes. If these data are representative of debtors throughout the country in 1998, then about 650,000 homeowners filed for bankruptcy that year.

Each bankruptcy story has its own particularities, but Don Wilson tells a fairly familiar story. He is thirty-six years old. He went to college, but he didn't graduate. He has never been married. He explains his experience as a homeowner in Havertown, a suburb of Philadelphia: "The reason for my bankruptcy is that I tried my luck in the ownership of a house and found out that I got in over my head, and from then on I kept sinking deeper in debt to when I can't get out, and as it looks to the point where the future looks bleak on the status of my house." Don has moderate unsecured debt—$2,079—which, on an income of $24,636, he seems to have managed without too much difficulty. He owes no credit card bills and no unpaid taxes. But his secured debt is $87,980, of which $85,000 is a home mortgage. Don had a period of unemployment during the two years before he filed, but he does not blame that for his bankruptcy. Instead, he explains that he bought a house that he simply could not afford.

What is likely to happen to Don in bankruptcy? As he already knows, if he cannot keep up with the payments, he will lose the house. Bankruptcy can rid him of his unsecured debt, but that will do little to change the financial squeeze he faces. Don is in Chapter 13, which means that he will have time to pay off the mortgage payments he skipped and get on track with his mortgage company again. But he will have to keep current on the mortgage payments while he catches up on the past due amounts, which means he will face higher monthly house payments than ever before.

A financial planner would have told Don not to file bankruptcy. He could simply sell the house. According to Don's report, the house is worth $160,000, which gives him about $75,000 in equity, so he could likely pay off all his mortgage debt and his other debts as well. Don could start over. He might lose some of whatever he put into the house by way of down payment or repairs, leaving him where he was back before he bought a house—minus any down payment he had saved. On the other hand, if Don waited until the last minute and the house was about to suffer foreclosure (and the far-below-market sale price foreclosures bring), the financial planner would tell him to file Chapter 7 to stop the foreclosure and let the bankruptcy trustee sell the house. In other words, Don has the option to sell the house himself (if he has time) and use his equity to pay off his creditors, or Don may let the trustee in bankruptcy sell the house (if Don is facing foreclosure) and the trustee will use the equity to pay off the creditors. Either way, Don loses his house and the equity is used to pay the creditors. Because he lives in a state with no homestead exemption, he cannot protect the equity in his property at state law, but if he files for bankruptcy he can preserve $15,000 of the equity for himself to start over again.

But the desire to hang on to a home overcomes the quiet reasoning of a financial planner. According to his files, Don plans to repay his mortgage debts in full. He intends to catch up on the payments, including interest and penalties, making up where he has fallen behind. He plans to stretch out his nonmortgage debt payments so that he can concentrate his financial efforts on his home mortgage. The house is sinking him, but Don is not ready to give it up.

For Don to succeed in Chapter 13 and to keep his home, he must pay *all* his mortgage arrearages, including the past due payments, outstanding penalties, and accumulated interest. Because he has substantial equity in the house and the bankruptcy laws require a debtor to pay creditors at least as much as they would have gotten in liquidation, Don will also have to propose a full payment for his small amount of unsecured debt.[21]

What are the chances that Don will be able to complete his Chapter 13 payments? If he is like other debtors in bankruptcy, the answer is: not good. More than two out of three debtors who file for Chapter 13 are unable to continue their payments through to a successful conclusion.[22] Don may make up some of his back payments on his mortgage, but the odds are he will fail to pay off his plan in full and keep his house.

Don represents the two-edged sword of homeownership that reveals itself in the bankruptcy files. The proportion of homeowners in bankruptcy is lower than in the population generally. As mentioned above, about 64.2 percent of all Americans were homeowners in 1991, which means that about a third more Americans in the general population own homes than in the bankruptcy sample.[23] The debtors in bankruptcy are not a perfect cross-section of Americans. Instead, bankruptcy is more likely to occur among nonhomeowners. At the same time, the proportion of homeowners such as Don is not small. About half of all the debtors who file for bankruptcy own homes when they file.[24]

Even among the nonhomeowning population in bankruptcy there are debtors with homeownership problems. The half of the debtors who are not homeowners include some families who once lived in their own homes but fell back to renter status before they filed their bankruptcy petitions. Of the 2,010 debtors who explained their reasons for filing bankruptcy, 28 mentioned homes they had lost through foreclosure. These debtors' foreclosure sales had not yielded enough money to pay off their home mortgages, and they were in bankruptcy to deal with the remaining debts they were legally obligated to pay even after their homes had been sold to others.[25] These debtors represent another 1.4 percent of the sample who were trying to cope with the lingering implications of homeownership.

This number may still understate the number of debtors who had already lost homes before they filed. Because the foreclosure data are not based on an answer to a systematic question, such as "Did you lose your home before filing?" the available information is only incidentally reported. Some debtors happened to mention losing their homes as part of an open-ended statement of the reason for bankruptcy. Debtors who lost their homes but who did not have large deficiencies to make up with their mortgage companies would have been unlikely to mention this as a factor in their filing decisions. Others who wrote "too much debt" or "creditors are after [me] for what I cannot pay" may have had in mind the mortgage debts they still owed on homes that were long gone—or they may have had in mind other debts. All that we can state with certainty is that some fraction of the debtors listed as renters had been homeowners not long before their filings, suggesting that the bankruptcy risk for homeowners is larger than these numbers reflect.

The data reported here may understate the financial risks faced by homeowners in yet another way. The consumer bankruptcy data are gathered only from debtors who filed for Chapter 7 and Chapter 13. These two chapters are where most individual debtors file, but people are legally permitted to file for Chapter 11 as well. They rarely have reason to do so because the Chapter 11 procedures, which are designed for business bankruptcies, are more complex and more expensive. For debtors reluctant to file for Chapter 7 because they would risk being forced to liquidate all their assets, Chapter 13 is often the preferred alternative.[26] But Chapter 13 puts a cap on secured debt ($350,000 at the time these data were gathered). For debtors trying to save a home with a large mortgage (or a second or third mortgage that put the total secured debt beyond $350,000), the only alternative is to file for Chapter 11. There is some indication that homeowners in financial trouble in parts of the country with very expensive real estate markets may have filed for Chapter 11 rather than in Chapter 13 or Chapter 7.[27]

These data show regional variation, but based on the comments from the debtors and on the Chapter 11 data from California, it is a reasonable estimation that about half the individuals who declare bankruptcy are homeowners, with the number climbing above two-thirds in some states.[28] The remarkable aspect of this finding is not that homeowners are underrepresented in bankruptcy but that the underrepresentation is relatively modest. The pressing question is how did so many homeowners—perhaps more than 650,000 nationally in 1998 alone—get into so much trouble?[29]

## Mortgages: Certification of Economic Stability

The presumptive financial security of homeowners is evident in the process by which they purchase their homes. Homeowners nearly always purchase their homes—especially their first homes—with the help of a home mortgage. More than 90 percent of homebuyers need a mortgage to purchase a home.[30] In most cases, homebuyers made a down payment. The average down payment for a home purchased in 1991 was 22.6 percent of the purchase price, or about $30,350.[31] First-time homebuyers had lower down payments, but even they managed to muster, on average, an impressive $17,500 to enter the housing market.[32] Even if the typical debtor in bankruptcy did not enter the housing market recently or with a median down payment, these data suggest that at some point these debtors amassed substantial assets to acquire a home and demonstrate a reasonable prospect of economic security.

Some homeowners managed to buy their homes without meeting the stringent criteria and large down payments imposed by private lenders. The federal government sponsors programs that are specifically designed to help people get home mortgages for which they otherwise would not qualify. The Veterans Administration, for example, guarantees loans without requiring a down payment for certain first-time homebuyers who have served in the armed forces. With a somewhat weaker showing of financial capacity and a lower cash investment to protect, it is not surprising that borrowers on VA loans default at about twice the rate of borrowers on conventional loans.[33] Federal Housing Administration (FHA) purchasers enjoy special mortgage insurance subsidies as well, permitting buyers with lower down payments to qualify for home mortgages through subsidized mortgage insurance. These loans, too, have higher default rates, generally more than twice that of conventional mortgages.[34] The federal government has also provided below market interest rate loans to moderate-income families trying to purchase homes through the Homeownership Assistance Program and has encour-

206

aged banks to make similar loans through the Community Reinvestment Act.[35] Some buyers are subsidized in other, less formal ways. Parents or families may give or lend money for a down payment, permitting a first-time home buyer to stretch beyond the federal purchasing guidelines.

Whether most bankruptcy filers are the more tentative homeowners—either the new owners who have been subsidized in one form or another or those who have somehow slipped through the lending net—we cannot determine. The bankruptcy files contain no information about whether the bankrupt debtors were first-time buyers or home purchasers, whether they put up small down payments or substantial ones, whether they had owned their homes for a short time or many years, or whether they bought their home with the assistance of a government program or through conventional financing. The files contain only the bare information about the value of the real estate and the size of the mortgage against it.

There is one clue that a substantial portion of the homeowners in financial trouble may be among the more recent arrivals in the housing market. General housing trends show that first-time buyers are concentrated in their twenties and early thirties, with a median age for first-time buyers of about thirty-one.[36] As we already noted, these first-time buyers tend to have smaller down payments and, as a result, smaller equities in their homes.[37] Younger people also tend to have somewhat lower incomes.[38] The bankruptcy sample contains a substantial subset of debtors who are among the youngest homeowners. One in four of the homeowners in bankruptcy is still in his or her twenties, and more than 40 percent of homeowners are under thirty-five. By comparison, among homeowners in the general population, only 17 percent are under age thirty-five.[39] Young homeowners are more than twice as likely to be in bankruptcy as their older counterparts.

These data suggest that some of the homeowners in bankruptcy are those who had not accumulated much wealth in their home equity or who had made mortgage payments for only a few years. Moreover, it is a fair inference that many of the young homeowners fell into trouble relatively soon after they acquired their first home, if only because their youth prevented them from having been homeowners for any extended time. This disproportionately large fraction of bankrupt young homeowners suggests that young homeowners may be particularly vulnerable to financial disruption.

But nowhere is it clearer that bankrupt debtors are a cross-section of all Americans than among the files of the homeowners. Although a substantial portion of the homeowners are likely first-time buyers, an even larger fraction are not. Sixty percent of the homeowners in bankruptcy are over thirty-five, and about half are over fifty, making it likely that an even more substantial portion of the homeowners in bankruptcy either have been in their homes for an extended time or have already moved on from their first homes into subsequent homes.[40] The sizeable fraction of homeowners in bankruptcy who are over thirty-five suggests a real vulnerability for established home-owners as well as their younger counterparts.

Notwithstanding the age differences among homeowners, there is an overriding and powerfully important similarity: in virtually all these cases the borrowers evidenced strong credit records and proofs of earnings adequate to meet their projected monthly ex-penses. Whether they were applying for loans from FHA or conventionally, whether their folks were putting up part of the down payment or they had saved for years, they needed to pass a home mortgage application. To succeed in that application, virtually all of the homeowners now in bankruptcy were, at one time, able to demonstrate in careful detail that they had steady incomes, strong credit histories, manageable outstanding debt, and cash on hand for down payments, closing costs, and emergencies. Without those qualifications, they could not have received a mortgage.

Nearly all would-be homeowners who apply for a mortgage must meet fairly rigid criteria showing that their mortgage payments, including taxes and insurance and a set-aside for maintenance and repairs, would not disrupt a reasonable budget. Unlike many other credit markets, the home mortgage market has a fair degree of standardization. To run a profitable mortgage lending operation, most mortgage lenders, from private companies to banks, need to be able to sell their mortgages in the secondary mortgage market. To generate marketable loans, lenders must demonstrate that their borrowers meet standardized lending criteria.

Key among the criteria are those established by the Federal National Mortgage Association (Fannie Mae, to its friends). A loan that does not meet these guidelines will be effectively barred from much of the secondary mortgage market and therefore be unattractive to most mortgage issuers. Fannie Mae guidelines require that "monthly housing expenses should not represent more than 25 to 28 percent of gross monthly income."[41] For the homeowners in bankruptcy, then, not only has someone determined that their credit is solid but, at least according to this widely used rule of thumb, that their projected budget is also manageable.[42]

That these debtors could survive the most searching financial scrutiny most Americans will ever face only to find themselves in bankruptcy a few years later is a stark reminder that even solid financial security can be fleeting. The bankruptcies of these homeowners represent a stunning fall from a perch of seeming financial security that had been certified by a mortgage lender as within the government guidelines of financial security.

The irony of the homeowners' fall into bankruptcy is sharp. Not only did many of them survive rigorous financial scrutiny, but even those who stretched beyond their capacity to buy and those who jumped into real estate markets they only dimly understood, were in some sense prudent people. When they bought their homes, many of these debtors were people who were making an effort to save rather than to consume. They were not the heedless grasshoppers who ran up credit card bills and waited until tomorrow to think about what to do. Nor were they the people who failed to plan for their futures. Instead, these were the people who saw themselves as purchasing a huge asset, acquiring both social status and an important long-term, tax-favored investment.

Such attitudes are generally borne out by the facts of economic life for middle-class Americans. Not only are homeowners wealthier than renters, homes represent the bulk of personal wealth for most people.[43] About 42 percent of the net worth of individuals in the United States is held in their homes.[44] A home is an asset that typically rises in value both as real estate becomes more valuable and as the homeowner pays down the balance due on the mortgage.[45]

The investment aspect of homeownership is a powerful factor in home-purchase decisions. In areas with declining real estate values, and hence increasing affordability, it would seem that new home buyers would flock into the market to take advantage of increasing

209

opportunities to become homeowners. Instead, however, in such declining markets new home purchases drop, even when the data are controlled for other economic factors. The reason, according to a leading housing expert, is that in a falling market nonhomeowners do not regard the investment potential for real estate as high, and they stay out of the housing market.[46] Conversely, in a rising market as affordability becomes more problematic, nonhomeowners stretch harder to buy homes and all buyers work harder to buy homes that will require a greater fraction of their incomes for mortgage payments in the belief that the investment will pay off over time.[47] People may love their homes, but these data suggest that they love them as much for what they represent in investment potential and financial security as for their large closets and charming flower gardens.

In some ways, homeowners represent an entrepreneurial slice of the middle class. These are the people who take on significant debt, planning to deny themselves other pleasures for some years and acknowledging that they may even struggle financially for a while. They undertake these burdens in the belief that they will ultimately own property of substantial value. Some of the bankrupt homeowners obviously took on too much risk, but there is no reason to believe that very many exceeded government guidelines on debt on their mortgages. The question for the remainder of this chapter is how these credit-worthy, asset-buying homeowners ended up comprising about half of the bankruptcy sample.

## Oh, Those Crazy Eighties

It is impossible to write a book about homeowners in the 1990s and beyond without pausing to reflect on the wild housing market of the 1980s. That decade offered homebuyers unprecedented opportunities to ride an economic roller-coaster, and some took the ride with little cash investment. Pundits encouraged homeowners to view their homes as economic opportunities, suggesting that they use various creative financing devices to acquire as much real estate as they could, bolstered by the "fact" that housing prices would always rise. Infomercials and popular books explained how folks could get rich in the real estate market with no money down. Real estate speculation resembled an epidemic, as boom and bust cycles traveled from the Sunbelt to the Northeast to the West Coast. While the real-estate craziness of the 1980s explains many business bankruptcies and the massive savings-and-loan debacle, it provides only a part, and not the major part, of the explanation for the large number of homeowners we found in bankruptcy in 1991.

It is true that the 1980s home mortgage marketplace was not always the sober, reflective monolith that a review of lending regulations evokes. During the early 1980s, mortgage rates shot through the roof with double-digit inflation, but then tumbled downward again as inflation was brought to heel.[48] Savings and loan institutions lent billions to developers to turn sugar beet fields into housing developments and marginally profitable apartment houses into high-rise condos. To double up on their profits, lending institutions financed construction loans and then made mortgage loans to the new homebuyers. When real estate markets began to soften, lending institutions redoubled their consumer lending efforts, working with failing developers to finance more consumer buyers so that the developers would not default on their huge construction loans.

As one region of the country after another saw real estate values plunge, buyers faced the unpleasant reality that they not only could not pay for what they had bought, but they also could not sell their property for enough money to cover their current loan balances. Lenders, overwhelmed by bad commercial and residential real estate loans (along with many other varieties of bad loans) went bust in record numbers.[49] For the ten-year period from 1971 through 1980, 79 insured banks were closed in the United States because of financial difficulties.[50] In the twelve-year period 1980 to 1992, 1,506 banks insured by the Bank Insurance Fund (BIF) were closed or merged into other, stronger banks.[51]

It may never be possible to document the lapses in prudent lending practices that accompanied the rise and fall of the real estate markets in the 1980s, but the important point for us is that there is ample evidence that for individual, middle-class borrowers, the financial problems of homeownership were not primarily those that arose in the unusual real estate market fluctuations of the 1980s.

Mortgage delinquency rates, a good measure of the number of shaky borrowers, climbed steadily throughout the 1970s and into the early 1980s. But the rate leveled off about 1985 and then began to de-

211

cline slowly.[52] In general, as the markets fluctuated more wildly and busts chased booms around the country, the proportion of debtors who could not meet their mortgage obligations remained fairly constant. The real estate debacles of the 1980s, and the consequent failures of financial institutions, were more likely fueled by the speculators and entrepreneurs who tried their hands at office buildings, shopping centers, and apartment houses. These data suggest that individual homeowners were not the ones who pushed their lenders into liquidation, nor was a unique homeowners' buying spree responsible for the large number of homeowners in bankruptcy in the early 1990s.

The bankruptcy data from an earlier period reinforce the idea that it was not the 1980s real estate market that suddenly drove homeowners into the bankruptcy courts. In 1981, well in advance of the boom and bust cycles of the 1980s, 52 percent of the individual debtors in our bankruptcy sample were homeowners. This means that homeowners comprised a larger fraction of the bankrupt population before the 1980s than they did a decade later. To be sure, the absolute number of homeowners in bankruptcy rose dramatically during the 1980s, but so did the absolute number of renters in bankruptcy. Proportionately the two remained in rough equilibrium, suggesting that whatever ills befell Americans during the decade, they were not misfortunes that fell disproportionately on those buying homes in fluctuating real estate markets. These data suggest that although the wild gyrations of the 1980s may have caught some debtors, the vulnerability of homeowners to financial catastrophe is a persistent problem.[53]

The impact of unstable real estate markets in the 1980s may have been felt in more subtle ways. A few debtors may have been the aggressive recipients of free and easy lending practices. But the bulk of the debtors in bankruptcy—like the bulk of their counterparts in the population generally—did not try get-rich-quick schemes in real estate. Instead, they purchased in high markets, perhaps taking on somewhat more debt than was entirely prudent. The market came back to haunt them when they later discovered either that declining business conditions cut their expected incomes or that they could not bail out from an expensive house by selling it for more than they had paid.

**HOUSING**

Ralph and Mary Ellen Mackley tell a tale familiar in the bankruptcy files. They live in Port Arthur, a small town in east Texas. Ralph has a college degree, and Mary Ellen is a high school graduate. Ralph was forty-three and unemployed at the time they filed their bankruptcy petition. Mary Ellen was thirty-seven and stayed home full time with their children. They explained why they filed: "We purchased a home near Austin, Texas at the height of the real estate and construction boom of 1985. The economy slowed down and people began to default on payments to me for work completed. I subsequently was unable to continue making the payments and the property went into foreclosure. I am now being sued for the deficiency." Not only could Ralph and Mary Ellen not manage their monthly payments on the Austin home, but when they lost the house in a foreclosure sale, they still owed more than the mortgage amount. They were responsible for the difference, in effect paying on their mortgage long after the home was gone—while they rented a house elsewhere. Ralph and Mary Ellen filed in Chapter 7, where they discharged their outstanding debts. Bankruptcy did not save anything for them; it put them back up to zero on their balance sheet—which, they seemed to think, was a substantial improvement.

The real estate fluctuations of the 1980s hit Ralph and Mary Ellen twice: they bought high, which put the squeeze on them when their income dropped, and they couldn't bail out by selling their home once the market fell. If the market had remained steady, Ralph and Mary Ellen could have avoided a foreclosure by selling the property on their own when they couldn't make the mortgage payments, using the sale proceeds to pay off the outstanding mortgage debt. They might even have ended up with something to tide them over through Ralph's unemployment. Ralph and Mary Ellen ended up in foreclosure only because their mortgage exceeded what their house would bring by the time of the sale. As an aside, we note that Ralph and Mary Ellen are not among the homeowners in our sample. They are listed as nonhomeowners in our data, even though they had a serious homeownership problem to deal with. Their Austin house was long gone, and they had not been able to buy another house in Port Arthur, so at the time of filing, they were renters.

Notwithstanding a home's powerful symbol of middle-class stability, our data show that homeowners flocked to the bankruptcy courts, taking up about half the seats of those who declare themselves economic failures.

## Homeowners and Renters: Better Off, Worse Off

The homeowners who file for bankruptcy tell their stories in encapsulated form: they are both richer and poorer than the other debtors who file for bankruptcy. They are the debtors with higher incomes and larger assets—and they are the debtors who are carrying substantial mortgages in addition to a mountain of other debt. The basic financial data for the homeowners who filed for bankruptcy, along with a comparison group of the nonhomeowners, are available in Table 7.1. The data reported here show that homeowners have higher incomes than renters. At the median, a homeowner in bankruptcy earns $22,800, while a renter earns only $14,600. The bankrupt debtor who is a homeowner has an income about one-and-a-half-times larger than that of a bankrupt renter. In this sense, bankruptcy reflects the rest of the world, where those with higher incomes are homeowners and those with lower incomes are not.

The assets listed reinforce the view that homeowners are the more affluent among bankrupt debtors. Homeowners in bankruptcy report median assets valued at $61,400, while renters in bankruptcy report assets worth less than $3,800. The principal difference, of course, is the value of the home, but nonhome assets are also higher among homeowners than among nonhomeowners. In other words, homeowners own more personal property than do nonhomeowners, at the median about $6,700 versus $3,800. Homeowners apparently use their higher incomes to purchase substantially more assets, including their homes, which they bring with them into bankruptcy. Their renter counterparts, by comparison, come into bankruptcy with little property.

The picture of relative affluence disappears, however, with an examination of the debt columns. The debt burdens of homeowners are three times larger at the median than those of renters. The debt information is subdivided to show the kind of debt they incurred. Homeowners and nonhomeowners have indistinguishable unsecured debt, but their secured debts are dramatically different. Homeowners report median secured debts of $50,500 compared with median secured

**Table 7.1**  Comparison of homeowners and renters in bankruptcy

| OWN HOME? | Total annual income | Total assets | Total debt | Amount of home mortgate | Non-mortgage debt |
|---|---|---|---|---|---|
| YES | | | | | |
| Mean | 25,194 | 79,297 | 85,652 | 58,066 | 27,236 |
| s.d | 13,084 | 66,121 | 93,529 | 83,413 | 48,998 |
| 25th percentile | 15,600 | 41,682 | 34,786 | 21,500 | 8,200 |
| Median | 22,790 | 61,427 | 63,000 | 44,000 | 17,447 |
| 75th percentile | 31,623 | 87,438 | 100,307 | 68,000 | 33,991 |
| Valid cases | 286 | 296 | 298 | 291 | 290 |
| Missing | 14 | 4 | 2 | 9 | 10 |
| | | | | | |
| NO | | | | | |
| Mean | 16,342 | 6,744 | 31,281 | 0 | 32,494 |
| s.d. | 8,949 | 11,332 | 51,773 | 0 | 55,254 |
| 25th percentile | 10,704 | 1,746 | 11,617 | 0 | 11,588 |
| Median | 14,574 | 3,775 | 19,082 | 0 | 18,908 |
| 75th percentile | 21,408 | 8,100 | 30,979 | 0 | 31,194 |
| Valid cases | 346 | 379 | 374 | 314 | 306 |
| Missing | 38 | 5 | 10 | 70 | 78 |
| t-value | 9.34 | 18.67 | 9.00 | 11.88 | 1.23 |
| significance level | *** | *** | *** | *** | ns |

ns = not significant at $p < .05$
*** $p < .001$

*Source:* Consumer Bankruptcy Project II, 1991.

debts of $2,000 for nonhomeowners. One obvious inference is that the difference in secured debt is attributable to the difference between owing money on a home mortgage and perhaps a car versus owing money only on a car.[54]

The more detailed data show that most of the difference in secured debt between homeowners and nonhomeowners is the home mortgage. Mean home mortgage debt for homeowners was $58,000, with median debt somewhat more modest at $44,000. When home mortgages are stripped from the secured debt, the differences between homeowners and nonhomeowners disappear. In other words, homeowners borrow money to buy cars, purchase furniture on time, and offer their personal property as collateral for loans at about the same level as nonhomeowners. The difference in the debt burdens between the two groups results from the ever-present mortgage.

The burden of the home mortgage is driven home by the fact that, even with their larger incomes, homeowners in bankruptcy carry total debts that are about two and a half times larger than their annual incomes.[55] As we regularly note throughout this book, including mortgages in a debt-to-income ratio is somewhat misleading; no one expects the home mortgage to be paid in full right away. And yet, unlike most renters, who can go through bankruptcy and discharge most outstanding debts without losing a single asset, the homeowner faces a steady stream of principal, interest, taxes, and insurance payments that must be maintained before, during, and after bankruptcy or the homeowner will be forced to give up the house for sale or foreclosure.[56]

The point here is not to try to measure the relative pain of bankruptcy for homeowners and renters; economic failure is undoubtedly painful for both. Instead, the point is that about half of the debtors file for bankruptcy with the higher incomes, higher assets, and higher debt burdens that come with homeownership. They are both richer and poorer as they file. These solidly middle-class people face painful choices as they try to cope with unmanageable debts while they try to find some way to keep their homes.

## Homeowners, Bankrupt and Not

The comparison of bankrupt homeowners with bankrupt renters demonstrates the mixed financial blessing of homeownership. But when homeowners in bankruptcy are compared with the group from which they emerged—homeowners in the general population—the depths of their financial troubles are etched in even sharper relief. This comparison between homeowners in bankruptcy and homeowners in the general population also provides some inferential clues about how these homeowners, drawn from among the most financially secure Americans, got into so much trouble.

Bankrupt homeowners seem to lack the income security of their nonbankrupt neighbors. When homeowners who filed for bankruptcy were compared with renters who filed, homeowners were the more affluent debtors. They earned 154 percent of the income of their renter counterparts. In the population generally, however, the gap

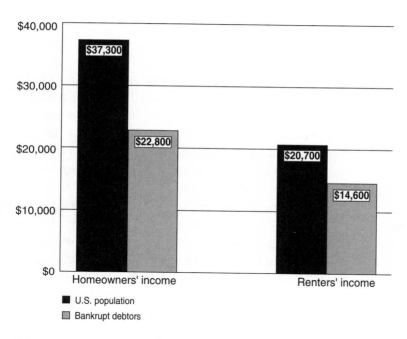

$40,000

$30,000

$20,000

$10,000

$0

$37,300

$22,800

$20,700

$14,600

Homeowners' income

Renters' income

■ U.S. population
▢ Bankrupt debtors

Fig. 7.1 Income comparisons of bankrupt debtors and U.S. population for homeowners and renters, 1991. *Note:* All numbers are reported in 1991 dollars. *Source:* Consumer Bankruptcy Project II, 1991; U.S. population calculated from *Statistical Abstract: 1993,* 458, table 713.

between homeowners and renters was larger. At the median, the incomes of homeowners were 187 percent of renters.[57] Homeowners outside bankruptcy support their home mortgages and other obligations on incomes that are relatively much larger than the incomes of renters.

The differences in the relative burdens of homeowners in and out of bankruptcy can be demonstrated with another comparison of income. Incomes of all bankrupt debtors are depressed relative to the incomes of Americans generally (fig. 7.1). In 1991 renters in the general population earned median incomes of about $20,700, while renters who filed for bankruptcy earned less at about $14,600.[58] This means that bankrupt renters earn about 70 percent of the income renters earn in the general population. Homeowners, by comparison, face a broader chasm. Outside bankruptcy the median homeowner earns about $37,300, while the median family income for home-

**HOUSING**

owners in bankruptcy is $22,800.[59] Homeowners in bankruptcy have incomes slightly less than two-thirds—about 61 percent—as large as the incomes of homeowners in the general population.[60]

The double comparisons of income show that homeowners are in a tight squeeze. In bankruptcy, they look more like renters than do their counterparts outside bankruptcy. Moreover, the income gap between homeowners in the general population and homeowners in bankruptcy is larger than the income gap for renters. The income differences are particularly important in the case of homeowners because of the significant debt loads they carry.

Homeowners in and out of bankruptcy are united not only by their decision to buy a home but also by their need to take on substantial mortgages to do so.[61] In 1991 the median outstanding mortgage—combining old mortgages and new—of homeowning Americans generally was $44,334.[62] The same year, homeowners in the bankruptcy sample owed a median mortgage debt of $44,000. Bankrupt homeowners thus carry nearly identical mortgage debt burdens as nonbankrupt homeowners.

The mortgage debts may be similar, but the relative burdens imposed by those debts are not. Bankrupt debtors with their lower incomes are necessarily devoting larger shares of their incomes to paying those mortgage debts. It is possible to develop some measure of the relative burden homeowners face in keeping their homes. Homeowners in the United States spend, on average, about 18 percent of their annual incomes for principal, interest, taxes, and insurance for their homes.[63] Fannie Mae, as we noted earlier, has determined that "monthly housing expenses should not represent more than 25 to 28 percent of gross monthly income."[64] Those whose incomes exceed such levels are dubbed by housing experts as "house poor."[65] They are, according to the experts, spending such a large fraction of their income on housing that they are placing their financial security in jeopardy.

Using the Fannie Mae guidelines, the Census Bureau estimates that about 10 percent of American homeowners are "house poor."[66] By this estimate, about one in ten homeowners in the population generally is at risk of being sunk financially by housing costs. When homeowners in bankruptcy are compared with homeowners generally, the proportion of "house poor" owners rises sharply.[67] About 69 percent of the homeowners in bankruptcy exceed the Fannie Mae guidelines for housing expenditures.[68] By this calculation, seven out of ten of the homeowner debtors are "house poor."

Another measure of financial health is nonmortgage debt. Nonmortgage debt tends to be short-term, high-interest debt, consuming a relatively larger fraction of immediate income. A homeowner could withstand a relatively larger burden of mortgage debt if other debt were only nominal. Unfortunately, homeowners are not insulated from the need (or desire) for consumer debt, and they have substantial nonmortgage debt burdens. The nonmortgage debt burden per household in the population generally is about $8,000. Bankrupt debtors have more than twice as much short-term, high-interest debt: their median nonmortgage debt is $17,500.[69]

It is possible to combine the comparisons of income, mortgage debt, and nonmortgage debt for homeowners in bankruptcy with homeowners in the general population. In every comparison, the news is bad for the homeowners in bankruptcy. They carry similar mortgage debts and higher nonmortgage debts than their homeowner counterparts in the general population, and they do so on substantially lower incomes. Although homeowners might survive lower incomes or higher consumer debt, especially if their mortgage debt was somewhat lower than average, the combination of all three factors may be lethal (fig. 7.2).

Bankrupt homeowners' debts outstrip their incomes by every measure. The homeowners who file for bankruptcy are loaded with inescapable mortgage obligations, on top of which they frequently carry more than twice the nonmortgage debt of other homeowners — all on incomes that are a third lower than other homeowners. For some, like Don Wilson, bankruptcy comes to the first-time homebuyer in over his head. For others, like Ralph and Mary Ellen Mackley, homeownership is a comfortable indication of their overall economic stability until a cutback in income makes the house an impossible burden. Perhaps the homeowners in bankruptcy have tried too hard to be middle class, or at least too hard to maintain the ultimate symbol of the middle class. The resulting financial collapse should not be surprising.

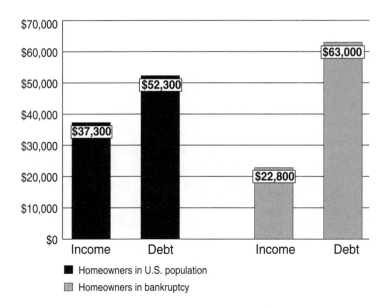

Fig. 7.2 Homeowners' debt and income for bankrupt debtors and U.S. population, 1991. *Source:* Consumer Bankruptcy Project II, 1991; U.S. population calculated from *Statistical Abstract: 1993,* 458, table 713. Debt was calculated for homeowners by adding median mortgage debt of $44,300 and median nonmortgage debt of $8,000 (Bureau of the Census, *American Housing Survey for the United States in 1991,* Current Housing Reports, Ser. H150/91 [Washington, D.C., 1993], table 3.15). To preserve a similarity of approach, the debt for bankrupt homeowners was calculated by adding the median mortgage and nonmortgage debt from table 7.1.

## Home Equity—America's Hidden Savings

The discussion thus far has omitted an important question: What happened to the value of the house? After all, a mortgage is only part of the financial picture of homeownership. One person may owe $50,000 on a home valued at $100,000 while a second owes $50,000 on a house valued at $50,000. Both have the same substantial debt with which they must deal, and both may face losing their homes if their incomes are inadequate to meet their mortgage payments. But no one would describe the two as being in the same financial circumstances. Surely the first homeowner, with a reserve of value in the family home, is in better financial shape.

For most Americans, home equity represents their single biggest source of personal wealth.[70] Homeowners have more value tied up in home equities than in savings accounts and certificates of deposit, stocks and mutual funds, cars, retirement accounts, and other real estate combined.[71] For these people, the home mortgage is a burden, to be sure, but it represents continuing payments on their largest asset.

The Census Bureau has studied the relation between mortgages and home value, trying to determine the wealth that each homeowner has built up over time. The bureau reports that when mortgage debt and home values are matched for each homeowner, at the median, Americans' mortgages average only 57.4 percent of the value of their homes. In 1991 the median home equity for homeowners was $43,078.[72] This means that the national median equity in a home is larger than the national median income for a year—not a bad nest egg to tuck away.

When we match the data on the same debtor-by-debtor basis for the families in bankruptcy, a different picture emerges. Don Wilson's substantial equity was very much the exception. At the median, the debtors in bankruptcy carry mortgages that are 87.3 percent of the value of their homes. The median home equity for homeowners in bankruptcy is a relatively paltry $5,500.[73]

Equity was calculated on a debtor-by-debtor basis by subtracting all listed mortgages from the listed value of the home (fig. 7.3).[74] If the mortgages listed were greater than the home value, equity was reported at zero, rather than a negative number. In one sense, this approach inflates the report of equity by boosting negative equities to zero, but it gives a more accurate representation of the amount of positive value to be protected. The data demonstrate that the homes of bankrupt debtors represent substantially less value than the homes of most other homeowners.[75]

A quarter of the debtors have no home equity.[76] The mortgage on their property equals or exceeds the value of the home for one in four of the homeowners in bankruptcy. These debtors have no financial reserve tucked away in the homes that they are trying to protect through the bankruptcy courts. In effect, the bankrupt homeowners are tenaciously hanging on to their homes that are no longer financial assets. The debtors negotiate with their mortgage lenders to pay off their mortgages in full; if instead they turned the homes over to their lenders, the lenders would be unlikely to recover payment in

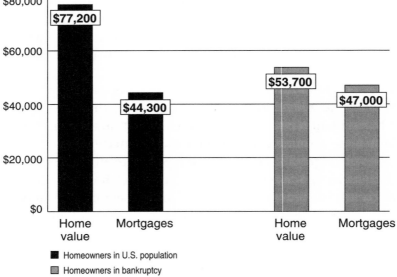

$80,000

$60,000

$40,000

$20,000

$0

$77,200

$44,300

$53,700

$47,000

Home value    Mortgages                Home value    Mortgages

■ Homeowners in U.S. population
▢ Homeowners in bankruptcy

Fig. 7.3 Home equity, in and out of bankruptcy. *Source:* Consumer Bankruptcy Project II, 1991; U.S. population calculated from *Statistical Abstract: 1993*, 725, table 1237; Bureau of the Census, *American Housing Survey for the United States in 1991*, Current Housing Reports, Ser. H150/91 (Washington, D.C., 1993), table 3.15.

full for the outstanding mortgages. Finally, the debtors end up in bankruptcy, still clinging to their homes. It should also be noted that the equity the debtors list is probably higher than the amount that would be obtained at a foreclosure sale. Such sales are notorious for fetching low prices.[77] The debtors are likely listing equities based on what they believe their homes would bring on the real-estate market, not the much lower values associated with forced sales.[78]

While the mortgage lender was often played in the early movies as an evil man with a long mustache that curled up on the ends, today many mortgage lenders hate the idea of taking homes almost as much as the homeowners hate losing them. It is unlikely that a buyer will show up at a foreclosure sale with enough money to pay off the large mortgage. Instead, the mortgage lender will probably have to buy the property and remarket it after the foreclosure sale. Most mainstream mortgage lenders are not in the real estate business and do not want to be.[79] They were looking forward to a secure thirty-year income stream, and instead they have an expensive and

**HOUSING**

often unprofitable mess to clean up. Legal fees for foreclosures are high, the loans are often delinquent by months or even years, and the condition of the property can be very uncertain. As a result, some mortgage lenders are eager to see a troubled borrower file for a Chapter 7 bankruptcy, since the other debts can be discharged and the debtor can cure the defaults on the mortgage debt and continue regular home payments. Having eliminated their other debts, the debtors are much better able to service the mortgage and maintain the property and are less likely to end up in foreclosure. In Chapter 13, where debtors continue their payments over time, it is not clear if as many homeowners are able to stabilize financially and save their homes, but at least they are trying to work it out so that they can pay without forcing the property into foreclosure.

The home equity that is supposed to represent Americans' great tucked-away savings does not exist for a substantial subset of middle-class people who are house-poor. Whether the equity never existed or whether it disappeared in a falling market, it is gone by the time the debtors declare bankruptcy.

## Multiple Mortgages

The way Americans have incurred mortgage debt has changed significantly in the past two decades. In 1981 second mortgages accounted for less than 4 percent of outstanding home mortgage debt. By 1991 second mortgages were 12 percent of home mortgage debt, a three-fold rise in ten years.[80] Second mortgage debt has grown at a faster pace than all other forms of consumer debt except credit card debt.

One reason for this rise in second mortgage debt was the introduction of a new financing device: the home-equity line of credit. The homeowner signs a mortgage securing any money borrowed in the future under a line of credit from the lender. Thus the homeowner may owe nothing on the first day of the mortgage but will add to the amount of the mortgage with each charge. Alternatively, the mortgage often finances old unsecured debts, so the mortgage begins by securing the previously unsecured debt load, with more to be added with future charges. In either case, any default on the loan may lead to foreclosure of the mortgage and sale of the home. Unlike traditional fixed-term, fixed-amount second mortgages, these new devices provided borrowers with a line of credit that permitted borrowing, repayment, and borrowing again on a revolving basis. In 1980 fewer than 1 percent of all financial institutions offered home-equity lines of credit; by 1989, 80 percent of banks and 65 percent of savings and loans made such loans.[81] Consumer demand for such loans rose with changes in the tax code that eliminated the deductibility of consumer interest except for mortgage-type loans.[82] In addition, changes in federal banking regulations made such loans more attractive for lenders.[83] Home-equity loans provided a convenient, and seemingly clever, way to finance any number of new purchases. Such loans grew spectacularly from $1 billion in 1981 to $132 billion in 1991. Traditional second mortgages also grew substantially, from $59 billion to $225 billion in the same period.[84] Overall, the amount of mortgage debt increased three times faster than the value of the homes securing that debt.

The contemporary role of second mortgages—or at least one important role—is demonstrated by what has happened in the bankruptcy courts. Debtors in bankruptcy carry total mortgage obligations that are about the same as the obligations of their cohorts outside bankruptcy. But the path by which they obtained their current mortgage debt is noticeably different. Nearly all the debtors in bankruptcy have a mortgage on their property.[85] For about two-thirds of the homeowners, the first mortgage is the only mortgage, but the remaining third of the bankrupt debtors had second mortgages.[86] A handful (about 3.5 percent) had third mortgages, about half a percent had four or more, and we picked up one couple in the sample who listed ten mortgages against their home.[87] This is a far higher rate of second and subsequent mortgages than in the population generally. Bankrupt debtors are twice as likely to have second mortgages as homeowners with mortgages in the general population, and the rate of third or subsequent mortgages among the bankrupts is ten times higher.[88]

The data on multiple mortgages suggests that a substantial fraction of the homeowners in bankruptcy have built up their mortgage debt by borrowing against their homes after the initial purchase. As we noted earlier, the mortgage debt for homeowners in bankruptcy is $44,000, compared with a similar figure for homeowners generally of $44,334. Because our data indicate that about a third of the bankrupt debtors accumulate their mortgage debt through multiple mortgages compared with only about 12 percent of the population generally, the figures suggest that the homeowners in bankruptcy are more likely to have smaller first mortgages, supplemented by second and third mortgages. The bankrupt homeowners would have had smaller first mortgages if, on average, they had bought more modest homes initially, if they had made sizeable down payments, or if they had lived in their homes long enough to pay down their mortgages substantially. In any case, by the time they hit bankruptcy, the homes were loaded with debt that nearly exceeded their value.

What does it mean that homeowners in bankruptcy have high proportions of second and even third mortgages? It is possible that second mortgage debt was yet another trap for homeowners. Because they were homeowners, they had better access to credit.[89] They may have taken out lines of credit secured by their homes, spent the money on anything from the kids' school shoes to spur-of-the-moment vacations, then found themselves saddled with debt they could not afford.[90] Second and third mortgages convert ordinary consumer debt into debts that may cost the family its home. The data are consistent with this story.

It is possible, however, that the homeowners purchased and spent like all other Americans until they hit a serious financial setback. They may have had a hospital bill they could not pay or a divorce that required attorney's fees and apartment deposits and extra day-care costs. They may have bought a lot on credit cards, foolishly spending beyond their means — or they may have used credit cards to get them through periods of unemployment or emergencies that demanded cash. The homeowners in bankruptcy may have already hit a substantial bump in the road long before they filed for bankruptcy. The difference is that homeowners, unlike renters, may have bailed themselves out, paying off the hospital, the attorney, or the credit card company with cash from a second or third mortgage. The data are also consistent with this story.

Homeowners who tap into their home equity may see themselves as clever, avoiding catastrophe by tapping into the riches represented by equity in their homes. The television ads certainly congratulate the

225

borrowers for their astuteness. And for many, they may be right. The bankruptcy files are necessarily devoid of the homeowners who successfully used this financial stratagem, as they paid off their second mortgages over time and regained their financial balance.

But the bankruptcy data show that for some homeowners this stratagem is very risky. A home-equity loan might only delay the day of reckoning—and when the day comes, the cost will be higher. By paying off debts with second mortgages, debtors might transfer otherwise dischargeable debts such as credit cards and hospital bills to debts that must be paid upon penalty of losing the family home. If the debtor wants to keep the house, all mortgage debt—including second and third mortgages—must be paid in full, including all penalties and interests. The homeowners in bankruptcy are a living testament to how difficult that task can be.[91]

The data on home mortgages were collected principally in 1991. If similar data were collected again in 1999, they might show a more pernicious problem associated with second mortgages. According to a recent government report, banks introduced a new lending product in 1995: high-loan-to-value (HLTV) second mortgage. These HLTV mortgages add on to the first mortgage for a total obligation of 125 percent of the estimated value of the home—a $62,500 mortgage on a house worth $50,000. The report documents the phenomenal growth in these loans, with the total volume doubling every year. HLTV loans averaged about $30,000 with an interest rate about double that of ordinary first mortgages. The loans are marketed mostly to people who used them to consolidate credit card debt. In other words, financially pressed homeowners have flocked to more costly home-equity loans, increasing their debt burdens on their homes. As the popularity of these loans grows, it would not be surprising to see an increasing fraction of homeowners in the bankruptcy courts—and to see more of them lose their homes. It should be noted that, because these lenders know from the start that their loans will greatly exceed the value of their collateral, the value of the foreclosure right is not economic but *in terrorem*: the threat to throw the debtor into the street.

# The Homeowner Blues

The statistical information about homeowners in bankruptcy presents a stark picture that is reinforced by the debtors' own explanations of how they ended up in the bankruptcy courts. Most homeowners explain that they filed because the same problems that befell nonhomeowners hit them as well. Homeowners list about the same causes for bankruptcy as nonhomeowners—divorce, medical problems, credit card debt, and so on.[92] In only two important respects do homeowners in bankruptcy differ from nonhomeowners in how they explain their difficulties: for some, the home itself is the source of the problem; for others, job loss seems to have hit homeowners disproportionately hard.

Just over 6 percent of the debtors in bankruptcy list a specific problem related to their homes as the reason for filing for bankruptcy. Six percent is not a large fraction of the bankruptcy sample, and homeownership problems are not the main reason listed by the debtors. But 6.2 percent of the total sample is 14 percent of the homeowning sample, which means that one in every seven homeowners in bankruptcy lists the home not as a bulwark against catastrophe, but as a reason for seeking the shelter of the bankruptcy court.[93] If the sample is representative of the bankrupt population generally and the proportion remained about the same later in the decade, it would suggest that more than eighty thousand families filed for bankruptcy in 1998 specifically to deal with financial problems related to their homes.[94]

Homeowners describe their difficulties in a number of ways. For a small fraction of the debtors, about 3 percent of the homeowners, the house has become a burden they can no longer sustain. Like Don Wilson, some explain that the house was a larger financial obligation than they had anticipated. Some homeowners give more detailed explanations of why homes can be financial traps. Home maintenance is a routine chore for most homeowners; during 1991, more than six in ten homeowners spent money to keep up their homes, spending an average of $315.[95] For some, however, home maintenance and repair is a more global undertaking. The stories about buying old houses and fixing them up are traded around every social gathering in the cities and the suburbs. They have supplanted fishing stories as the way the next conversant can top the last one. But for some homeowners, a fixer-upper can spell financial disaster.

Myra Tennings Collins has a steady job in Nashville, where she recently bought a house. She has been divorced for a few years, and she has custody of the children. After a long court battle with her ex-husband, she lost $30,000 in promised payments that he discharged in his bankruptcy. Myra gets by on her income of $33,300. She explains that she thought she had gotten herself and the children back on track after the lawsuits ended: "I was able to locate a house we could have owner-financed. This is house I'm on verge of losing now. It's an older house. After moving in I was plagued with problems such as no plumbing (it had been disconnected because of leaks), electric, etc, etc, (which had to be resolved as they arose)." Myra learned that unlike renters, homeowners don't have the option to move off if the property is a mess. They must either fix the problem or live with it.

Like Don Wilson, Myra owes relatively little ($2,500) in unsecured debt, and she has no credit card debt or tax debt outstanding. But she owes $74,039 on the mortgage—considerably more than the $60,000 she lists as the value of the home. Also like Don, Myra is in Chapter 13. Once again, bankruptcy will not offer this troubled homeowner much help. It will provide no funds to repair the house. Even if she can make the mortgage payments, she will be paying $74,000 to buy a house worth only $60,000. Myra could best reestablish herself financially by giving up the house (either to sale or repossession) and using bankruptcy to discharge her deficiency debt. But Myra is determined to hang on. Her home has truly become the cement life raft to which she tenaciously clings.

The most frequent single reason for bankruptcy given by bankrupt homeowners (about half of those mentioning a housing-related problem) is that they are trying to pay off their mortgages, and they are in bankruptcy specifically to stave off losing their homes. They might describe the source of their problems as a combination of mortgage payments and other bills or some other difficulty, but these debtors frame their reason for filing as saving the house.

Edgar and Maria Rodriguez live in San Antonio, Texas. Both are in their forties. Edgar did not finish high school, and Maria is a high school graduate. Edgar is a barber. He has been steadily employed for several years, and last year he opened Rodriguez's Barber Shop, from which he draws a monthly salary of $900. Maria works as a part-time cashier in a nearby restaurant, and she, too, has been steadily employed. Their combined annual family income is $13,404. Through the years they have built up assets valued at $38,812, including their home, which they value at $35,000. They have household goods they estimate are worth $3,000, $200 worth of clothing, and a twelve-year-old Chevrolet Malibu worth $512. They have no other assets, no savings, no insurance, and no retirement accounts. They owe no unsecured debt, including any credit card debt. They owe a mortgage of $12,044 and another $1,360 secured by items they bought from Lacks Furniture. They explain why they filed for bankruptcy: "Because it can give us a little time to pay off our debts without them taking our home away." The Rodriguez family is in bankruptcy looking for time—not discharge of debt and not a way to escape an unaffordable home. They are also in Chapter 13, where they will have the chance to bring the mortgage payments up to date and pay off their secured debt to the furniture company in full. They will not discharge any debt.

229

## Working and Not Working

The questionnaire responses of the bankrupt debtors in our sample indicate that homeowners may be especially vulnerable to another problem—job loss. Homeowners might not lose their jobs any more often than renters, but homeowners are more likely to explain that job losses have pushed them into filing for bankruptcy than their nonhomeowning counterparts. Fully half—52.1 percent—of the homeowners in our sample explain that they filed for bankruptcy because they lost their jobs, compared with 39.7 percent of nonhomeowners.[96]

And yet, the data here are complex. While homeowners disproportionately describe job loss as the reason for their bankruptcy filing, when each debtor is asked specifically whether the debtor had had an income interruption within the two years before filing, about half the homeowners report income interruptions—the same rate as the remainder of the bankrupt population. In other words, although they actually lose their jobs at about the same rate, homeowners cite job loss as the reason for financial collapse more often than renters.

Homeowners in bankruptcy may be unemployed at the same rate as renters, but unemployment poses a much larger financial risk for homeowners than for renters. When David Caplovitz conducted his four-city research of the economic circumstances of all Americans (not just the bankrupt population), he found that only about 4 percent of the homeowners he interviewed were unemployed, compared with 21 percent of the renters.[97] Of course, only a small percentage of the currently unemployed will eventually need to file for bankruptcy. But the relatively high rate of unemployment among homeowners in bankruptcy, compared with the relatively low rate of unemployment among homeowners generally, suggests that unemployed homeowners may face a greater risk of bankruptcy than their renter counterparts.

Economists from the FDIC studied the relation between job loss and mortgage foreclosure. They found that while typical economic literature speaks in terms of debtors making rational decisions to give up their houses when they have little equity, mortgage foreclosure rates can better be understood as a function of "trigger events" that are economic calamities in the household. They focus on unemployment as one of the events tied to household insolvency and the likelihood of a mortgage foreclosure.[98]

Why should job loss pose such a threat to the financial security of homeowners? The fixed costs associated with homeownership may worsen the impact of any job loss. Perhaps the relentless commitment embodied in a home mortgage ruins homeowners when they face any extended job loss. Selling a home is often more expensive than leaving an apartment, and declining housing markets may make it impossible to cut housing costs quickly enough to respond to an interruption in income. The higher costs of moving may also make homeowners less inclined to move to try to find another job, or when they do move, if they can't sell the first home, their financial woes may multiply rather than disappear. Our data suggest that the home that protects families when they are working may become their financial trap when they are not.[99]

It is also possible that homeowners simply have a different mind-set in approaching their financial problems and that this difference leads them to catastrophe. Homeowners may be more persistent in their efforts to hang on to a home that they can no longer realistically afford—more reluctant to initiate a move that will disrupt the family and demonstrate dramatically how far they have fallen. It is even possible that homeowners have lost an option for dealing with debt that is available to less-encumbered renters: it is harder for them to move off and leave their creditors behind, establishing a new life else-where—and harder for them to stiff old creditors without the benefit of bankruptcy laws. We know from data comparing homeowners and renters generally that homeowners are much less mobile; perhaps in times of financial setback such immobility becomes a factor that pushes them into bankruptcy.[100]

## The Most Precarious Homeowners: African-Americans and Hispanic-Americans

Demographers have long documented the housing difficulties of racial minorities in the United States. African-Americans and Hispanic-Americans have had particular difficulties in obtaining and maintaining adequate housing.[101] Blacks comprise 11 percent of all American households, but they are 23 percent[102] of the precariously housed households.[103] Hispanics make up 6 percent of all households, but they account for 13 percent of all precariously housed house-holds.[104] During the 1980s, the rates of becoming precariously housed grew three to six times faster for minorities than for whites.[105]

For many demographers, the most troubling sign in the housing data during the 1990s is the difficulty facing African-American and Hispanic-American families in buying their own homes. Homeowner-ship rates among Hispanic-Americans slipped from 42 percent to 39 percent in the past decade, while rates for African-Americans re-mained stable at 43 percent. Both groups had homeownership rates markedly below the 67.9 percent for white Americans, with the mi-nority groups showing no sign of making up the gap.[106]

The economic pressures on young people trying to purchase their own homes, noted in the population generally, were particularly powerful in some minority communities. Although it was hard for all young people to set out and establish independent households, the decrease in household formation among blacks aged twenty-five and over, for example, was twice as great as among whites of the same age group.[107] Among whites, 52.2 percent of those aged twenty-five to thirty-four were living in their own homes, while only 30.1 percent of African-Americans in the same age group were living in a home they owned. Young Hispanic-Americans had even lower homeownership rates (26 percent) among the twenty-five to thirty-four-year-olds.[108]

The problem was equally serious at the other end of the age spectrum. As the population ages, Americans tend to move into their own homes. But the increases in homeownership among older Americans was lower for African-Americans and Hispanic-Americans than for white Americans.[109] More than eight out of ten whites (82.3 percent) aged sixty-five to seventy-four lived in their own homes, while 63.3 percent of blacks and 59.0 percent of Hispanics in the same age group were in their own homes.[110]

The significance of lower rates of homeownership for African-Americans and Hispanic-Americans reflects a myriad of social and economic problems. These numbers may reflect discrimination in housing and lending that restrict choices for minority families and drive up the cost of homeowning, as well as differential employment and educational opportunities that constrict economic opportunities. The effects of redlining, the practice by which mortgage lenders refuse to lend in predominantly minority neighborhoods to applicants of equal economic status to those buying outside the neighborhood, fall hardest on nonwhite homeowners. Although redlining is usually discussed in terms of limited access to home mortgage credit, the practice has other economic effects that may affect the economics of housing for minority homeowners.[111] Redlining has a double impact for minority homeowners. By making mortgage money scarce, it increases mortgage costs for minority purchasers, making comparable housing more expensive for a purchaser in a redlined area.[112] At the same time, it depresses the value of homes held by minority homeowners, reducing the marketability of their homes when they need to sell.

For purposes of this analysis, however, it is the intersection between race and housing that provides a unique perspective on the fragility of the middle class. Homes represent middle-class economic stability for a larger share of African-American and Hispanic-American families than for other Americans. The data on the net worth of American households illustrates this point. Net worth for white households was substantially higher than for black and Hispanic households in 1991, with median white households having an overall net worth of $44,408, black households a net worth of $4,604, and Hispanic households a net worth of $5,345.[113] The data on black and Hispanic households are depressed by the relatively larger fraction of each group that has limited assets.

For African-American households that have substantial assets, those assets are more likely to be homes than anything else. Among African-Americans, a substantially larger fraction of their wealth was tied up in a home than for white families (63 percent versus 41 percent).[114] For white families, wealth tends to be more diversified; the bulk of their assets is in their homes, but they also are more likely to hold a larger share of other financial assets, such as stocks, bonds, certificates of deposit, and savings accounts.[115] In other words, for more African-American and Hispanic-American families, whatever wealth they accumulate is tied up in homes. For these groups it is disproportionately true that a home represents a lifetime's accumulation of value.

To be sure, data about the net wealth of different racial groups would do little more than produce a rueful smile for most of the debtors who file for bankruptcy, regardless of their race. The bankrupt debtors have usually lost nearly every asset except their homes by the time they file—and some have lost their homes as well. There is financial equality among racial groups in bankruptcy; nearly all are busted. Bankrupt debtors do not have diversified portfolios; they have only the homes they are struggling so desperately to keep.

These data are consistent with yet another measure of stress among homeowning families. An "excessive payment burden" has been defined as the commitment of more than 35 percent of income to housing.[116] In 1990, outside of bankruptcy, minority homeowners were about twice as likely as whites to suffer excessive payment burdens. About 23 percent of black homeowners, 17 percent of Hispanic homeowners, and 12 percent of white owners had committed more than 35 percent of their incomes to paying their mortgages.[117] The effects of such financial stress show up in bankruptcy. The overall filing rate in bankruptcy 1997 was about fourteen families for every

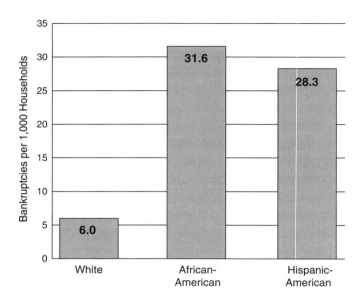

Fig. 7.4 Racial-ethnic composition of homeowners in bankruptcy, 1991. *Source:*
Consumer Bankruptcy Project II, 1991; U.S. population calculated from *Statistical Abstract: 1993*, 724, table 1236.

thousand families in the population. Homeowners do better because they are generally wealthier, but the salutary effects of homeownership are felt only by white homeowners.

If the data from our 1991 sample could be extrapolated to the whole country, white homeowners are far less likely to file for bankruptcy than are their black or Hispanic counterparts (fig. 7.4).[118] If we had a room filled with a thousand white homeowners, six would have filed for bankruptcy during 1997. If we had a room filled with a thousand African-American homeowners, thirty-two would have filed for bankruptcy during 1997. If we had a room filled with a thousand Hispanic-American homeowners, twenty-eight would have filed for bankruptcy. Black and Hispanic homeowners are about five times more likely to end up in bankruptcy trying to save their home.

The bleak picture for African-American and Hispanic-American homeowners is reflected in their own explanations for their bankruptcy filings. When these two groups are combined for statistical analysis, they collectively mention their efforts to keep their houses nearly twice as often as nonblack, non-Hispanic homeowners.[119]

**HOUSING**

About 15 percent of the black and Hispanic homeowners listed the struggle to keep their homes as a reason for filing their bankruptcies, compared with about 8.8 percent of the remaining homeowners.

Dwayne and Shawna Larue, from Nashville, Tennessee, are African-Americans. We began this chapter with their explanation of why they were filing for bankruptcy: "To keep our home is the main reason for filing bankruptcy. I have tried all other means." Dwayne is thirty-five, and Shawna is thirty-four. Both have had some college education, and both have been steadily employed. Together they bring home $56,808 annually, well above the median in the bankruptcy sample. They owe no credit card debt, no tax debts, no car loans, and no priority debts. Their total unsecured debt burden is $1,997. Their only significant debt is their home mortgage. They owe both a first and second mortgage, together totaling $115,254. They list the value of their home at $116,000, so they have virtually no home equity.[120]

With a stable home life, a substantial income, a decent education, and no medical problems or other catastrophes in their lives, Shawna and Dwayne should have been financially secure. They embarked on the path to prosperity as homeowners by buying a substantial home of considerable value. But they stretched hard for this home. The lack of equity in the home suggests that either they have been caught in a declining market or they did not have even a modest down payment. Shawna and Dwayne can't make it with this house, but they are determined to keep it. Because their total unsecured debt is less than $2,000, they are unlikely to discharge more than a small amount of debt. They are in bankruptcy, looking for time to make up the arrearage on their home mortgage so they can keep their house. It makes very little financial sense for Shawna and Dwayne to hang on to this house, but they are driven to try everything, even bankruptcy, if it will preserve their status as homeowners.

Once again, the bankruptcy data reframe pressing social questions. Many of the current policy discussions about housing circumstances of African-Americans and Hispanic-Americans center on their substandard housing, on their lower rates of homeownership, and on their reduced prospects for becoming homeowners. Government policy has focused only on the availability of mortgage money to finance a house, not on the pressures facing families trying to stay in them. The bankruptcy data direct attention to the African-Americans and Hispanic-Americans who have already accomplished much: the African-Americans and Hispanic-Americans who have purchased homes and who now encounter financial pressures that put their economic and social stability at risk. The data demonstrate that African-American and Hispanic-American homeowners face substantially greater financial pressures as a group than other racial and ethnic groups. The problem for African-Americans and Hispanic-Americans as a group is not only getting on board economically but staying on board throughout their lives.

Buying a home: This was supposed to be the good news, but changing circumstances may demonstrate that even good news can turn into a calamity. Homeowners have been caught in the rising tide of bankruptcies that have plagued all Americans, so that there are now about four times more homeowners in bankruptcy than there were in the early 1980s.[121] Surely these data prove that homeownership is no insulation against the financial pitfalls into which any of us may stumble.

The persistently high fraction of homeowners in bankruptcy—about half of all filers—demonstrates that the problems homeowners face are not quirks of a recession. The fact that homeowner bankruptcy rates remain relatively similar among debtors in different regions of the country suggests that isolated problems with a local economy are not exclusively to blame. The data, particularly the debt-income data, consistently demonstrate that a small but significant fraction of homeowners finds itself in serious financial trouble.

Whether their troubles were caused by the purchase of homes that were a stretch to buy, or whether these homeowners faced other disasters that later put their homes at risk, the debtors in the bankruptcy sample show a determined attitude about their houses. They worked hard for their homes, and they intend to try any means to keep them. They hang on to these houses even after it becomes clear that the houses themselves threaten their economic survival.

This chapter, the final one in the catalogue of the financial risks facing middle-class people, illustrates another truth about the people who are going broke in the midst of plenty: they make decisions that profoundly affect their economic futures, but those decisions

236

are only partly the rational decisions of costs and benefits; they are also decisions of the heart. Homeownership is about money, but it is also about status, about symbols, about community, about self-identification, about group identification, and about the built-in bookshelves that were a monthlong project involving Uncle Stanley and the older kids. When middle-class debtors fail economically, bankruptcy is their last chance to try to save the lives they believe in.

Chapter 8

# The Middle Class in Debt

Stability is the essence of the middle class. It is the source of disdain for the bourgeoisie as well as its goal and glory. But the economic dynamics of recent decades have placed important portions of the middle class at risk. Bankruptcy is a middle-class phenomenon, and the dramatic increases in bankruptcy filings must be understood to reveal a middle-class pathology. Something is amiss, at least financially, at the heart of American society. Although many middle-class people are prosperous in the midst of one of the longest economic booms in United States history, the middle class is not so secure as it once seemed.

More than one million bankruptcy filings a year means that more than a million American households are directly affected by bankruptcy annually. With about one hundred million households in the United States, in the space of a decade, even allowing for some overlap, that rate would imply that about 10 percent of the country would have lived through a personal bankruptcy.[1] Of course, that is the rate in a boom time. The rate may change if bad times return, as they always have in the past.

One explanation offered for the sharp increase in bankruptcies is that the bankruptcy law is "too easy." People are filing for bankruptcy frivolously, when they really could pay their debts if they would just buckle down and take some responsibility.[2] The difficulty with this argument is that it flies in the face of known facts. If people nowadays are filing bankruptcy more from convenience than from desperation, two things must be true: many bankrupts must have relatively payable debts, and there must be a growing number of such "can pay" bankrupts. In fact, the figures from our study, and the others we report in this book, show that the great majority of debtors in bankruptcy are overwhelmed by debt they could not possibly pay. These data also show that their incomes are lower and they are just as deeply indebted as were their predecessors in our 1981 study.[3] If the explanation based on easy laws and strategic behavior by debtors is not sufficient, what is the answer?

Studies of bankruptcy filings in the 1990s have begun to explore the leading causes of the financial collapse of middle-class households. The most important, beyond doubt, are the loss of income and long-term reduction in income that result from job loss and job changes. The central economic problem for ordinary, middle-class salaried workers is the risk of job loss. For the middle-aged middle class, job loss may be tantamount to forced retirement. The resulting trauma may be the most plausible explanation for the stability of wage rates (and the consequent lack of inflation) at a time of record-low unemployment: people are afraid to demand higher wages and slow to move to new opportunities at a time of increasing volatility in the employment market. The danger in this rapidly shifting economy is not only unemployment but changing employment and landing on a lower rung on the economic ladder.

Americans seem to react with profound ambivalence to the increasing volatility of employment. Our mixed emotions are nicely captured in the *New Yorker* cartoon in which Hermes and two other gods are talking. Hermes says, "It's called monotheism, but it looks like downsizing to me." We pat ourselves on the back for downsizing our way back to competitiveness and pity the Europeans for their staggering unemployment rates. At the same time, we shake our heads over the stories of fifty-year-old former factory foremen and bank managers tending airport kiosks and delivering pizza. Consistent with our history, Americans have opted for overall economic success at the price of severe economic inequality and serious economic hardship for some. In the past we have exchanged economic security for political and social mobility and economic opportunity.

239

**THE MIDDLE CLASS IN DEBT**

In the 1990s and into the new millennium, we have done it again. One consequence may be a loss of middle-class stability.

The point highlighted by our findings in the bankruptcy courts is the role of the *rate* of change. Only in the 1970s did the financial world finally discover that the rate of change in investment value—the beta—is a key aspect of financial analysis. Our findings may contribute to an appreciation that the same thing is true with respect to the central investment in the lives of most middle-class people: their jobs. It is the volatility of the job market,[4] not necessarily the end result, that is an essential factor in explaining the bankruptcies of the 1990s.[5] Debts may have seemed reasonable (even if at the high end of reasonable) when acquired, but they may have suddenly become crushing when the future held lesser prospects. Even if a laid-off employee lands an equivalent salary in a new job, the interval between jobs, with high interest rates running, may dig a debt hole that is too deep to escape.

To these difficulties we must often add the inevitable lag in adjustment to disaster. Human beings seem to require some period in which to accept the consequences of calamity, so that debts may actually increase (especially on credit cards thrust through the mailbox daily) while the head of a household reluctantly begins to absorb the fact that things are not going to get better soon.

Closely related to job loss as a cause of bankruptcy are medical problems. Our debtors report that the most serious consequence of illness or injury is loss of income, whether temporarily during recovery or rehabilitation or permanently following disability. In significant part, this result follows from the very structure of America's safety nets for the ill or injured. Worker's compensation and public and private disability plans are deliberately designed to provide a fraction of the employee's previous salary. Such support may provide enough to live on, but it leaves little margin for repaying debts, especially if the debts were stretching the available resources back at the previous income level. Even if recovery or rehabilitation makes the loss of income temporary, the accumulation of consumer interest during that period will make the debts very hard to repay.

Although loss of income was the most important consequence of medical problems, our debtors say that unpayable medical debts were also a major factor. The striking increase in medical costs over the past two decades has been well documented and much discussed. Despite the prevalence of third-party payers in the form of employer-provided benefits, many middle-class Americans are still paying a lot of their own medical bills. That number grows every time people are laid off from long-term jobs with benefits and reemployed as temporary or contract workers without benefits. Although many doctors and hospitals perform a substantial amount of charity work, there are still many people burdened with large medical debts.

Just as bankruptcy is our primary indicator of financial crisis in middle America, so the divorce rate signals its social turmoil. The family is the center of middle-class life, but nowadays many families break up and re-form, increasing social volatility in tandem with increased economic volatility. A standard of living established by two living together—and most often contributing two salaries—must decline when the two separate. The change in circumstances is even greater when children are involved. The most profound human emotions and the most serious disruption of personal context are inextricably linked with great financial pressure.

The financial results are all too often measured in bankruptcy. The financial burden falls more heavily on women, who are typically the custodial parents for the children of the marriage and who usually have lower earnings than their ex-husbands. Although there is some dispute about the size of the divorce penalty, most researchers agree that divorce has serious adverse financial consequences for men and women and that the consequences for women are much more serious than they are for men. There is also agreement that the key to financial recovery from divorce is remarriage, especially for women. Thus it is not surprising that we find a far higher percentage of unmarried people in our bankruptcy sample than among Americans generally.

The basic reason that we frequently find the shards of a broken marriage in the bankruptcy courts is familiar: the debts incurred at one level of net disposable income are too great to be satisfied by a lower income. In this context, the calculation may also change because even if the income(s) remain the same, the expenses of living apart are greater. The net result is identical. The husband heavily burdened with alimony and support payments, whether made willingly or under threat of jail, may find that bankruptcy, by eliminating his other debts, provides the only way to focus enough of his earnings on

**THE MIDDLE CLASS IN DEBT**

those divorce obligations he cannot escape. The wife left with rusty job skills, children to raise, and unstable support payments may find herself in bankruptcy as well, using the filing to erase old debts if her family is to free up enough income to put a roof over their heads, groceries on the table, and otherwise survive financially. There are no doubt many others who manage to stay out of the bankruptcy courts who are severely burdened in much the same ways, but the financial pressures on families in the aftermath of divorce are unmistakable.

It seems strange to think of homeownership as part of the litany of middle-class woe, but our research indicates that it holds an important place in financial distress. Homes join credit card debt as one of the voluntary sources of money troubles. No one wants to be laid off or to become sick or injured, and the mix of fault that leads to each divorce is unique to every marriage. But homes are bought and credit charges are run up voluntarily, even eagerly. Like credit card debt, home mortgages are the subject of a constant hard sell, but homeownership is different in its respectability. Friends are unlikely to send congratulations for maxing out a Visa card, but they will buy a drink to celebrate qualifying for a mortgage on the soon-to-be-purchased dream house. Even in the frenzy of modern credit use, there is a widespread feeling that credit cards are dangerous and that their overuse signals irresponsibility. Buying a home, by contrast, is rarely condemned and often applauded.

Yet homeownership gets people into financial trouble in similar ways: they buy more than they can truly afford and they have too little margin left when disaster strikes. The initial difference is the social cachet; the long-term difference is the personal and social attachment to the home. When trouble strikes homeowners, some will file for bankruptcy because their mortgage obligations have become unmanageable. As with support obligations, by eliminating all other debt they can focus their incomes on making the mortgage payments and saving their homes. For many, the desperation to keep a home extends beyond their attachment to the kitchen wallpaper and the barbecue in the backyard. If they are unable to pay other debts, their neighbors and friends may never know, but leaving a home for an apartment is hard to explain away. The move is a public announcement of downward mobility.

It must be significant that second-mortgage lending has increased so dramatically in the past decade or so, a development related to the fact that the amount of mortgage debt has climbed much faster than the value of the homes securing that debt. In 1998 Texas became the last state to abolish most of its stringent limitations on second mortgages. In the ensuing months, the state has seen an explosion of advertising urging Texans to create second mortgages as a source of credit. Because Texas is the second-most populous state, a further, rapid rise in second mortgages nationally seems very likely. Debtors are using their homes to secure loans for home improvements, college tuition, and taking care of elderly parents, but they are also putting their homes at risk for what has long been considered ordinary consumer debt—credit cards and other lines of credit to be drawn on one charge at a time. In spite of their potentially revolutionary impact, the implications of second mortgages—and third and fourth mortgages in many cases—are largely unexplored. For whatever reasons, with about half the debtors in bankruptcy identified as homeowners, it is clear that the American dream of homestead security is in serious jeopardy. More homeowners are struggling harder than ever to hang on to their chief symbol of participation in the middle class, and the bankruptcy courts are often their last stop to try to stabilize economically before they face foreclosure.

We have identified five factors contributing to consumer bankruptcy: job and income loss, sickness and injury, divorce, homeownership, and too much credit. When we look at the data we have gathered on these bankrupt debtors and put it in the context of larger economic trends, we conclude that the first four of these are the necessary preconditions to increasing financial failure, and frequently the triggering causes, but they are not sufficient in themselves to explain a 400 percent increase in bankruptcy filings since 1985.[6] Increasing job volatility and the rising cost of medical debts have undoubtedly contributed, not just to the failure, but to the increasing rate of failure, of middle-class families. They are important, but are probably not enough by themselves to explain the rapid rise in financial failure. Historically high divorce rates have also contributed, but they have remained relatively stable for nearly twenty years. Mortgage rates have fallen steadily since the sky-high rates of the early 1980s, giving homeowners the opportunity to reduce somewhat the financial risks associated with homeownership. Concluding that these factors, important as they are, do not seem sufficient to explain the increase in financial failure, we look to two additional factors: the reallocation of national wealth away from the middle of the middle class and the dramatic rise in consumer credit, especially credit cards.

The central paradox we address is the rise in middle-class financial failure in the midst of prosperity. The paradox is to some extent only apparent, because much of the middle class is not enjoying most of that prosperity. It is a cliche, but also a truth, that the top and the bottom of the income scale have done much better in the past twenty years than the middle class.[7] To a large extent, the income side of debt-income ratios has remained almost stagnant for most middle-class people.

Our data fit together with a number of other sources to suggest strongly that greatly increased consumer debt is the crucial additional explanation for the great increase in economic distress leading to bankruptcy. Every financial problem confronting every family is made worse by an overlay of consumer debt. During the past decades, with a sharp rise since the mid-1980s, American families, collectively and individually, have increased their debt burdens, making themselves vulnerable to every other problem that may come their way. Any job loss can be devastating, but a working family can withstand a short time without a paycheck coming in or can adjust to a smaller check—if there is some flexibility in the weekly budget. But for every week of income that is committed to pay off last month's fast-food purchases and last year's nursery furniture, a family's chance of withstanding an economic collapse goes down. A divorce that divided $40,000 of income to support two households was painful, but much more manageable, in 1973 when the family owed about $250 in credit card debt. By 1998, when a similar family might owe about $11,500 in such debt, a trip to the divorce court would be much more likely to be accompanied by a second trip to the bankruptcy court. Medical debts of $10,000 can stagger any family, but when they are piled on top of $20,000 of credit card debt, the house of cards collapses. The same pattern is true for every problem, from the most catastrophic to the mildest. As more families carry more debt, the number of Americans ripe for financial implosion grows exponentially.

Our data show that the amount of unsecured debt that carries into bankruptcy as a proportion of peoples' income has stayed about the same. At the same time, that same ratio—unsecured, mostly installment debt as a percentage of income—has risen greatly in the general population.[8] Thus it is reasonable to conclude that more people are reaching the "tip point" of debt-income ratios that leads many of them to file for bankruptcy. Why is this debt rising?

The most persuasive explanation, from our data and other sources, is the dramatic rise of the credit card. In the studies we report, the proportion of ordinary consumer debt incurred on credit cards carried into bankruptcy rose substantially from 1981 through 1991 to 1997. Although the ratio of total unsecured debt to incomes remained steady for the debtors in bankruptcy, the fraction of debt that was devoted to credit cards climbed sharply. From six weeks' worth of income in 1981 to six months' worth of income in 1991 to nine months' worth of income in 1997, the debtors in bankruptcy demonstrate that they follow the growing national trend to charge more and more of their expenses on credit cards.[9]

In a world in which credit cards are rapidly taking over much of the world of unsecured credit (now used to pay department stores, drug stores, doctors, lawyers, and even the Internal Revenue Service), they stand surrogate for almost the whole universe of everyday consumer credit. Although big-ticket items, such as automobiles, are often financed by specialist companies and a fair number of loans, especially "consolidation" loans, are made by finance companies in the traditional way, there is a strong push toward a day when all or most nonmortgage credit will revolve around credit cards and their issuers. Both in bankruptcy and out of bankruptcy, the credit card category is swallowing the entire consumer credit industry, so that speaking of "credit cards" comes closer to describing all consumer credit.

Technically, credit card debt is merely one category of consumer debt, along with the personal loans from finance companies and banks and the installment sales of cars, furniture, and appliances. But three characteristics of credit card debt make such debt very different from other consumer debt. First, the credit decision is different. Unlike traditional loans, credit card debt continues to be extended long after the initial application, at a time when the lender knows little about the borrower's current finances. Second, the borrowing decision is different. The debt itself is incurred a little bit at a time, so that even large amounts of debt do not involve a single, sober decision to take on $25,000 or even $2,500 of debt. And third, the payment schedules are different. The user may become ever more indebted while paying the minimum required every month exactly on time. Together the three characteristics suggest that credit card debt endangers the financial health of the middle class.

There has been much complaint about the fact that card issuers obtain relatively little information about consumers before issuing lines of credit of thousands of dollars. About half of all new solicitations are preapproved, indicating that the decision to extend credit has been made with no information other than a zip code or ordering preferences from certain mail order catalogues. Often creditors rely on "credit scores" obtained from credit agencies whose information is incomplete, dated, and often inaccurate. If the issuers do ask debtors for information, it is often no more than to name the current employer and state annual income, so they frequently have little idea of the consumer's existing obligations to other creditors. To a large extent, all they know is that the debtor has had an income of a certain amount and a payment record identified by a credit agency as good, fair, or poor.

Although lack of preissuance investigation is a serious problem, this complaint overlooks the more profound difference between traditional loans and credit card credit. Traditional loans are discrete, but a credit card invites a continuous flow of borrowing. The credit card issuer is like the lender in making some judgment at the start of the relationship but is very unlike the lender in that the bulk of the credit is actually extended at a later time—often years later. Most issuers, it appears, make little or no attempt to review the borrower's financial status after the initial issuance of the card except to raise the limit. The result is an absence of the credit judgment we have traditionally associated with lending, an almost complete disconnection between the circumstances of the borrower and the granting of the credit at the time it is granted. Modern credit has become like life insurance: after the initial exam, you keep the benefit as long as you pay the premium. For credit cards the premium is the minimum payment. The credit line is extended on an actuarial basis, like insurance. The issuer is lending to a category of people, most of whom will pay. Any individual borrower is a statistical black marble or a red one, but the issuer does not know which is which until the end. Instead, the creditor absorbs the risk, flush in the profits from lending to the ninety-nine of each one hundred customers who pay—slowly, with interest, over time. Spending resources—or constricting lending—to eliminate the red marble that will end up not paying is not cost effective for many lenders.

The second unique feature of credit card debt is that it is incurred bit by bit.[10] One need not have a deep understanding of human nature to appreciate the risks of incremental foolishness. There are many mistakes we would not make all at once that we will make a little at a time. As we remarked of Betina Darvilian in Chapter 4, it is the potato chip problem: it is hard to eat just one. She would never have asked for a $42,000 loan for odds and ends and no lender would ever have given it to her, but over a period of years she kept charging and making her minimum payments, and the eight all-purpose card issuers and five retailers kept on extending more credit to her. Every failed dieter understands the process intimately.

With traditional lending, there was a certain weight to the decision to put one's assets or future income at risk. Even with the friendly folks at Local Finance, a prospective borrower had to go into the office, answer a number of financial questions, and be told a specific amount that would be due each month on the loan. With a credit card, each decision to borrow is made in the midst of a busy life, with the kids at the local deli after the Little League game and in a miserable moment at the garage when the bill for the new transmission is presented. Rarely does the typical person carefully assess his or her financial future at that moment, taking account of the effects of compound interest or the global economy's effects on job stability. And even when the bill comes, it is very easy to look only at the box that says "minimum payment due." It is, in short, much easier to make a big financial mistake bit by bit than all at once.

The minimum payment feature is the third great difference from traditional lending. It permits a borrower to pay the full amount requested on time every month and yet every month be deeper in debt. Given high consumer interest rates, it is quite possible to charge nothing in a given month, make the minimum payment, and owe still more on the card than last month. The reason is negative amortization, the practice of setting the minimum monthly payments below the interest charges. Card issuers are not required to reveal their amortization practices and very few do, but industry analysts note that lower monthly payments, even below the amount of interest charged, increase total revenues by increasing the time it takes to repay the loans and hence the total interest eventually repaid. Even when credit card issuers use positive amortization and minimum payments exceed the outstanding interest, industry analysts estimate that using a typical minimum credit card pay-down rate, it would take thirty-four years to pay off a $2,500 loan, and total payments would exceed 300 percent of the original principal.[11] The unsophisticated are likely to miss the fact that their regular payments—often rewarded periodically with an increase in credit limit—are not staying even with their mounting indebtedness. If they are fortunate, they will learn the lesson before the debt mounts out of any possible reach.

The minimum payment system for many people operates like the infamous company store in nineteenth-century mining and manufacturing towns. The workers there had no choice but to buy at the company-owned stores and often paid inflated prices, so that they found they could never get out of debt no matter how hard they worked. The modern card user has many options, but the system is designed to encourage the same result: an ever-refreshed stream of debt that never dries up. After a few years, even if they do not spend another penny on their credit cards, these people are like those in the old Tennessee Ernie Ford song, "another day older and deeper in debt."

Our point is not to demonize the credit industry but to understand how consumer lending has changed and how the changes affect both commercial lenders and consumers. The industry is in the business of selling money. It raises large amounts in the capital markets of the world and must lend it out quickly at rates high enough to reward its investors. Like any other industry, it devotes time, money, and the creative energies of very bright people to selling as much of its product as possible. In the course of its marketing, the industry's risk-reward calculations since the early 1980s have changed because of the availability of vastly higher consumer interest rates than before. Rates of 18 percent or higher are commonplace today. Twenty years ago charging such rates was illegal, except for some relatively small niches carved out legally for small-loan companies. Usury was socially despised, and rates over 20 percent were often associated with shadowy alleyways and large men wearing brass knuckles.

All that changed with the sky-high inflation of the late 1970s and early 1980s. With inflation in double digits, Congress and the Supreme Court effectively legalized what had been usury, overriding the restrictive state laws.[12] Once one state raised its usury limits and creditors rushed in to make their loans from such protected places, many of the other states followed suit, if only to keep more lenders from relocating to usury-havens. From that time in the early 1980s, consumer credit has exploded, with only slight pauses. Year by year it increased, and not surprisingly, the bankruptcy rate increased with it. In 1998 the Federal Deposit Insurance Corporation published an article by one of its analysts showing the close statistical connection between the abolition of usury laws, the large increase in consumer credit, and the dramatic rise in consumer bankruptcies.[13] The result of much higher interest rates has been to make higher default rates acceptable to the credit industry in exchange for a much larger debt base.

In 1991 the financial industry spent about $650 million dollars advertising its product: money.[14] Every indication is that the barrage has intensified since then. Jim Palmer and Terry Bradshaw (baseball and football hall-of-famers, respectively) pitch easy credit with relentless friendliness. The automobile classified section in virtually every newspaper in America echoes the billboard in Austin, Texas, that proclaims, "Bad Credit? No Credit? Bankruptcy? NO PROBLEM." Web site advertising has now taken up the same chant, promising access to credit to everyone as they sponsor various consumer buying guides.[15] As one would expect with such a marketing blitz, the product is selling better every year. Installment debt as a percentage of disposable income rose to a historic high in 1998 despite—or because of—record prosperity.[16] Being financially responsible in the face of all that hype is arguably harder than it used to be.

To return to the comparison with another American obsession, weight loss, anyone who has gone on a diet has noticed the enormous pressure in our society to eat. Although some people have an incentive to sell us expensive ways to lose weight, far more people are trying their creative best to stuff us full. Many social functions

**THE MIDDLE CLASS IN DEBT**

require eating, and it is still assumed that hospitality is directly proportional to the size and caloric density of the spread. Mothers who for generations urged their children to clean their plates have now been supplanted by food ads everywhere exhorting us to eat. The better grocery stores and shops are filled with sample tables. Their scents, and the aroma of the ubiquitous bakery, make a shopping trip a torture of temptation for someone trying to lose weight.

The same feelings of temptation must press on laid-off workers who see that "NO PROBLEM" billboard or hear Jim or Terry urge them to take a line of credit and know that cash will be on the way. Companies mail unsolicited "live checks" for thousands of dollars to people struggling to pay the rent and utilities, worried about a car with failing brakes and an overdue bill from the doctor. It takes great willpower for the recipients to tear up these checks. From that perspective, the miracle may be that not everyone in America is in bankruptcy under the unrelenting bombardment of cleverly concocted enticements to spend money. Few advertisers seem to have an incentive to tell us to spend less and put something away for a rainy day.

Having said all that, consumer credit is not dispensed at gunpoint. Millions of Americans have reached historic levels of debt as compared with disposable income because they want things and they want them now. Many have been foolish enough to ignore the risk that they might suffer layoff or illness or divorce and have left no margin for error in their financial lives. About 7 percent of our sample of debtors list their own stupidity or bad planning as a cause of their bankruptcies.[17] We have not listed "irresponsibility" as a cause of bankruptcy because it is too hard to define or quantify, but we are not unmindful of its effects.[18] The anguished regret expressed by so many bankrupt consumers is an important part of the data we have gathered. In a recent survey, Canadian insolvency practitioners identified debtor "overextension" as the most important cause of bankruptcy.[19] The message is that there are a number of solidly middle-class people in our country—people who get up every morning and go to work and get the kids to school—who cannot handle credit.[20] These people are the object of an endless seduction by an industry willing to play to their weakness and successful at doing so. The result is a major fissure in middle-class stability and a growing social problem. Kathy Wood is a twenty-nine-year-old college graduate with a steady job: "My credit began in college. Because I was usually current with payments, several credit agencies came to me with opportunities for more credit. My debt got out of hand over the years. I began to advance cash to myself through open credit lines just to make payments and survive on a monthly basis. Because my salary was spent on payments, I had to continue to charge items and borrow money. It became a cycle of which there was no end."

The bankruptcy data demonstrate the unmistakable interaction of all these factors in producing the present bizarre combination of record prosperity and record bankruptcies. The current prosperity has been accompanied by unprecedented downsizing, which mismatches prior debts and future income for a lot of people. This stunning boom has also left behind the sick and injured and the divorced and not-remarried, with the same result. The volatility and unpredictability of modern life in a global economy have encountered a people who have grown used to living on the economic edge through the magic of expensive consumer credit.

We reported in Chapter 7 that job loss and housing are frequently linked as a cause of bankruptcy. That connection may illustrate the confluence of overextension and bad luck. The classic middle-class vulnerability may be a house-poor or, at least, house-stretched family struck by a layoff of one spouse. Or it may be a family struck by sickness or injury to one spouse that reduces or eliminates one of the incomes that supported the original mortgage application. Add even a modest bulge in credit card debt and the recipe for bankruptcy is complete.

One additional financial factor is rarely mentioned in our data but may emerge as an important middle-class frailty in the next study of economic failure: student loans. The middle-class burden of educating its children has escalated dramatically in the past twenty years. The cost of higher education has increased, both for consumers and for the institutions themselves.[21] Tuition at four-year colleges doubled at both public and private institutions between 1985 and 1994.[22] From 1985 to 1992, loans from the two major federal student loan programs rose more than 60 percent.[23] More families are extending themselves to the limit to finance college educations and more students are leaving school staggering under loans they have promised to repay. Those trends may not be immediately revealed in

251

bankruptcy because student loans are generally not dischargeable in bankruptcy. Like the homeowner desperate to hang on to a home or the ex-husband who must make support payments in order to avoid wage garnishments or worse, the young person facing a mountain of student loans may end up in bankruptcy not to cut down on the student loans, because the law will not permit such an action, but to get rid of any other debts so that a larger fraction of take-home income can go to paying down the debts incurred for an education. If the ex-student has little debt other than the student loans, there is no help in bankruptcy court—or anywhere else.

The impact of burdening so many young people with high levels of educational debt at the outset of their adult lives is just beginning to be felt. Many young people begin their first permanent jobs encumbered with debts that exceed several years' income. For the students who do not land good-paying jobs, the realities of supporting a five- or six-figure student loan on a restaurant server's salary plus tips can be crushing. Even those with better-paying jobs learn that if they want to buy a home and start a family, student loans that already exceed the price of a moderate house may make them too overburdened to be considered an acceptable risk. The long-term effects of student loans may be an important and growing source of middle-class financial strain that is only beginning to become apparent. Of course, this emerging threat to the middle class may simply be the one most visible to those of us who work in academe.

## The Fix?

This grim view of the increasing risks facing middle-class Americans leads us inevitably to the American Question: How do we fix it? Many savants offer "solutions" to downsizing, rising medical costs, and family breakups, but we would not pretend to have solutions to the problems that have created the fragile middle class. We are somewhat more comfortable addressing a smaller, but still expansive question: How do we reverse the trend of increasing failure among the middle class?

One proposal that has floated around for years but gained sudden currency in Congress in 1998 is to change the bankruptcy laws to make the federal government a sort of super collection agency. According to a proposed revision of the bankruptcy laws that handily passed the House of Representatives in the fall of 1998, no family would be allowed to get a legal discharge from their debts if they could pay off as little as 20 percent of their unsecured debts by paying a little each week for seven years while living on a minimal budget devised by the IRS.[24] The approach has the appeal of making citizens "more responsible" by cutting off their access to a Chapter 7 discharge if they demonstrated any capacity to repay.

The problem with this approach is that it confuses the cure with the disease. The problem is not bankruptcy itself; bankruptcy is merely the treatment. The core problem is that people are falling out of the middle class because of overwhelming debts. Bankruptcy is nothing more than a legal remedy for an untenable financial situation. The data—ours and those of every other independent academic and government researcher—show that the families in bankruptcy are in dire financial shape. Even if they are denied access to bankruptcy, the problem of deeply indebted families remains.

Indeed, the proposed solution to close the doors to the bankruptcy courts would only increase the rate of fall from the middle class. Financially pressed families use bankruptcy today to deal with debts that far exceed their annual incomes. Without access to bankruptcy, how many families will lose their homes in the struggle to pay credit cards, finance companies, and mortgage companies all at once? How many workers will decide that putting in overtime—or punching a time clock at all—makes no sense when a creditor can grab a significant portion of their wages? How many ex-spouses will conclude that it makes more sense to move from state to state working for cash, evading both consumer debt and support obligations at the same time? How many families that today manage to avoid divorce in the midst of bankruptcy will collapse under the strain of seven years of living a spartan life while trying to repay old debts?

Some of those squeezed out of Chapter 7 might try repayment plans. The House proposals involve pressing debtors into seven-year repayment plans based on budgets dictated by the IRS for its taxpayer collection negotiations. Given that about two-thirds of bankruptcy repayment plans do not succeed today, even though they are voluntary, it is likely that some number of people in financial trouble will drift in and out of bankruptcy for years. They will pay for a while,

253

then fail in their plan repayments and be dismissed, only to face the revival of all their old debts, now swollen with compounded interest and penalty fees. Later they will return to bankruptcy court when the cacophony of collection calls and the sting of wage garnishments becomes too much to bear. Others will despair and enter an underground economy in order to keep going, while still others will work harder to find strategic methods to play the system and evade their creditors. This is a social experiment that could get very ugly.

Another solution is to leave things just as they are. The credit industry has made record profits for years. Indeed, the commercial banks have been saved by consumer credit. After nearly a decade of bad real estate loans and other investment disasters, they have watched much of their big corporate lending business disappear, preempted by new sources of capital for companies in the greatly expanded and diversified world capital markets that have emerged in recent years. For many institutions, profit on consumer debt has meant the difference between failure and prosperity. Consumer credit is now twice as profitable as all other bank lending activities, and profits have grown right along with the rise in the bankruptcy rate.[25] One could say let the borrowers merrily charge on. If some of them default, the high rates paid by the rest more than make up the losses.

Two responses might come from opposite ends of the philosophical spectrum. One is the industry's response, couched in the charge that all the rest of us poor suckers are paying higher rates for our credit because of the deadbeats who default and go into bankruptcy. That would be a good argument if it were true, but there is no evidence that it is true and some evidence that it is false. For reasons that are not entirely clear, the consumer credit market is not very competitive as to interest rates. Like the airlines in the old days, which competed on food, attractiveness of flight attendants, leather seats, and everything else except fares, the credit card companies offer frequent-flyer miles and "gifts" for charges, and even participation in lotteries, but the great majority do not offer lower permanent rates. Low introductory rates—now called "teasers"—are offered for three to six months to induce debtors to switch to a new card, but the big issuers do not offer lower interest rates for the long haul. Economists have been puzzled at this lack of rate competition in a free market.[26]

Some speculate that the reason is that the people who notice interest rate differences are the well-off and sophisticated customers who are the very people who do not carry card balances and are therefore indifferent to rates on credit cards. Those who carry card balances, the argument goes, are not savvy about finances or are too financially pressed to care about the rates.[27]

Whatever the explanation may be, there is no evidence that consumer interest rates have risen and fallen with the rates of defaulted consumer debts, so there is no basis to think that fewer defaults would produce lower interest rates for the rest of us. A little history may be instructive: the single biggest cost for a credit card issuer is the cost of funds for the money it lends to borrowers who repay over time. Between 1980 and 1992, the rate at which banks borrow money fell from 13.4 percent to 3.5 percent. During the same time, the average credit card interest rate rose from 17.3 percent to 17.8 percent.[28] Thus during the period that the credit card issuers' largest cost was plummeting, they were raising the price of credit to their consumers. Because a change in the write-off rates based on bankruptcy filings would be only a tiny fraction of this change in costs, history suggests that changes in bankruptcy filings are highly unlikely to produce any discernible change in the cost of a credit card.

Even if fewer defaults would produce lower interest rates for the rest of us, that goal cannot be served merely by barring people from bankruptcy. A bad debt write-off costs the same whether the debtor just never paid or declared bankruptcy and then never paid. For the rest of us to get lower rates, the people kept out of bankruptcy still have to find the money to pay. The studies we report in this book show that the great majority of debtors do not have the money. The most recent academic study of the House bankruptcy bill estimates that about 3 percent of the debtors currently filing for Chapter 7—fewer than thirty thousand families out of a million—would have paid *anything,* even under the harsh guidelines of the proposed bill.[29] It is wise to remember that much of the debt discharged in bankruptcy had already been written off by the issuer as "uncollectible" because the issuer had determined that the debtor was so unlikely ever to have the resources to repay that spending another dollar on debt collection was throwing good money after bad.

Although creditors may lobby for tougher bankruptcy laws, the only available evidence suggests that they would collect very little more from hard-pressed consumers. More critically, the effects on families that cannot find a way to deal with overwhelming debts may involve ramifications for work and family life that the proponents of change have overlooked.

The second objection to a status quo approach might come from humanists and communitarians at the other end of the philosophical spectrum. They would point to the human wreckage at the convergence of overindebtedness and rapid economic change, even with the bankruptcy laws we have now. They would point to shattered families, the loss of a lifetime's work, untreated illnesses, and other social harms produced by a combination of excessive credit and extreme economic distress. They would point out that bankruptcy is a weak solution to a growing problem. Bankruptcy permits debtors to declare their failure and wipe out some of their debts, but it does nothing more. It leaves most of those who file with substantial debts for homes, cars, taxes, alimony, child support, and educational loans. It offers them no stability in their jobs, no additional health coverage, and no improvement in their family circumstances. Bankruptcy is a thin—some would say hopelessly thin—safety net in an increasingly precarious world.

For these critics, bankruptcy offers too little. The solutions must come elsewhere. At this point, such critics might advocate regulation of consumer credit, stricter restrictions on layoffs by companies, enhanced unemployment compensation, better retraining and job placement services, universal health insurance, subsidized child care and other support for single parents, free access to a university education, and so forth to shore up the failing finances of the shakiest members of the middle class. In short, they must move from bankruptcy policy to larger and less focused questions about the economic stability of the middle class.

While the consumer credit industry wants to solve the problem of middle-class failure by locking the doors to the bankruptcy courts, their counterparts want to solve failure by legislating it away long before it reaches the bankruptcy courts. The conflicting approaches share a certain myopia: they both overlook the interrelated roles of the social safety net, unregulated consumer credit, and consumer bankruptcy. Perhaps an international comparison would shed some light on this dynamic relationship.

For decades, our Western European counterparts have tried to insulate their middle classes from economic risks. After World War II, they built an extraordinary social safety net, providing benefits to shore up the middle class and decrease the impact of job loss, medical catastrophe, and, eventually, family breakup. They subsidized higher education, taking on what has become one of the biggest costs many middle-class families face. They also directly regulated consumer credit and supported banking systems that sharply curtailed the easy availability of short-term, high-interest consumer credit.

With their extraordinarily protective approach to economic risk, these countries never had anything like an American-style bankruptcy discharge for consumers. With a bankruptcy system that provided little protection for families in trouble, their consumer bankruptcy filing rates remained low. In 1980, for example, at a time when the American consumer bankruptcy rate was 1.30 for every 1,000 citizens, the filing rate for "consumer insolvency" in England and Wales was 0.08 per 1,000 citizens and in Scotland 0.03 per 1,000.[30] In other words, in 1980, when we account for differences in population size, there were about 130 families in bankruptcy in the United States for every 8 families in England and Wales and every 3 families in Scotland in similar circumstances.

Our Canadian cousins help fill in the picture. They offer a stronger social safety net than our own, but it is considerably smaller and stiffer than its European counterparts. On one hand, for years they restricted consumer credit more than in the United States but less than in most European countries. On the other, unemployment assistance is both stronger and longer than in the United States but does not match the extensive benefits offered in Great Britain. The Canadian consumer bankruptcy system is also intermediate, offering neither the ready access to a consumer discharge of the United States nor the traditionally restrictive approach of the Europeans. In 1980 the Canadian consumer bankruptcy rate fell between the two extremes as well, at 0.85 per 1,000. In other words, Canada had about 85 filings for each 130 American filings and for each 8 English and Welsh filings.

**THE MIDDLE CLASS IN DEBT**

In the United States we have opted for dynamic economic change even at the cost of economic risk and instability. We have chosen economic opportunity at the risk of economic hardship. We prefer a world of winners and losers. But a world of winners and losers requires a way to cope with the losers. If they revolt in the streets or withdraw from the economy, the costs of their failure are displaced to the winners who cannot enjoy their prosperity in safety. The bankruptcy discharge is an important part of the traditional, market-driven American approach to risk. Bankruptcy reduces the pain of loss while it lets the losers get back in the game. As far back as Henry Clay, Americans decided that collectively we would all be better off to cut the losers loose from their old debts so they could try the game again.[31] Their future energies, their willingness to work and to pay taxes and to invest in their middle-class ways of life would yield more benefits for all of society than would any marginally increased payoffs for huge financial companies that resulted from yoking people to their debts forever.

258

Recent events in the economies of Western Europe demonstrate the close connection between bankruptcy and economic regulation. After years of phenomenal profits in the United States, Mastercard and Visa "discovered" Europe, making it their next new growth market. Local banks responded in kind, learning from their American counterparts that consumer lending can be a lucrative business. As part of a general trend toward deregulation, and with specific pressure from the banks that saw new markets opening up, European governments began deregulating the consumer credit industry in the late 1980s. The resulting explosion of consumer debt has been as extraordinary in Europe as it was in the United States. Consumer lending in the United States doubled from 1986 to 1997, from $658,181 million to $1,254,103 million. The United Kingdom, starting with a smaller base, saw a somewhat higher proportional jump, from 30,150 million pounds to 77,548 million pounds in the same time period. Canada experienced a similar leap, with consumer credit increasing from $56,882 million (Canadian) in 1986 to $138,408 million (Canadian) in 1997.

Along with the rise in consumer debt has also come widespread consumer distress. As a result, a number of European countries are now experimenting with a bankruptcy discharge for the first time in their histories.[32] Canadians, also facing growing consumer credit and the resulting financial collapse of an increasing number of families, have strengthened their consumer bankruptcy laws, although with the same mixed viewpoints we have.[33] The bankruptcy rates have risen in both parts of the world. The consumer insolvency rate in England and Wales has jumped from 0.08 in 1980 to 0.47 in 1997, nearly a 600 percent increase. Canada's consumer bankruptcy rate climbed more than 350 percent from its 1980 level of 0.85 to its 1997 rate of 3.00. The connections between increases in consumer debt and increases in consumer failure are unmistakable in these countries just as in the United States.

Yet substantial differences remain. In both Europe and Canada, even with much talk of a somewhat fraying social safety net, the risks facing individual families remain much more cushioned than in America, and the bankruptcy rates reflect those stronger safety nets.[34] Even as debt levels and bankruptcy levels have risen in Europe, Canada, and the United States, the absolute differences in filing rates still show the United States as the runaway leader in consumer financial collapse. In 1997 the U.S. bankruptcy rate was 5.1 per 1,000, giving America 510 bankruptcies for every 300 Canadian bankruptcies and every 47 English and Welsh bankruptcies. The bankruptcy laws in countries with stronger social safety nets are designed to serve—and evidently need to serve—a much smaller proportion of the citizenry than in the United States.

These data suggest that the need for a more protective consumer bankruptcy law is directly proportional to the size of the social safety net and the availability of consumer credit. Like any good three-legged stool, change the length of one leg and the shift will be felt by the other two. The United States offers families more sanctuary in bankruptcy—at the same time that it permits a wide-open consumer credit economy coupled with less protection from the economic consequences of other problems such as job losses, medical problems, accidents, and family breakups. If consumer credit were more restricted or if more family risks were shared with taxpayers, the bankruptcy system would play a less significant role in rescuing failing families. The European and Canadian approaches, by contrast, make the game safer—but less competitive.

The comparison with the British and Canadian economic systems suggests that asking how to fix the fragile state of the American middle class is to ask the wrong question. There is no fix. There is only a question about how a government should deal with the risks facing its citizens. For those who believe that the risk itself should be borne collectively rather than individually, the obvious answer is to increase the strength of the social safety net and restrict consumer lending. Bankruptcy laws can be rather modest, reserved only for the most extraordinary cases. For those who believe that the risk should be borne individually, however, consumer bankruptcy provides critical relief that heads off social unrest and keeps the maximum number of players in the economic game.

Bankruptcy is the ultimate free-market solution to bad debt. It forces individual creditors who made voluntary lending decisions to bear the costs of their bad credit decisions out of the profits from their good loans. So far, that part of the equation has worked extraordinarily well, with consumer lenders enjoying more than a decade of the lending industry's highest profits, despite writing off more bad loans than ever. Bankruptcy is the market-driven choice to deal with privatized, rather than socialized, risk. For the family facing financial collapse, however, a trip to the bankruptcy court may be considerably less attractive than standing in line at an unemployment office or using an identification card to obtain free medical care. Bankruptcy may be ameliorative, but it is not pleasant. The sting of losing is still sharply felt by those who must publicly declare that they are "bankrupt." Not all ways to deal with risk are equally attractive to the losers.

One of the redeeming paradoxes of this country is that a people so individualistic and so competitive nonetheless overwhelmingly identify themselves as members of a single class, the middle class. Some see it as glorious and some as boring, but it is within the perceived reach of nearly all citizens. A clerk and a secretary sharing a one-room apartment in Newark will give the same response to a question about class identification on a survey questionnaire as a hard-charging executive and a management consultant spouse in a fourteen-room manse in Grosse Pointe. The social reality may be considerably more complex, but the perception has a profound importance of its own.

One consequence of the Great Depression was a federal commitment to protect and extend this great, amorphous middle class. Literally hundreds of government programs, from housing subsidies and tax breaks to small business loans, were designed to further that end. Indeed, one way to describe the New Deal as a reaction to the Great Depression is that the federal government became committed to maintaining middle-class stability in the face of economic change and to expanding the ranks of the middle class to include as many Americans as possible. One way to describe the political direction of the country since the Reagan Revolution is the dismantling of that government structure in favor of one with more flexibility, more inequality, more opportunity, and more risk. On that basis, one inevitable cost can be seen to be the increased vulnerability of the American middle class to financial catastrophe.

There is no easy fix for the fragile middle class. As we opt for deregulation and higher profits, we also opt for higher rates of personal failure. The tradeoff is thrilling for some and offensive to others. At this juncture, we can do little more than understand that in every choice to deal with risk, a game that produces winners also produces losers, and that for every policy to encourage winning, there must be some thought about mechanisms to deal with losing.

261

We began this book by using bankruptcy as the lens to understand failure. We end it with the thought that bankruptcy is not merely the passive lens through which we might see the failure. It appropriately belongs near the center of the economic policy stage, offering itself as the treatment for those injured in a competitive, high-risk game. Correctly calibrating the kind and amount of bankruptcy treatment is central to the long-term survival of the always interesting, often dangerous American Experiment.

Appendix 1

# Data Used in This Study

This appendix is designed to provide the interested reader with information concerning the study design, data collection, and data analysis reported in this volume. We also discuss small data sets collected by bankruptcy judges that were made available to us for analysis and use in this book. Appendix 2 provides some information about other recent studies of bankruptcy to which we refer.

The General Plan of Data Collection

This is a book about the middle class, but our data collection began in the United States Bankruptcy Courts. Only after we began analyzing the data did we conclude that we had a portrait of a distressed segment of the middle class. There had been hints of middle-class bankruptcy participation in our earlier study—especially, for example, in the findings about the occupational background of the bankrupt debtors in the early 1980s. The definitive information, however—educational status—was missing in that data set.

Consumer Bankruptcy Project Phase I was based on data collected only from the schedules filed by bankruptcy petitioners.[1] The petition data include detailed financial information concerning debts and assets, more limited information concerning income, some information concerning occupation or the petitioner's own business, and almost no information about demographic background. After our study, bankruptcy petitions were redesigned to include more detailed information on the bankrupt debtor's number of dependents and the family budget, but demographic information remains fragmentary. No interviews with debtors were attempted because by the time we had drawn the data, we knew that the debtors would be difficult to locate.

Consumer Bankruptcy Project Phase II, conducted with cases filed in 1991, was designed to provide demographic data that were unavailable in 1981. We developed a questionnaire that included information concerning age, marital status, citizenship, and educational background. We also included questions concerning employment that parallel the questions used by the U.S. Census Bureau to determine the unemployment rate. We provided a place for respondents to indicate race or ethnicity, and we asked the respondents to answer a free-response question about the reasons for their bankruptcy. We asked respondents for their name and case number. For a subsample of these respondents, we collected and coded the petition data on file in the courthouse for their cases.

This design involves the trade-off among the desired criteria for a good study. Petition data are systematic but omit important information; a survey of individual debtors provides the important information but is less systematic than the petition data. In Consumer Bankruptcy Project Phase I we valued systematic representation over richer data. For this study, we valued richer data and sacrificed some of the systematic quality of the former study.

An alert reader will immediately ask, Why not use both petition data and interview data? The answer to that question is that we, and a number of other researchers, have tried to do both, but questioning individual debtors remains difficult.[2] Response rates are often lower than desired, and many debtors refuse to answer questions. We believe that debtors' reticence is a sign that a substantial stigma remains attached to bankruptcy. Most recent analyses of the "decline in stigma of bankruptcy" do not use any direct measure of stigma. Instead, the proxy for declining stigma is the rising bankruptcy rate. When asked, "How do you know that stigma has declined?" the analyst will point to the rising bankruptcy rate. When asked, "Why has the bankruptcy rate increased?" the analyst will reply that the stigma has declined. The circularity of this argument is obvious.

Petition studies avoid the stigma issue because the debtor has no choice about participating in the study. By filing bankruptcy, the debtors have assumed a statistical chance of having their petitions drawn into a study. The court docket is the universe of bankruptcy filings; drawing a systematic sample from these filings is easy, and the major drawback is the geographic distribution of courthouses (and thus the expense of collecting the data) and the possibility that a case might occasionally be lost or misfiled. Parenthetically, we note that the number of cases we have ever been unable to find is fewer than five. The U.S. Bankruptcy Courts do an excellent job of maintaining records of filings.

Choice of District

In Consumer Bankruptcy Project Phase I, we studied Illinois, Pennsylvania, and Texas. For that 1981 study, in which a comparison of Chapter 7 debtors with Chapter 13 debtors was crucial to our argument, we took three states with differing state exemption laws but with districts displaying a great variability in the ratio of Chapter 7 filings to Chapter 13 filings. Texas, with its generous state exemptions, and Illinois, with its meager exemptions, were the two more extreme cases, with Pennsylvania the intermediate case. These states also vary in the types of nonbankruptcy collection devices available to creditors. Illinois allows wage garnishment, for example, but Pennsylvania and Texas do not.

For Phase II, we wanted to repeat the original three states for comparison purposes, and we added California and Tennessee. California led the nation in absolute numbers of bankruptcies with 139,372 cases filed in 1991. California ranked ninth among the states with a per-household filing rate of one case for every 74 households. California, like Texas, allows debtors a relatively generous exemption. In terms of cases filed per household, Tennessee ranked first, with one filing for every 43 households, or 42,733 cases.[3] Tennessee has modest exemptions and has historically had a high proportion of Chapter 13 filings.

We studied all three districts in Illinois and Pennsylvania, all four districts in California and Texas, and two of the three districts in Tennessee. In one district of Tennessee we did not receive permission to do the study; in one district of California, we received permission relatively late in the study and so the timing of the data collection was somewhat different from other districts.

Within each state, we selected one district and collected the bankruptcy petitions that matched our 150 sampled cases. This enhanced sample consisted of the Central District of California, which contains Los Angeles; the Northern District of Illinois, which contains Chicago; the Eastern District of Pennsylvania, which contains Philadelphia; the Middle District of Tennessee, which contains Nashville; and the Western District of Texas, which contains San Antonio. The choice of these large urban districts probably gives us a financial view of the debtors that is somewhat skewed toward urban problems, although each district also contains rural and suburban areas. From an examination of the zip codes of the petition data, we were able to confirm that the debtors in the sample came from rural and suburban areas of the districts as well as from the central cities.

Some of the petition data were collected in the court itself; other petitions had already been stored in the federal data warehouses. The petition data were photocopied and sent to the authors for coding and combination with the questionnaire data.

## Methods

Before entering the field, we submitted our questionnaire and procedures to the University of Texas process for the protection of human subjects. Simultaneously, we submitted the materials to the University of Pennsylvania process, because one of the coauthors was then a professor at that institution. As part of these procedures, we promised to maintain our respondents' confidentiality. In asking the cooperation of the judges and trustees, we also promised confidentiality for our respondents. A short paragraph of instructions with the questionnaire included a notice that we would preserve the respondents' confidentiality. All of the personnel engaged in the research in any capacity signed statements pledging to protect the confidentiality of our respondents. In the text of this book, we quote our respondents' verbatim remarks, but we have changed their names and in some cases changed identifying information (such as the exact name of an employer) to preserve their anonymity.

We believe that this promise is essential to the quality of the research. Professor Philip Shuchman has criticized our adherence to the rubrics for protecting human subjects, arguing that the bankruptcy files are public data.[4] Moreover, current research canons provide several loopholes that we could have used: the study is not federally funded; the study population is not impaired; we are using ordinary survey methods, not an experiment of some sort; the court data are in the public domain. On the other hand, the University of Texas at Austin prescribes completing the human subject protection paperwork even to claim that the study is exempt from the procedures. And the American Sociological Association, to whose code of ethics one of us is professionally committed, exhorts researchers to protect their subjects' identity. In dealing with a behavior that is already stigmatized (critics notwithstanding), and given the embarrassing and painful accounts many debtors recorded, we believe that it would have been inappropriate to compromise their anonymity. We also believed that we would get greater cooperation in completing questionnaires with a promise of anonymity.

267

With the permission of the bankruptcy judges, court clerks or trustees distributed questionnaires to debtors who had filed for bankruptcy during the first two quarters of calendar year 1991. Because Section 341 meetings are often held some months after the initial filing, some of the questionnaires we collected were for petitioners who had filed for bankruptcy in 1990. These questionnaires were not further analyzed. Because of the lag time between filing and Section 341 meeting, we continued to collect data in most districts throughout the calendar year 1991 and several months into 1992, even though cases filed during the first half of the year constituted our universe. In the Southern District of California, because of a low response rate, we collected data for filings throughout 1991.

Limiting the universe to the first half of the year raises the issue of the seasonality of bankruptcy filings. In our previous work, we noted that contrary to conventional wisdom, there was little seasonality in bankruptcy filings.[5] Inspection of weekly filing data for Texas and California in 1991 confirmed our conclusion that filings show little seasonality across months. There was marked seasonality in Texas by weeks, but this seasonality seemed to coincide with the first Tuesday of the month, the traditional date on which mortgages are foreclosed. This weekly seasonality does not affect our data, because our data were collected in every week. Moreover, the cumulative filing line, which is nearly straight, indicates that there is little month-to-month seasonality. Ed Flynn, who studied the monthly variations in filing from 1985 through 1991, characterizes them as "slight."[6] The monthly filing rate, the quarterly rate, and the cumulative filing rate for the year showed little pattern of seasonality.

In some districts, the questionnaire was given to the attorney or the debtor at the time of filing to be returned at the Section 341 meeting. In most districts, however, questionnaires were distributed to the debtors at the time of the Section 341 meeting, a mandatory meeting held with a bankruptcy trustee and any creditors who wish to attend and ask questions of the debtor. Section 341 meetings are typically scheduled from three weeks to three months after the bankruptcy filing, with the variation attributable to the trustees' schedules, the city in which the bankruptcy is filed, and the chapter of filing. An unknown number of cases have such incomplete filings that they are dismissed before the Section 341 meeting. On the other hand, all of the cases that will eventually reach confirmation (in a Chapter 13) or discharge (in a Chapter 7) must come at least this far, and so the sample probably represents what we might call "completed" bankruptcies.

Debtors were advised that completion of the form was voluntary and that their responses would be anonymous. Debtors come to the Section 341 meeting with their attorneys, and there is often a lengthy wait in a hallway for their hearing to begin, during which the debtors would have had opportunity to consult with their legal counsel about completing the form. Debtors were explicitly informed that anyone could help them with the questionnaire. They could complete the questionnaire during their waiting period, although some of the debtors took their questionnaires home to write us more complete answers. One petitioner wrote a four-page, single-spaced explanation of the reasons for his bankruptcy. The debtors were encouraged to leave their questionnaires with their case trustee or with the clerk at the courthouse or to mail it back to us. We left prepaid envelopes with the court clerks for the return of the questionnaires. We received questionnaires in all of these ways. We also received a few telephone calls from debtors who wished to amplify their responses.

We viewed the presence of the attorney as a bonus, because debtors who were doubtful about completing the questionnaire, or who did not know how to answer a particular question, could immediately ask their attorney for advice.

## Questionnaire

The questionnaire was deliberately designed to be only one page long to help reduce respondent fatigue and make the task appear manageable. All but two of the questions were pre-coded, requiring only a check mark to complete. There were two columns of answers to allow for separate answers by a joint petitioner, if there was one. A facsimile of the questionnaire appears as figure A.1.

Most of the demographic questions were identical in wording to questions asked in the 1980 census. Two additional questions concerned marital interruption and work interruption during the two years preceding the bankruptcy filing. We thus learned of marital and job interruptions that had possibly occurred as early as January 1989.

The final, open-ended question asked the respondents for the reasons for their bankruptcy. We suggested that respondents answer on the back of the questionnaire, which gave them a full page to respond. Some respondents did not write anything; others wrote extensive commentaries and continued on separate sheets of paper.

Most of these responses were read by one of the investigators or by one of the research assistants, even if the questionnaire was not eventually selected into the sample. In a few places in the text of the book, we have added comments made by petitioners who completed questionnaires but whose questionnaires were not included in the final sample.

## Language

In both Texas and California, and to a growing extent in Philadelphia and Chicago, many members of the population do not speak

# FORM 1.1: INDIVIDUAL DEBTOR QUESTIONNAIRE

Directions: This form should be completed for any *person* filing for bankruptcy in any chapter. In the case of a joint filing, the questions should be answered for both petitioners. Completion of this form is voluntary.

NAME(S) of PETITIONER(S): _____

CASE NUMBER: _____

| Question | First or Principal Petitioner | Second Petitioner (if joint) |
|---|---|---|
| 1. Sex | male<br>female | male<br>female |
| 2. Age (print each person's age at last birthday). | _____ | _____ |
| 3. Marital status (check one box for each person). | now married<br>separated<br>widowed<br>divorced<br>never married | now married<br>separated<br>widowed<br>divorced<br>never married |
| 3a. Has this person experienced a *change* in marital status since 1 Jan. 1989? | yes<br>no | yes<br>no |
| 4. Education (check one box for highest level of school COMPLETED). | no school<br>8th grade or less<br>9th, 10th, or 11th grade<br>12th grade, no diploma<br>high school graduate<br>some college<br>bachelor's degree<br>advanced degree | no school<br>8th grade or less<br>9th, 10th, or 11th grade<br>12th grade, no diploma<br>high school graduate<br>some college<br>bachelor's degree<br>advanced degree |
| 5. Is this person a citizen of the U.S.? | yes, by birth or parentage<br>yes, by naturalization<br>no | yes, by birth or parentage<br>yes, by naturalization<br>no |
| 6. Since 1 Jan. 1989, has this person experienced an interruption of at least two weeks in work-related income? (for example, through layoff or illness) | yes<br>no<br>not employed during this time | yes<br>no<br>not employed during this time |
| 7. If not currently holding a job, did this person actively SEEK work during the past four weeks? | yes, sought work<br>no<br>has a job now | yes, sought work<br>no<br>has a job now |
| 8. [optional] What is this person's ancestry, racial or ethnic origin? | _____ | _____ |

9. On the back, in your own words, please indicate what you believe to be the reasons for your bankruptcy.

Fig. A.1 Individual debtor questionnaire used in Consumer Bankruptcy Project II, 1991.

English. In particular, the Spanish-speaking segment of the population has grown substantially. Although we did not know in advance how well the Spanish-speaking population would be represented in bankruptcy, we decided to provide the questionnaire in both Spanish and English. Census Bureau officials had made a similar decision with census forms during the preceding year.

We used the Census Bureau's Spanish translation of the questions that appeared both on our questionnaire and on the census questionnaire. For the remaining questions, we asked two graduate students to provide translations: a Mexican-American student who grew up in Texas speaking Spanish, and a Central American student who also grew up speaking Spanish, but in another country. We sought two translations to be careful about any idiomatic expressions that some respondents might not have understood. Where translations differed, we asked the two students to discuss the difference and recommend one wording. Then we had the entire Spanish questionnaire back-translated into English. This was a precaution taken to ensure that the Spanish correctly captured the sense we intended in the English version of the questionnaire.

We received a substantial number of Spanish questionnaires in California and a few in Texas. We again asked Spanish-speaking graduate students to assist us in translating the written comments into English. In some cases, we also needed their interpretation of colloquial expressions; for example, we learned that "he was run off" (the literal interpretation of the Spanish) was an expression for having been fired from a job.

From discussions with court personnel in the Central District of California (Los Angeles), we believe that there might have been immigrants who spoke neither Spanish nor English who did not complete questionnaires. We have been told that the courts face difficulties in providing translators for the many languages that debtors use. It is possible, then, that our study underrepresents some immigrants. It is more reasonable to suppose that naturalized citizens would complete the questionnaire. We assumed that those who are naturalized would speak enough English (required for naturalization) to be able to understand at least some of the questions in our questionnaire.

## Coding and Recoding of Data

The pre-coded answers in the questionnaire were generally those used by the Census Bureau in the 1990 census. Respondents' answers were transferred to an Excel spreadsheet, adding only additional codes for item nonresponse and for the absence of a second petitioner.

The open-ended question concerning race or nationality was coded using a truncated listing of racial and ethnic groups developed from the Census Bureau's codes for the 1990 census. Where people listed two or more identities (e.g., Irish-German), we coded the first one listed. In the analysis, we ended up combining all respondents from European origin (except Spanish) with others who identified themselves only as white.

For the question asking about the reason for bankruptcy, we often received lengthy responses. We developed content codes from a separate sample of 150 cases from the Northern District of Illinois. Each researcher read the separate sample and developed a series of codes for commonly mentioned reasons. We discussed our trial codes and collated these reasons into a lengthy list of reasons, grouped into larger categories. For example, the list of job-related reasons included layoff of the petitioner, layoff of the spouse, cutback on hours of work, reduced overtime, closure of the petitioner's business, closure of the employer's business, and so on.

The three researchers and a research associate independently coded one hundred questionnaires and then discussed our coding. Based on the discussion and some additional revision of the codes, we each coded an additional fifty questionnaires. The original level of coder interreliability was around 67% but eventually rose to over 90%. We finally used sixty separate codes, with a code for nonresponse to this item and a code for answers that we could not understand or adequately code elsewhere.

Because debtors often provided a lengthy narrative of their reasons for bankruptcy, we coded up to five answers in the order in which they were mentioned. Some respondents listed the most important reason first; others listed the reasons in chronological order. In analyzing the reasons, we usually analyzed any response in which a particular reason (say, job-related reasons) was reported. When an analysis is different—for example, if only the first-named reasons are being analyzed—the text clearly indicates that fact.

In the text, we often quote verbatim from the debtors' narratives. Although the narrative comments appear with assumed names for the debtors, the narratives are genuine and not composites. The narratives of our sample cases were typed into a word-processing database. Because of the variation in handwriting, there were occasional words or phrases that were imperfectly deciphered. The voice evident in the comments varies; sometimes, the writer is obviously the wife in a joint filing; in others, it is clearly the husband. In some cases it is not clear whether the written comments are those of the primary or secondary filer. The quoted comments are presented in the text exactly as written; interpretations or clarifications are placed in square brackets. Although some respondents signed their names and gave their addresses, we omitted these details if we quoted them. We left the names of employers in the verbatim quotations if the employer was a large corporation with many employees. We disguised the names of smaller employers to avoid the risk of breaching confidentiality. Because we had the comments in a database, it was also possible to search for words or groups of words to provide additional analytic texture.

The 150 cases that had been selected for five of our districts were used to create an enhanced subsample with information taken from the bankruptcy forms filed with the courts. The bankruptcy petitions filed with the court provided information on occupation, income, debts, assets, and expected distribution of assets. We used the occupational codes used by the General Social Survey and previously used for the U.S. Census. This information was coded by trained coders and followed a codebook modeled on the one developed in the earlier phase of the Consumer Bankruptcy Study. Our experience in the earlier study led us to omit a number of variables that had not been useful in that study.

Financial data were coded in nominal dollars but are usually reported in inflation-adjusted dollars in this volume. One conventional standard for assessing inflation is the federal government's Consumer Price Index (CPI), which is currently indexed to 1982–84.

**APPENDIX 1**

The value of the index for all items in 1981 was 90.9 and for 1991 the value was 136.2. Another way to look at this index is that it took $1.36 in 1991 to buy a 1982–84 dollar, and in 1981 it took only $0.91 to buy a 1982–84 dollar.[7] An adjustment for inflation may be done in either direction, either by presenting constant 1981 dollars or constant 1991 dollars. In our comparisons between 1981 and 1991, we have adjusted for inflation by applying a multiplier based upon the CPI. By the same principle, when presenting more recent data, we used an adjustment to 1997 dollars. The index value for 1997 was 160.5, indicating that it took $1.60 in 1997 to buy a 1982–84 dollar, or $1.18 to buy a 1991 dollar.[8]

This adjustment is probably reasonably accurate for current income, and it is frequently performed to compare real income for different dates. The adjustment is convenient but less accurate for debts. Debts may have been incurred over a period of years under a variety of inflationary conditions. Long-term debts in particular may have been relatively "dearer" or "cheaper" at the time of the bankruptcy petition compared with the date they were incurred. We have adjusted the debt totals by the CPI for the sake of comparability across the decade, although we recognize that the debt obligation is for nominal, not real, dollars.

We also examined the accuracy of this inflation adjustment for the three areas of the country we were studying. The government publishes cost-of-living data for selected years and cities.[9] In 1980, the year before our first study, the overall CPI for U.S. cities was 82.4; in the Chicago metropolitan area, the index was 82.2, and in Philadelphia it was 82.1. San Antonio is not separately listed among the cities for which we had reports, but two other large Texas cities are: in Houston the index was 82.7, in Dallas–Fort Worth 81.5. At the time of the first study, therefore, the cost-of-living differences across these major cities were small.

The differences were greater in 1991, when the overall city index stood at 136.2. The CPI for Los Angeles was 124.6, for Chicago 124, and for Philadelphia 127.2. San Antonio was much lower at 93.1, and Nashville was even lower at 91.7.[10] The housing component is calculated separately, and its value was a whopping 196.23 for Los Angeles, 173 for Chicago, 139.3 for Philadelphia, 90.9 for Nashville, and only

85.1 for San Antonio. This means that a person living in Los Angeles would pay $1.96 for housing for every $.91 that a person living in Nashville paid. The reader might wish to keep these differences in mind in examining our data for districts.

A federal judicial district encompasses more geography than the single metropolitan area, so that the CPI for the area as a whole may not be the same as that for the metropolitan area. The Western District of Texas, for example, includes the metropolitan areas of San Antonio, El Paso, and Austin and many smaller cities such as Waco, Laredo, and New Braunfels. With such a large area, there might be substantial differences in cost of living that are not reflected in the data for the large metropolitan area. A review of the regional data, however, suggested that the generalizations we made in the preceding paragraph also apply to larger regional areas.[11]

## Sampling and Sample Size

We received about 59,000 questionnaires, excluding perhaps nearly another 1,000 questionnaires from cases that had been filed in 1990. Based on an estimated 118,040 nonbusiness filings in these districts during the first six months of 1991, our overall response rate was about 49.9% (table A.1).[12] To have a reasonable number of cases for analysis, we randomly selected 150 cases from each district to analyze in our final sample. Questionnaires were sampled using a random start and a systematic draw from the total number of questionnaires. The size of the sample eventually drawn was 2,452. A few of the sampled questionnaires were completely blank, and we replaced them with another random draw from among the remaining questionnaires. Illegible questionnaires were kept in the sample, although if we could not decipher their responses the debtors were excluded from the analysis of reasons for bankruptcy. The elimination of statistical outliers is discussed below.

The use of 150 cases as an adequate sample size for each district is justified in our previous work.[13] The number of filings and the number of questionnaires in each district obviously differ from each other, and these differences are disguised in the use of a constant sample size. This choice poses a problem if either of the following

**Table A.1** Questionnaires returned in this study, with response rates

| District | Number of usable questionnaires | Estimated response rate (%) |
|---|---|---|
| California | | |
| Central | 5,841 | 11.1 |
| Eastern | 4,080 | 42.2 |
| Northern | 5,150 | 49.4 |
| Southern | 904 | 7.3 |
| Illinois | | |
| Central | 3,960 | 61.6 |
| Northern | 9,909 | 57.0 |
| Southern | 1,494 | 67.0 |
| Pennsylvania | | |
| Eastern | 5,374 | 55.2 |
| Middle | 1,152 | 69.4 |
| Western | 1,877 | 32.4 |
| Tennessee | | |
| Middle | 8,756 | 71.3 |
| Western | 2,004 | 15.8 |
| Texas | | |
| Eastern | 102 | 6.2 |
| Northern | 1,050 | 12.6 |
| Southern | 3,746 | 43.4 |
| Western | 3,484 | 61.6 |

*Source:* Consumer Bankruptcy Project II, 1991.
*Note:* Number of questionnaires limited to cases filed in 1991; estimated response rate is based on one-half the number of nonbusiness Chapter 7 and Chapter 13 filings in the district during fiscal 1991.

situations pertains: the districts are quite different from one another or the people who respond are very different from the people who do not respond.

We addressed the first issue by cross-tabulating our variables of interest by state and district to look for significant district-level differences. Most of these tests showed no significant differences and so they are not reported in the text. Occasionally, however, there were significant district differences and they are reported, often without interpretation because we were not certain that an interpretation was possible. An example was the significantly greater proportion of joint petitions in Texas. We reported this finding in Chapter 3, but we are unable to offer an interpretation of why this difference has occurred.

**APPENDIX 1**

The next issue is whether the people who answered our question-naires are very different from the people who refused to answer the questionnaire. The term for this difference is nonresponse bias, and it is addressed in the next section.

## Nonresponse Bias

In 1991 debtors had the choice to complete or to ignore our question-naire. In examining the 1991 data we must thus ask whether those who refused to respond ("nonrespondents") differed from those who responded ("respondents"). Such a difference is important because of the likelihood that any nonresponse bias is systematic—that is, that the nonresponders may differ from the respondents according to some characteristic that is related to the object of the study. To take a hypothetical example, suppose that the people who were most ashamed of their bankruptcies were also the least likely to cooperate with our study. In such a case, our sample would be biased in terms of the emotional state of the debtors.

Debtors could not avoid filing their papers in the court, however, so the court docket is a complete universe. One way to study non-response bias is to compare the papers filed by the nonrespondents with those of the respondents to see if there are any differences. We estimated nonresponse bias by comparing the financial data in the bankruptcy file from a sample of 77 nonrespondent petitioners in the Eastern District of Pennsylvania with the court records of the sample of 150 respondents. By comparing the court docket with the com-pleted questionnaires, it was possible to list and then to systemati-cally sample the nonrespondents. We were then able to compare non-respondents with respondents on the financial variables that both groups had listed in their bankruptcy petitions. We were not able to compare them on demographic criteria, however, because the court files do not contain such data.

Data on family income, total assets, total debt, and secured and unsecured debt levels for 145 respondents and 77 nonrespondents in the Eastern District of Pennsylvania are shown in table A.2. Data are reported for the mean and standard deviation, as well as for the 25th percentile, median, and 75th percentile. These latter three in-dicators mark three points in a distribution. The 25th percentile is

**Table A.2**  Distribution of income, assets, and debts for bankruptcy petitioners in the Eastern District of Pennsylvania, by response status[a,b]

**Respondents**

| Distribution | Family income | Total assets | Total debt | Secured debt | Unsecured debt |
|---|---|---|---|---|---|
| Mean | 17,368 | 32,452 | 46,417 | 26,601 | 19,815 |
| s.d. | 10,505 | 46,045 | 55,942 | 45,775 | 28,343 |
| 25th percentile | 10,104 | 3,113 | 15,581 | 0 | 6,816 |
| Median | 15,900 | 14,500 | 28,293 | 8,846 | 14,514 |
| 75th percentile | 22,620 | 43,966 | 53,698 | 36,488 | 24,081 |
| N | 137 | 138 | 138 | 138 | 138 |
| Outliers Removed | 1 | 1 | 1 | 1 | 1 |
| Missing[c] | 7 | 6 | 6 | 6 | 6 |

**Nonrespondents**

| Distribution | Family income | Total assets | Total debt | Secured debt | Unsecured debt |
|---|---|---|---|---|---|
| Mean | 20,352 | 58,965 | 68,936 | 42,802 | 26,290 |
| s.d. | 10,636 | 99,687 | 89,416 | 63,535 | 59,292 |
| 25th percentile | 14,394 | 6,764 | 20,818 | 4,453 | 8,082 |
| Median | 18,000 | 36,200 | 35,487 | 23,399 | 13,977 |
| 75th percentile | 24,640 | 68,792 | 81,452 | 49,151 | 29,471 |
| N | 77 | 77 | 75 | 77 | 75 |
| Missing | 0 | 0 | 2 | 0 | 2 |
| Statistical Test t-value *p ≤ 0.05 | 1.99* | 2.21* | 1.98* | 2.16* | 1.08 |

*Source:* Consumer Bankruptcy Project II, 1991, published in *American Bankruptcy Law Journal* 68 (1994): 152.
*Notes:* [a] Cases with extreme values on assets, total debt, or income are removed. Outliers removed are beyond the cutoff points used in *As We Forgive Our Debtors,* adjusted to 1991 dollars using the Consumer Price Index (*Statistical Abstract: 1992,* 468, table 737). The original 1981 figures were multiplied by 1.498 to get the adjusted cutoff points (Income > 97,393; Assets > 749,175; Total debt > 749,175).
[b] Respondents filled out the Questionnaire (Form 1.1) while the nonrespondents chose not to reply.
[c] Six cases from the Eastern District of Pennsylvania (all six cases are "respondents") were removed from this analysis because of invalid secured debt information.

the value below which one-quarter of the cases fall. The median is the point that divides the distribution in two: half of the cases have values greater than the median, and half have values below the median. The 75th percentile is the value below which three-quarters of the distribution falls. In a "normal" curve, the ideal, bell-shaped distribution, the median and the mean would be the same; to the extent that the mean is greater than the median, the distribution is being skewed by large values.

The t-test, reported at the bottom of each column, is a measure of whether the two distributions are significantly different. Nonrespondents here have significantly higher family incomes, assets, total debt, and secured debt than respondents. Because the nonrespondents have both higher total debts and higher incomes, the total debt-income ratio of the respondents, 2.99, is not significantly different from the total debt-income ratio of the nonrespondents, 2.90.[14] The two groups do not differ significantly on unsecured debt, although the median for the nonrespondents diverges sharply from the mean, indicating a skewed distribution.

We repeated the analysis by comparing the respondents from the Texas and Illinois samples with the Pennsylvania nonrespondents. The results, reported in table A.3, show that for every indicator, the t-test value is not significant, indicating that the Pennsylvania non-respondents do not differ statistically from the Texas and Illinois respondents. Moreover, the respondents did not differ significantly from the nonrespondents in either the total debt-income ratio nor the nonmortgage debt income ratio.[15] In contrast to the data in table A.2, then, table A.3 suggests that the nonrespondents in Pennsylvania look very much like the respondents in other states.

This investigation of response bias alerts us that the respondents in the Eastern District of Pennsylvania differ in financial circumstances from both the nonrespondents and the respondents in the other two districts. In some previous work, we have suggested that the active Legal Services program in Philadelphia might have led both to more lower-income debtors and to more debtors who cooperated with our study.[16] The fact that the nonrespondents are fairly homogeneous with the respondents in Illinois and Texas, however, reduces the chance that the nonresponse bias would undercut our findings about the middle-class identity of the debtors.

## Statistical Tests

When the word *significant* is used in the text, it is used in the sense of statistical significance. Analyses in this study were done using both SPSS and SAS, statistical packages commonly used in the social sci-

**Table A.3** Distribution of income, assets, and debts for respondent bankruptcy petitioners in the Western District of Texas and Northern District of Illinois, compared with nonrespondents in the Eastern District of Pennsylvania[a,b]

**W.D. Tex. and N.D. Ill. Respondents**

| Distribution | Family income | Total assets | Total debt | Secured debt | Unsecured debt |
|---|---|---|---|---|---|
| Mean | 22,021 | 41,285 | 52,847 | 31,412 | 21,127 |
| s.d. | 12,461 | 52,127 | 53,107 | 40,361 | 32,309 |
| 25th percentile | 13,065 | 3,219 | 16,140 | 2,800 | 7,301 |
| Median | 19,872 | 18,763 | 32,522 | 11,421 | 12,626 |
| 75th percentile | 28,444 | 64,425 | 73,161 | 55,200 | 22,975 |
| N | 292 | 294 | 292 | 295 | 292 |
| Outliers Removed | 4 | 4 | 4 | 4 | 4 |
| Missing | 7 | 5 | 7 | 4 | 7 |

**E.D. Pa. Nonrespondents**

| Distribution | Family income | Total assets | Total debt | Secured debt | Unsecured debt |
|---|---|---|---|---|---|
| Mean | 20,352 | 58,965 | 68,936 | 42,802 | 26,290 |
| s.d. | 10,636 | 99,687 | 89,416 | 63,535 | 59,292 |
| 25th percentile | 14,394 | 6,764 | 20,818 | 4,453 | 8,082 |
| Median | 18,000 | 36,200 | 35,487 | 23,399 | 13,977 |
| 75th percentile | 24,640 | 68,792 | 81,452 | 49,151 | 29,471 |
| N | 77 | 77 | 75 | 77 | 75 |
| Missing | 0 | 0 | 2 | 0 | 2 |
| Statistical Test t-value | −1.08[c] | 1.50[c] | 1.49[c] | 1.50[c] | 1.01[c] |

*Source:* Consumer Bankruptcy Project II, 1991, published in *American Bankruptcy Law Journal* 68 (1994): 153. *Notes:* [a]Cases with extreme values on assets, total debt, or income are removed. Outliers removed are beyond the cut-off points used in *As We Forgive Our Debtors*, adjusted to 1991 dollars using the Consumer Price Index (*Statistical Abstract: 1992*, 468, table 473). The original 1981 figures were multiplied by 1.498 to get the adjusted cut-off points (Income > 97,393; Assets > 749,175; Total debt > 749,175).
 [b]Respondents filled out the questionnaire (Form 1.1) while the nonrespondents chose not to reply.
 [c]Not statistically significant at $p \leq 0.05$.

ences. We used a criterion level of 5%, meaning that there would be a 5% or smaller probability that a finding had occurred by chance. Given the nature of our sample, a relatively simple set of statistical tests seemed appropriate. Comparisons of nominal and ordinal variables (state, district, chapter, marital status, occupation, etc.) were typically performed with chi-square tests, and comparisons of interval variables (income, debt, assets) were normally done with t-tests. Occasionally we report zero-order correlations or other statistics. Although multivariate analyses are not reported in the text, we performed a number of analyses that we did not deem sufficiently interesting to include.

The analysis of the financial variables deserves a particular word of mention. There is inherently a great deal of variability in the analysis of debt, income, and assets. For a variable such as sex, our respondents agreed to classify themselves in only two ways, male or female. The analysis of financial data requires summarizing and describing many values. An indicator such as debt takes on a different value for every case in the study. The mean, or arithmetic average, is the usual way to summarize such a series of values, but the mean is susceptible to distortion by a few very large numbers. For example, a single debtor with a million-dollar debt will substantially raise the mean of the debt owed by a group of 100 randomly selected debtors. This distortion will be transmitted to the standard deviation, the most commonly used measure of dispersion, because the value of the mean is used to compute the standard deviation. If a test of statistical significance is done, such as the t-tests that we commonly used, the error will be compounded because both the mean and the standard deviation are used to compute the t-test.

One way to reduce the distortion is to remove the outliers, or the cases with extreme values, before offering the summary statistics. In our 1981 study, we plotted all values and then visually identified the cases with extreme values. This resulted in removing 6 cases reporting income greater than $65,000; 5 cases with assets greater than $500,000; and 17 cases with debts in excess of $500,000. Because one debtor was an outlier on two criteria, a total of 27 debtors were eliminated from the statistical analysis.[17] For our 1991 study, we had available to us a computer program that estimated outliers based on the techniques of exploratory data analysis.[18] We also adjusted our 1981 criteria for inflation and calculated outliers using the visual techniques we had used in the earlier study. The two techniques—the computer approach and the visual approach—identified the same set of outlying cases. In this book we have chosen to use our 1981 criteria because there is no practical difference achieved by using the more elaborate statistical criteria. Five cases are eliminated as outliers from the analysis of respondents. There were no outliers among the nonrespondents whom we analyzed separately.

## Comparison Data

In the text a number of comparisons are made with published or publicly available data. Data on bankruptcy filings are taken from electronic or print publications of the Administrative Office of the U.S. Courts. Demographic comparisons to the general population are usually made using 1990 Census data. Labor force comparisons are usually based upon the Current Population Survey, which is conducted each month by the Bureau of Labor Statistics and the Bureau of the Census. We used the General Social Survey for occupational data.

Financial data on the general population come from several sources. The Federal Reserve occasionally publishes a Survey of Consumer Finances. The Census Bureau conducts the Survey of Income and Program Participation. These two sources provide information on assets, debts, and net worth. Both the census and the Current Population Survey provide information on income.

Comparative data on housing, medical care, and credit card use came from a variety of sources, some public and some private, for which there are references in the relevant chapters. Two bankruptcy judges shared data they had collected on cases appearing before them. Their data, although necessarily limited in geographic coverage, offer depth and texture to our study. A third judge conducted a multidistrict survey, the results of which were reported to Congress.

## Los Angeles Data Set

The Honorable Barry Russell, bankruptcy judge in the Central District of California, gave us access to data he had collected between 1975 and 1985, with a short lapse in 1979. Judge Russell was interviewed by Teresa A. Sullivan on August 8, 1995, about the collection of the data. The judge explained that cases were assigned randomly to him and to the other judges in the district. He collected data through a combination of questioning and observation. As he said in his interview,

"I eyeballed age, sex, and race. There was one transvestite—I wasn't quite sure about that one. Other things I specifically asked, such as why they filed."

Judge Russell discovered patterns in his data that we were able to confirm in our study, including the increased representation of women as bankruptcy filers; the prevalence of divorce as a triggering mechanism; and the role of credit cards. He was also able to disprove some hypotheses. He found, for example, that there were very few debtors filing for a second or third time and that few people were in bankruptcy because of gambling problems.

## Ohio Data

The Honorable Barbara Sellers gave us data she had collected during 1997 in the Southern District of Ohio. She tabulated these data by hand, and with her permission, we transcribed the data to a spreadsheet for more systematic analysis. Judge Sellers selected the first 100 Chapter 13 cases and the first 50 Chapter 7 cases assigned to her during 1997. Every case in that group was studied. Assignment of cases in the Southern District of Ohio is random among the judges. Judge Sellers used only her own cases in order to eliminate any differences in outcomes that might be influenced by the judge.

Judge Sellers recorded about 75 pieces of information for each case. We received her handwritten sheets of information in June 1997. Following the same protocols that were used to code and report data from the Consumer Bankruptcy Project Phase I and Phase II, we coded the data into machine-readable form.

Because Judge Sellers's selection of cases produced a disproportionate share of Chapter 13 cases, given the filing data for the district, the analysis of the data from this district was weighted in the 75–25 proportion of Chapter 7 to Chapter 13 cases that existed in 1997 in her district. To enhance the accessibility of our data for other researchers, we did not sample the Chapter 13 cases, instead using a straightforward weighting process.

Judge Sellers inferred the reasons for bankruptcy from her reading of the cases; she did not interview the debtors. The Consumer Bankruptcy Project Phase II data came from direct written responses by the debtors. The Phase II data then could be seen as more subjective first-person responses and the Ohio data as third-person inferences from a knowledgeable observer.

## Multidistrict Study

The Honorable Randall J. Newsome, president of the National Conference of Bankruptcy Judges and a judge in the Northern District of California, asked other bankruptcy judges to conduct a small random sample of Chapter 7 cases filed in 1998. He presented testimony to Congress in 1999 reporting on 65 surveys of randomly selected Chapter 7 cases closed within 1998; the eventual database with a sample size of 5,235 is in the public domain. Professor Gary Neustadter analyzed the data and found a median gross annual income of $21,540 among the Chapter 7 debtors in 1997.[19]

## Michelle White

Economist Michelle White has done a number of analyses of bankruptcy. Many of these analyses featured econometric models of publicly available data (for example, data from the 1992 Survey of Consumer Finance).[20] She has made an important contribution to the collection of original bankruptcy data, however, because she had a question about previous bankruptcy added to the Panel Study of Income Dynamics, an excellent longitudinal study conducted by the University of Michigan. This survey is now in the public domain and available to other researchers. Although the survey has so far been analyzed in cross-section, it offers the possibility of a longitudinal linkage back to earlier years to the study. A longitudinal analysis might make it possible for researchers to answer the elusive question about what happens to debtors once they leave the bankruptcy courts.

## Age Data

The development of age data in our questionnaire offered the opportunity for a number of additional checks of data and for further exploration of our substantive findings reported in Chapter 2. Age data

**Table A.4**   Overall and age-specific bankruptcy filing rates, 1991 (per 1,000 population)

| Age group | Rate per thousand |
|---|---|
| Total, ages 20 and older | 4.93 |
| 20–24 | 3.69 |
| 25–29 | 6.18 |
| 30–34 | 7.55 |
| 35–39 | 7.12 |
| 40–44 | 7.74 |
| 45–49 | 7.17 |
| 50–54 | 4.16 |
| 55–59 | 4.49 |
| 60+ | 0.84 |

*Source:* Consumer Bankruptcy Project II, 1991, based on 600 cases from four districts: Northern District of Illinois, Eastern District of Pennsylvania, Middle District of Tennessee, and Western District of Texas.

are a sensitive indicator of overall data quality because misreporting of age data can be quantified. Careless reporting, or reporting by less-educated populations, often reveals "heaping," or overreporting of ages ending in 5 and 0. That is, respondents round off their ages rather than reporting the ages exactly. We studied age data from four districts in our enhanced sample and found little evidence of age heaping using Whipple's Index and Myers' Blended Index.

285

Chapter 2 discusses in some detail the baby boomer representation in bankruptcy. No one has, to our knowledge, previously developed a schedule of age-specific bankruptcy filing rates, so it is impossible to know if the baby boomers are different from earlier, smaller cohorts in their credit and bankruptcy practices. It is possible, however, to estimate age-specific bankruptcy filing rates for the primary filers from our data, and the schedule is presented in table A.4. This table was constructed using the data from the Northern District of Illinois, the Central District of California, the Eastern District of Pennsylvania, and the Western District of Texas. In this table we assumed that the proportion of filings at each age observed in our four districts would apply nationwide. A comparison with the other districts in the study showed few differences. Using our assumption of a constant relationship to age, we distributed the 1991 nonbusiness bankruptcy filings by age to form the numerators for the rates. Second, the schedule of rates assumes that use of the 1990 census figures introduces

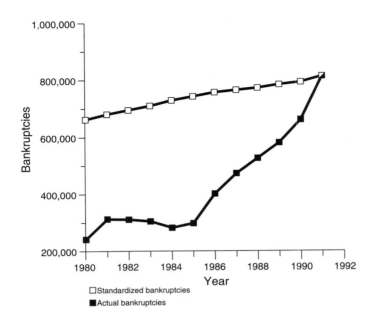

Fig. A.2  Actual and age-standardized U.S. bankruptcy filings, 1980–91.

minimal error into the denominators. We used the census data as the denominators for our age-specific rates.

The overall bankruptcy filing rate in 1991 was 4.9 per 1000 persons aged 20 or older. The age-specific filing rate ranges from 7.7 per thousand for ages 40–44 to 0.8 per thousand for ages 60 and older. The rate exceeds 7 per thousand for the age groups between 30 and 50, including the three baby boom groups between ages 30 and 45 (born 1946 through 1961). The age structure of the United States changed substantially throughout the 1980s as the baby boom cohorts aged from 16–34 in 1980 to 27–45 in 1991. The population was growing in the very age groups that have the largest age-specific filing rates in 1991. The changes in age structure suggested that at least some of the growth in bankruptcy filings might be an artifact of age structure.

We applied the 1991 age-specific bankruptcy filings to U.S. age structures to indirectly standardize the actual numbers of bankruptcy filings from 1980 through 1991 (fig. A.2). The line marked "actual" refers to the number of nonbusiness bankruptcies that were actually filed in the years indicated. The line marked "standardized"

**APPENDIX 1**

refers to the number of bankruptcies that would have been filed had the 1991 age-specific bankruptcy filing rates been in effect. In 1980, there would have been about 662,000 bankruptcies if the 1991 age-specific rates had been applied to the actual 1980 age structure (instead of the 241,685 that actually occurred). The standardized figure is 18% below the actual 1991 figure of 812,685. Thus, age structure alone accounted for about 18% of the increase in bankruptcies in 1991 compared with 1980.

Appendix 2

# Other Published Studies

In this appendix, we review some of the published studies in the field. For the most part, we discuss only studies that have gathered original data. Of course, our reference here or in the notes is not an endorsement of any study, given that we have not directly analyzed a study's data ourselves. We do comment on certain reported aspects of some of these studies. Occasionally the methodological description may have been too sketchy for us to make thorough critiques. In other studies, the design is obviously deficient in ways that we note. Even so, if the publication has occurred in a scholarly site, we take some comfort in knowing that the editor has scrutinized the work or, even better, has subjected it to peer review. The studies about which we are most dubious are those that are proprietary (so that no further data analysis can be done by others), that are sketchy in their methodological description, and that are published in informal formats rather than in professional literature.

Empirical research in bankruptcy has flourished during the past decade. This appendix is not intended to be a comprehensive literature review. For the most part, we have emphasized studies that touch on points raised in this book. A great deal of recent work, however, has focused on the issue of whether debtors in Chapter 7 can repay. Because this issue is related to our finding that the debtors in bankruptcy have very low incomes, we devote some attention to these recent studies.

A study published in 1999 by the General Accounting Office has compared four studies of these studies that attempt to estimate whether debtors can pay.[1] The studies, which find that between 3.6% and 15% of debtors could repay, differ in terms of methods, assumptions, and hypothesized statutory changes. Although each of the studies finds a proportion of debtors who could repay given certain assumptions, the GAO reviewers note that some debtors already reaffirm debts in Chapter 7 and that nearly two-thirds of the Chapter 13 debtors do not complete their plans.

## Executive Office for the U.S. Trustees

The Executive Office of the U.S. Trustees studied 1,955 Chapter 7 no-asset cases closed during the first six months of 1998 in the 84 (out of 90) judicial districts that had U.S. trustees.[2] The number of sample cases in each district was proportional to each district's share of the national total of Chapter 7 cases filed in calendar year 1997. Each trustee was asked to send the appropriate quota of cases, so that the sample, though large, is not random. The GAO review raises the issue of whether the cases might be affected by judgments of the trustees. Only 300 debtors had any positive net annual income above the national median income. The authors estimated how much debt could be repaid if 25%, 50%, 75%, or 100% of the available income to pay unsecured nonpriority creditors were used for this purpose. The authors concluded that the final return to the unsecured nonpriority debtors was likely to be less than $1 billion annually.

289

## Credit Research Center

John M. Barron and Michael E. Staten, both affiliated with the Credit Research Center of Georgetown University (and previously affiliated with Purdue University) published a study in October 1997.[3] The General Accounting Office subsequently evaluated this study.[4] Barron and Staten's sample was drawn from a single location in each of 13 judgmentally chosen districts for a period of one or two months. The usual time frame was May or June 1996, but the months varied somewhat. The sample size was 2,441 Chapter 7 and 1,357 Chapter 13 filings. The cases were those filed during the first few days of the month in each district. This study resulted in an estimate that 30% of Chapter 7 debtors could repay a "substantial portion of their debts." This study was funded by the credit industry and has not at this writing been published in a professional journal.

A forerunner of this study was done with cases filed in the summer of 1981. This study, done by Credit Research Center researchers when they were at Purdue University, examined the records of 1,199 debtors in Chapter 7 in an effort to see if they could repay their debt in a Chapter 13–type plan that would hold the debtors to the poverty level for five years.[5] Homeowners were permitted to make their mortgage payments, but otherwise income over the poverty level was devoted to repayment. We have previously criticized this study for recommending Chapter 13–style plans without having examined how well Chapter 13 works, and also for mistakes in the legal analysis and methodology.[6]

## Ernst and Young

The accounting firm Ernst and Young analyzed a nationally representative sample of nonbusiness Chapter 7 filings from all 90 bankruptcy districts during the calendar year 1997.[7] The sample of 2,142 cases was randomly drawn from all Chapter 7 filings during the year, and it was adjusted to exclude an estimated percentage of cases that were dismissed and in which the petitioners received no discharge. This study indicated that 15% of the Chapter 7 debtors could repay a substantial portion of their debts, defined as all nonhousing secured debt, all unsecured priority debt, and 20% of the unsecured nonpriority debt. This study was subsequently analyzed and compared with the Credit Research Center's study.[8] One article has been published in a professional journal.[9]

## Creighton University Study

This study was conducted by two law professors, Marianne B. Culhane and Michaela M. White, with funding from the American Bankruptcy

Institute.[10] They studied a random sample of cases that were filed in 1995 in seven judgmentally selected bankruptcy districts. The sample size was 1,041 filings. The cases had all closed as nonbusiness Chapter 7 cases by the time the sample was drawn, although some had originally been filed in other chapters. Their study was similar to that of Ernst and Young in many of its definitions and overall assumptions, but it found that only 3.6% of the debtors could repay a substantial portion of their debt. This study, along with the Ernest and Young study and the Credit Research Center Study, have been reviewed comparatively in a report from the General Accounting Office.[11]

## SMR Research Corporation

SMR Research Corporation also released a study in 1997.[12] The principal study method was an analysis of a database containing aggregate data for more than 3,000 U.S. counties. The variables included median household income, mean average disposable after-tax income, bankruptcy filing data, the percentage of the population in the 1990 census who had at least one year of college, and some other aggregated data. It is not clear how SMR is able to allocate bankruptcy filings to the county of residence. Presumably such an allocation could be done with zip codes from petition data, but there is no mention of the use of data from the bankruptcy courts.

The conclusions of the analysis are reported rather than the statistical analyses, but the unnamed authors conclude that the poorest counties also had low bankruptcy filing rates. The authors headlined this conclusion by saying that bankruptcy is a "middle class and upper middle class problem." They also reported that counties had, on average, 45.2% of the population with some college education and that counties right at that average had the highest bankruptcy rates. By examining state-level health insurance rates and bankruptcy filing rates, they conclude that lack of medical insurance is a cause of bankruptcy.

Although these two findings might seem to confirm our own findings earlier in the analysis, other findings are discrepant. Using the unemployment rate for counties, for example, SMR authors argue that job loss has no relationship to bankruptcy. They also argue that lawyer advertising has reduced the stigma of bankruptcy and that gambling debts are an important cause of bankruptcy—two findings for which we have no affirmative evidence and some skepticism.

## Visa Bankruptcy Study

Visa conducted a study of more than 65 macroeconomic and social variables to explain trends in personal bankruptcy filings at both state and national levels. The econometric model that was eventually developed used 16 years of filing data. The most important explanatory variables in the model were growth in total employment, share of population aged 25–44, divorce rate, median existing home prices, "social factors trend variable" (a parenthetical note adds, "e.g., legal advertising"), number of bank credit card accounts per adult, and ratio of consumer installment debt service to personal disposable income. There was some difference in significance at the state and national levels; unemployment rates, for example, are more important at the state level than growth in total employment, and divorce rates are not significant at the state level.[13]

## GKM

Gerard Klauer Marrison and Company issued an industry report in 1996 on the loss risks of bank credit cards.[14] The authors attribute escalating credit card losses to the proliferation of cards issued and suggest that data on bankruptcy filings might become a new leading indicator. The authors conducted an informal survey of approximately 30 personal bankruptcy attorneys in five large states. The states are not named, nor is the method of locating the attorneys specified. As a result of this survey, the authors conclude that the 1990–91 rise in bankruptcy filings was cyclical (that is, related to the business cycle) but that the subsequent increases in bankruptcies are due to the ease of obtaining credit and preapproved credit cards. They also offer as conclusions that the stigma of bankruptcy is diminishing (the proof is the number of filings); that fraud is not a major factor; that bankruptcy lawyers are aggressively advertising; and that although the law is not more favorable to debtors, few petitioners are refused a discharge.

**APPENDIX 2**

## Susan Kovac

Kovac, an assistant general counsel with the Tennessee Department of Human Services, studied 247 filings drawn from the Northern Division of the Eastern District of Tennessee during fiscal year 1986 (July 1, 1985 through June 30, 1986). The sample was limited to judgment-proof filers in Chapter 7—that is, filers with no assets available to creditors. Of these petitioners, 33 were long-term unemployed, 105 were recently unemployed, and 84 were workers who had been at work for the preceding two years. The author argues that garnishment or the threat of garnishment was an impetus to bankruptcy for this sample. She found considerable gender differences in financial situations, with women in all work categories worse off than men.[15]

## Gary Klein and Maggie Spade

Gary Klein, an attorney with the National Consumer Law Center, and Maggie Spade, the center's director of research, conducted a study of self-representation in the Massachusetts bankruptcy courts.[16] This study, which was funded by the National Conference of Bankruptcy Judges, studied pro se cases in the District of Massachusetts. The researchers reviewed 172 cases filed pro se in Massachusetts during November 1990 and during February, May, August, and November 1991, along with a control sample of 91 debtors represented by counsel. The sample was drawn by discarding every third pro se debtor from the universe. The control sample was drawn by taking the next case in numerical order following every other one of the pro se cases. In follow-up telephone calls, the researchers were able to contact 24 pro se debtors for a survey. They also interviewed court personnel.

The data showed significant differences between pro se debtors and debtors represented by counsel. Pro se debtors were less likely to receive a discharge and much more likely to have their cases dismissed, especially in Chapter 13.[17] The pro se debtors were poorer, with only 52% having incomes above 150% of the federal poverty level, compared with 81% of the represented debtors. Nevertheless, the represented debtors were hardly rich, with only 39% of them making more than $24,000.[18]

## Ian Domowitz and Colleagues

Ian Domowitz, an economics professor at Northwestern University, has written a series of studies on bankruptcy. Domowitz and colleagues have studied a random sample of Chapter 7 and Chapter 13 cases from five court districts in the second and third quarters of 1980. The districts are Southern and Eastern New York, Southern Ohio, Eastern Kentucky, and Central California. The General Accounting Office collected the data from petitions; the sample size in the analysis was 575 Chapter 7 cases and 252 Chapter 13 filings.[19] The authors use the Survey of Consumer Finances as a control sample. Domowitz and Robert L. Sartain find that medical debt has a large impact on the conditional probability of bankruptcy but that credit card debt is the largest single contributor to bankruptcy at the margin. The authors also note that homeowning is associated with a different debt structure and more commonly associated with Chapter 13 filing.

294

## Michael Herbert and Domenic Pacitti

Law professors Michael J. Herbert and Domenic E. Pacitti studied the distribution of assets in Chapter 7 cases that were closed during 1984–87.[20] Their study used the universe of Chapter 7 cases closed in the Richmond Division of the Eastern District of Virginia from October 1984 through January 1987. The authors note that the distinction between business and nonbusiness bankruptcies was not always clear; in analyzing consumer cases, they assumed that an ambiguous case was a business case and eliminated it from consideration. An asset distribution was made in 204 cases out of 4,723 cases closed under Chapter 7. Nearly 96% of the Chapter 7 cases were thus no-asset cases. The authors concluded that only secured creditors realized much from Chapter 7 estates.

## Oliver Pollak

History professor Oliver Pollak studied 5,680 nonbusiness bankruptcies filed in Nebraska (a single district) during the period July 1, 1996, through June 30, 1997. The raw court records were coded for gender, chapter, zip code, and case number. This procedure was repeated for 925 of 3,779 filings for calendar year 1987, for 317 of the 1,937 filings for 1977, and for 178 of the 1,211 filings in 1967. It was not clear on what basis cases were sampled from the earlier decades. A substantial increase in the proportion of filings by women occurred over this time, from a low of 11.1% in 1970 to a high of 32.4% in 1996–97.[21]

## Philip Shuchman

Law professor Philip Shuchman conducted several empirical studies in which he gathered empirical data from bankruptcy files to examine specific statutory issues.[22] These studies presented data in descriptive format. Details on how the samples were drawn were usually sketchy. For these reasons, and because measures of dispersion were not reported, it has been difficult for subsequent researchers to make meaningful comparisons with other studies. These studies did demonstrate, however, that the schedules filed with the courts were potentially important sources of information that could be coded and analyzed.

## The Brookings Study

In some ways the progenitor of all the other research, the Brookings Study was a large-scale study of bankruptcy based on case analyses and interviews in eight districts.[23] The sample was chosen randomly from cases that were closed in 1964. Four hundred interviews were conducted with debtors, and credit bureau records were examined. The study also included interviews with judges, clerks, trustees, and some creditors. In a separate survey, the researchers mailed a questionnaire to more than 1,000 trial attorneys. The researchers incorporated responses from a Gallup Poll that asked questions about bankruptcy.

## One-District Studies

A number of small studies of a single district were conducted throughout the late 1960s and 1970s. These studies were often doctoral dissertations or master's theses. Taken as a group, they offer some insight into both the methods and the lines of inquiry that would be pursued in subsequent decades. Several reviews of these small studies are available.[24]

296

# Notes

## Chapter 1: Americans in Financial Crisis

1. In 1996 for the first time more than 1 million consumer bankruptcies were filed. See Department of Justice, Administrative Office of the U.S. Courts, *Report of the Director of the Administrative Office of the U.S. Courts* (1997). The first-quarter filings accelerated the upward trend from prior years. By comparison, during the first fiscal year in which the current bankruptcy law was in effect, 243,618 nonbusiness cases were filed. See Department of Justice, Administrative Office of the U.S. Courts, *Report of the Director of the Administrative Office of the U.S. Courts* (1980), 559, table F3B6. See House, Banking and Financial Services Committee, *Hearing on Consumer Debt Before the House Banking and Financial Services Committee,* 104th Cong., 2d sess., Sept. 12, 1996 (statement of Chairman James A. Leach).

2. We have published the part of the Consumer Bankruptcy Project Phase II data that represent an update of the Phase I study from the perspective of those interested in current operation of the bankruptcy system. See Teresa A. Sullivan, Elizabeth Warren, and Jay Lawrence Westbrook, "Consumer Debtors Ten Years Later: A Financial Comparison of Consumer Bankrupts, 1981–1991," *American Bankruptcy Law Journal* 68 (Spring 1994): 121.

3. See Bureau of the Census, *Statistical Abstract of the United States: 1994* (Washington, D.C., 1994), 548, table 849.

4. We did not distribute questionnaires to Chapter 11 debtors. See Appendix 1.

5. The debtor signs a form to accompany the bankruptcy petition stating, "I ____, declare under penalty of perjury that I have read the foregoing Schedule of Current Income and Expenditures, consisting of ____ sheets, and that it is true and correct to the best of my knowledge, information, and belief." The bankruptcy laws are unforgiving about falsification. A debtor will receive no discharge of any debt in bankruptcy if the debtor "knowingly and fraudulently,

in or in connection with any case (A) made a false oath or account." 11 U.S.C. § 727(a)(4). Most debtors are represented by counsel who inform the debtor of these requirements and who themselves can face liability for passing on falsified documents.

6. Because the home is usually the debtor's single valuable asset, the creditors, the bankruptcy trustee, and the court are likely to look most closely at the statements of valuation to see if they fit with their own perceptions about local real estate markets. If anyone has a question, the court can require a certified appraisal of the property, but such requests for appraisals are rare.

7. The National Bankruptcy Review Commission expressed concern over the possibility of errors in debtors' schedules and recommended a procedure to institute random audits of the filing papers. Even as it made such a recommendation, however, the commission noted that the move was designed to "increase confidence in the accuracy of the scheduled information" but that it had no "hard evidence that debtors intentionally misrepresent their finances on statements and schedules." The commission concluded that errors were more likely the result of financial affairs of individual debtors that are in "complete disarray. Bills and pay stubs, if available at all, often are brought to lawyers' offices in a shoe box or a paper bag." National Bankruptcy Review Commission, *Bankruptcy: The Next Twenty Years*, vol. 1 (Washington, D.C.: GPO, 1997), 107–11.

8. About 56% of American adults (111 million people) were married and living with their spouses in 1998. Bureau of the Census, *Marital Status and Living Arrangements: March 1998 (Update), P20-514* (Washington, D.C., 1998).

9. In theory they can "redeem" the car by paying its full value to the lienholder in cash, but few consumer debtors have enough cash to do that.

10. Chapter choice is a complex issue. Aside from the legal advantages to Chapter 13, some people file Chapter 13 because they want to pay their creditors as best they can. Some want to do so for moral reasons. Others think that a Chapter 13 payment effort will improve their future credit rating, although that is doubtful in most districts. On the other hand, Chapter 7 debtors often re-affirm some of their debts, agreeing to repay some creditors notwithstanding the bankruptcy discharge, so that they receive a less-fresh start than they otherwise would. Furthermore, Chapter 7 may simply be unavailable. In some parts of the country, the federal courts bar debtors from Chapter 7 if the judge believes they are able to pay a substantial part of their debts at some level of sacrifice and hardship. See, e.g., In re Walton, 866 F.2d 981 (8th Cir. 1989). Various informal forces at work in parts of the country also push debtors toward Chapter 13 even when Chapter 7 might seem a better choice for them. See Teresa A. Sullivan, Elizabeth Warren, and Jay Lawrence Westbrook, "The Persistence of Local Legal Culture: Twenty Years of Evidence from the Federal Bankruptcy Courts," *Harvard Journal of Law and Public Policy* 17 (Summer 1994): 801–65. The result of all these factors cutting in favor of one type of proceeding or the other is that there are many filings in each of the two chapters, although Chapter 7 filings remain the majority of cases in most areas. The proportion of filings in each chapter varies greatly around the country, one of many instances of regional variation in a supposedly uniform national statute. Ibid., 813.

11. Briefly, debtors in Chapter 13 have to pay the lienholder only an amount

298

equal to the value of the property securing the debt, not the whole amount of the debt. The rest of the debt is then treated as unsecured, just like a telephone bill or credit card charges.

12. In some parts of the country debtors can attend consumer-finance education programs, but such programs are not widespread.

13. See William Whitford, "The Ideal of Individualized Justice: Consumer Bankruptcy as Consumer Protection, and Consumer Protection in Consumer Bankruptcy," *American Bankruptcy Law Journal* 68 (Fall 1994): 397; Sullivan, Warren, and Westbrook, *Local Legal Culture*, 817, n. 6.

14. See, e.g., Henry S. Farber, "Are Lifetime Jobs Disappearing? Job Duration in the United States: 1973–1993," National Bureau of Economic Research Working Paper No. 5014 (1995). A survey of bankruptcy professionals (lawyers, trustees, and others in the system) yielded similar reasons, but with some interesting differences (three primary reasons: ease of obtaining credit, job loss, and financial mismanagement). G. Ray Warner, *Report on the State of the American Bankruptcy System* (Washington, D.C.: American Bankruptcy Institute, 1996), 6.

15. Department of Labor, News Release No. 94-434 (1994). The survey covered long-tenured workers displaced in 1991–93 and asked about their status in February 1994. A "displaced" worker by government definition is one who has been laid off (not fired or quit), and a "long-tenured" displaced worker is one who was with the prior employer for at least three years.

16. Council of Economic Advisors, Job Creation and Employment Opportunities, *The United States Labor Market, 1993–96* (1996): 9.

17. Bureau of Labor Statistics, Worker Displacement Survey, 1995–97 (Aug. 19, 1998) (http://stats.bls.gov/newsrels.htm).

18. See Department of Labor, "Displaced Worker Summary" (Washington, D.C., Aug. 19, 1998), 347.

19. Median incomes for all families increased less than 1% from 1980 to 1993, in constant 1993 dollars. See Bureau of the Census, *Statistical Abstract of the United States: 1995* (Washington, D.C., 1995), table 731.

20. See, e.g., Bureau of the Census, "Middle Class Income—All Households" (showing that between 1981 and 1991 every segment of the population fell in its percentage of national income, except for the highest fifth, which rose substantially). This trend continued through four more years of prosperity. Bureau of the Census, *Statistical Abstract of the United States: 1997* (Washington, D.C., 1997), table 725. Most of the increase actually went to the top 5%.

21. See *Statistical Abstract: 1997*, table 779.

22. See Glenn B. Canner and Charles A. Luckett, "Payment of Household Debts," *Federal Reserve Bulletin* 77 (1991): 218; Glenn B. Canner, Arthur B. Kennickell, and Charles A. Luckett, "Household Sector Borrowing and the Burden of Debt," ibid. 81 (1995): 323. In these two articles, the authors argue that the debt burdens on consumers are not as serious as the statistics suggest, primarily because they associate the increases with consumers with higher net worth and income. However, their focus is on overall effects, not the effects on large numbers of marginal households. So, e.g., their most recent figures show that percentage of households with brutal, often-unpayable debt levels—above 30% of income— have increased by more than 50% from 1983 to 1992; see table 7. These figures

also show that these overburdened households are among the least-affluent in net worth.

23. *Statistical Abstract: 1997*, tables 798 and 806.

24. Diane Ellis, "The Effect of Consumer Interest Rate Deregulation on Credit Card Volumes, Charge-Offs, and the Personal Bankruptcy Rate," *Bank Trends* 98-05 (FDIC, Division of Insurance, March 1998): 98.

25. John Drake, "Credit Card Crunch: Lenders' New Rules Hit Consumers," *Houston Chronicle*, Nov. 11, 1998, A1 (citing a study by Consumer Action and Consumer Federation of America of 117 types of cards from 74 banks).

26. Jennifer M. Gardner, "Worker Displacement: A Decade of Change," *Monthly Labor Review* (April 1996): 45, 52, and table 6.

27. Bureau of the Census, "Children Without Health Insurance," *Census Brief/ 98–1* (March 1998): 1.

28. Bureau of the Census, *Dynamics of Economic Well-Being: Health Insurance, 1991 to 1993*, 70-43, 2, table A (1995).

29. More than 4 million households shifted an estimated $26 billion from credit card debt to home-equity loans in a 24-month period from 1996 to 1998, according to a recent study commissioned by the Consumer Bankers Association. Cited in Linda Punch, "The Home-Equity Threat," *Credit Card Management*, September 1998, 1. The industry notes high growth in home equity lending, particularly subprime lending of high loan-to-value ratio loans. American Banker-Bond Buyer, "Introduction and Summary," *Mortgage-Backed Securities Letter* 13 (Dec. 14, 1998): 1.

30. Federal Reserve, "Family Finances in the U.S.: Recent Evidence from the Survey of Consumer Finances," *Federal Reserve Bulletin* (January 1997): 21, table 14: Aggregate and median ratios of debt payments to family incomes, and shares of debtors with ratios above 40% and those with any payment sixty days or more past due, by selected family characteristics, 1989, 1992, and 1995. The Federal Reserve data in this table show that since the early 1990s, Americans with incomes below the poverty level nearly doubled their credit card usage, and those in the $10,000–25,000 income bracket came in a close second in the rise in debt. By contrast, those with incomes above $50,000 reduced their credit card debt.

31. This new segment of the consumer credit industry has been profiled in two very interesting and thorough articles: "Merchants of Debt," *New York Times*, July 2, 1995; "Bankrupts Who Drive Are Lucrative Market to a Growing Lender," *Wall Street Journal*, June 28, 1995. By 1998–99 a number of these subprime lenders had encountered serious financial difficulties themselves. See, e.g., Heather Timmons, "United Cos. Warns It May Default on $1.2B in Debt," *American Banker*, Feb. 4, 1999, 164.

32. See Juliet B. Schor, *The Overspent American: Upscaling, Downshifting, and the New Consumer* (New York: Basic Books, 1998). This interesting study must be read with the understanding that her "Telecom" sample represents a slice of the middle class distinctly above average. Ibid., 200, App. table B.1.

33. "The Downsizing of America," *New York Times*, Mar. 3, 1996. It was the longest series run by the *Times* since the "Pentagon Papers" in 1971. See "All Worked Up," *New Yorker*, Apr. 22, 1996, 51.

Chapter 2: Middle-Class and Broke

1. Robert W. Hodge and Donald J. Treiman, "Class Identification in the United States," *American Journal of Sociology* 73 (March 1968): 535, 547.

2. Kenneth M. Dolbeare and Jannette Kay Hubbell, *U.S.A. 2012: After the Middle-Class Revolution* (Chatham, N.J.: Chatham House, 1996), 3.

3. Mary R. Jackman and Robert W. Jackman, *Class Awareness in the United States* (Berkeley: University of California Press, 1983), 216–17. When given four options for social class (lower, working, middle, upper), roughly 96% of the population places itself in either the working class or the middle class. This pattern is evident in data from the National Opinion Research Center's annual General Social Survey from 1974 through the 1990s. Nancy J. Davis and Robert V. Robinson, "Do Wives Matter? Class Identities of Wives and Husbands in the United States, 1974–1994," *Social Forces* 76 (March 1998): 1063–86. The cultural ubiquity of the American middle class is described by Barbara Ehrenreich, *Fear of Falling: The Inner Life of the Middle Class* (New York: Pantheon, 1989). Ehrenreich attributes the "discovery of poverty" in the 1960s to an accompanying myth of general affluence.

4. Michele Lamont, *Money, Morals, and Manners: The Culture of the French and American Upper-Middle Class* (Chicago: University of Chicago Press, 1992), 65–66.

5. Erik Olin Wright, "Class Boundaries in Advanced Capitalist Societies," *New Left Review* 98 (1976): 3–41.

6. Philip Shuchman, "New Jersey Debtors, 1982–1983: An Empirical Study," *Seton Hall Law Review* 15 (1985): 544–45.

7. Ibid., 546.

8. Thomas J. Stanley and William D. Danko, *The Millionaire Next Door* (Atlanta, Ga.: Longstreet Press, 1996).

9. Alex Markels, "Down But Not Out,"*American Demographics* 20 (November 1998): 59, 61.

10. Frank Levy, "Incomes and Income Inequality," in Reynolds Farley, ed., *State of the Union: American in the 1990s,* vol. 1 (New York: Russell Sage, 1995), 1–57. Douglas S. Massey and Deborah S. Hirst, "From Escalator to Hourglass: Changes in the U.S. Occupational Wage Structure 1949–1989," *Social Science Research* 27 (March 1998): 51–71. Public policy changes have contributed to the erosion; see Dolbeare and Hubbell, *U.S.A. 2012,* 5–12. William P. Kreml characterizes these policy changes as ranging "from subsidy to abandonment." Kreml, *America's Middle Class: From Subsidy to Abandonment,* 2d ed. (Durham, N.C.: Carolina Academic Press, 1997).

11. Moreover, many of the college educated have had to take jobs that used to be filled by high school graduates. Daniel E. Hecker, "College Graduates in 'High School' Jobs: A Commentary," *Monthly Labor Review* 118 (December 1995): 28; John Tyler, Richard J. Murnane, and Frank Levy, "Are More College Graduates Really Taking 'High School' Jobs?" *Monthly Labor Review* 118 (December 1995): 18–27. Frederic L. Pryor and David Schaffer, "Wages and the University Educated: A Paradox Resolved" *Monthly Labor Review* 120 (July 1997): 3–14, argue that it is differences in literacy that channel some of the college-educated into better jobs and some into worse jobs.

12. Paul Ryscavage, "A Surge in Growing Income Inequality?" *Monthly Labor Review* 118 (August 1995): 52–62. Also see Kreml, *America's Middle Class,* 153–56.

301

13. Bureau of the Census, <http://www.census.gov/hhes/income/histinc/f12.html> (June 3, 1998).

14. Massey and Hirst, "From Escalator to Hourglass," 52.

15. See *Wall Street Journal,* Dow Jones Newswires, Dec. 23, 1998.

16. Some economists have tried to develop an econometric estimate of declining stigma, but their work indicates that the number of people in the survey who admitted to having been in bankruptcy was less than half the number expected, based on national filing rates. The percentages should have been the same because the survey is a large one, representative of the general population. Scott Fay, Erik Hurst, and Michelle White, "The Bankruptcy Decision: Does Stigma Matter?" (paper presented at the seminar "Law and Economics," Harvard University, Feb. 24, 1998, table 1). The economists nonetheless believed that the data showed that stigma had declined.

17. In terms of income and occupational prestige, bank officers are well off. Median weekly earnings for all financial managers in 1997 was $717, or about $37,500 annually. Bureau of Labor Statistics, *Employment and Earnings* 45 (January 1998): 209, table 39. Bank officers earned even more. The occupational prestige score for a bank officer is 72, well above the median level of 39 for the labor force. (A further discussion of occupational prestige scores follows below.) By either criterion, Willis Creighton was at least middle class and perhaps, when such distinctions are made, upper middle class.

18. In the 1994 Business Bankruptcy Project, we called owners and operators of small businesses that had failed. We identified ourselves as academic researchers and assured confidentiality. Nonetheless, many of the people we tried to interview denied that their businesses had filed for bankruptcy.

19. Robert Dolphin, Jr., "An Analysis of Economic and Personal Factors Leading to Consumer Bankruptcy," Bureau of Business and Economic Research, Occasional Paper No. 15 (East Lansing: Michigan State University, 1965).

20. Fifteen such studies were consulted for the Brookings Study. David T. Stanley and Marjorie Girth, *Bankruptcy: Problem, Process, Reform* (Washington, D.C.: Brookings Institution, 1971), 219–20. Another good review of this literature appears in Ramona K. Z. Heck, "Identifying Insolvent Households," *Journal of Home Economics* 72, no. 4 (1980): 14–17.

21. Congress, Report of the Commission on the Bankruptcy Laws of the United States, H.R. Doc. No. 137, 93d Cong., 1st sess., pt. 1 (1973).

22. Stanley and Girth, *Bankruptcy,* 42. Stanley and Girth did not endorse nor deliberately promulgate a stereotype. Inevitably, their work was used selectively by later readers.

23. Ibid., 41–46. The preponderance of males may be partly explained by the lack of a joint filing procedure before 1978. For both husband and wife to declare bankruptcy required that each of them file a petition and pay the filing fee. Instead of this expensive procedure, there was often an informal practice of letting the husband file without requiring his wife to file as well. Among the women who were in the Stanley and Girth study, 17% were divorced, compared with only 6% of the men. In terms of age, 19% were in their twenties, 32% were in their thirties, and 30% in their forties. Stanley and Girth are careful to note that there might be some bias among their respondents because they were hard to find and many were unwilling to be interviewed. Ibid., 41.

24. Ibid., 42, footnote omitted.

25. Ibid., 43–44. Then as now, the entrepreneurs were overrepresented in bankruptcy. Former business owners constituted about 13% of the "straight bankruptcy" (i.e., Chapter 7) cases and 1% of the Chapter 13 cases. At the time that Stanley and Girth wrote, chapter numbers were designated by Roman numerals, and so their sample was actually in Chapter VII or Chapter XIII.

26. General Accounting Office, *Bankruptcy Reform Act of 1978—A Before and After Look*, GAO/GGD-83-54 (Washington, D.C., 1983), 22. Also see Teresa A. Sullivan, Elizabeth Warren, and Jay Lawrence Westbrook, *As We Forgive Our Debtors: Bankruptcy and Consumer Credit in America* (New York: Oxford University Press, 1989), 63–83.

27. Sullivan, Warren, and Westbrook, *As We Forgive*, chap. 8. Oliver B. Pollak, examining 5,441 consumer filings in Nebraska for 1996–97, found that 40.6% of filings were joint and 32.4% were by women filing alone. Pollak, "Gender and Bankruptcy: An Empirical Analysis of Evolving Trends in Chapter 7 and Chapter 13 Bankruptcy Filings, 1996–1997," *Commercial Law Journal* 102, no. 3 (1998): 333–38. By comparison, he reports that the proportion of single-filing women was 14.6% in 1967, 11.1% in 1977, and 22.2% in 1987. Forty-one percent of a 1997 Canadian sample of bankrupt debtors were women. Saul Schwartz and Leigh Anderson, *An Empirical Study of Canadians Seeking Personal Bankruptcy Protection* (Carleton University, 1998), 3. For additional commentary on women in bankruptcy, see Zipporah Batshaw Wiseman, "Women in Bankruptcy and Beyond," *Indiana Law Journal* 65 (Winter 1989): 107–21; Karen Gross, *Failure and Forgiveness* (New Haven and London: Yale University Press, 1997), 68–70, 245–46. For a longer view of the role of women in the bankruptcy system, see Karen Gross, Marie Stefanini Newman, and Denise Campbell, "Ladies in Red: Learning from America's First Female Bankrupts," *American Journal of Legal History* 40 (January 1996): 1–40. For a more contemporary view about the roles of women in the bankruptcy system from bankrupt to lawyer, see "The Effects of Gender in the Federal Courts: The Final Report of the Ninth Circuit Gender Bias Task Force," *Southern California Law Review* 67 (1994): 745; Commission on Gender, Commission on Race and Ethnicity, "Report of the Third Circuit Task Force on Equal Treatment in the Courts," *Villanova Law Review* 42 (1997): 1355.

28. Philip Shuchman, "Social Science Research on Bankruptcy," *Rutgers Law Review* 43 (Fall 1990): 185. Shuchman completed several empirical studies himself.

29. Bureau of the Census, *Statistical Abstract of the United States: 1994* (Washington, D.C., 1994), 549, table 850. There were also another 67,714 business bankruptcies, at least some of which involved small business owners and their families. Because married couples are entitled to file jointly, the number of filings does not represent the number of petitioners.

30. In 1991, 252,137,000 people resided in the United States in 94,312,000 households. Ibid., 27, table 26; 61, table 70.

31. Some fragmentary data indicate that the families of bankrupt debtors may be larger than average. See Sullivan, Warren, and Westbrook, *As We Forgive*, 81, n. 13. Stanley and Girth reported that the average debtor had four people dependent on him. Stanley and Girth, *Bankruptcy*, 42. Heck notes, "A variety of other studies found the typical family size to be between 4 and 6 members." Heck, "Identifying Insolvent Households," 14, 15.

303

32. Department of Justice, Administrative Office of the U.S. Courts, <http://www.uscourts.gov/judicial_business/f00sep97.pdf> (June 4, 1998). In the first quarter of 1998, consumer bankruptcy filings rose 6.4% over the first quarter of 1997. American Bankruptcy Institute, "Bankruptcy Filings in First Quarter of 1998 Increase Six Percent from Same Period Last Year," press release, June 3, 1998.

33. Sullivan, Warren, and Westbrook, *As We Forgive,* 149–51.

34. Married filers ranged from 55% of the bankrupt debtors in the Southern District of Texas to 58% in the Eastern District, all significantly higher than the sample average. There are other interesting geographic variations in the representation of women. The proportion of primary filers who were female ranged from 16% (Eastern District of Texas) to 44% (Western District of Tennessee). The differences by district were statistically significant.

35. Primary filers vary somewhat by district in terms of age. The modal age group, ages 30–34, accounts for 18.3% of the sample but 23.9% in the Middle District of Tennessee and only 9.5% in the Eastern District of Texas. The Eastern District of Texas was unusual in that 27% of the primary filers were older than 50. A more detailed discussion of baby boomers, life-cycle issues, and bankruptcy filing appears in Teresa A. Sullivan, Elizabeth Warren, and Jay Lawrence Westbrook, "Bankruptcy and the Family," *Marriage and Family Review* 21, nos. 3–4 (1995): 193, 207.

36. Calculated from Bureau of the Census, *Statistical Abstract of the United States: 1992* (Washington, D.C., 1992), 18, table 18. This figure is based on people older than 17. In each state that we studied, the median ages of the adult population were close to those of the debtors: 38.3 in California, 40.2 in Illinois, 42.1 in Pennsylvania, 40.7 in Tennessee, and 36.2 in Texas. Calculated from Sullivan, Warren, and Westbrook, "Bankruptcy and the Family," 26, table 27.

37. For a more detailed discussion of these data and the circumstances of older bankrupt debtors generally, see Teresa A. Sullivan, Elizabeth Warren, and Jay Lawrence Westbrook, "From Golden Years to Bankrupt Years," *Norton Bankruptcy Law Adviser* 9 (July 1998): 1–14.

38. Paul C. Light, *Baby Boomers* (New York: W. W. Norton, 1988), 43–44. Light uses 1946–64 as the dates for the baby boom; if we use his dates, the proportion of the sample in the baby boom grows to 63%. Sullivan, Warren, and Westbrook, "Bankruptcy and the Family," 19.

39. Calculated from Bureau of the Census, *Statistical Abstract of the United States: 1993* (Washington, D.C., 1993), 16, table 16.

40. We would expect the median age in bankruptcy to be higher than the overall median age, principally because children under 18 are included in the overall median but are, as a practical matter, unlikely to file for bankruptcy. The overall median age was 33.1. *Statistical Abstract: 1993.* In their study of Canadian debtors, Schwartz and Anderson find that 32% of their sample were under 30, 55% were between 30 and 50, and 13% were over 50. The median age was 34. As in the American sample, the 30–50-year-old group is overrepresented. Schwartz and Anderson, *Empirical Study,* 4.

41. By 1994, the median income of households in the United States ($32,264) had not yet recovered to its 1989 prerecessionary peak ($34,445 in 1994 dollars). Bureau of the Census, <http://www.census.gov/hhes/income/highlite.html> (July 5, 1996).

42. Teresa A. Sullivan, Elizabeth Warren, Jay Lawrence Westbrook, "Baby Boomers and the Bankruptcy Boom," *Norton's Bankruptcy Law Adviser* 4 (April 1993): 1–4.

43. The significance test was run using five-year age groups; the ten-year age groups used in the figure make the differences sharper.

44. Calculated from middle series projection for 1997 from Bureau of the Census, *Statistical Abstract of the United States: 1996* (Washington, D.C., 1996), 17, table 17.

45. Calculated from Bureau of the Census estimated age data for July 1, 1997 <http://www.census.gov/population/estimates/nation/intfile2-1.txt> (June 3, 1998). Boomers were a smaller proportion of the adult population than they had been in 1991, when they were 39.2% of all adults because young cohorts (the children of the boomers) came into the young adult years in large numbers, shrinking the proportion of boomers. At the same time, boomers were beginning to experience the force of mortality.

46. Some studies based on aggregated data have suggested that bankruptcy rates were high where there were large populations of minority group members. To conclude that it is therefore the minority group members who are declaring bankruptcy demonstrates a failure of logic known as the ecological fallacy. Such studies implicitly support the overrepresentation hypothesis developed in the text. See L. Shepard, "Personal Failures and the Bankruptcy Reform Act of 1978," *Journal of Law and Economics* 27 (October 1984): 419–37.

47. E. Franklin Frazier, *Black Bourgeoisie* (New York: Collier, 1962).

48. Fewer blacks own homes, and blacks own homes of lower value regardless of their socioeconomic status or household structure. Hayward Derrick Horton and Melvin E. Thomas, "Race, Class, and Family Structure: Differences in Housing Values for Black and White Homeowners," *Sociological Inquiry* 1 (February 1998): 114–36. Similarly, a smaller proportion of Hispanic Americans own their own homes. Home ownership rates among Hispanics slipped from 42% to 39% in the last decade, while rates for African Americans remained stable at 43%. Both groups had homeownership rates markedly below the 67.9% for white Americans, with the minority groups showing no sign of making up the gap. Timothy S. Grall, *Our Nation's Housing in 1991* (1991), Bureau of the Census, Current Housing Report, Ser. H121/93-2 (Washington, D.C., 1993).

49. Sociologist Troy Duster has noted: "In 1939, the Federal Housing Authority's manual that provided the guidelines for granting housing loans explicitly used race as one of the most important criteria." The manual stated that loans should not be given to any family that might "disrupt the racial integrity" of a neighborhood. Indeed, section 937 of the FHA manual stated, "If a neighborhood is to retain stability, it is necessary that properties shall be continued to be occupied by the same social and racial classes." Duster concludes that "on this basis, for the next 30 years, whites were able to get housing loans at 3 to 5 per cent, while blacks were routinely denied such loans. For example, of 350,000 new homes built in Northern California between 1946 and 1960 with FHA support, fewer than 100 went to blacks." Duster, "Open Forum," *San Francisco Chronicle,* Jan. 19, 1995.

50. David Caplovitz, *Consumers in Trouble: A Study of Debtors in Default* (New York: Free Press, 1974). In an earlier study, Caplovitz had documented how poor

residents in cities were more likely to misunderstand credit arrangements, to receive defective merchandise, and to pay higher prices. David Caplovitz, *The Poor Pay More* (New York: Free Press, 1963).

51. Caplovitz, *Consumers in Trouble*, 20.

52. Ibid., 21. The income gap between defaulting black and white debtors was much smaller than that between blacks and whites more generally.

53. Ibid., 249

54. For a more detailed discussion of local legal culture and bankruptcy, see Teresa A. Sullivan, Elizabeth Warren, and Jay Lawrence Westbrook "The Persistence of Local Legal Culture: Twenty Years of Evidence from the Federal Bankruptcy Courts," *Harvard Journal of Law and Public Policy* 17 (Summer 1994): 801–65.

55. Lack of access, it should be noted, is a matter not of law but of institutional incorporation. If one does not know any lawyers and has never heard of bankruptcy as a remedy, then even crushing financial problems will not be resolved in bankruptcy court. Herbert Jacob had already indicated that debtors in trouble are more likely to seek bankruptcy if they already know someone in bankruptcy. Herbert Jacob, *Debtors in Court* (Chicago: Rand-McNally, 1969). Caplovitz's studies suggested that blacks (and, by inference, Puerto Ricans) were perhaps underrepresented in bankruptcy, given their propensity to be in financial difficulties. One possible reading is that minority group members who needed the protection of bankruptcy were less likely than majority whites to receive it. Again, this difference was not because of overt discrimination but because of limited access to lawyers as problem solvers. Caplovitz's finding, although influential in many circles, is quite different from that of other authors.

56. The authors believed that there was some nonresponse bias: "The 400 who were found and were willing to be interviewed probably were more stable, better satisfied, and in better financial condition than those who had disappeared or who refused to be interviewed." Stanley and Girth, *Bankruptcy*, 41.

57. Ibid., 45.

58. The most notable overrepresentation occurred in the Northern District of Alabama, in which 78% of the debtors interviewed were black compared with two large cities in the district: 40% of the population of Birmingham were black, as were 34% of the population of Anniston. This large difference is striking. In Oregon, by contrast, 5% of the petitioners were black versus 4% of the population of Portland. Given the small sample size, the differences in the Oregon proportions may not be statistically significant. Exact sample sizes for each district were not reported in the table; the percentages are reported in Ibid., 46, table 4.1.

59. Ibid., 45. They also asserted a disproportion of those with a French-Canadian background in Maine. In 1990, 9.7% of the population of Maine reported French ancestry <http://www.census.gov/the-bin/themapit.pl/themapit/www/themes/830701568-US.theme?OLDMAP=%2Fftp%2Fpub%2Fthemapit%2Fwww%2Ftemp%2Fismaps%2F836512978.map&EXMENU=2%2399%2323%239.693484&EXOPT=EQ> (July 4, 1996).

60. Ibid., 46, table 4.2.

61. In 1960, the Bureau of the Census identified the population of the five Southwestern states who had Spanish surnames. This measure tends to underrepresent the proportion of the population who are of Spanish origin. A self-

identification procedure was followed in subsequent censuses to allow each person to identify himself or herself by racial or ethnic category.

62. Stanley and Girth, *Bankruptcy,* 45–46.

63. This is in fact what one law professor found. Shuchman, "New Jersey Debtors." He studied debtors whose names were gathered from attorneys and law students. In Newark, where the study was conducted, 58.5% of the population enumerated in the 1990 census was black. *Statistical Abstract: 1992,* 36, table 38.

64. The largest city in the district is not necessarily the source of most of the petitioners, although some studies using aggregate data find a positive association between urbanization and bankruptcy filing rates, leading to the speculation that urban dwellers may be more prone than others to file for bankruptcy. Shepard, "Personal Failures," 42–44, table 446. In both the Middle District of Tennessee and in the Eastern District of Pennsylvania, about 25% of the sample was black. This compares with 24.3% of the population of Nashville and 39.9% of the population of Philadelphia. *Statistical Abstract: 1993,* 36–37, table 38.

65. One factor that certainly affected the differences between Caplovitz and ourselves (and Brookings) is that we and the Brookings researchers use large samples of people who have filed for bankruptcy and, as data in this chapter indicate, we have drawn a large group of people with middle-class characteristics. Caplovitz, by contrast, intended to study only the poor.

66. The comparable proportion of "Spanish speaking" in the Western District of Texas in 1964 was 36%. Stanley and Girth, *Bankruptcy,* 46, table 4.2.

67. *Statistical Abstract: 1992,* 33, table 35.

68. Ibid.

69. Ibid.

70. Bureau of Labor Statistics, *Employment and Earnings* 36 (January 1989): 183–84, table 11; 45 (January 1998): 174–75, table 11.

71. An important study of this difference is Melvin L. Oliver and Thomas M. Shapiro, *Black Wealth, White Wealth: A New Perspective on Racial Inequality* (New York: Routledge, 1995); see also Dalton Conley, *Being Black, Living in the Red: Race, Wealth, and Social Policy in America* (Berkeley: Calif., 1999).

72. Ibid.

73. A series of illustrative case studies is analyzed by Michael D. Woodard, *Black Entrepreneurs in America: Stories of Struggle and Success* (New Brunswick, N.J.: Rutgers University Press, 1997).

74. Duster, "Open Forum."

75. See Bureau of the Census, <http://www.census.gov/hhes/wealth/wlth 934a.html> (July 4, 1996).

76. Ibid.

77. One-third of all immigrants enumerated in the 1990 census resided in California. B. R. Chiswick and T. A. Sullivan, "The New Immigrants," in Reynolds Farley, ed., *State of the Union: America in the 1990s,* vol. 2 (New York: Russell Sage Foundation, 1995), 211, 227. Schwartz and Anderson, who studied Canadian bankrupt debtors in 1997, found that 15% of their sample were foreign-born, approximately the same proportion as in the Canadian population generally. Asian immigrants were somewhat underrepresented in bankruptcy considering their fraction of all immigrants. Schwartz and Anderson, *Empirical Study,* 6. Note that Asian Americans were also underrepresented.

78. Calculated from Bureau of the Census, *County and City Data Book* 1994, 12th ed. (Washington, D.C.: Bureau of the Census, Data User Services Division, 1994). Although the representation may not be disproportionate, large numbers of foreign-born petitioners do put a strain on the bankruptcy courts in terms of providing adequate translation services.

79. See the 1972 Report of the Commission on the Bankruptcy Laws, pt. 1.

80. *Statistical Abstract: 1994,* 158, table 234. This table is based on persons aged 25 and older in 1993. The data are for married women with spouse present.

81. The differences by state are important to investigate because of differing sample sizes. Both Texas and California have four districts, so we had a potential sample size of at least 600 debtors in those states. Illinois, Pennsylvania, and Tennessee each have three districts, but we had access to only two of the Tennessee districts, so the case bases in these states are necessarily smaller. The Texas and California samples are better educated and thus could skew the sample. But even in Illinois, Pennsylvania, and Tennessee, the debtors are very well educated relative to the remainder of the population. Again, the Canadian comparison closely tracks our findings. Schwartz and Anderson report that "overall, the educational attainment of our sample of debtors seeking bankruptcy protection was slightly higher than that of all Canadians in 1995." Schwartz and Anderson, *Empirical Study,* 5. As with the American sample, the Canadian debtors with some postsecondary education were less likely than the general population to have earned a certificate or degree.

82. The states differ among their general populations in terms of educational attainment. In California, only 46% of the population has not attended college, compared with 53.5% in Texas, 53.8% in Illinois, 62.9% in Tennessee, and 63.9% in Pennsylvania. *Statistical Abstract: 1993,* 159, table 236. Based on these data, the Pennsylvania debtors look somewhat less educated than the remainder of the states. For further comments on the Pennsylvania sample, see Appendix 1.

83. Based on 11.4% of 880,399 and 15.3% of 880,399.

84. Ulrich Beck, *Risk Society: Towards a New Modernity,* trans. Mark Ritter (Beverly Hills, Calif.: Sage, 1992), 99. The argument is that those who will not take risks but seek only a paycheck will find fewer opportunities available to them. Risk-takers will be economically self-directed and have the opportunity for vast successes. Of course, as Millie's case shows, they also have the opportunity for economic failure.

85. The gravestones in some cemeteries indicate the importance of occupation. Some are labeled "CPA," "lawyer," or "teacher" in addition to the dates of birth and death.

86. Thorstein Veblen, *The Theory of the Leisure Class* (1899; reprint ed., New Brunswick, N.J.: Transaction, 1992).

87. We used scores developed by the National Opinion Research Center; see Robert W. Hodge, Paul M. Siegel, and Peter M. Rossi, "Occupational Prestige in the United States, 1925–1963," *American Journal of Sociology* 70 (November 1964): 286–302. These scores have been equilibrated to the occupational codes that were used in the 1970 census. *Codebook for the Spring 1974 General Social Survey* (Chicago: National Opinion Research Center, 1974), 117–36. We used the 1970 census occupational codes and the prestige scores that corresponded to the codes. This was the same coding method that we used for our 1981 data.

In the 1980 census, a different coding scheme was used that relied heavily on the concept of industry as well as the concept of occupation. See Gloria Peterson Green, Khoan tan Dinh, John A. Priebe, and Ronald R. Tucker, "Revisions in the Current Population Survey Beginning in January 1983," *Employment and Earnings* 30 (February 1983): 7–15. Both coding systems are in use today, but many sociologists still prefer the 1970 version. Randy Hodson and Teresa A. Sullivan, *The Social Organization of Work,* 2d ed. (Belmont, Mass.: Wadsworth, 1995), 49–54.

We coded only the occupations reported on the schedules. These data were corroborated, however, by spontaneous comments the debtors made in which they identified their occupations and industries. Many of these comments are presented and discussed in Chapter 3.

88. Sullivan, Warren, and Westbrook, *As We Forgive,* 89–91. The higher scores in 1991 are statistically significant in comparison with the 1981 scores. In the Canadian study, Schwartz and Anderson use a 16-category classification of occupations that they then collapse somewhat further, and they find that those with relatively low skill levels are still disproportionately represented among the bankrupt debtors. Schwartz and Anderson, *Empirical Study,* 10–11.

89. The national sample is the National Opinion Research Center's General Social Survey for 1990. Again, although the numbers are substantively similar, because of the large sample size the difference is statistically significant.

90. For the secondary filers, the range of scores was 16–63, with a mode of 36. Some typical occupations at this level include secretary (36), nurse's aide (36), and maintenance technician (35). Fifty percent of the secondary filers fell between scores of 28 and 47.

91. Sullivan, Warren, and Westbrook, *As We Forgive,* 108.

92. Many people identified themselves unambiguously as self-employed, using such phrases as "work for myself" or "owner-manager." Others gave more ambiguous responses that could indicate they were self-employed or could indicate they worked for someone else, using such terms as "consultant."

93. *Statistical Abstract: 1993,* 459, table 715. The median income for all households (i.e., not just families) is $30,126. Mean income for all households was $37,922, versus $20,314 for the debtors. See ibid., table 714. In general, family incomes are higher than household incomes. We are not able to distinguish between the debtors' family income and their household income. This figure includes all income reported on the petition for both husband and wife. Because the unrelated members of a debtors' household are not required to be listed on the petition (e.g., a roommate or boarder), the figure we report is probably closer to the family income concept than to the household income concept. The figures in this and the following footnote are nominal dollars for the years in question, not adjusted for inflation.

94. See Bureau of the Census, <http://www.census.gov/hhes/income/income 97/prs98asc.html> (Jan. 14, 1999). The 1996 median is used here. The Ohio median was even higher, $51,835 for four-person families. These data come from the Bureau of the Census website, <http://www.census.gov> (June 3, 1998).

95. These data are in constant 1989 dollars for the sake of comparability. These five states differ from one another in their level and distribution of income. All five states have a median household income that is below the national *family* median of $36,404; three states are also below the national *household* median of

$30,126. California is the best off with a median income of $35,748, and Tennessee is worst off with $24,807. The median household incomes for Tennessee, Texas, and Pennsylvania are below the national median for all households.

96. In an earlier description of the data from Illinois, Pennsylvania, and Texas, we noted the higher incidence of low-income debtors in the Pennsylvania sample. At the time the sample was drawn, Philadelphia had a volunteer lawyer program to increase access to the bankruptcy courts for low-income individuals. We cited some evidence suggesting that this program increased the number of poorer debtors in the sample. Teresa A. Sullivan, Elizabeth Warren, and Jay Lawrence Westbrook, "Consumer Debtors Ten Years Later: A Financial Comparison of Consumer Bankrupts, 1981–1991," *American Bankruptcy Law Journal* 68 (Spring 1994): 121–54. California has a reportedly higher incidence of "typing services" and other low-cost operations that make bankruptcy available to those who cannot afford the services of a lawyer. The higher proportion of low-income debtors in California may be attributable to an increased accessibility.

97. In Tennessee, only 44% of the population falls into this range.

98. The data cited in Sullivan, Warren, and Westbrook, "Ten Years Later," suggest that the ability to hire a lawyer may be an important determinant in the decision to file bankruptcy. Even then, debtors only slightly below the poverty line may need bankruptcy whereas debtors well below the poverty line (incomes of $5,000 and less) do not.

99. *Statistical Abstract: 1993*, 469, table 735. This is the income cutoff for a nonfarm family of four. Although the index contains graduations for combinations of family size and residence, this figure is commonly referred to as "the" poverty index.

100. Ibid., 471, table 740.

101. Ibid., table 741. The comparison data for the sample show that 208 petitioners were below poverty, 433 above, with 95 cases missing; these data are from five districts. There is a significant association between being below the poverty level and filing in Chapter 7. There is also a significant association between being in poverty and filing in California, Pennsylvania, and Tennessee.

102. Bureau of the Census, "Forty-Six Million Were Poor for Two or More Months in 1990, a New Census Report Says," press release, Feb. 3, 1995. These data are based on the Survey of Income and Program Participation, a longitudinal study of a cross-section of American families.

103. "Education Marks a Widening Income Divide," *Wall Street Journal*, June 28, 1996.

104. Similar tables based on 1991 data from the three districts in Illinois, Pennsylvania, and Texas and comparing 1981 and 1991 data for the three districts are in Sullivan, Warren, and Westbrook, "Ten Years Later," 28. Table 1 in the text differs by adding in data from the Middle District of Tennessee and the Central District of California. The resulting income differences are fairly small. For example, median income in the five districts is $17,964, compared with $18,000 in the three districts. The asset differences are larger: $12,655 in the five districts, down from $16,765 in the three districts. Thus the five-district group reported in the text is even more asset-poor than the group discussed in our earlier article. The 1981 data have been adjusted to 1991 dollars using the Consumer Price Index. The article discusses the adjustment for inflation; see 148–49.

105. Elizabeth Warren, "The Bankruptcy Crisis," *Indiana Law Journal* 73 (Fall 1998): 1079–10.

106. Marianne B. Culhane and Michaela M. White, *Means-Testing for Chapter 7 Debtors: Repayment Capacity Untapped?* (Washington, D.C.: American Bankruptcy Institute, 1998), 1–8. For a more detailed discussion of this study, see Appendix 2.

107. In 1998 the House of Representatives passed H.R. 3150 with a stringent means test for Chapter 7 debtors, but the legislation did not pass the Senate.

108. U.S.C. §727(a)(4).

109. At least 84.6% of all Americans owned some assets. These data come from the Survey of Income and Program Participation and are reported at Bureau of the Census, <http://www.census.gov/hhes/wealth/wlth93b.html> (July 4, 1996), tables A and B (hereafter cited as "Wealth, 1991"). The data are presented in constant 1993 dollars, but the dollars reported in the text have been deflated to 1991 dollars using the Consumer Price Index, using the factor 0.94. Calculated from *Statistical Abstract: 1994*, 488, table 747. The Federal Reserve System conducted its Survey of Consumer Finance in 1989 and 1993, but not in 1991. In 1989, 84% of Americans owned a vehicle. *Statistical Abstract: 1993*, 476, tables 751 and 752.

110. "Wealth, 1991." Among Americans as a whole, three-quarters (74.4%) of all assets are nonfinancial, with about a quarter financial (25.6%). In terms of nonfinancial assets not mentioned in the text, roughly one-fifth of American households, 20.9%, reported owning investment real estate, 14.2% reported some interest in a business, and 7.4% reported other nonfinancial assets. Although relatively fewer families own these types of assets, their value amounts to 37% of assets. *Statistical Abstract: 1993*, 476, table 751 and 752.

111. Bureau of the Census, "Median Value of Interest-Earning Assets Down and Home Equity Up in 1993 Compared with 1991," press release, Sept. 25, 1995. These data are based on the Survey of Income and Program Participation, not on the Consumer Finance Survey. The figure has been adjusted to 1991 dollars.

112. The highest debt total reported in the sample is $10,417,775. This case was filed by a 44-year-old widowed white male in the Eastern District of Pennsylvania. He has a college degree and has had a job interruption, but he has a job now. The reason he gave for his bankruptcy was that a real estate development failed, resulting in $2.5 million in unpayable debt. His case is not otherwise analyzed in our statistics, however, because we removed extremely high values for debts. The cutoffs for outliers are the same as the ones used in Sullivan, Warren, and Westbrook, *As We Forgive*, though corrected for inflation, and the outliers are removed to prevent statistical distortions of the data. The outliers were incomes greater than $97,393, assets greater than $749,173, and total debt greater than $749,175.

113. The standard deviation is $60,548, the 25th percentile is –$21,774, and the 75th percentile is –$2,390.

114. "Wealth, 1991," tables B and 4. The figure presented here was in 1993 dollars and was adjusted to 1991 dollars as described in the note to Appendix 1.

115. It is sobering to note that a homeless person with no assets and no debt presents a better balance sheet than the overwhelming majority of the debtors in the bankruptcy sample.

311

1. Texas Employment Commission, "Fact Sheet on Job Growth and Development in San Antonio" (Austin: Texas Employment Commission, n.d.).

2. Bureau of the Census, *Statistical Abstract of the United States: 1994* (Washington, D.C., 1994), 422–24, table 656.

3. Ibid., *Statistical Abstract of the United States: 1993* (Washington, D.C., 1993), 467, table 731. The equivalent figure for male workers was $35,850, another 50% above the female average. The average for women in Jeanne's age group, 55–64, was $22,451, still more than 40% higher than Jeanne's earnings.

4. Department of Justice, Administrative Office of the U.S. Courts, Annual Reports, various years.

5. *Statistical Abstract: 1993,* 416, table 658.

6. Interestingly, nearly one-third of these unemployed people did not list a job-related reason for their bankruptcy, perhaps because some other reason was even more salient. Instead, they explained their financial failures in terms of a mortgage foreclosure or a generic inability to pay their bills or a similar financial event.

7. Furthermore, the question was only asked of Chapter 7 debtors, so our 1981 data are limited to them. Teresa A. Sullivan, Elizabeth Warren, and Jay Lawrence Westbrook, *As We Forgive Our Debtors: Bankruptcy and Consumer Credit in America* (New York: Oxford University Press, 1989), 85–86.

8. Ibid., 85–86.

9. In response to a question in the court papers about tenure on the debtor's current job, 23 of the debtors in Judge Sellers's sample reported "0" years. If that can be taken as reflecting unemployment, then 20.3% of those debtors were unemployed at the time of bankruptcy.

10. Bureau of Labor Statistics, *Employment and Earnings* 45 (April 1998): 128, table C.2. The seasonally adjusted unemployment rate for Ohio in 1997 ranged from a low of 4.4% in June, July, November, and December to a high of 5.0% in January. By any estimate this would be considered a good year in terms of unemployment.

11. These are also 1991 figures. *Statistical Abstract: 1993,* 413, table 652, and 414, table 654.

12. To quote a recent journalistic account of this behavior, "Many downsized Americans don't intend to change their spending habits. Instead, they 'share a stubborn inclination to live and spend at their previous income levels.'" Editorial, "We're Born, We Spend," *American Demographics* 20 (November 1998): 6.

13. The highest proportions were found in California, where 55.8% in the Central District of California and 50.4% in the Northern District of California reported job-related reasons for bankruptcy. In Jeanne Salem's district, the Western District of Texas, 48.1% gave a job-related reason. The Western District of Texas was also the most likely district to report that a spouse had lost a job or was unemployed; 12.8% of the cases reported this, versus 0.7% (the lowest rate) in the Southern District of Illinois. Even in the district with the lowest proportion reporting a job-related reason, the Middle District of Tennessee, one-third reported a work-related reason (33.1%).

14. One study of how unemployment affects health has concluded that a

312

1% increase in the unemployment rate translates into 37,000 deaths, 4,000 state mental hospital admissions, and 3,300 state prison admissions. Barry Bluestone and Bennett Harrison, *The Deindustrialization of America* (New York: Basic Books, 1982). There is a large literature of ethnographic and survey research on individuals who have been laid off that documents the negative consequences of joblessness that go beyond economics. See, e.g., G. J. Meyer, *Executive Blues: Down and Out in Corporate America* (New York: Dell, 1995).

15. Bureau of Labor Statistics, *Mass Layoffs in 1990* (Washington, D.C., 1992); Bureau of Labor Statistics, *Mass Layoffs in 1988* (Washington, D.C., 1989).

16. Bureau of the Census, *Statistical Abstract of the United States: 1996* (Washington, D.C., 1996), 404, table 635. The development of this measure is described in Bureau of Labor Statistics, "Displaced Workers of 1979–1983—How Well Have They Fared?" *Displaced Workers, 1979–83,* by Paul O. Flaim and Ellen Sehgal (Washington, D.C., 1985).

17. Bureau of Labor Statistics, "Displaced Workers Summary," USDL 98-347 (Washington, D.C., Aug. 19, 1998).

18. Two economists with the FDIC write, "Since the bulk of business failures typically occur among small firms, the growth in the number of such firms in the 1980s helps explain the persistence of high business failure rates. More to the point, a rise in business failure rates coincident with an increase in household dependency on small business success suggests more than a casual linkage between business failures and residential mortgage foreclosure rates." Peter J. Elmer and Steven A. Seelig, "The Rising Long-Term Trend of Single-Family Mortgage Foreclosure Rates," FDIC Working Paper 98-2 (1996), 6. The authors also note that the unemployment rate does not explain the trend, and they suggest that the unemployment rate does not adequately depict the risk for homeowners, an inference our data would also support.

19. Thomas S. Moore, *The Disposable Work Force* (New York: Aldine de Gruyter 1996), 21.

20. Bureau of Labor Statistics, "Recent Job Losers Less Likely to Expect Recall," *Issues in Labor Statistics* (Washington, D.C., 1992).

21. Thomas J. Lueck, "Thousands of Executives Seeking Wall Street Jobs in Bleak Market," *New York Times,* Jan. 17, 1988.

22. According to an employment consulting group, there was a 75% increase in permanent job reductions from 1990 to 1991. More startling is the fact that permanent job reductions increased from 1997 to 1998 by 56%. The number of reductions in 1998 was the highest of any year in the 1990s, despite widespread prosperity. This information is from Challenger, Gray & Christmas, Inc., of Chicago, which bills itself as the first and oldest outplacement firm in the country. Fax letter from Challenger, Gray & Christmas to Jonathan Pratter, Tarlton Law Library, University of Texas at Austin, June 3, 1999.

23. Louis Uchitelle, "Job Losses Don't Let Up Even as Hard Times Ease," *New York Times,* Mar. 22, 1994; Louis Uchitelle and N. R. Kleinfield, "On the Battlefields of Business, Millions of Casualties," *New York Times,* Mar. 3, 1996.

24. Juliet Schor, *The Overworked American* (New York: Basic Books, 1992), 19. In companies that have downsized, the remaining workers report working harder.

25. *Statistical Abstract: 1996,* 411, table 642.

26. *Statistical Abstract: 1992,* 384, table 613.

313

27. Bureau of Labor Statistics, *Employment and Earnings* 39 (May 1992): 155–59.

28. Bureau of the Census, "Statistical Brief: Income and Job Mobility in the Early 1990s," SB/95-1 (Washington, D.C., March 1995). For the population as a whole, unemployment is much more widespread than unemployment compensation. In 1994, when almost 8 million workers were unemployed (about 6.1% of the labor force), there were only 2.7 million insured unemployed (about 2.5% of the labor force). *Statistical Abstract: 1996,* 416, table 650.

29. If they really own their home free and clear, then the home will be exempt in Texas, which means that their creditors cannot force its sale to pay off debts. Sometimes, however, debtors have a home mortgage that is not listed in the schedules, despite clear regulations to the contrary. See a further discussion of the phenomenon of failure to report home mortgages in the chapter on housing.

30. Randy Hodson and Teresa A. Sullivan, *The Social Organization of Work,* 2d ed. (Blemont, Calif.: Wadsworth, 1995), 134–35.

31. She reports on interviews with laid-off managers. Kathleen S. Newman, *Falling from Grace: The Experience of Downward Mobility in the American Middle Class* (New York: Free Press, 1988).

32. Ibid.

33. Meyer reports multiple downsizing and provides a detailed account of the impact on his morale and family. A recent account suggests that denial and the refusal to adjust living expenses to the unemployment check is more widespread, and not limited to executives such as those surveyed by Meyer. Alex Markels, "Down But Not Out," *American Demographics* 20, 11 (November 1998): 59–66.

34. Bureau of Labor Statistics. "Worker Displacement Increased Sharply in Recent Recession," news release USDL 92-530, Aug. 19, 1992. Moore offers an argument from economic theory for the lower earnings after displacement. Moore, *Disposable Work Force,* 26–28.

35. Bureau of the Census, "Statistical Brief: Income and Job Mobility in the Early 1990s."

36. Jennifer M. Gardner, "Recession Swells Count of Displaced Workers," *Monthly Labor Review* 115 (June 1993): 14–23.

37. The study was done by Louis Jacobson, Robert LaLonde, and Daniel Sullivan with a longitudinal, administrative data set from the state of Pennsylvania. Jacobson, LaLonde, and Sullivan, *The Costs of Worker Dislocation* (Kalamazoo, Mich.: W. E. Upjohn, 1993). The study is quoted by Moore, *Disposable Work Force,* 29.

38. See discussion in Chapter 7 about failure to report home mortgages.

39. The Bureau of Labor Statistics has developed several alternative measures of unemployment, of which U5 is the commonly accepted definition: total unemployed as a percentage of the civilian labor force. This figure was 5.5% in 1991. The most restrictive definition, U1, was 1.9% and it is persons unemployed 15 weeks or longer as a percentage of the civilian labor force. The only definition that takes the partially employed into account is U6, defined as total full-time job-seekers plus one-half part-time job-seekers plus one-half total on part-time for economic reasons as a percent of the civilian labor force less one-half of the part-time labor force. The value of U6 for 1991 was 9.2%. *Statistical Abstract: 1994,* 415, table 657. Only half of the part-time workers are included in the count to

provide a rough approximation of full-time equivalent workers. The problem with U6 for our purposes is that the components due to part-time job seekers and persons on part-time for economic reasons are not disaggregated. Even the difference between U6 and U5 is difficult to interpret because the denominators are different.

The values of U5 and U6 varied through the 1980s and into the 1990s as follows:

|      | U5   | U6   |
| ---- | ---- | ---- |
| 1980 | 7.1  | 9.2  |
| 1985 | 7.2  | 9.6  |
| 1986 | 7.0  | 9.4  |
| 1987 | 6.2  | 8.5  |
| 1988 | 5.5  | 7.6  |
| 1989 | 5.3  | 7.2  |
| 1990 | 5.5  | 7.6  |
| 1991 | 6.7  | 9.2  |
| 1992 | 7.4  | 10.0 |

40. Bureau of the Census, "Statistical Brief: Income and Job Mobility in the Early 1990s." By contrast, 7% of men and 12% of women moved from part-time to full-time work.

41. Robert E. Parker, *Flesh Peddlers and Warm Bodies: The Temporary Help Industry in the United States* (New Brunswick, N.J.: Rutgers University Press, 1994).

42. The definition of a contingent worker is "[a worker] who does not have an implicit or explicit contract for ongoing employment. Persons who do not expect to continue in their jobs for personal reasons such as retirement or returning to school are not considered contingent workers, provided that they would have the option of continuing in the job were it not for these personal reasons." Bureau of Labor Statistics, "Contingent and Alternative Employment Arrangements, February 1997," USDL 97-422 (Washington, D.C., December 1997), 2.

43. Ibid., 2–3. The median weekly earnings of full-time contingent workers were 82% of the earnings of noncontingent workers.

44. Bureau of Labor Statistics, *Employment and Earnings* 45 (February 1998): 18, table A.7. Overall unemployment was only 4.7%; 13, table A.3.

45. *Statistical Abstract: 1996*, 429, table 668.

46. Ibid., 430, table 670.

47. See the discussion at note 18, above.

48. Hodson and Sullivan, *Social Organization of Work*, 133–35. For the social-psychological consequences of prolonged unemployment, see Moore, *Disposable Work Force*, 44–46.

49. Bureau of the Census, "Statistical Brief: Income and Job Mobility in the Early 1990s."

50. Clare Ansberry, "Workers Are Forced to Take More Jobs with Few Benefits," *Wall Street Journal*, Mar. 11, 1993.

51. The relation between marital status and giving any job reason is statistically significant.

52. There was a significant association with job prestige, such that 60% of

315

those with prestige scores lower than 49 tended to report job problems, but smaller fractions of those with higher scores had job problems. Prestige was tabulated in increments of ten points.

53. Moore, *Disposable Work Force,* 33.

54. Ibid.

55. For those who did not have any current employment, there was a significant association both with reporting a work interruption and with mentioning a job-related reason for bankruptcy. These workers were also more likely to be actively seeking work. Both the respondents reporting job disruptions and those who reported job-related reasons for their bankruptcies were significantly more likely to be in Chapter 7 than to be in Chapter 13.

56. The relationship between race and job reason is significant. The relationship between race and seeking work is not significant.

57. See, e.g., Lester C. Thurow, *The Zero-Sum Society: Distribution and the Possibilities for Economic Change* (New York: Basic Books, 1980); Gary Burtless, ed., *A Future of Lousy Jobs? The Changing Structure of U.S. Wages* (Washington, D.C.: Brookings Institution, 1990); and Bennett Harrison and Barry C. Bluestone, *The Great U-Turn: Corporate Restructuring and the Polarizing of America* (New York: Basic Books, 1988).

58. G. Pascal Zachary and Bob Ortega, "Workplace Revolution Boosts Productivity at Cost of Job Security," *Wall Street Journal,* Mar. 10, 1993.

59. Newman, *Falling from Grace.*

60. Reasons that were not correlated with assets included consumer, specific debt reasons, family reasons, medical reasons, and general reasons. None of the correlations achieved significance.

61. There is no difference between renters and homeowners in the report of an actual income interruption. For whatever reason, the homeowner was more likely than the renter to attribute the bankruptcy to the job interruption.

62. Bureau of Labor Statistics, "The Employment Situation: January 1998," news release USDL 98-37, Feb. 6, 1998, 4–5, table A.1.

63. Bureau of Labor Statistics, *Employment and Earnings* 45 (April 1998): 128, table C.2.

64. Ibid., 133, table C.3.

65. For a more detailed discussion of the Ohio data, see Appendix 1.

66. We downloaded variable marginals from the website for the Institute for Survey Research. This institute, located at the University of Michigan, has for many years conducted the Panel Study of Income Dynamics (PSID), a longitudinal study of American families and their finances. The PSID is supported by the National Science Foundation and has been the source of many studies about Americans' work and earnings.

67. In 1998 three economists noted that the PSID data underestimates the number of bankrupts. Scott Fay, Erik Huest, and Michelle White, "The Bankruptcy Decision: Does Stigma Matter?" (paper presented at the Seminar in Law and Economics, Harvard University, Feb. 24, 1998), table 1. Given national filing rates, considerably more former bankrupt debtors should have been found in the sample.

68. Bureau of Labor Statistics, "Contingent and Alternative Employment Arrangements," table 8.

69. Bureau of Labor Statistics, *Employment and Earnings* 45 (April 1998).

70. Allen Sloan, "A Real Lump of Coal: Cost-Cutting Companies Hand Out Pink Slips," *Newsweek,* Dec. 14, 1998, 50; "The Numbers Game," NewsHour with Jim Lehrer, transcript, Dec. 4, 1998.

71. Steve Rhodes, "Hurts So Good," *Newsweek,* Jan. 18, 1999, 42–43.

72. Markels, "Down But Not Out," 60–61.

73. Louis Uchitelle, "Downsizing Comes Back, But the Outcry Is Muted," *New York Times,* Dec. 7, 1998.

74. Economists from the FDIC looked at the economic problems that can beset families, forcing them to lose their homes. They cited the importance of job loss in causing mortgage defaults but argued that the small business failure rate should be taken into account along with the unemployment rate to understand more clearly how many people have lost their incomes. Peter Elmer and Steven Seelig, "Insolvency, Trigger Events, and Consumer Risk Posture in the Theory of Single-Family Mortgage Default," *Real Estate Finance Journal* 14 (Winter 1999): 25–33.

## Chapter 4: Credit Cards

1. The *Nilson Report* is used extensively throughout this chapter. The report, a bimonthly trade publication, is the product of independent research conducted by the Nilson Company. It is the primary source for data about credit cards; both the Federal Reserve Bank and the Census Bureau rely on data generated by the Nilson Company.

Credit card purchases in 1995 were $753.52 billion, compared with cash purchases of $703.79 billion. *Nilson Report* 632 (November 1996): 6–7. In 1994, credit card purchases were $648.18 billion, compared with cash purchases of $664.40 billion. Ibid., 599 (July 1995): 6–7. Checks outstrip both plastic and cash and have for many years, but the numbers are not strictly comparable. Check volume includes house payments, alimony and child support, payments when credit card invoices are paid by check, and so on.

2. Bureau of the Census, *Statistical Abstract of the United States: 1996* (Washington, D.C., 1996), 520, table 799.

3. Ibid., tables 799 and 66.

4. *Nilson Report* 632 (November 1996): 6–7. Nilson estimates that credit card transactions will more than double to just under $2 trillion dollars charged on more than 28 billion transactions. These data are based on domestic purchases only. Checks are predicted to decline in total dollar volume and cash to rise slightly, but both will lose significant market share as payment systems.

5. Donald R. Katz, *The Big Store* (Harmondsworth: Penguin, 1987), 173. Katz spins a fascinating yarn about the rise and fall of Sears, giving an incidental history of retailing in the twentieth century. He documents Sears's reliance on consumer credit, showing how constriction in consumer lending led directly to a constriction in sales and a decline in the company's profitability.

6. Also in 1910, Arthur Morris, a lawyer in Norfolk, Virginia, opened the Fidelity Savings and Trust Company, the first major commercial business devoted solely to consumer lending. James Medoff and Andrew Harless, *The Indebted Society: Anatomy of an Ongoing Disaster* (Boston: Little, Brown, 1996), 10. Finance company lending saw especially strong growth during the Depression, with com-

panies making their money from small loans (the legal limit was $300 in 1937) repayable in five to 20 months.

7. Ibid., 11.

8. Franklin National Bank of Long Island is credited with creating the first bank card in 1951, but it failed to capitalize on the idea with a nationwide system. Bank of America developed the BankAmericard, which later became Visa, in 1958, followed by MasterCharge, which later became MasterCard, in 1966. George Ritzer, *Expressing America: A Critique of the Global Credit Card Society* (Thousand Oaks, Calif.: Pine Forge Press, 1995), 36–37. For a fascinating discussion of Bank of America's early attempts at mass marketing, see Joseph Nocera, "The Day the Credit Card Was Born," *Washington Post Magazine,* Dec. 4, 1994, 17.

9. American Express expanded its business from 800,000 cards outstanding in 1960 to 26 million cards outstanding in the United States alone in 1991. To reach the broadest market, American Express in 1991 marketed a green card, a gold card, a corporate card, a platinum card, Optima green and gold cards, an Optima Platinum card, and an Optima Independent card. American Express customers used these cards to make purchases totaling $77.85 billion that year. *Nilson Report* 509 (October 1991): 17.

10. There are holdouts, to be sure. Perhaps a quarter of all adults still do not carry a credit card. Peter Yoo, "Charging up a Mountain of Debt: Accounting for the Growth of Credit Card Debt," *Review: Federal Reserve Bank of St. Louis,* March–April 1997, 4. Yoo, an economist at the Federal Reserve Bank of St. Louis, analyzes the Survey of Consumer Finances to conclude that by 1992, 72% of all households had at least one credit card. Federal Reserve, "Family Finances in the U.S.: Recent Evidence from the Survey of Consumer Finances," *Federal Reserve Bulletin* (January 1997): 17 (reporting that 67% of all families have bank-type cards).

11. Among those without cards are the 10% of American families that do not have *any* relationship with a bank or other financial institution. One in ten families has no relationship with any kind of depository or nondepository financial institution. Bureau of the Census, *Statistical Abstract of the United States: 1993* (Washington, D.C., 1993), 507, table 790. In 1991, Nilson estimated that of 116 million employed Americans, 23% (27 million) had no banking relationship of any kind. *Nilson Report* 491 (January 1991): 7. Many of these people, however, lived in families where another adult in the family had a deposit account or other arrangement with a financial institution. Only one-third of Hispanics have a credit card, and about 30% of Hispanics have a checking account. Brad Edmondson, "Hispanic Americans in 2001," *American Demographics* 19 (January 1997): 16–17. In addition, individuals without credit cards include many of the elderly, newly arrived immigrants, people not in the workforce, prisoners, the very poor, the mentally impaired, economic dependents, transients, recovering charge-aholics, and a few cranky souls who just don't want the darn things. Nilson reports that "unbanked" Americans represent a "growing trend" of people who will be served by checking/ cashing services. *Nilson Report* 624 (July 1996): 9.

12. Federal Reserve, "Family Finances."

13. Bureau of the Census, *Statistical Abstract of the United States: 1997* (Washington, D.C., 1997), 520, table 798.

14. Federal Reserve, "Family Finances," 17 (discussing bank card debt). Some observers suspect that federal reports on consumer debt understate the total

credit card amount outstanding. Stephen Brobeck, Executive Director of the Consumer Federation of America, compares the Federal Reserve Bank's reported revolving credit with the Survey of Consumer Finances, which relies on self-reported data about bank card debts, and notices a large discrepancy in the amount of reported debt. The self-reported debt is far lower than the amount of debt reported by credit card issuers. Brobeck concludes that "this discrepancy suggests that, overall, households may underreport credit card debt by 50 percent or more." Brobeck, "The Consumer Impacts of Expanding Credit Card Debt," *Consumer Federation of America,* February 1997, 4. A simple calculation gives strong support to Brobeck's argument: the government reports 50 million families making credit card payments on an estimated $500 billion in outstanding credit card debt, which would suggest an average of $10,000 per family.

15. Moody's Investor Services pegs total average cost of credit card debt at 18.72% in 1997. See, e.g., "Charge It Costs More," *Morning Star* (Wilmington, N.C.), July 7, 1997. For the 1991 calculations, interest rates were calculated at 18.43 percent, the December 1991 weighted average of all outstanding bank cards. *Nilson Report* 513 (December 1991): 1.

16. Federal Reserve, "Family Finances," table 11.

17. Ibid.

18. Ibid. Later in the chapter, however, we note that the creditors are working actively to change this fact.

19. Families with middle-aged heads of households also took on heavier consumer debt burdens. Those in which the head of the household was in the 35–44 age range had the highest short-term debt burdens, so that they made monthly payments of about 18% of their incomes on their short-term, high interest debts. Ibid., table 14. Aggregate and median ratios of debt payments to family incomes, and shares of debtors with ratios above 40% and those with any payment sixty days or more past due, by selected family characteristics, 1989, 1992, and 1995. By comparison, families with the head of household older than 75 were paying less than 4% of their monthly incomes on consumer debt. Ibid.

20. George M. Salem and Aaron C. Clark, "Bank Credit Cards: Loan Loss Risks Are Growing," *GKM Banking Industry Report,* June 11, 1996, 25. Other numbers are sometimes used. The difficulty in pinning down any number is that the credit card companies themselves are not forthcoming about the amortization rates of their cards, and they often have several "products" that bear both different interest rates and different repayment periods.

21. *Statistical Abstract: 1997.*

22. *Statistical Abstract: 1993,* table 705. Per capita income in Los Angeles in 1991 was $25,676.

23. We count married couples filing jointly as having experienced a job interruption if either of the spouses reported being employed and losing a job. We also count those who are not employed, such as homemakers, those on disability, and the permanently unemployed who are not actively looking for work, as having experienced no interruption in their work. If those people are removed from the calculation and only those who hold jobs or who are actively looking for work are included, then 82.5% of the bankrupt debtors experienced a job interruption.

24. AT&T sued a bankrupt debtor for fraud because she had run up charges

on her credit cards that she could not possibly repay. To its surprise, AT&T found that its own lending practices were put under the microscope. Judge Robert Mark denied AT&T's request, excoriating the company for its credit practices, including its practices of "targeting" families already in financial trouble. AT&T Universal Card Services Corp. v. Chinchilla, 202 B.R. 1010, 1015–20 (Bankr. S.D. Fla. 1996).

25. The most lucrative and fastest-growing segment of the highly profitable consumer credit industry is selling credit to people already in financial trouble. The so-called subprime market, which includes high loan-to-value ratio mortgages, car loans, and ordinary credit card debt, is "estimated at $200 billion and growing by an estimated 50 percent a year." Jessica Skelly, "Subprime Under Siege," *Retail Banker International,* Nov. 19, 1998, 8. Lenders' attraction to people already in financial trouble has been demonstrated by the growth in lending from collection agencies. It seems that some debt collectors have figured out that if they buy bad debt—debts the customer has already stopped paying— and lend these people more money at substantial interest rates, they will make a profit. Eric Weiner, Dow Jones News Service, Jan. 10, 1999 (reporting on Credit-Trust's program to lend money to consumers whose loans the banks have already determined are uncollectible).

26. Teresa A. Sullivan, Elizabeth Warren, and Jay Lawrence Westbrook, *As We Forgive Our Debtors: Bankruptcy and Consumer Credit in America* (Oxford: Oxford University Press, 1989), 111.

27. Ibid., 118.

28. Ibid., table 6.1, reported here in constant 1995 dollars.

29. Quoted in Carol Smith, "How to Fail in Business: Many Find Road to Bankruptcy Is Paved with Credit Cards," *Los Angeles Times,* May 30, 1993. Arthur Andersen and National Small Business United, a trade association, conducted another survey of 750 businesses. Their finding was similar. They reported that 26% of the owners were using credit card debt to fund their companies. Cited in Michael Selz, "Can't Meet Payroll? Businesses Use Plastic to Get Cash Infusions," *Wall Street Journal,* Aug. 19, 1994.

30. Study reported in Robert Schwab, "Credit Cards Bankrolling Small Firms," *Denver Post,* Jan. 17, 1999.

31. Cited in Smith, "How to Fail in Business."

32. Quoted in ibid.

33. Quoted in Selz, "Can't Meet Payroll?"

34. Quoted in ibid.

35. James B. Arndorfer, "Bank One, Amex Join Forces for Preapproved Credit Lines," *American Banker,* Apr. 15, 1996, 1.

36. James B. Arndorfer, "Fair Isaac Creating Software for Banks to Target Prospects," *American Banker,* May 13, 1996, 13.

37. *Nilson Report* 646 (June 1997): 1, 4–5. The *Nilson Report* notes that business use of credit cards jumped sharply between 1990 and 1996 and is projected to continue its steep climb through 2005.

38. See Chapter 6 for a discussion of 1994 changes in the bankruptcy law that make it more difficult for one spouse to discharge the joint debts of a couple. When Fred filed in 1991, there were no restrictions of any kind on whether one spouse could discharge the couple's joint debts.

39. The actual number is 59%. By 1996, the Visa study shows 62% of their bankruptcy sample listing credit card debt. Calculated from Visa Consumer Bankruptcy Reports, *Bankruptcy Petition Study,* 1997, 21. Apart from other difficulties with the Visa study (see Appendix 2), the Visa number may not be reliable because the relative proportions of Chapter 7 and Chapter 13 filings reported are not consistent with the filings in the districts that are studied. Because of the differences in data collection and reporting, these data should not be interpreted as indicating a trend.

40. The bankruptcy data reported here understates total credit card debt. The bankruptcy data represent only bank card debt, which is composed of bank cards (such as most MasterCard and Visa cards) and independent or nonbank-affiliated multi-use cards (such as American Express and Diners Club cards). The bankruptcy data are narrower than the reported credit card debt because of differences in reporting and recording information. With bankruptcy data, bank card debt is the only debt in the bankruptcy files that can be identified in the files with certainty as credit card debt. Bankruptcy schedules do not currently contain enough data to permit a reliable, detailed analysis of other types of card debt. Bankruptcy files do not always distinguish between retail credit cards and other credit transactions with merchants. We could assume that all store debt is credit card debt, but that would ignore our earlier finding in 1981 that a substantial portion of store debt was in fact the debts that small businesses owed to their suppliers. Sullivan, Warren, and Westbrook, *As We Forgive,* 108–27. If we counted all store debt as credit card debt, we would probably overstate credit card debt somewhat. This makes the reporting dilemma clear: to omit all store debt understates the influence of credit card debt, but to include all store debt overstates the influence of credit card debt. Without somewhat different reporting procedures in bankruptcy, a closer fix on the influence of credit card debt remains elusive. In the text discussion we report figures that understate credit card debt in conjunction with the more inclusive calculations, recognizing that the problems we identify are probably bigger than we have stated.

41. In the 1981 study, when we looked only at wage earner debtors, we discovered that about 88% of those bankrupt filers had some credit card debt (banks and stores together). However, the data are not entirely comparable. See Sullivan, Warren, and Westbrook, *As We Forgive,* 108–27.

42. Gary Klein and Maggie Spade, "Self-Representation in the Bankruptcy Court: The Massachusetts Experience" (typescript, 1995), app. 5: Public Records and File Review Code Sheets, 5.

43. For additional discussion of the Ohio data, see Appendix 1.

44. We report the California data because they are recent and they add to the picture of the growing credit card problem. We do not rely on them for the heart of the analysis, however, because the California numbers are not representative on two grounds: Chapter 7 debtors tend to have more credit card debt than Chapter 13 debtors, and more California debtors have credit card debt than debtors in other states. Even so, finding 95% of a sample of debtors suggests that the credit card problems are pervasive. For more discussion of Judge Newsome's data, see Appendix 1.

45. Iain Ramsay of Osgoode Hall Law School in Toronto conducted a careful study of Canadian debtors who filed for bankruptcy in 1994. He reports that

321

81% of the debtors had credit card debts. Ramsay, "Individual Bankruptcy: Preliminary Findings of a Socio-Legal Analysis," *Osgoode Hall Law Journal* 37 (1999): 15.

46. Michael Allen, "Bankruptcy Filing Doesn't Have to Be Credit's Final Chapter," *Wall Street Journal,* Feb. 19, 1991. Either they pay off the outstanding balance on one or more of their credit cards before they file or they continue to make their regular payments to some issuers without listing those debts on their bankruptcy schedules. In both cases, the debt remains unrecorded and the card issuer gets paid in full, so it is unlikely that the issuer will learn of the bankruptcy and cancel the card. Failure to list card debt violates the Bankruptcy Code, which unambiguously provides that *all* debt must be listed. This practice also puts a debtor at risk of losing the discharge entirely by making a material misrepresentation to the court. 11 U.S.C. §§ 521(1), 523(a)(3). Nonetheless, trustees and attorneys describe this as "a common practice." Allen, "Bankruptcy Filing." Many consumer bankruptcy attorneys can tell about debtors who offered to pay their fees with credit cards they planned to conceal from the court.

47. The irony is that they need not worry. Credit availability following bankruptcy is high. Some credit card issuers specialize in lending to people emerging from bankruptcy, and virtually all issuers have made credit cards available to customers with a bankruptcy on their records. See, e.g., Dr. Michael Staten, Director, Credit Research Center, Krannert School of Management, Purdue University, "Working Paper No. 58: The Impact of Post-Bankruptcy Credit on the Number of Personal Bankruptcies" (typescript, January 1993). Websites now routinely carry click-on advertisements at the top of restaurant guides and other consumer services heralding "Bad Credit, No Credit, Bankruptcy?" and offering more credit.

48. A related phenomenon occurs with respect to reaffirmations of debt. With a few exceptions for such debts as alimony, taxes, or fraud, debtors who file for Chapter 7 bankruptcy are discharged from personal liability on their debts. Notwithstanding this discharge, Visa estimates that more than 50% of the Chapter 7 debtors agree to be bound again on some of the debts they discharge. Visa, *Consumer Bankruptcy: Bankruptcy Debtor Survey Preliminary Report,* April 1997, 3 (reporting that 54.1% of the debtors reaffirmed one or more debts). The economic irrationality of the move evidently does not deter some debtors. The amounts reaffirmed are not trivial. Even the Purdue Study reports that the debtors reaffirm an average of $11,311 of non-mortgage debt on median incomes of $17,712. Michael Staten, "Do Consumers Take More Bankruptcy Relief Than They Need?" presentation to Merchants Research Council, February 1997. Neither of these studies meets the standards of statistical reporting or reliability (see discussion in Appendix 2), but the reports support others' conclusions that debtors reaffirm many of their debts.

49. In addition to the data reported in the text, a credit industry study provides another look at the credit card burdens of debtors in bankruptcy. These data are from a report of a four-city Visa study covering 1988, 1992, and 1994. Because the Visa study did not report data for each year separately, we used 1992 as the year for standardization to convert the report in 1997 dollars, but we recognize that the 1997 estimate may be either too high or too low—if more of the data came from a later year or an earlier year. Also, because the Visa data are disaggregated into different kinds of credit card debt and there are no reported

322

Ns for the individual cells, it is not possible to reaggregate the data to make them comparable to the data reported in the text. The synthetic debt-income ratio completed here differs somewhat from the debtor-by-debtor debt-income ratio we report in the text in part because the distributions of both debt and income are not normally distributed and each debtor is not at the same point on both distributions. For more discussion of the Visa studies, see Appendix 2. Despite these limitations, the Visa data reinforce the view that the credit card burden of debtors in bankruptcy is substantial.

Visa Data, 1988–96

| Chapter 7 | California (1992) | Tennessee (1993) | Massachusetts (1993) | Illinois (1993) |
|---|---|---|---|---|
| Bank card | $14,351 | $7,579 | $14,127 | $11,264 |
| Discover | $2,595 | $2,460 | $3,013 | $2,571 |
| Retail card | $2,707 | $2,282 | $3,952 | $2,987 |
| American Express | $5,512 | $4,158 | $4,833 | $3,614 |

| Chapter 13 | California (1992) | Tennessee (1993) | Massachusetts (1993) |
|---|---|---|---|
| Bank card | $11,540 | $4,731 | $14,283 |
| Discover | $2,336 | $2,520 | $3,054 |
| Retail card | $2,338 | $1,342 | $4,487 |
| American Express | $5,178 | $2,582 | $5,423 |

50. Data corrected to 1997 constant dollars.

51. It is possible to make a rough extrapolation of total credit card debt from the 1991 data on bank card debt. In 1991, bank card debt accounted for 73% of revolving debt in the country generally. Similarly, about 72% of all people who carried any credit cards carried bank cards. *Nilson Report* 507 (September 1991): 5. If bankrupt debtors behaved like other consumers, at least in a proportional distribution between bank card debt and other kinds of credit card debt, they probably have total credit card debt about a third higher than we report. This would leave the mean debtor with total credit card debt of about $15,800 and the median debtor with total credit card debt of about $9,500 in 1997 dollars. These numbers are close to the actual numbers recorded in the Ohio study in 1997.

52. Visa reported its own study of credit card debt, identifying such debts on a disaggregated basis, so that reports were separated for bank cards, American Express, Discover, retail cards, and "other." It was not possible to aggregate the data in a reliable manner because of the inconsistent reports on both the dates the data were collected (over eight years) and the inconsistent and incomplete information collected (e.g., there were no data on Chapter 13 debtors from one of the four states represented, and it was not possible to tell what district in a state that the data came from for proper weighting of reported Chapter 7 and Chapter 13 data). Even if the data were aggregated, it would not be possible to compare the Visa data with the Consumer Bankruptcy Project Phase I and Phase II or with the Ohio data because Visa does not report standard deviations, which are essential for making statistical comparisons among data groups.

53. Our Canadian cousins seem to experience much the same phenomenon.

Iain Ramsay found that the mean outstanding credit card debt for Canadians filing in 1994 was $7,633. In addition, Ramsay notes that 44% of the debtors had "store debt," with a mean amount owed of $12,225. Ramsay, "Individual Bankruptcy."

54. Federal Reserve, "Family Finances," 17.

55. Of course, if amount of credit card debt carried by families generally is understated as some experts allege, then the general population looks more like the bankrupt population. See discussion in note 14, above.

56. Among the 1997 California debtors, the debt loads were even worse. In a California sample of 100 Chapter 7 debtors, 93 had some credit card debt. Of those debtors, 57% had more than $20,000 in debt, and 13% had more than $50,000 in debt. The prize debtor in the California sample was a man who owed $198,118 on his credit cards.

57. The 1991 data on bank card debt show similar patterns, but the credit card debt loads are not so extreme as the 1997 samples show. In 1991, 400 debtors listed some specific amount of bank card debt. Of these, 149 listed more than $10,000 on their bank credit cards (Visa, MasterCard, American Express, Discover, etc.). Of those 149, 67 owed more than $20,000. Seven debtors in the bankruptcy sample had run up bank card debts of more than $50,000, and the prize debtor was a Californian who owed MasterCard and Visa $168,142. (Dollar figures reported in 1997 dollars for easier comparability.)

58. *Statistical Abstract: 1996,* table 791.

59. OCC Advisory Letter 96-7, Sept. 26, 1996 (96-7.txt at <www.occ.treas. gov>); *FDIC Quarterly Banking Profile Graph Book* (4th Quarter 1997).

60. In just three years between 1992 to 1995, the median card balance jumped another 40% for American households, from $1,100 to $1,500. Calculations from *Statistical Abstracts* and from "Family Finances in the U.S.: Recent Evidence from the Survey of Consumer Finances," *Federal Reserve Bulletin* 17 (January 1997). The number of cards in circulation surged as well, with 35% growth from 1990 to 1996.

61. Mailed credit card solicitations grew by 20% in 1997 alone. "Solicitations Reach Three Billion, But Response Falls," *Credit Card News,* Apr. 1, 1998. They grew another half-billion in 1998 *American Banker,* Apr. 8, 1999. Telephone solicitations for credit cards are not included in these tables.

62. *Statistical Abstract: 1997,* table 798.

63. The data reported in Sullivan, Warren, and Westbrook, *As We Forgive,* from the Consumer Bankruptcy Project Phase I for 1981 are only for wage earning debtors, whereas the 1991 Phase II report includes both self-employed and wage earning debtors. The data reported in *As We Forgive* indicate that in 1981 the self-employed had lower proportionate credit card debt as a fraction of total unsecured debt, which suggests that the numbers reported here for 1981 might have been lower if all debtors had been included. In that case, the increase between 1981 and 1991 might be greater than we report, particularly since more entrepreneurs are now using credit cards when their businesses get into trouble.

Philip Shuchman reports comparable numbers for his 1979–81 study of consumer debtors. Although he does not report adequate information for statistical comparability, such as the standard deviations from the reported means, he indicates that the mean total credit card debt is $2,537 and the median is $1,786

324

(which translates to $4,480 at the mean and $3,155 at the median in 1997 dollars). Shuchman seems to be using "credit card debt" to refer to bank card debt rather than combined retail and bank card debt, although that is not clear from the report. Shuchman, "The Average Bankrupt: A Description and Analysis of 753 Personal Bankruptcy Filings in Nine States," *Commercial Law Journal* 88 (June–July 1983): 297, table P. In a single-district study in 1982–83, he reports mean credit card debt of $3,155 and median credit card debt of $2,178 for those who had some bank credit card debt (which translates into $5,088 at the mean and $3,512 at the median when adjusted to 1997 dollars). Shuchman, "New Jersey Debtors, 1982–83: An Empirical Study," *Seton Hall Law Review* 15 (1985): 541, 568, table 30.

64. Susan Kovac conducted a single-district study in 1985–86 examining the poorest debtors in bankruptcy—those who had no assets in excess of their state law exemptions. Among this subset of debtors, she found less credit card debt than with bankrupt debtors generally. Kovac reported that the debtors owed $3,714 on bank cards at the mean, which would translate into $5,445 in 1997 dollars. Because she is dealing with a poorer subset of all the debtors in bankruptcy, the data are not comparable to those in the text. They are useful, however, to fill out the picture of debt for the lowest-income debtors. Kovac, "Judgment-Proof Debtors in Bankruptcy," *American Bankruptcy Law Journal* 65 (Fall 1991): 675, table J, 722 (reported in constant 1997 dollars). As more creditors enter the subprime market, deliberately targeting less credit-worthy customers, this picture may be changing. David A. Moss and Gibbs A. Johnson argue that the downward shift in the lending profile in the 1990s has changed the "bankruptcy multiplier" as poorer and poorer families take on credit and find themselves in bankruptcy more quickly than their middle-income counterparts. Moss and Johnson, "The Rise of Consumer Bankruptcy: Evolution, Revolution, or Both?" *American Bankruptcy Law Journal* 73 (Spring 1999): 311, 345.

65. Calculated from Federal Reserve, "Family Finances," 17, and *Statistical Abstract: 1996*, table 709 (reporting median income in 1994 of all households at $32,264). The comparison between the population generally and the bankrupt debtors is not entirely accurate. The census data are based on pre-tax income and the bankruptcy data are based on post-tax income, which means the divergence is even greater than reported here.

66. Ordinarily we calculate a debt-income ratio by comparing each debtor's debts with that same debtor's income. Table 4.2 represents such calculations for the Consumer Bankruptcy Project Phase II (CBP II) and for Judge Sellers's Ohio data. We have only aggregated data from the Visa study, and so we calculated a synthetic debt-income ratio by comparing the mean debt to the mean income. Adjusting the figures to 1997 dollars we found the following:

|  | Visa | CBP II |
|---|---|---|
| Annual income | 24,380 | 23,927 |
| Total debt | 121,284 | 65,158 |
| Bank card debt | 8,507 | 6,782 |
| Synthetic total debt-income ratio | 4.975 | 2.511 |
| Synthetic bank credit card debt-income ratio | 0.349 | 0.297 |

*Note:* The Visa figures were calculated from summary data. The debt-income ratios are the ratios of the mean debt to mean income. These data differ from the data in table 4.2 be-

325

cause the debtors occupy different positions on the distributions of debt and income and this information is lost in comparing averages only.

67. The median is somewhat more moderate at only $31 of each $100, but it still captures four months of income.

68. At the median in the 1991 sample, a debtor owed $31 of every $100 in take-home pay for bank card debt. These data are calculated only for debtors who have reported some credit card debt.

69. Bureau of the Census, "Statistical Brief: Housing Changes, 1981 to 1991," SB93-5 (Washington, D.C., May 1993).

70. Bureau of the Census, "Statistical Brief: House-Poor/House-Rich," SB91-19 (Washington, D.C., August 1991); Mary Naifeh, *House-Poor/House-Rich,* Bureau of the Census, Current Housing Reports, Ser. H150/89 (Washington, D.C., 1991). For a more detailed discussion of "house poor," and how many bankrupt debtors find themselves in this position, see the discussion in Chapter 7.

71. Although the data reported here are based on medians, the data at the mean are more extraordinary. The mean debtor in bankruptcy would have to commit nine months' income to pay the principal on the credit card bills and another month and a half of income in interest payments. If he or she paid off the credit card bills, this debtor would have six weeks' worth of income to live on for the whole year.

72. Interest rates for 1991 were calculated at 18.43%, the December 1991 weighted average of all outstanding bank cards. *Nilson Report* 513 (December 1991): 1 .

73. See Chapter 2 for a discussion of general financial information about debtors in bankruptcy. At the median, 1981 debtors listed $37,002 in total debt (in 1997 constant dollars), while 1991 debtors listed $34,795 (in 1997 constant dollars) and 1997 debtors listed $37,002.

74. See table 2.5 for a complete listing of 1981, 1991, and 1997 debt-income ratios.

75. When secured debt is deleted from the equation to show the effects of shorter-term consumer debt, the comparison remains the same: 1981 and 1991 debtors carry statistically indistinguishable debt loads. The 1997 data show the same results. Median debts for the 1997 Ohio debtors in bankruptcy are about $40,960, again statistically indistinguishable from the earlier debtors. Setting aside the effects of inflation, debt levels in consumer bankruptcy have been re-markably stable for more than 15 years.

For debtors in Chapter 7 only, the numbers are somewhat different. Debts are increasing, as is the ratio of debt to income. The pace is not nearly so rapid as the growth in credit card debt, however, and the overall trend can fairly be char-acterized as similar. See, e.g., Elizabeth Warren, "The Bankruptcy Crisis," *Indiana Law Journal* 73 (1998):1, 19, 29–31.

76. We speculate that the same was true for debtors in 1971, 1961, and 1951, but those data are lost to history, so the speculation remains unexplored.

77. Department of Justice, Director of the Administrative Office of the U.S. Courts, *Annual Report, 1981* (U.S. Bankruptcy Courts, 1991), 555, table F.3B.

78. Department of Justice, Director of the Administrative Office of the U.S. Courts, *Annual Report, 1991* (United States Bankruptcy Courts, 1991), table F.

79. Filings for the year-long period ending Mar. 31, 1999, per Department of Justice, Administrative Office of the U.S. Courts, "Second Quarter 1999 Shows a Slight Drop in Bankruptcy Filings," news release, May 21, 1999.

80. Studies by the Congressional Budget Office, the Federal Deposit Insurance Corporation, and independent economists link the rise in consumer bankruptcies directly to the rise in consumer debt. Diane Ellis, "The Effect of Consumer Interest Rate Deregulation on Credit Card Volumes, Charge-offs, and the Personal Bankruptcy Rate," *Bank Trends* 98-05 (FDIC, Division of Insurance, March 1998); Lawrence M. Ausubel, "Credit Card Defaults, Credit Card Profits, and Bankruptcy," *American Bankruptcy Law Journal* 71 (Spring 1997): 249; Kim Kowalewski, Chief, Financial and General Macroeconomic Analysis Unit, Congressional Budget Office, statement before the Senate Judiciary Subcommittee on Administrative Oversight and the Courts, Apr. 11, 1997, 4; Jagdeep S. Bhandari and Lawrence Weiss, "The Increasing Bankruptcy Filing Rate: An Historical Analysis," *American Bankruptcy Law Journal* 67 (Winter 1993): 1–12; Federal Reserve Bank of New York, "Bad Debt Rising," Don Morgan and Ian Toll, *Current Issues in Economics and Finance* (1997).

Charlene Sullivan compared consumer debts from the 1980s with debts from 1945 through 1970, concluding: "Growth in consumer credit alone relative to income was not associated statistically with bankruptcy rates, but the trend in total household debt relative to income was positively and significantly associated with the bankruptcy rates during the last ten years. The estimated coefficients indicated that a one percentage point change in the total debt to income measure was associated with a rise of 15.74 Chapter 7 [filings] and 3.7 Chapter 13 [filings] per 100,000 of the population." A. Charlene Sullivan, testimony before the House Banking Subcommittee on Consumer Coinage, Hearing on Fair Debt Collection Practices Act, Sept. 10, 1992, 8.

81. Kowalewski, statement before the Senate Judiciary Subcommittee on Administrative Oversight and the Courts, Apr. 11, 1997. See also Jay Lawrence Westbrook, "A Comparative Empirical Research Agenda in Consumer Bankruptcy," *Canadian Business Law Journal* 21 (1992): 30.

82. Saul Schwartz and Leigh Anderson document a similar finding in Canada. They report a 0.89 correlation between total consumer debt and bankruptcy filings from 1966 through 1996. Schwartz and Anderson, "An Empirical Study of Canadians Seeking Personal Bankruptcy Protection," 64–65, fig. 3. Their findings confirm those of Jacob Ziegel and his colleagues, who reported a correlation of 0.79 for the time period 1976–84. Ziegel et al., "Consumer Bankruptcies and Bill C-5: Five Academics Claim the Bill Turns the Problems on Their Head," *National American Insolvency Review* 13 (1996): 81–90.

83. Moss and Johnson, "Rise of Consumer Bankruptcy"; Ellis, "Effect of Consumer Interest Rate Deregulation"; Ausubel, "Credit Card Defaults."

84. A study paid for by the credit card issuers tries to refute the conclusion that a rise in consumer debt correlates with bankruptcy filings. The Visa–MasterCard study instead blames a decline in the "stigma" for bankruptcy filing. Congressional Budget Office economists reviewed the Visa–MasterCard study and pronounced it "unsound" and determined that "the report's claim about the importance of 'social factors' that Visa believes affect personal bankruptcy filings to be unfounded." Memorandum, "Evaluations of Three Studies Submitted to the

327

National Bankruptcy Review Commission," from Kim J. Kowalewski to Brady Williamson, Chairman, National Bankruptcy Review Commission 1 (Oct. 6, 1997).

85. While we remind the reader again of the limitations in the report of the Visa data that make any statistically valid comparisons impossible, the reports here are very consistent with the Visa reports. They report that bank card debt (which does not include Discover or American Express or any retail cards) accounted for 43.3%, 40.9%, 28.5%, and 24.7% of all the unsecured debt in their 1993–95 study of Chapter 7 cases in Illinois, California, Tennessee, and Massachusetts. Visa, *Bankruptcy Petition Study* (July 1997), 48. They report somewhat higher proportions for the three states in which they have Chapter 13 data.

86. *Nilson Report* 697 (April 1996): 9.

87. When Visa conducted its own survey of debtors, it gave specific options for the debtors to identify the reasons for the bankruptcy filings. Among the seven items offered to respondents and counted by Visa, none were "credit card debt." Visa was evidently confident that the problem lay elsewhere. See Visa, "Consumer Bankruptcy: Bankruptcy Debtor Survey," *Visa Consumer Bankruptcy Reports,* July 1996, 15; see Appendix 2.

88. When it turns out that we could have gotten better data using another research method, some people (including ourselves) may wonder why we didn't use it. Usually the answer is that we didn't think of it. But this time the answer is that we thought about it, and we decided that an open-ended question was better for other reasons. We got the debtors' own words, uncolored by any subtle suggestion of "right" answers.

If we had made up the selection list, we would have missed some very interesting answers, such as the significant fraction of the debtors for whom a medical problem spelled financial catastrophe not because they couldn't pay the medical debts but because they had to cut back on work. We would also have missed the debtor who explained that getting called up unexpectedly for military duty did her in or the man who explained that his bankruptcy was a result of the spotted owl controversy. See more discussion of this problem in Appendix 1.

89. This debtor does not blame credit cards for his financial demise, although he admits that his admittedly poor money management techniques involved the use of plastic: "I carelessly handled money and my credit. Because of this I can't afford to pay my bills or rent all at the same time. Each month I had to use credit cards to help pay living expenses and bills." With a monthly take-home pay of $1,408 and monthly expenses of $1,743 for rent, food, utilities, medical, clothing, car payment, and furniture payment, he is likely to have some difficulties paying off over $27,000 in credit card debt.

90. During the hearings of the National Bankruptcy Review Commission on consumer bankruptcy, one of the commissioners noted that his dog Bradley had recently received a credit application. Although he thought Bradley was a "fine fellow," the commissioner expressed his doubt about Bradley's ability to handle a line of credit. The credit card issuers at the meeting had no comment. Meeting of the National Bankruptcy Review Commission, May 23, 1996.

91. *Nilson Report* 254 (February 1981): 5.

92. Ibid., 507 (September 1991): 4–5.

93. OCC Advisory Letter 96-7, Sept. 26, 1996; *FDIC Quarterly Banking Profile Graph Book* (4th Quarter 1997).

94. Industry analyst Asheet Mehta explained that "card issuers are breaking all records in direct mail solicitations, and as competition intensifies, they are spending more and more to sign new customers. Mr. Mehta said the cost of opening a new account, only $40 in the early 1990s, has climbed to almost $100 and may hit $200 by 2000." Asheet Mehta, "Credit Card Industry Outlook Growing More Gloomy," *American Banker,* Sept. 24, 1997, 1.

95. Salem and Clark, "Bank Credit Cards," 5.

96. "Solicitations Reach Three Billion."

97. Salem and Clark, "Bank Credit Cards," 5. They express their estimate per adult Americans, but it is possible to convert to households to keep the analysis parallel.

98. As bankruptcy levels have risen, total credit card profitability has grown — credit card lending is now twice as profitable as all other lending activities. In the third quarter of 1997, credit card banks showed a 2.59% return on assets, compared to a 1.22% return on assets reported by all commercial banks. Federal Reserve Board, *The Profitability of Credit Card Operations of Depository Institutions* (August 1997). For a discussion of the higher profitability of credit cards over other forms of lending, see Ausubel, "Credit Card Defaults," 249.

99. Federal Reserve, "Family Finances," table 14. Aggregate and median ratios of debt payments to family incomes, and shares of debtors with ratios above 40% and those with any payment 60 days or more past due, by selected family characteristics, 1989, 1992, and 1995; Yoo, "Mountain of Debt," 4; David Wyss, "Surveillance Programs and Performance," *DRI/McGraw-Hill,* Apr. 15, 1997, 8.

100. Penny Lunt, "Card Profits Are Holding Steady, But Will Drop If You Don't Trim Expenses," *American Bankers Association Banking Journal,* March 1995, 43.

101. "For several years, subprime lenders were darlings of the investment markets. The number of subprime lenders grew 22 percent last year." Jim Barlow, "Subprime Lenders Feeling the Pinch," *Houston Chronicle,* Oct. 15, 1998.

102. Paul Beckett, "Citigroup Debut Comes with a Warning," *Wall Street Journal,* Oct. 9, 1998.

103. Federal Reserve, "Family Finances," table 14.

104. Yoo, "Mountain of Debt," 4.

105. Wyss, "Surveillance Programs and Performance," 8.

106. Federal Reserve, "Family Finances." Aggregate and median ratios of debt payments to family incomes, and shares of debtors with ratios above 40 percent and those with any payment 60 days or more past due, by selected family characteristics, 1989, 1992, and 1995.

107. Salem and Clark, "Bank Credit Cards," 9.

108. U.S. PIRG, "The Campus Credit Card Trap: Results of a PIRG Survey of College Students and Credit Cards" (September 1998): 2. Research conducted by Roper Starch Worldwide, Inc., in 1995, reported in Antoinette Coulton, "Easy Credit for Students Teaching Hard Lessons," *American Banker,* Oct. 17, 1996, found that 64% of college students had credit cards.

109. Coulton, "Easy Credit," 1.

110. Reported in ibid. One of this book's coauthors, who teaches a freshman seminar on credit cards, found that her students received, by all means, an average of 60 credit card solicitations each during their first semester on campus.

111. Industry analysts are highly critical of the level of underwriting (credit

scrutiny) for credit card debt, citing incomplete data from credit bureaus, failure to gather information on the customers' current income or employment status, no attempts to account for the debtors' changed circumstances, and no consideration of the amount of credit the debtor already has. Salem and Clark, "Bank Credit Cards," 7–8.

112. See note 61, above.

113. The actual estimate is 526,681. This calculation assumes 1,350,118 non-business consumer filings for 1997, with 83% having some credit card debt and 47% having a credit card debt-income ratio at or above 0.5, based on the Ohio data. We chose the Ohio data for the calculation because they are the latest figures and they include *all* credit card debt for *all* consumer filers. Other comparable data are Gary Klein and Maggie Spade's 1991 single-district data, which also included all credit card debt and reported 88% with some credit card debt ("Self-Representation in the Bankruptcy Court"), the 1981 Consumer Bankruptcy Project data, which also suggested 88% with some credit card debt, and Judge Newsome's 1997 California data, which showed that 93% of the sample of Chapter 7 filers had some credit card debt.

**Chapter 5: Sickness and Injury**

1. A large and important study of medical expenditures was conducted in 1977 and repeated in 1987. A. Taylor and J. Banthin, *Changes in Out-of-Pocket Expenditures for Personal Health Services: 1977 and 1987* (Rockville, Md.: National Technical Information Service, 1994), 1–21. The study indicated that more than 9 million families spent more than 20% of their incomes on medical care (as defined) during 1987; 12, table 7. During that decade, this category had increased by more than 1 million families. A new MEPS (Medical Expenditures Panel Survey) was done in 1996, but its expenditure results have not been published. See Joel W. Cohen et al., "The Medical Expenditure Panel Survey: A National Health Information Resource," *Inquiry* 33 (Winter 1997): 373.

2. Internal Revenue Service, *Statistics of Income Bulletin* 14 (Winter 1994–95): 177, table 1, col. 6. Since 1987, such deductions are allowed only if the taxpayer's expenses exceeded 2% of adjusted gross income.

3. Bureau of the Census, *Statistical Abstract of the United States: 1993* (Washington, D.C., 1993), 132, table 199 (621 million lost days in 1990).

4. Some intriguing recent research in England suggests that job insecurity can be the direct cause of increased sickness in a population of workers threatened with downsizing. Jane Elizabeth Ferrie et al., "An Uncertain Future: The Health Effects of Threats to Employment Security in White-Collar Men and Women," *American Journal of Public Health* 88 (July 1998): 1030.

5. The questionnaire data cited here are from 1991, but the cases filed in Ohio in 1997 are very similar. See the discussion of the Ohio data in Appendix 1. In our 1991 data, 19.3% of the sample mentioned medical reasons as one of the reasons for bankruptcy. About half of this number, or 10.1% of the sample, listed a medical reason as the first reason for bankruptcy. In the 1997 Ohio data, 21.4% of the sample were believed to have a medical reason for bankruptcy.

The credit industry also launched its own study in the mid-1990s. Visa sent out questionnaires to 5,000 individuals who had filed for bankruptcy during

1996. Debtors were asked an open-ended question: "What was the main reason you had to file bankruptcy?" Of the debtors who responded, 16.5% identified medical and health-related reasons. Later in the questionnaire, debtors were asked, "What was the 'last straw' that led to your bankruptcy filing?" Choices that could be checked off were repossession, litigation, medical, taxes, foreclosure, divorce, wage garnishment, and other. Of the debtors responding, 14.3% identified "medical" as the "last straw" before filing. Visa, *Consumer Bankruptcy: Bankruptcy Debtor Survey,* July 1996, 7–9. We report those findings simply as an indication from another source that medical problems may be a significant trigger for bankruptcy. For more discussion of this study, see Appendix 2. Many, but not all, earlier studies found medical reasons to be important in consumer bankruptcies. Joe Lee, "Bankruptcy Study Plan," *Senate Judiciary Committee Report 13* (1971), 18, 20.

6. About 3% of the sample specifically mentioned the birth of a baby as a precipitating event in their financial collapse.

7. Rashi Fein, *Medical Care, Medical Costs: The Search for a Health Insurance Policy* (Cambridge: Harvard University Press, 1986).

8. Henry J. Aaron, *Serious and Unstable Condition: Financing America's Health Care* (Washington, D.C.: Brookings Institution, 1991), 39.

9. A recent study reports that just from 1988 to 1992 medical expenditures rose from 15% of total national consumption to almost 17%. Gregory Acs and John Sabelhaus, "Trends in Out-of-Pocket Spending on Health Care, 1980–92," *Monthly Labor Review* 118 (December 1995): 35. Aaron says that U.S. expenditures for health care are by far the highest in the world, overall and per capita. Aaron, *Serious and Unstable Condition,* 79–80, table 4.1.

10. Thomas A. Durkin and Gregory E. Elliehausen, *1977 Consumer Credit Survey* (Washington, D.C.: Federal Reserve Board, 1978), 80, table 15.1.

11. Ibid., 83, table 16.3.

12. General Accounting Office, *Tax Policy: Many Factors Contributed to the Growth in Home Equity Financing in the 1980s,* report to the Honorable William J. Coyne, House of Representatives, GAO/GGo-93-63, March 1993, 16, table 2.

13. Ibid. The 1977 consumer survey did not break out second-mortgage medical debts separately in this way but stated that 36% of second-mortgage debts were taken out under a heading of "other" purposes that included medical reasons. Durkin and Elliehausen, *1977 Consumer Credit Survey,* 92, table 18.3.

14. Public Health Service, *National Medical Expenditure Survey: Estimates of the Uninsured Population, Calendar Year 1987* (Rockville, Md.: Agency for Health Care Policy and Research, 1990), 5, table 1. The survey was based upon a sample of 15,000 households interviewed four times during the calendar year 1987.

15. These numbers are strongly supported by a survey done by the National Opinion Research Center at the University of Chicago. In that poll of a telephone sample of almost 4,000 people, 19% indicated that they were uninsured at the time of the survey or had been uninsured within the prior year. Karen Donelan et al., "Whatever Happened to the Health Insurance Crisis in the United States? Voices from a National Survey," *Journal of the American Medical Association* 276 (October 1996): 1346.

16. Bureau of the Census, *Dynamics of Economic Well-Being: Health Insurance, 1991 to 1993,* by Robert L. Bennefield (Washington, D.C., 1995), 2, table A. The bu-

reau concedes that the Public Health estimates are likely to be more accurate. See <http://www.census.gov/hhes/hlthins/cover96/cov96asc.html> (Apr. 10, 1997).

17. Bureau of the Census, *Statistical Abstract: 1993*, 117, table 165. This table gives another set of figures, even though the source for these tables is also the Census Bureau. The reason for the difference seems to be that these tables cite a different Census Bureau study, the *Current Population Survey*, which is taken each quarter. Nonetheless, this table shows relatively small changes from 1985 to 1991, a finding consistent with the other data sources. Thus the differences mentioned are not differences in the real world but reflect the different approaches to measurement.

18. The preliminary estimate from the 1996 MEPS is that 44 million people, 17% of the population, were uninsured at some point during 1996. Karen M. Beauregard, Susan K. Drilea, and Jessica P. Vistness, *The Uninsured in America: 1996: Health Insurance Status of the U.S. Civilian Noninstitutionalized Population* (Rockville, Md.: Agency for Health Care Policy and Research, 1997).

19. See also Charles J. Dougherty, *American Health Care: Realities, Rights, and Reforms* (New York: Oxford University Press, 1988), 11; General Accounting Office, *Canadian Health Insurance: Lessons for the United States,* Report to the Chairman, Committee on Government Operations, House of Representatives, 1991, 21. Dougherty estimates that 35 million people were uninsured in the mid-1980s, whereas the GAO report estimates that 32 million people under age 65 were uninsured.

20. Bureau of the Census, *Dynamics of Economic Well-Being*, 4, table B. The exact time period was 32 months.

21. Ida Hellender et al., "The Growing Epidemic of Uninsurance: New Data on the Health Insurance Coverage of Americans," *International Journal of Health Services* 25 (1995): 377; Gregory Acs, "Explaining Trends in Health Insurance Coverage Between 1988 and 1991," *Inquiry* 32 (Spring 1995): 102.

22. Bureau of the Census, *Census Brief: Children Without Health Insurance* (Washington, D.C., March 1998), 1.

23. Peter J. Elmer and Steven A. Seelig, "The Rising Long-Term Trend of Single-Family Mortgage Foreclosure Rates," *Real Estate Finance Journal* 14 (Winter 1999): 25–33.

24. Stephen Long and Jack Rogers, "Do Shifts Toward Service Industries, Part-Time Work, and Self-Employment Explain the Rising Uninsured Rate?" *Inquiry* 32 (Spring 1995): 111. There was some trend for workers to shift into workplaces less likely to be covered by health insurance. That cause combines with falling family incomes, reducing capacity to pay health insurance premiums. Acs, "Explaining Trends in Health Insurance Coverage."

In 1994, 52.9% of workers were in group health plans. The least likely employees to have health insurance were those in services (32.1%), sales (43.3%), and farming, forestry, and fishing (21.4%). Also less likely to have coverage were part-time workers (19% covered) and workers in small firms (27.5% covered in firms with fewer than 25 persons). Bureau of the Census, *Statistical Abstract of the United States: 1996* (Washington, D.C., 1996), 430, table 670. Except for the farm-forestry-fishing group, these low-benefit areas were among those with the most rapid job growth. Between 1983 and 1994, overall nonfarm employment grew by 2.1% annually, but employment in "services" grew by 4.4%. Ibid., 411, table 642. Union representation declined from 23.3% of the labor force in 1983 to 16.7% in 1995.

332

Ibid., 438, table 684. And several observers argued that most new jobs were being created by small employers. David Birch argues that as many as two-thirds of new jobs are created in firms with fewer than 20 workers. Birch, "Generating New Jobs: Are Government Incentives Effective?" in Robert Friedman and William Schweke, eds., *Expanding the Opportunity to Produce: Revitalizing the American Economy Through New Enterprise Development* (Washington, D.C.: Corporation for Enterprise Development, 1981), 10–16. For a discussion and partial rebuttal of this argument, see Randy Hodson and Teresa A. Sullivan, *The Social Organization of Work*, 2d ed. (Belmont, Mass.: Wadsworth, 1995), 409–10.

25. Pamela Short and Jessica Banthin, "New Estimates of the Underinsured Younger than Sixty-Five Years," *Journal of the American Medical Association* 274 (October 1995): 1302.

26. Steven Findlay and Joel Miller, National Coalition on Health Care, *Down a Dangerous Path: The Erosion of Health Insurance Coverage in the United States*, May 5, 1999 (<http://www.nchc.org/releases/erosion.html>).

27. Bureau of the Census, *Statistical Abstract of the United States: 1997* (Washington, D.C., 1997), 430, table 669.

28. More recently, additional pressure has been exerted by a substantial increase in uninsured people coming off the welfare rolls, because welfare and Medicaid are linked. *Losing Health Insurance: The Unintended Consequences of Welfare Reform*, Families USA Foundation Report No. 99-103 (Washington, D.C.: Families USA Foundation, May 1999).

29. The Brookings study from the mid-1960s reported about 28% of the debtors as citing "family problems" as a cause of bankruptcy. D. Stanley and M. Girth, *Bankruptcy: Problems, Process, Reform* (Washington, D.C.: Brookings Institution, 1971). Those researchers lumped together as "family problems" both medically related difficulties and births and deaths. If we added births and deaths to our medical category, we would get about the same figure as a percentage of debtors reporting these sorts of problems as causes of bankruptcy.

30. Larry Sitner et al., "Medical Expense as a Factor in Bankruptcy," *Nebraska State Medical Journal* 52 (1967): 412; Barry Gold and Elizabeth Donahue, "Health Care Costs and Personal Bankruptcy," *Journal of Health Politics, Policy, and Law* 7 (Fall 1982): 734. Unfortunately, these studies did not report standard statistical information, so it is hard to use them for data comparisons.

31. Senate Judiciary Subcommittee on Courts, Statement of Philip Shuchman, *Bankruptcy Reform Act of 1978, Future Earnings*, 97th Cong., 1st sess., 1981, pt. 2, 69 and 78; Philip Shuchman, "New Jersey Debtors, 1982–83: An Empirical Study," *Seton Hall Law Review* 15 (1985): 541; Philip Shuchman, "The Average Bankrupt: A Description and Analysis of 753 Personal Bankruptcy Filings in Nine States," *Commercial Law Journal* 88 (June–July 1983): 288. Unfortunately, these studies were rendered much less useful by a failure to report standard deviations, which are necessary to make meaningful statistical comparisons. The larger of the studies, "Average Bankrupt," is vague concerning its sampling framework. Such omissions make any meta-analysis impossible.

32. Teresa Sullivan, Elizabeth Warren, and Jay Lawrence Westbrook, *As We Forgive Our Debtors: Bankruptcy and Consumer Credit in America* (Oxford: Oxford University Press, 1989), 168–69. We looked at medical debts as a percentage of overall debt and found that in most bankruptcies they were a small part of debt. How-

333

ever, we recognized that medical debt and many other effects of illness or injury might not be revealed by the financial statements in the court files.

33. Shuchman, *Bankruptcy Reform Act*, 72; Shuchman, "Average Bankrupt," 295. Shuchman also suggested that medical debt might be a more important factor in the bankruptcies of single women. Shuchman, "Average Bankrupt," 289, n. 7. We found that single-filing women had a significantly greater ratio of medical debt to income than did joint-filers or men filing alone. Sullivan, Warren, and Westbrook, *As We Forgive*, 171.

34. Susan D. Kovac, "Judgment-Proof Debtors in Bankruptcy," *American Bankruptcy Law Journal* 65 (Fall 1991): 675. Note that her work was drawn from the one district in Tennessee that we did not study.

35. Ibid., 711, table G. The table provides a helpful comparison among the several studies.

36. For example, Sullivan, Warren, and Westbrook, *As We Forgive*, 169 (11% of unsecured debt).

37. Unfortunately, the Tennessee study also fails to report standard deviations, making statistical comparisons between studies impossible.

38. For example, Kovac suggests that the much greater impact of medical debt in her sample might result from her using more current income figures for the debtors, but that point would not explain the dramatic differences in medical debt as a percentage of total unsecured debt between her study and the others reporting that information. She also suggests that the presence of garnishment in Tennessee might explain the difference. Kovac, "Judgment-Proof Debtors," 719. Leaving aside the assumption that medical providers might be especially aggressive collectors, which may be true, that explanation seems weak given that garnishment was permitted in Illinois, representing three of the ten districts studied in *As We Forgive*, and there were no state-level differences in medical debts in that study. Sullivan, Warren, and Westbrook, *As We Forgive*, 169–70. If garnishment by medical creditors were a strong factor leading to bankruptcy, there should have been more medical debt in 1981 in our Illinois sample than in Texas and Pennsylvania.

39. Kovac, "Judgment-Proof Debtors," 687. She systematically eliminated business cases and cases where debtors were part of a more affluent family. As a result, her debtors had a mean annual income of about $5,000, far below the poverty level and far below the mean incomes in the other studies discussing this issue.

40. Sullivan, Warren, and Westbrook, *As We Forgive*, 328.

41. See Chapter 4 for a discussion about increased access to debt for those below the poverty line.

42. Ian Domowitz, statement before the Senate Judiciary Subcommittee on Administrative Oversight and the Courts, Apr. 11, 1992.

43. Sullivan, Warren, and Westbrook, *As We Forgive*, 169.

44. See Chapter 4 for a discussion of debtors' failure to list credit card debt.

45. Shuchman learned in interviews in New Jersey that medical debt is sometimes not scheduled for that reason. Shuchman, "Average Bankrupt," 295, n. 34. We found the same phenomenon with home mortgages. Sullivan, Warren, and Westbrook, *As We Forgive*, 135.

46. The hospitals and doctors are consistently clear about the distinction,

334

although they do not always break out the figures. E.g., Marsha C. Holleman et al., "Uncompensated Outpatient Medical Care by Physicians," *Medical Care* 29 (1991): 654; Robert L. Ohsfeldt, "Uncompensated Medical Services Provided by Physicians and Hospitals," *Medical Care* 23 (1985): 1338.

47. Saul J. Weiner, "Assessing Bad Debt in New Hampshire and Vermont Office-Based Practices," *Family Practice Resident Journal* 13 (1993): 331.

48. Kovac, "Judgment-Proof Debtors," 710.

49. Sullivan, Warren, and Westbrook, *As We Forgive*, 169, n. 3.

50. Judge Sellers's 1997 Ohio data indicate that "medical bills" were an important cause for about 3.5% of the bankruptcies she studied. She did not have a category for loss of medical insurance.

51. To the extent it has any validity, the credit industry study reinforces the strength of our finding. As we noted earlier, the study cannot be confirmed and insufficient data are reported to meet even the basic criteria for academic studies. Its survey questionnaire is directed at the debtors, 16.5% of whom identify medical problems as the reasons for their bankruptcy filing. Because there is no breakdown in the analysis, it is not possible to identify separately medical debt problems and problems of lost income following illness or an accident. However, the combined total is very similar to the combined total in our 1991 and 1997 data, in which 19% of the debtors identified medically related problems as their reason for filing bankruptcy. Visa, *Consumer Bankruptcy: Bankruptcy Debtor Survey*, July 1996, 7–9.

52. Kovac, "Judgment-Proof Debtors," 711.

53. About 54% of the debtors listing a medical reason also listed a job-related reason.

54. One recent study reports that in Canadian bankruptcies medical debts are "rare and small in size." Saul Schwartz, "The Empirical Dimensions of Consumer Bankruptcy: Results from a Survey of Consumer Bankrupts," *Osgoode Hall Law Journal* 37 (1999): 83.

55. See Iain Ramsay, "Individual Bankruptcy: Preliminary Findings of a Socio-Legal Analysis," *Osgoode Hall Law Journal* 37 (1999): 15.

56. Census Bureau, *Statistical Abstract: 1997*, 138, table 208 (621 million lost days in 1990, 642 million lost days in 1994).

57. See, for example, Diane B. Hill, "Employer-Sponsored Long-Term Disability Insurance," *Monthly Labor Review* 110 (July 1987): 16; Chester Arthur Williams, *An International Comparison of Workers' Compensation* (Boston: Kluwer Academic, 1991), 65.

58. Social Security Bulletin, Annual Statistics Supplement (1991): 349. Consider that a "prudent" cost for housing is one-third of income, compared with the 20–40% of income that could be lost to disability.

59. Emily A. Spieler, "Perpetuating Risk? Workers' Compensation and the Persistence of Occupational Injuries," *Houston Law Review* 31 (1994): 119, 247–49.

60. Hill, "Employer-Sponsored Long-Term Disability Insurance."

61. Ibid., 150, table 5.A1, and 349. On the other hand, SSDI benefits are not taxable and can sometimes exceed predisability net pay. Monroe Berkowitz and M. Anne Hill, "Disability in the Labor Market: An Overview," in Berkowitz and Hill, eds., *Disability Policy in the United States, Sweden and the Netherlands* (Ithaca, N.Y.: Cornell University Press, 1986), 12.

62. For example, Colleen Mulcahy, "Disability Rehab Programs Really Pay Off," *National Underwriter #17* 98 (1994): 2. Interestingly, insurance companies and other active participants in the field consistently take this view, while the dissenting view—that rehab programs are of questionable value—is found primarily in the academic community. E.g., Berkowitz and Hill, eds., *Disability Policy.*

63. On the other hand, experience in other nations reflects that where serious disability persists such programs have only limited success in returning workers to nonsheltered jobs. Richard Burkhauser, "Disability in the Labor Market," in Berkowitz and Hill, *Disability Policy,* 278–80.

64. More than one in five debtors with job problems (21.8%) also reported a medical problem.

65. No significant difference is found among the five states or the 16 districts.

66. There was no significant difference among the proportions of whites, Hispanics, blacks, Asians and Pacific Islanders, and "others" in the sample. We also found no significant differences in comparing whites with all others, blacks with all others, or Hispanics with all others.

67. Acs and Sabelhaus, "Out-of-Pocket Spending," 12.

68. Approximately equal proportions of male and female first-named petitioners reported medical debts.

69. See earlier discussion in this chapter, at note 33.

70. See discussion in Chapter 6.

71. For those who mention medical debts, mean income is $19,804 and debt-income ratio is 2.39. For those who do not mention medical debts, both means are insignificantly higher: $20,575 income and 2.60 debt-income ratio.

72. Acs and Sabelhaus, "Out-of-Pocket Spending," 12, table 7.

73. Those over 65 are only 2.4% of the sample, but they are 4.2% of the people citing medical reasons for bankruptcy. Age is significantly associated with citing a medical reason for bankruptcy.

74. See Stanley and Girth, *Bankruptcy.*

75. See generally Elmer and Seelig, "Rising Long-Term Trend."

76. See Ohsfeldt, "Uncompensated Medical Services."

77. There is virtually nothing in the literature about the effect of nonpayment on the willingness of doctors to provide further services. There is evidence that doctors are able to cost-shift or adjust their practices to mitigate the effects of nonpayment, although it is not clear if that fact affects their inclination to write off or to pursue delinquent patients. John M. Eisenberg, *Doctors' Decisions and the Cost of Medical Care: The Reasons for Doctors' Practice Patterns and Ways to Change Them* (Ann Arbor, Mich.: Health Administration Press Perspectives, 1986), 32–33.

78. David Blumenthal, "The Social Responsibility of Physicians in a Changing Health Care System," *Inquiry* 23 (1986): 270. See also Joel Weissman, "Uncompensated Hospital Care: Will It Be There If We Need It?" *Journal of the American Medical Association* 276 (September 1996): 823; Nancy Cross Dunham et al., "Uncompensated and Discounted Medicaid Care Provided by Physician Group Practices in Wisconsin," *Journal of the American Medical Association* 265 (June 1991): 2982; Mark Green, "Who Are New York City's Uninsured?" (Public Advocate's Office, February 1997), iii.

79. Eisenberg, *Doctors' Decisions,* 32–33.

**NOTES TO PAGES 160–68**

80. Jack Hadley, Earl P. Steinberg, and Judith Feder, "Comparison of Uninsured and Privately Insured Hospital Patients: Condition on Admission, Resource Use, and Outcome," *Journal of the American Medical Association* 265 (January 1991): 374; Holleman et al., "Uncompensated Outpatient Medical Care," 656, 658. Holleman and colleagues explain that care may be substandard even where physicians are donating their services, because of the unavailability of expensive tests and various ancillary services. In general, however, it is difficult to document the difference in care for those who do not have insurance or substantial financial resources, because few studies have been reported. Aaron, *Serious and Unstable Condition,* 77.

81. *Medicaid Source Book: Background Data and Analysis (a 1993 Update),* Report to the Subcommittee on Health and the Environment, Committee on Energy and Commerce, 103d Cong., 1st sess. (1993), 174, table 3.2. These were the high, initial eligibility incomes. After 12 months on welfare, they dropped to $784 and $284 per month, respectively.

82. Ibid., 194, table 3.6.

83. R. J. Blendon, "Three Systems: A Comparative Survey," *Health Management Quarterly,* 1st Quarter 1989, 2–10.

84. The program reported that after the interviews, Michael died. It did not say whether his mom and dad had proceeded to file bankruptcy.

85. Thomas Bodenheimer and Kevin Grumbach, "Paying for Health Care," *Journal of the American Medical Association* 272 (August 1994): 634 (reporting estimates for 1991). About the same percentage is reported for 1995. Center for Cost and Financing Studies (CCFS) of the Agency for Health Care Policy and Research, *Trends in Personal Health Care Expenditures, Health Insurance, and Payment Sources, Community-Based Population, 1987–1995* (March 1997), 3. CCFS states that the percentage had declined from 26% in 1987. Another source, however, suggests that out-of-pocket expenditures are rising as a percentage of family budgets when insurance costs are included. Acs and Sabelhaus, "Out-of-Pocket Spending," 37. Both studies are based on extrapolations rather than on direct surveys.

337

## Chapter 6: Divorce

1. These changes are taking place throughout the industrialized world. See, e.g., "Marriage: Why Do We Still Bother?" *Independent,* Aug. 18, 1996, 16.

2. Annemette Sorensen, "Estimating the Economic Consequences of Separation and Divorce," in Leonore J. Weitzman and Mavis Maclean, eds., *Economic Consequences of Divorce: The International Perspective* (New York: Oxford University Press, 1992), 263–82; Greg J. Duncan and Saul D. Hoffman, "A Reconsideration of the Economic Consequences of Marital Dissolution," *Demography* 22 (1985): 485.

3. "Report from PAA," *Population Today* 23 (June 1995): 3. See also Barbara D. Whitehead, *The Divorce Culture* (New York: Alfred A. Knopf, 1997), 8.

4. See, e.g., Sylvia Lane, "Petitioners Under Chapter XIII of the Bankruptcy Act," *Journal of Consumer Affairs* 3 (Summer 1969): 26. There have been several aggregate level studies that have shown a positive association between divorce rates and bankruptcy filing rates. Ramona K. Z. Heck, "An Econometric Analysis of Interstate Differences in Nonbusiness Bankruptcy and Chapter Thirteen Rates," *Journal of Consumer Affairs* 15 (Summer 1981): 13; Duncan and Hoffman, "Economic

Consequences of Marital Dissolution"; General Accounting Office, *Bankruptcy Reform Act of 1978—A Before and After Look*, GAO/GGD-83-54 (Washington, D.C., 1983). Another sample, however, had relatively low proportions of divorced debtors. William J. Preston, "A Comparison of the Rationale and Socio-Economic Characteristics of Straight Bankruptcy and Chapter XIII Petitioners in the Denver, Colorado Area" (Ph.D. diss., Colorado State College, 1969). It is also a common finding among students of divorce that economic problems play a major role both before and after the divorce. See Ramona K. Z. Heck, "Identifying Insolvent Households," *Journal of Home Economics* 14 (Winter 1980): 14. One recent book argues that divorce leads to economic problems more than results from them. Whitehead, *Divorce Culture*, 93. We have previously reviewed the relationship between family problems and bankruptcy in Teresa A. Sullivan, Elizabeth Warren, and Jay Lawrence Westbrook, "Bankruptcy and the Family," *Marriage and Family Review* 21 (Winter 1995): 193.

5. Allen M. Parkman, *No Fault Divorce: What Went Wrong?* (Boulder, Colo.: Westview, 1992), 95, table 5.2.

6. Lenore J. Weitzman, *The Divorce Revolution: The Unexpected Social and Economic Consequences For Women and Children in America* (New York: Free Press, 1985), 327. Parkman and Weitzman tell the story of a California assemblyman, James Hayes, who was involved in a brutal alimony battle with his wife of 25 years while playing a leading role in the adoption of the California no-fault statute. At one point, he was able to cut his wife's alimony to $200 a month, with the trial judge telling her "to get a job," even though she had only one year of college and a quarter-century as a homemaker. The decision was overturned on appeal. Parkman, *No Fault Divorce*, chap. 4; see also Weitzman, *Divorce Revolution*, 211. Judge Roslyn B. Bell reports a number of similar horror stories under Maryland's 1980 statute in a 1986 study of Montgomery County, Maryland. Bell, "Alimony and the Financially Dependent Spouse in Montgomery County, Maryland," *Family Law Quarterly* 22 (Fall 1988): 225.

7. See, for example, Pamela J. Smock, "The Economic Costs of Marital Disruption for Young Women over the Past Two Decades," 30 *Demography* (August 1993): 353. Men may also do worse after divorce, at least initially, but the findings on this point are mixed.

8. Weitzman, *Divorce Revolution*. A number of earlier scholarly works had pointed to the gender gap in financial outcomes following divorce. See Thomas J. Espenshade, "The Economic Consequences of Divorce," *Journal of Marriage and the Family* 41 (August 1979): 615; Saul Hoffman and John Holmes, "Husbands, Wives, and Divorce," in Greg Duncan and James Morgan, eds., *Five Thousand American Families: Patterns of Economic Progress* (Ann Arbor: Survey Research Center, Institute for Social Research, University of Michigan, 1976), 23–75. Such studies are reviewed in Karen C. Holden and Pamela J. Smock, "The Economic Costs of Marital Dissolution," *Annual Review of Sociology* 17 (1991): 51. Weitzman's study, however, attracted media attention and subsequently the attention of lawyers and judges.

9. Weitzman, *Divorce Revolution*, 326–28, table 21. A subsequent reanalysis of her data showed the decline for women to be 27% and the increase for men to be 10%. Richard A. Peterson, "A Re-Evaluation of the Economic Consequences of Divorce," *American Sociological Review* 61 (June 1996): 528; Lenore J. Weitzman, "The Economic Consequences of Divorce Are Still Unequal: Comment on Peterson,"

338

American Sociological Review 61 (June 1996): 537; Richard R. Peterson, "Statistical Errors, Faulty Conclusions, Misguided Policy: Reply to Weitzman," *American Sociological Review* 61 (June 1996): 539. Even though Weitzman's study is controversial and her reported numbers are disputed, the overall effect of divorce on women, and the greater economic suffering that divorce inflicts on women, are generally well established in the scholarly literature.

10. There is great controversy over the cause of this economic deprivation. Herbert Jacob, among others, has done extensive work challenging the idea that no-fault divorce is the cause of increased economic suffering by divorced women. E.g., Jacob, "Another Look at No-Fault Divorce and the Post-Divorce Finances of Women," *Law and Society Review* 23 (February 1989): 95, 111–12. But Jacob agrees that the postdivorce economic situation of women is miserable. Ibid., 113.

11. S. D. Hoffman and G. J. Duncan, "What Are the Economic Consequences of Divorce?" *Demography* 25 (November 1988): 641.

12. For example, Duncan and Hoffman, "Economic Consequences of Marital Dissolution," 489, table 2. Duncan and Hoffman's study indicated that income drops for both spouses in the year following a divorce or separation, although women's income declines more sharply. They found that men's income declined by 7% in the year following divorce. Women's income in that first postdivorce year dropped by almost 20% from their predivorce levels. A study published in 1993 based on data from the 1970s and the 1980s produced figures closer to Duncan and Hoffman's than to Weitzman's. This study showed only a 20% decline in the postdivorce income of white women in the first year following divorce combined with a relatively modest gain for men. Smock, "Economic Costs of Marital Disruption," 359–60. The studies are hard to compare, because the published papers are often vague about the components of income—what is included and excluded. E.g., some of the studies do not make it clear if they deduct ordered alimony and support from the man's income. In general, they do. See also Richard V. Burkhauser et al., "Wife or Frau, Women Do Worse: A Comparison of Men and Women in the United States and Germany After Marital Dissolution," *Demography* 28 (August 1991): 353 (after adjustment for family size, taxes, and government benefits, men's incomes fell on average 6% and women's incomes fell 24%, with almost half the men enjoying an increase in income postdivorce); Sorensen, "Economic Consequences of Separation and Divorce" (women's incomes decline between 10% and 30% in the first year following divorce; men's incomes rise). A large part of the difference in findings turns on adjustments for child custody.

13. Bell, "Alimony," 318. Another picture of the income differences between "stable" and "unstable" families is provided by the Panel Study of Income Dynamics, discussed in Sara McLanahan and Gary Sandefur, *Growing Up with a Single Parent: What Hurts, What Helps* (Cambridge: Harvard University Press, 1994). There are a number of interesting (and perplexing) twists in these data, but the central finding is that single-parent families with adolescent children have incomes less than half of two-parent families. Ibid., 80–81, table 4.

14. Smock, "Economic Costs of Marital Disruption," 366. She offers and then refutes a variety of explanations and ends by not being able to explain the lack of improvement for postdivorce women. The tendency of both sexes to move in with adult relatives following divorce has the potential to improve their financial situations. Ibid., 362–63. An intriguing gender difference is that men are more

339

likely to do so. Women, by contrast, apparently do not move in with relatives nearly so often. Katherine S. Newman, *Falling from Grace: The Experience of Downward Mobility in the American Middle Class* (New York: Free Press, 1988), 218, n. 45.

15. 11 U.S.C. §§ 523(a)(5) and 1328(a)(1) (1994).

16. 11 U.S.C. § 362(b)(2) (1994).

17. Ibid. In 1991 there was no special priority of payment for alimony or child support in the bankruptcy case itself, although they were nondischargeable and could be pursued following bankruptcy. The recent changes have given them a priority, as discussed in note 19, below.

18. For an overview of the 1994 amendments, see Michaela M. White, "Divorce After the Bankruptcy Reform Act of 1994: Can You Stay Warm After You Split the Blanket?" *Creighton Law Review* 29 (1996): 617.

19. 11 U.S.C. § 523(a)(15) (1994).

20. 11 U.S.C. § 507(a)(7) (1994).

21. 11 U.S.C. § 1322(a)(2) (1994).

22. Michael J. Herbert and Domenic E. Pacitti, "Down and Out in Richmond, Virginia: The Distribution of Assets in Chapter 7 Bankruptcy Proceedings Closed in 1984–1987," *Richmond Law Review* 22 (1988): 303 (documenting that the overwhelming majority of Chapter 7 business or consumer bankruptcies have nothing left after paying secured and priority creditors).

23. Parkman, *No Fault Divorce,* 73, table 5.1. The marriage rate per thousand unmarried women aged 15 and older went from 90.2 in 1950, to 55.7 in 1986. By 1988, the rate was 54.6. Bureau of the Census, *Statistical Abstract of the United States: 1994* (Washington, D.C., 1994), 100, table 140.

24. Parkman, *No Fault Divorce,* 73, table 5.1. The divorce rate more than doubled from 1950 to 1987, going from 10.3 to 20.8 per 1,000 married women. The rate peaked in 1980 at 22.5, declined to 20.4 in 1990, and has bounced between 20.5 and 21 since then. Bureau of the Census, *Statistical Abstract of the United States: 1997* (Washington, D.C., 1997), 105, table 145.

25. From 1970 to 1992, the number of unmarried couples rose from 1.2% of the number of married couples to over 6%. Calculated from Bureau of the Census, *Statistical Abstract of the United States:1993* (Washington, D.C., 1993), tables 62 and 63, 54. This is a topic on which the census takers suspect misreporting.

26. As of March 1993, 27% of all children lived in single-parent households. About 35% of those households were headed by a never-married single parent. Bureau of the Census, *Monthly News,* August 1994, 1.

27. Commission on Interstate Child Support, Report to Congress (1992), 5. The comparable figure for Canada in 1991 was 953,640 lone-parent families, involving 1.5 million children. In Canada's 1996 census, the numbers had risen to 1.14 million families and 1.8 million children. Statistics Canada website: <http://www.statcan.ca/english/census96/oct14/fam1.htm> (Jan. 16, 1999).

28. Teresa A. Sullivan, Elizabeth Warren, and Jay Lawrence Westbrook, *As We Forgive Our Debtors: Bankruptcy and Consumer Credit in America* (Oxford: Oxford University Press, 1989), 149. Another study from about the same time reports larger numbers. Philip Shuchman, "New Jersey Debtors, 1982–83: An Empirical Study," *Seton Hall Law Review* 15 (Summer 1985): 541–92, listed joint filers, single filing women and single filing men in two studies from the early 1980s. He observed

that in his 1979–81 multidistrict study 31% of the debtors filing for bankruptcy were women filing alone and 32% were men filing alone. In his 1981 study of New Jersey debtors, the proportion of women filing alone was 24%, that of men filing alone 32%. The differences between our reports and Shuchman's reports may arise from how the sample was drawn: Shuchman's New Jersey data were taken from 186 files provided by "volunteer" lawyers, which may mean that they are not representative of the filing population generally. He was able to locate and interview 62 of those 186 debtors. Shuchman compared the files of the 62 debtors interviewed with 40 additional files obtained from the bankruptcy court in Newark, although he does not indicate how those 40 files were chosen. He states that the comparison of the 40 court files with the 62 files of interviewees "indicate that the interviewed debtors were fairly representative of the larger group of 186 [provided by the lawyers]." Ibid., 542. A note states that "the debtors" resided in six counties that differed substantially as to racial composition and other important characteristics. Ibid., 542, n. 8. We have difficulty evaluating the result. Our own data were taken from a systematic sample of the bankruptcy files. Compare Shuchman, 541 ("For the research described here, we began not with the bankruptcy court files, but rather with the files of four cooperative lawyers in New Jersey"), with Sullivan, Warren, and Westbrook, *As We Forgive*, 18–19 (explaining the procedures for drawing a systematic sample of about 150 debtors from each of ten judicial districts). Shuchman does not explain how the sample was drawn for his nine states study, other than to say that it relies on "the cooperation of many volunteers—lawyers, law teachers and law students," whom he thanks by name in a footnote. Shuchman, "The Average Bankrupt: A Description and Analysis of 753 Personal Bankruptcy Filings in Nine States," *Commercial Law Journal* 88 (June–July 1983): 288. Although Shuchman lists both the 31% and 24% rate of filing for single females in his two studies, he does not explain the significance or the source of the difference. We are unaware of any statistical tests of significance to test the differences reported.

341

29. In our 1981 study, at least 12% of the single filing women mentioned elsewhere in their files the presence of a spouse. Sullivan, Warren, and Westbrook, *As We Forgive*, 150. All the joint filing debtors must be married. 11 U.S.C. § 302(a) (1988). The single filers may be married or not, which means that filing data will not yield an accurate picture of marital status.

30. Bankruptcy laws permit only married couples to file joint bankruptcies. By permitting both to discharge their debts for only one filing fee, the law encourages couples to file together. But if a sizable portion of the debts are those of only one spouse—such as the debts from a failed business or the consequences of an uninsured automobile accident—one spouse may file alone. The other spouse may stay outside the system, hoping to preserve a good credit record. Thus, the proportion of single filers is not coextensive with the proportion of single people filing for bankruptcy.

31. Throughout this section we report data from all the districts collectively. We have checked these data to see if important differences among districts emerge. While there are some differences—e.g., the Texas debtors were somewhat more likely to be married than were debtors in the other states—in most cases there were no statistically significant differences among the districts.

32. The question specifically asked about change since Jan. 1, 1989, and it was administered between Jan. 1, 1991, and June 30, 1991 (later in a few districts), so it would have covered more than two years for some debtors.

33. Shuchman has an intriguing entry in his article on New Jersey debtors filing in 1982–83. In table 49, labeled "How Credit Problems Arose," he identifies six cases, 10% of the cases reporting, as "marital problems." Debtors could give more than one reason. Shuchman, "New Jersey Debtors." He also notes that a few divorces were pending. For a description of his sample, see note 28, above.

34. Interestingly, in one study Shuchman lists "medical problems" in 53% of the cases and job loss in no cases. See ibid., 586, n. 27.

35. Reported problems included divorce, separation, alimony, care for family members, births, or deaths as a cause of their financial troubles. In part, these data suggest that when family lives become chaotic and emotionally stressful, the problems may have significant financial aspects. The reasons for family disruption are widely varied, supporting Tolstoy's remark that all unhappy families are unhappy in their own ways.

36. Of those who had recently experienced a marital disruption, 39% also mentioned a family problem as the reason for the bankruptcy.

37. See also Shuchman, "New Jersey Debtors," 551; Shuchman, "Average Bankrupt," 289.

38. We calculate this adjustment based on the fact that we have 180 debtors under age 25, of whom 88 are married (including ten who are separated).

342

39. The proportion divorced in the general population could be as high as 11.4% with some adjustment. This proportion was calculated by adding all divorced persons and all persons who were married, spouse absent. The national figure is based upon the population aged 15 and older in 1991. Bureau of the Census, *Statistical Abstract of the United States: 1992* (Washington, D.C., 1992), 46, table 55. The 10% figure for "divorced" remained the same in 1998. Bureau of the Census, "Marital Status and Living Arrangements: March 1998" (update), 20–514.

40. Our figures might be inflated by the fact that our sample includes a lower percentage of young people. Figure 6.2 corrects for this age structure by removing all people younger than 25 from both our sample and the comparative national figure.

41. See Iain Ramsay, "Individual Bankruptcy: Preliminary Findings of a Socio-Legal Analysis," *Osgoode Hall Law Journal* 37 (1999): 315; Saul Schwartz and Leigh Anderson, "An Empirical Study of Canadians Seeking Personal Bankruptcy Protection" (Carleton University, 1998), 4–5. Ramsay reports that 25% of the bankrupt debtors in Canada are divorced or separated, a much higher percentage than the general population. Schwartz found 29% "formerly married."

42. There is a significant relationship between filing status (joint, single male, and single female) and divorced or separated status of the first petitioner.

43. Women filing alone are significantly more likely than men filing alone to mention a family disruption as the cause of the divorce.

44. These comparisons are once again between single filing men and single filing women. This result is significant.

45. The difference is statistically significant.

46. The association between being female and claiming a broader family reason for bankruptcy is significant.

47. A recent empirical study examined every bankruptcy case in which some party sought a ruling as to whether a marital debt would be discharged. It found that most of the cases in which such a ruling is sought involved a male debtor. In one district in that study, 92% of those cases involved male debtors. Seventy-five percent were male in a second district. Peter Alexander, "Divorce and the Dischargeability of Debts: Focusing on Women as Creditors in Bankruptcy," *Catholic University Law Review* 43 (1994): 351 . Both of these districts are included in our study, although our study is based on cases filed in the preceding year. Even though the presence of a request for ruling does not perfectly identify cases in which discharge of a marital debt is attempted, the study's finding is consistent with the conventional view that males file most cases discharging marital debts.

48. There is one sense in which changing a household does not seem to increase financial risks: death. Those who have lost a spouse comprise only 3% of the bankruptcy sample, but 8.6% of the over-25 population; see figure 6.1. The underrepresentation of the widowed may be related to the underrepresentation of the elderly in our sample. Only 2.4% of the bankruptcy sample is aged 65 years or more, compared with 16.3% of the adult population. Among people aged 65–74 years, 9.2% of men and 35.3% of women are widowed. See *Statistical Abstract: 1992*, 43, table 48. Even so, although those who lose a spouse through death lose the additional income that the spouse provided, the possibility of insurance may cushion the financial blow in a way that has no counterpart in divorce. Moreover, there is no effort to establish two households from the income that supported just one household, as there is in divorce.

49. *Statistical Abstract: 1993*, 102, table 146.

50. Calculated from Duncan and Hoffman, "Economic Consequences of Marital Dissolution," 487, n. 2, table 1. About three-quarters of the white men and more than half the white women were remarried in five years. For black men and women, the figures were 57% and 42%, respectively.

51. Ibid., 487. This result holds true for both white and black women, even though black women's income falls more than that of whites, fewer black women get remarried, and it takes those who do remarry longer to catch up.

52. Smock, "Economic Costs of Marital Disruption," 359, table 1. Remarried white women had incomes almost double those of single white divorced women. Even on a per capita basis, remarried white women's incomes were more than 125% higher than their single counterparts. The figures for black women, though less extreme, were comparable. As with Duncan and Hoffman, Smock generally counted cohabiting women as remarried.

53. Duncan and Hoffman, "Economic Consequences of Marital Dissolution," 485.

54. Four hundred fifty-three debtors reported themselves as having been divorced or separated, but reported no divorce or separation (marital disruption) within two years before bankruptcy. Only 69 reported remarriage. Although some of these responses may have been errors, the comments of these debtors explaining their reasons for filing bankruptcy reveal that in most cases they had been divorced or separated more than two years before bankruptcy.

55. For those in bankruptcy who specifically identified divorce as the problem that led them into financial trouble, only 12% had remarried by the time they filed for bankruptcy.

56. Commission on Interstate Child Support, Report to Congress, 5. This figure includes unmarried women as well as divorced and separated women.

57. Bell, "Alimony," 306.

58. Weitzman and others account for the additional financial burdens that women usually bear as the custodial parent by making an adjustment for income per capita—that is, dividing the income by the number of people in the household. If the former husband and wife each had $30,000 in income after divorce but the wife had custody of two children, these researchers would say that the true income level for the wife and children postdivorce is $10,000, because the wife's $30,000 has to be divided among three people. Others argue that per capita adjustments overcompensate. These critics make "needs" adjustments based on various standards, such as Bureau of Labor Statistics budgets. Thus, they adjust the wife's $30,000 income by a factor of increased expense that the BLS budget makers would assign to a family with three members as opposed to a family with one member to give them the lifestyle equivalent to a single person with a given income. Those adjustments are much smaller than a straight per capita formula, and they would produce an income figure for the ex-wife lower than $30,000 but higher than $10,000.

59. James B. McLindon, "Separate But Unequal: The Economic Disaster of Divorce for Women and Children," *Family Law Quarterly* 21 (Fall 1987): 351.

60. Burkhauser et al., "Wife or Frau," 356.

61. See Ramsay, "Individual Bankruptcy." Schwartz found only 15% of the "unmarried" Canadian bankrupts had a dependent under 21, but it is unclear if that category included the formerly married. Schwartz and Anderson, "Empirical Study of Canadians," 4–5.

62. 11 U.S.C. § 523(a)(5) (1988). Many have used bankruptcy to avoid their obligations to pay predivorce debt, a point discussed earlier in this chapter.

63. Some studies have argued that garnishment often precipitates bankruptcy. See, e.g., G. A. Brunn, "Wage Garnishment in California: A Study and Recommendation," *California Law Review* 53 (1965): 1214; D. Stanley and M. Girth, *Bankruptcy: Problems, Process, Reform* (Washington, D.C.: Brookings Institution, 1971).

64. Duncan and Hoffman, "Economic Consequences of Marital Dissolution," 487. It should be noted that their data lumped together divorce and separation. It also counted as "marriage" a long-term cohabitation, where long-term was roughly a year or more.

65. In a study of 2,000 families in four cities back in the early 1970s, David Caplovitz found that financially stressed families were more likely to rely on increasing income or on cutting their expenses as strategies but that about 8% of the families used credit as a means of dealing with inflationary pressures. Caplovitz, *Making Ends Meet: How Families Cope with Inflation and Recession* (Beverly Hills, Calif.: Sage, 1979), 114.

66. Ibid., 121–22.

67. Ibid., 121. By contrast, a majority of the couples in his sample asserted that financial troubles had actually brought them closer together, suggesting a sharply dichotomous reaction among families.

# Chapter 7: Housing

1. Melvin L. Oliver and Thomas M. Shapiro quote some elderly white homeowners who see their homes as a burden rather than an asset, but this view is not widely shared. Oliver and Shapiro, *Black Wealth, White Wealth: A New Perspective on Racial Inequality* (New York: Routledge, 1995).

2. Dowell Myers and Jennifer R. Wolch, "The Polarization of Housing Status," in Reynolds Farley, ed., *State of the Union: America in the 1990s*, vol. 1 (New York: Russell Sage, 1995), 269; David Listoken, "Federal Housing Policy and Preservation: Historical Evolution, Patterns and Implications," 2 *Housing Policy Debate* (1991): 157–86, 167.

3. Listoken, "Federal Housing Policy and Preservation, 167.

4. Myers and Wolch, "Polarization of Housing Status." Home owners are those who live in a dwelling unit owned either by the person interviewed or the person's spouse.

5. G. T. Kurian, ed., *The New Book of World Rankings*, 3d ed. (New York: Facts on File, 1991), table 182. Home ownership rates ranged from a reported high of 100% (Mongolia) to a low of 8% (Nigeria). Among industrialized nations, South Korea outstripped the United States with 86.9% of the population housed in their own homes. Other reports of European housing put homeownership rates in the European Community higher, so that Ireland is reported with an 81% homeownership rate, Spain is 78% homeowners, and Greece is 77% homeowners. Italy, Portugal, Luxembourg, and the United Kingdom are near the reported rate for the United States at 67% each. Dutch Ministry of Housing, *Statistics on Housing in the European Community* (1993), 61.

6. Myers and Wolch, "Polarization of Housing Status," 292–93. Homeownership rates declined from 64.4% in 1980 to 64.2% in 1990. See ibid., 295; Bureau of the Census, "We the Americans: Our Homes" (September 1993), 3, fig. 3.

7. Housing affordability is generally measured by the fraction of income dedicated to housing. For home owners, an affordability index of 100 indicates that a median income household is able to qualify for a median-priced home under a stated set of assumptions. An index of 90, e.g., indicates that the household earns only 90% of the needed income. The 1980 affordability index was 79.9, compared with an affordability index of 112.9 in 1991, when these data were collected, and 134.3 by 1994. Department of Housing and Urban Development, Office of Policy Development and Research, *U.S. Housing Market Conditions* (February 1995), table 9. Housing affordability was especially low during the early 1980s because high inflation drove up mortgage rates, which in turn increased the monthly payments required for home mortgages and put such mortgages out of the reach of more families. Although housing affordability declined for homeowners, the situation was worse for renters, with low-end renters squeezed particularly hard by the rise in rents.

8. Many inadequate rental units have also been removed from the market. One-room rentals, e.g., dropped by 41% from 1985 to 1989. Myers and Wolch, "Polarization of Housing Status," 274. The number of renters renting either one or two rooms was cut in half, and the proportion of renters in one or two room units dropped from 10% in 1981 to 5% in 1991. Bureau of the Census, "Statistical Brief: Housing Changes, 1981 to 1991," SB93-5 (Washington, D.C., May 1993).

9. Myers and Wolch, "Polarization of Housing Status," 276.

10. In the decade from 1981 to 1991, the proportion of homeowners living in at least seven rooms increased from 23% to 28%. Bureau of the Census, "Statistical Brief: Housing Changes, 1981 to 1991." Homeowners living in one or two room houses dropped from 4% in 1981 to 2% in 1991. The term "generously housed" is used among housing analysts to refer to households with more than 120% of the state median household income, payment burdens of less than 15% of income, and occupancy rates of 0.33 persons per room or fewer. Myers and Wolch, "Polarization of Housing Status," 305. By this definition, during the 1980s the proportion of all households that were generously housed grew rapidly—in spite of a small drop in the total proportion of generously housed families. Ibid., 312.

11. Ibid., 279.

12. Ibid., 271.

13. Ibid.

14. Ibid.

15. Median incomes of homeowners are nearly twice as high as median incomes of renters. Calculated from median income data in Bureau of the Census, "Statistical Brief: Housing Changes, 1981 to 1991."

16. *Statistical Abstract of the United States: 1993* (Washington, D.C., 1993), 725, table 1237.

17. Bureau of the Census, "We the Americans: Our Homes," 7, fig. 10.

18. David Caplovitz, *Making Ends Meet: How Families Cope with Inflation and Recession* (Beverly Hills, Calif.: Sage, 1979), 174–76.

19. Whether, when, and how many Americans will make it on board is the principal focus of housing policy makers. The housing picture of the 1990s is not entirely rosy. A small but troubling fraction of the population remains homeless, and overcrowding has increased for the first time in 50 years. Myers and Wolch, "Polarization of Housing Status," 280. When substandard housing was eliminated from the market, housing costs for poorer people increased. Ibid., 276. Pressure also increased for all those who had not yet acquired a home. During the early 1990s, affordability improved over the rates a decade earlier, when home mortgage rates were at their peak, but 51% of all families in the U.S. in 1991 could not afford a median-priced home in their areas. Bureau of the Census, "Fewer Families Can Afford to Buy a House," *Census and You* 28 (September 1993): 9. See also P. J. Fronzcek and H. A. Savage, *Who Can Afford to Buy a House in 1991?* Bureau of the Census, Current Housing Reports, Ser. H121/93-3 (Washington, D.C., 1993). During the 1980s, the rate of homeownership fell slightly— from a peak in 1980 of 64.4% to a slight decline of 64.2% by 1990, the first decline in 50 years. Myers and Wolch, "Polarization of Housing Status," 295. The homeownership rate for young families, those who traditionally have prompted the growth in homeownership in this country, was down substantially. Ibid., 294.

20. Government policies, directed almost exclusively at housing affordability and purchasing issues, are also premised on the assumption that homeownership confers safe status. A few scholars have questioned the single-focus aspect of housing policy that presses toward homeownership for all Americans. Among the most notable are Susan Wachter and Michael Schill, whose work is discussed below.

21. Bankruptcy Code §§ 1322(b)(2),(5) and 1325 (b)(1).

22. William Whitford, "The Ideal of Individualized Justice: Consumer Bankruptcy as Consumer Protection, and Consumer Protection in Consumer Bankruptcy," *American Bankruptcy Law Journal* 68 (Fall 1994): 397, 411 (finding a 31% completion rate in Chapter 13); Teresa A. Sullivan, Elizabeth Warren, and Jay Lawrence Westbrook, *As We Forgive Our Debtors: Bankruptcy and Consumer Credit in America* (New York: Oxford University Press, 1989), 215–17 (estimating a 32% completion rate in Chapter 13); Michael Bork and Susan Tuck, "Bankruptcy Statistical Trends: Chapter 13 Dispositions" (Working Paper 2), *National Association of Chapter Thirteen Trustees Quarterly* 7 (1995): 31 (36% of the Chapter 13 cases filed between 1980 and 1988 received a discharge).

23. The data about overall rates of homeownership are derived from the tables showing that 301 of 686 debtors are homeowners.

24. There was substantial variation among the districts in 1991, but one district seems aberrational for legal reasons. The home ownership rate in the four sample districts in Illinois, Texas, Tennessee, and Pennsylvania was a combined 48.1%. The sample from the fifth state, California, was only 20.2%. Because these data were drawn at a time when a debtor in Chapter 13 could have a maximum secured debt of only $350,000, there is evidence that high home prices and concomitantly larger mortgages forced many financially troubled California homeowners into Chapter 11, which was outside the reach of our sample. The California number thus understates the proportion of homeowners in bankruptcy. The California phenomenon is discussed in more detail later in this chapter.

347

The Ohio data, collected in 1997, suggest even higher homeownership rates. In Ohio, homeowners constituted at least 66% of the sample. We say "at least" because we can identify home mortgages in 66% of the cases. Judge Sellers did not make a separate entry for home ownership, so that a homeowner with no mortgage would have been omitted from the list. Any understatement from this fact, however, is probably small. With only one district, it is difficult to know whether the difference in the 1997 Ohio data comes from an increase in homeowners filing bankruptcy from 1991 to 1997 or from more homeowners filing in Ohio than in the other states we sampled. See Appendix 1 for a description of Judge Sellers's study.

25. In most states, a debtor who defaults on a mortgage remains liable on the mortgage debt until it is paid off. If the mortgage company forecloses on the mortgage, the money from the sale will be used to pay off the mortgage, but if it is less than the outstanding mortgage amount, the debtors will be liable for the deficiency. Such "deficiency judgments" leave the debtor in the difficult position of paying off the remaining portion of a mortgage for a home they no longer own.

26. A larger fraction of homeowners choose Chapter 13 than do their renter counterparts. In our sample, almost 60% of homeowners were in Chapter 13, while only about 25% of nonhome owners were in Chapter 13.

27. Our data show that California, the state with the second highest median home value in the country, had the lowest proportion of homeowners in our Chapter 7–Chapter 13 sample. Bureau of the Census, *1990 Housing Highlights Financial Facts* (June 1992), table 1. Median home value in 1990 in California was $195,500, compared with a median home value of $69,700 for Pennsylvania, the

state ranked 25th in median home values. California ranks behind Hawaii on median home value and ahead of every other state in the union. Only 20 out of 103 California debtors in the sample were homeowners. Among those 20, 19 were in Chapter 7, and only one California homeowner was in Chapter 13. In all the other districts, there were more homeowners in Chapter 13 than in Chapter 7. The proportion of home owners in the bankruptcy sample in Chapter 7 and Chapter 13 varied among the other four states we studied: Texas (62.4%), Pennsylvania (50.3%), Tennessee (44.4%), and Illinois (35.6%). But California was aberrationally low, showing a homeownership rate in Chapter 7 and Chapter 13 of only 19.4%. One study in California suggests that at about the time these data were drawn, 16% of the California debtors filing for Chapter 11 were not businesses, but were instead homeowners who were trying to save their homes and whose debt limits were too high for Chapter 13. Lisa Fenning and Brian Tucker, "Profile of Single Asset Real Estate Cases," American Bankruptcy Institute Annual Spring Meeting, April 1994, reprinted in *L.A. County Bar Association Commercial Law and Bankruptcy Section Newsletter,* June 1994, 4. The study population is "all 256 Chapter 11 petitions in cases assigned to [Judge Fenning] from January 1, 1992, through December 31, 1993." Four percent of all Chapter 11s were termed "small real estate cases," and they contained both a house and a modest second income-producing property. The "house" cases, where only the home was an asset, were 12% of the Chapter 11 filings. The house cases were filed in Chapter 11 rather than Chapter 13 because the debt levels exceeded the Chapter 13 limits. The two categories together, houses and small real estate, constituted 42 cases and 16% of the Chapter 11s. If those Chapter 11 debtors were added back into this sample, the California proportion of homeowners would rise, also increasing the proportion of homeowners in the five-state sample. It is impossible to project precisely the proportion of homeowners that would be added to the bankruptcy sample if homeowners filing in Chapter 11 were added to the sample. The California data are unlikely to be representative of the rest of the country. Moreover, the California data were collected in a way that would exclude from their classifications home owners who also had other substantial debt burdens.

Because the proportion of debtors in Chapter 11 is only a small fraction of all the bankruptcy filings, however, the effects of adding Chapter 11 homeowners should be modest. In other states as well, some homeowners may be closed out of Chapter 13 because of its restricted debt limits and are dealing with their debts in Chapter 11. In 1994, Congress amended the bankruptcy laws, raising the permissible debt limit in Chapter 13 to $1 million of combined secured and unsecured debt, in part to respond to this problem. This may mean that for filings after 1994, California homeownership data may come into closer alignment with other districts, and the overall totals of homeowners in Chapter 13 may be higher than these data suggest. If Chapter 11 homeowners were included in our sample, the magnitude of the risk facing homeowners would be clearer. Now that the debt limits in Chapter 13 exceed $1 million, the proportion of homeowners in Chapter 13 even in very expensive areas may have increased because fewer would be closed out by their high mortgage debts. The proportion of Chapter 7 filers may also have risen as homeowners come to see bankruptcy as more accessible. In 1997 bankruptcy judge Randall Newsome of the Northern District of California looked at 100 Chapter 7 consumer cases in his court. He found that

348

34%—a sharp rise over the California numbers from 1991—of the debtors were homeowners. For more on this study, see Appendix 1.

28. The regional variation on homeowners among the states is significant, but we believe we have captured the overall picture with these data. In another study conducted in 1991, Gary Klein and Maggie Spake of the National Consumer Law Center looked at 100 Massachusetts bankruptcy cases. They discovered that about 46% of the bankrupt debtors were homeowners. Klein and Spake, "Self-Representation in the Bankruptcy Court: The Massachusetts Experience," 5, app. 5 (typescript on file with authors, 1995). The Massachusetts data supplement our information on homeownership rates in bankruptcy. With those data and our own, we have systematic studies from New England, the mid-Atlantic, the South, the Southwest, the upper Midwest, and the West coast.

29. The estimate is based on about half of the 1.350 million filings in that year. The only 1997 data suggests a higher filing rate—66%—but that estimate is based on a single district. With wide regional variation and perhaps wide variation from year to year, we are reluctant to make an estimate more precise than about half of the filings.

30. Fewer than 10% of all buyers have as much as half the purchase price at the time they buy their homes. Bureau of the Census, *American Housing Survey for the United States in 1991,* Current Housing Reports, Ser. H150/91 (Washington, D.C., 1993), table 3.15. Only 7.1% of home buyers (6.9% of first-time buyers and 8.8% of repeat buyers) were able to purchase their homes without a commercial fixed-rate or variable mortgage. Of the remainder, some may have paid cash and others may be financing through families or friends. Chicago Title and Trust Co., "1997 Home Buyers Survey Highlights—National Census," *Guarantor,* Spring 1998, 8.

31. Calculation from Bureau of the Census, *Statistical Abstract of the United States: 1994* (Washington, D.C., 1994), 744, table 1226.

32. Ibid.

33. Ibid., table 812. The delinquency rate for Veterans Administration loans in 1991, e.g., was 6.8%, while the delinquency rate for conventional mortgages was 3.3%.

34. Ibid. The delinquency rate for Federal Housing Authority loans in 1991, e.g., was 7.3%, as compared with a delinquency rate for conventional mortgages of 3.3%.

35. For a thoughtful discussion of the potential impact of these programs, see Michael H. Schill and Susan M. Wachter, "The Special Bias of Federal Housing Law and Policy: Concentrated Poverty in Urban America," *University of Pennsylvania Law Review* 143 (1995): 1285, 1308–28. The authors argue that federal mortgage assistance programs may have destabilized inner-city neighborhoods first by redlining areas with significant proportions of minority households and then by causing abandonment and deterioration of these same neighborhoods.

36. In 1991, first-time buyers had a median age of 30.7 and repeat buyers had a median age of 39.8. *Statistical Abstract: 1993,* 734, table 1226.

37. Down payments, on average, were about twice as large for repeat buyers than they were for first-time buyers. Ibid.

38. Median income for householders in ages 25–34 in 1991 was $30,842, compared with a median income for householders ages 45–54 of $43,751. Ibid., 458, table 713.

349

39. Calculation from ibid., 725, table 1237.

40. The age profile of homeowners in bankruptcy does not differ from the age profile of renters in bankruptcy.

41. "How Much House Can You Afford?" Fannie Mae Website <http://www.homepath.com/hsp6.html> (1997).

42. Standards differ somewhat, from those debtors who have a 90% or lower loan-to-value ratio and spotless credit to those eligible for special "affordable housing" programs who have a 95% loan-to-value and some adverse credit. Not surprisingly, those debtors who met the higher credit standards had the lowest default rates (1.0%), whereas those who met the lower standards had higher default rates (6.6%). The affordable housing guidelines represent only a fraction of outstanding mortgage loans; even those more relaxed guidelines are based on the premise that the debtor had a reasonable probability of repayment. Gordon H. Steinbach, "Ready to Make the Grade," *Mortgage Banking* 37 (June 1995): 39.

43. See note 15, above.

44. The next largest form of asset was interest-bearing assets at financial institutions, which made up 14% of all assets. All other forms of asset ownership— owning a business, stocks and mutual funds, rental property, vehicles, other real estate, IRAs and KEOGH plans, and other assorted assets, each made up 7% or less of total assets. Bureau of the Census, "Statistical Brief: Household Wealth and Asset Ownership, 1991," SB94-2 (Washington, D.C., February 1994). The calculation includes both homeowners and renters alike. If only homeowners are considered, the proportion of wealth concentrated in homes is considerably larger.

45. The climb in median sales prices on existing homes from 1970 ($23,000, unadjusted dollars) to 1992 ($140,000, unadjusted dollars) far outpaces inflation. *Statistical Abstract: 1993,* 720, table 1227.

46. See Myers and Wolch, "Polarization of Housing Status," 300–301.

47. But more people try to buy homes in rising markets. Ibid., 302 ("Regional economic growth tends to push up incomes and tighten housing markets, thereby spurring house values and homeownership due to expectations of appreciation").

48. Conventional mortgage rates went from 8.56% in 1970 to 9.14% in 1975. In 1980, the sharp rate climb began, with rates of 12.7% (1980), 15.1% (1982), 12.5% (1984), and 10.0% (1985). Rates subsided after 1985, remaining in the 9–10% range until 1992, when rates dropped to 8.2% and continued a further slide. *Statistical Abstract: 1993,* 515, table 811 (using effective, not nominal, interest rates).

49. In 1989, e.g., the Office of Thrift Supervision approved 354 mergers of savings institutions. Of those, 36 were voluntary, while 318 were transfers of all the assets to the Resolution Trust Corporation as part of its program to eliminate failing institutions by merging them with stronger ones. Bureau of the Census, *Statistical Abstract of the United States: 1991* (Washington, D.C., 1991), 505, table 817. The number of commercial and savings banks covered by the Bank Insurance Fund closed down by the regulatory authorities climbed from 11 in 1980 to 221 in 1988, the peak year for such closings. *Statistical Abstract: 1993,* 509, table 795.

50. Bureau of the Census, *Statistical Abstract of the United States: 1986* (Washington, D.C., 1986), table 829.

51. Calculated from *Statistical Abstract: 1993,* 509, table 795; Bureau of the

350

Census, *Statistical Abstract of the United States: 1990* (Washington, D.C., 1990), 497, table 807.

52. Mortgage delinquency rates were 3.13% (1970), 4.37% (1975), 4.97% (1980), 5.83% (1985), 4.7% (1990), and 4.3% (1995). Bureau of the Census, *Statistical Abstract of the United States: 1997* (Washington, D.C., 1997), table 796; *Statistical Abstract: 1991*, table 827; *Statistical Abstract: 1986*, table 843.

53. The Ohio data, collected in 1997 and reported on earlier in the book and in this chapter, show even higher homeownership rates. Ohio homeowners constituted at least 66% of the sample. With only one district reporting, however, it is difficult to know whether the difference in the 1997 Ohio data comes from an increase in homeowners filing bankruptcy from 1991 to 1997 or from more homeowners filing in Ohio than in the other states we sampled.

54. In our earlier, more detailed study of consumer bankruptcy files, cars were the most frequently listed collateral for debtors' secured loans, with home mortgages coming in second. All other property combined formed only a small fraction of collateral for secured loans. Sullivan, Warren, and Westbrook, *As We Forgive*, 310, table 17.4.

55. Because their nonmortgage debts are very similar and the homeowners have relatively larger incomes, the nonmortgage debt-income ratios between the two groups differ somewhat. At the median, the homeowner owes 0.8 of one year's salary in nonmortgage debt (s.d. = 1.44), while the renter owes 1.14 year's salary in nonmortgage debt (s.d. = 2.32). When mortgage debt is included, the ratio, of course, shifts wildly, with homeowners' debt climbing to two and a half years' income (s.d. = 3.08), whereas nonhomeowners' debt is half as large, at one and a quarter years' income (s.d. = 2.88).

56. Although state law or federal law imposes limits on the amount of property debtors can keep when they file for bankruptcy, only a handful of Chapter 7 debtors have assets valued higher than those minimum levels. Michael J. Herbert and Domenic E. Pacitti, "Down and Out in Richmond, Virginia: The Distribution of Assets in Chapter 7 Bankruptcy Proceedings Closed in 1984–1987," *Richmond Law Review* 22 (1988): 303. Most debtors who file for bankruptcy face the loss of their property because it is collateral for a loan for which they may be unable to maintain the payments rather than because they have property valued in excess of the legal exemption levels. Sullivan, Warren, and Westbrook, *As We Forgive*, 304–12.

57. Calculated from median income data in Bureau of the Census, "Statistical Brief: Housing Changes, 1981 to 1991."

58. *Statistical Abstract: 1993*, 458, table 713.

59. Ibid.

60. Calculated from Consumer Bankruptcy Project Phase II data and Bureau of the Census, "Statistical Brief: Housing Changes, 1981 to 1991." In an earlier report based on three states, we reported the proportion as 52%. Teresa A. Sullivan, Elizabeth Warren, and Jay Lawrence Westbrook "Consumer Debtors Ten Years Later: A Financial Comparison of Consumer Bankrupts, 1981–1991," *American Bankruptcy Law Journal* 68 (Spring 1994): 121–54, n. 26. The proportion reported here, 61%, is higher but still of little comfort to the bankrupt homeowners.

61. See data cited at note 30, above.

62. Bureau of the Census, *American Housing Survey, 1991*, table 3.15.

351

63. Bureau of the Census, "Statistical Brief: Housing Changes, 1981 to 1991."

64. "How Much House Can You Afford?"

65. Bureau of the Census, "Statistical Brief: House-Poor/House-Rich," SB91-19 (Washington, D.C., August 1991).

66. Ibid.

67. It is not possible to make a direct comparison of the national data with the data in bankruptcy because of limitations in the way both kinds of data are collected and reported, but a rough comparison is possible. At the median, in 1991 homeowners with mortgages made monthly mortgage payments of $761. Bureau of the Census, *American Housing Survey, 1991,* table 2.19. The median mortgage in 1991 was $44,334. Ibid., table 3.15. At the median, then, the monthly payment for a homeowner with a mortgage was 1.72% of their principal balance. For this calculation, we projected that the bankrupt debtors, who have median mortgages similar to those of homeowners generally, paid the same fraction of their mortgage in their monthly payments. We computed the projected mortgage payment debtor by debtor, assuming that each debtor paid about 1.72% of the reported principal balance. Of course, the payment-mortgage balance ratio will depend in part on how long the homeowner has held the mortgage. The proportion of younger home owners in the bankruptcy sample may suggest that they have a higher payment–mortgage balance ratio. In addition, the debtors have a higher proportion of second mortgages, and second mortgages carry higher interest rates, so the 1.72% is likely to understate the typical payment burden borne by the debtor in bankruptcy relative to homeowners generally.

68. It is possible to use an alternate calculation. We can construct a projected house payment for each debtor that is roughly equivalent to the government data. In 1991 the median interest rate was 9.1% for all existing first mortgages (old and new). Ibid., table 3.15. One-quarter of our debtors had second and third mortgages. The interest rates on such loans are quite diverse, depending in part on the loan-to-value ratio; they typically run about four points higher than the rates on first mortgages, although it is not uncommon for a high LTV loan to carry twice the interest rate of a conventional first mortgage. American Banker-Bond Buyer, "Introduction and Summary," Mortgage Backed Securities Letter, Dec. 14, 1998, 1; Consumers Bankers Association, "1998 CBA Home Equity Loan Study," <http://www.cbanet.org/Surveys/homeq4.htm>; Ted Cornwell, "High LTV Seconds Are Expanding Dramatically," *National Mortgage News,* Dec. 2, 1996, 31 (citing Moody's Investors Service). We also know that around the country property taxes and insurance were about 15% of total housing expenses, based upon information supplied by the National Association of Home Builders to construct calculations for the Housing Affordability Index, Arizona Real Estate Center, L. William Seidman Research Institute, College of Business, Arizona State University. If we combine and weigh these factors, we estimate that the bankrupt debtors are paying about 16% of their outstanding mortgage obligation each year in principal, interest, taxes, and insurance. By dividing the number derived from that calculation for each debtor by that debtor's annual income, we can estimate the proportion of the bankrupt debtor's income that is going to house payments. Using this calculation we would conclude that more than half, but less than three-quarters, of the debtors are "house poor" under the Fannie Mae guidelines.

352

69. Calculated from *Statistical Abstract: 1994,* 61, table 70. Based on the reported data, the mean per capita nonmortgage debt is $7,896.

70. Bureau of the Census, "Statistical Brief: Household Wealth and Asset Ownership, 1991."

71. Ibid.

72. Ibid., table C. Among only the homeowners who have some home mortgage debt, equity values are somewhat smaller, but they are still substantial. The typical homeowner in the population with a median home mortgage of $44,334 would be purchasing a home worth about $77,237. Bureau of the Census, *American Housing Survey, 1991,* table 3.15.

73. Mean, 16,620; s.d., 34,464; 1st, 1,000; median, 5,500; 3d, 20,528; N, 288; missing, 14.

74. It is possible that the debtors do not tell the truth about the value of their homes on their bankruptcy petitions but do tell the truth to the Census Bureau. As we noted in the Introduction, however, the debtor signs a bankruptcy petition under penalty of perjury, a bankruptcy trustee reviews the schedules, and the bankrupt's creditors can raise objections to any of the disclosed information. Large discrepancies, especially in an item as difficult to conceal as a home, are unlikely. Moreover, in Texas and California, which provide generous homestead exemptions, there is no incentive for debtors not to list full value; they can keep all the value no matter how high it goes in Texas and they can keep up to $200,000 in value in excess of the mortgage in California. If the debtors cannot pay off their mortgages and the property must be sold, they will nonetheless retain the excess value if valuable homes are sold through foreclosure. It is possible that some debtors shave value, but because there are no incentives for falsehoods and the debtors face significant penalties if they are not truthful, it is hard to develop a plausible story about why the valuations would be significantly underreported.

75. One reason that home equity is lower for the debtors in bankruptcy is because their homes, on average, are less valuable than the homes of most other families who are carrying about the same mortgages. In fact, the government data may understate the value of American homes. The data are gathered from voluntary surveys. At the beginning of one Census Bureau report on housing values, the follow caveat appears: "wealth tends to be under reported." It explains the potential bias in its own data and how the data should be used to minimize the effects of those biases. Bureau of the Census, "Household Wealth and Asset Ownership: 1991," Statistical Brief 94-2 (February 1994), v. The available evidence suggests that the difference between the financial status of the bankrupt homeowners and homeowners generally is even larger than the report in the text suggests. The median value of the homes listed in the bankruptcy files was $53,750. For homeowners generally, the median value of homes in 1990 was $79,100. The pattern persists throughout the price ranges. A quarter of the homes owned by debtors in bankruptcy were valued at less than $35,000, compared with a quarter of the homes held by Americans generally that were valued at less than $49,500. Bureau of the Census, *Statistical Abstract: 1993,* 726, table 1239. At the top end, a quarter of the homes held by bankrupt debtors were valued above $75,000, compared with a quarter valued above $137,800 for the popula-

353

tion generally. Homeowners in bankruptcy are the nearby neighbors of all other homeowners, but these data suggest that most of them are living in somewhat more modest homes.

76. For 22.57% of the homeowners listed in bankruptcy, the mortgage debts exceeded the value of the home.

77. See BFP v. Resolution Trust Corp., 511 U.S. 531, 569 (1994).

78. Debtors are also unlikely to account for the costs of selling their houses. A sale through a real estate broker can typically cost 8–9% of the purchase price by the time fees, commissions, inspections, and transfer taxes are calculated. Those expenses come out the homeowners' share of the proceeds—not the mortgage company's.

79. There are exceptions. Some investor groups develop, buying homes in depressed neighborhoods, selling them to low-income families, repossessing and selling again to another family—all at sturdy profits. There are no systematic data about such investor groups, however, and it is not clear whether they operate in substantial numbers in many real estate markets.

80. General Accounting Office, *Tax Policy: Many Factors Contributed to the Growth of Home Equity Financing in the 1980s* (Washington, D.C., 1993), 9.

81. Ibid. During the 1980s, home value grew at an average annual rate of 1–1.9%, while home mortgage debt grew at an average annual rate of 6.6%.

82. Ibid. The Tax Reform Act of 1986 disallowed the deduction of personal interest while maintaining the mortgage interest deduction, making mortgage-backed borrowing more attractive than other forms of consumer borrowing.

83. Julia Forrester, "Mortgaging the American Dream: A Critical Evaluation of the Federal Government's Promotion of Home Equity Financing," *Tulane Law Review* 69 (1994): 373, 417–23. Forrester criticizes government policies that have put more Americans at risk for losing their homes, arguing that such policies have "a complete lack of justification under any rational federal policy." Ibid., 456.

84. General Accounting Office, *Tax Policy*, 8, table 1. Even with the explosion in second mortgages, however, most American homeowners remain unwilling to risk their homes to borrow more money. Among homeowners with mortgages in the general population, 13.7% have a second mortgage, and 0.3% have a third or subsequent mortgage. Calculated from Bureau of the Census, *American Housing Survey, 1991,* table 2.19.

85. Every homeowner in Illinois and every homeowner in California in our sample reported a home mortgage. One debtor in Tennessee, two in Pennsylvania, and nine in Texas did not. It is thus possible that 12 of the debtors in this sample owned their homes outright. We do not believe, however, that this is the case. Because home owners nearly always plan to continue to make their mortgage payments after the bankruptcy is concluded, if the debtor is current on the mortgage payments, the debtor and the debtor's attorney may fail to list the home mortgage. There will be no change in the status of the home mortgage lender; it remains able to collect in full on the original mortgage terms. As a result, neither the debtor nor the attorney may see any need to notify the lender. We saw evidence of this earlier in the 1981 Consumer Bankruptcy Project, where attorneys and judges indulged debtors who were current on their mortgages and who did not want the mortgage company to know of the filing. Sullivan, War-

ren, and Westbrook, *As We Forgive,* 134–35. The concentration of no-mortgage debtors in one district also supports the inference of a local custom that makes it unnecessary to list the home mortgage if the debtor remains current on all payments. The practice is not legally correct because all assets and debts must be disclosed, but it may fall into a "no-harm, no-foul" category because the lender retains a valid mortgage and is eventually paid in full. For our analysis of mortgage debt, we list these 12 debtors as "missing" mortgage information, along with the nine other debtors who clearly indicated a mortgage, but failed to list the exact amount.

86. Among all the home owners in our sample, 27.2% had more than one mortgage. At the time this sample was drawn, Texas, unlike any other state in the country, prohibited attachment of a mortgage for any reason other than initial purchase, property taxes, or home improvements. The Texas constitution, reflecting the state's early settlement by those forced off their land by their creditors, permitted only purchase money mortgages, materialmen's liens for home improvement, and tax liens to encumber the homestead. Texas Constitution, Art. 16, § 50 (West 1993). In 1997 the lenders finally prevailed on a constitutional amendment to permit second mortgages, although it is chockablock with conditions and exceptions. Such mortgages became enforceable January 1, 1998. If we omit Texas from the calculation because of the legal impossibility of adding typical second mortgages to the property after it is purchased, the proportion of homeowners in the sample with two or more mortgages rises to a third.

87. People sometimes ask whether it is possible, or at least credible, that someone would have ten mortgages on a home. It is, of course, possible to record any number of mortgages on a home so long as the homeowner and the mortgagee agree to do so. It would be a rare lender, however, who would lend in a tenth position. Multiple mortgages are more likely to be the result of an entrepreneur offering the security of a mortgage against his or her home as part of a guarantee of business debt. In that case, the person is promising to pay the debt or lose their home, a promise that is valuable to a guarantor even if a foreclosure would not yield anything for the lender.

88. Calculation from Bureau of the Census, *American Housing Survey, 1991,* table 2.19.

89. Homeownership is usually about 15% of a credit score, with renters getting zero and homeowners getting full points. Sheldon Charrett, *The Modern Identity Changer: How to Create a New Identity for Privacy and Personal Freedom* (Boulder, Colo.: Paladin Press, 1997), 36. Analysts explain that an applicant who owns a home is more stable than one who rents, has a more sizable asset to protect, and is responsible for regular payments.

90. Borrowers report taking on second mortgages for a range of reasons, including home improvements, home purchase, debt consolidation, auto purchases, education, medical needs, and taxes. GAO analysis of Federal Reserve data from the 1989 Survey of Consumer Finances, reported in General Accounting Office, *Tax Policy,* 16, table 2.

91. Some debtors may use a second mortgage more strategically. In jurisdictions that limit the amount of the home equity that a debtor can protect in bankruptcy, multiple mortgages may actually be a benefit in the bankruptcy reckoning. The debtor under financial pressure who owns a home worth $75,000,

355

subject to a $35,000 mortgage, would have to declare home equity of $40,000 in a bankruptcy filing. In Illinois, Pennsylvania, and Tennessee, e.g., the debtor would have to sell the home, keep a predetermined portion of the value, and turn over the remaining value to the trustee in bankruptcy for distribution to all the creditors. The debtor who puts a second mortgage on the house, say for another $30,000, cuts the equity remaining in the house, so there need be no sale. Moreover, the debtor has $30,000 to spend—or to fend off bankruptcy or to pay out to a few preferred creditors while the remaining unsecured creditors get nothing. If bankruptcy comes, the debtor has both a first and second mortgage to pay off—but if the debtor can make the payments, the family home need not be sold.

92. There is no statistically significant difference between homeowners and non-homeowners on mentioning any family problem; no statistically significant difference between home owners and non-homeowners on mentioning any medical problem; and no statistically significant difference between homeowners and non-home owners on amount of credit card debt.

93. Calculated from the fact that homeowners are identified as 44.4% of our 1991 sample. As we indicated, however, this estimate is understated.

94. Calculated from 6.2% of the number of nonbusiness bankruptcies in 1997.

95. Bureau of the Census, "Keeping Up the Castle!" *Census and You* 29 (July 1994).

96. The difference is statistically significant.

97. Caplovitz, *Making Ends Meet,* 177, table 9.4.

98. The authors note that job loss can best be understood as the income lost either from unemployment or from the collapse of a small business. They observe a relationship "between business failures and residential mortgage foreclosure rates." Peter J. Elmer and Steven A. Seelig, "The Rising Long-Term Trend of Single-Family Mortgage Foreclosure Rates," FDIC Working Paper 98-2 (1996), 6.

99. Caplovitz also produced one confounding piece of evidence. He finds that homeowners are less stressed when they lose their jobs, which is certainly inconsistent with their increased likelihood that they are facing financial disaster. Caplovitz, *Making Ends Meet,* 177. He concludes that "homeownership does indeed lessen the pain for the unemployed." It may be that because Caplovitz interviewed a sample of homeowners generally rather than a sample of bankrupt homeowners that his data reflect the opening statistic in this chapter: fewer homeowners than renters file for bankruptcy. Perhaps homeowners are less likely to face the serious financial setback that lands them in bankruptcy, but for that smaller group experiencing an extended job loss that lands them in bankruptcy, the stress—financial and otherwise—is extraordinary. These bankrupt homeowners may simply have been outside his sample.

100. Renters moved at about twice the rate of homeowners in the four-year period 1985–89. *Housing Characteristics of Recent Movers: 1989,* Bureau of the Census, Current Housing Reports, Ser. H121/91-2 (Washington, D.C., 1991).

101. This section concentrates on the housing data available for African Americans and Hispanics. Generally, the data for these two groups is similar, while housing data for Asians follows different patterns, sometimes making them indistinguishable from whites and sometimes making them different from

all other groups. Although there are differences between Asians and other groups in general housing patterns, the bankruptcy data reveal no differences in housing data for Asians when compared with non-Asians. The bankruptcy finding, however, may be an artifact of the very low proportions of Asians in the bankruptcy sample, which makes statistical significance almost impossible to achieve. Only when Asians are combined with whites do differences among ethnic groups (whites and Asians compared with blacks and Hispanics) become statistically significant.

102. See Myers and Wolch, "Polarization of Housing Status," 305.

103. See ibid., 308. To give more texture to their discussions of housing circumstances, housing analysts developed the phrase "precariously housed." This includes all renters whose household incomes fall below 50% of their state median income levels but at least half of whose income is allocated to rent. A second tier of "precariously housed" individuals experiences overcrowding as well, with occupancy rates exceeding 1.5 per room. Ibid., 305.

104. Ibid., 308, table 4. Blacks and Hispanics are more likely to live in crowded conditions, with 2.9 and 4.1 residents per household, at the mean, than whites, with 2.6 residents per household. Elizabeth Sweet, "Roster Research Results from the Living Situation Survey" (typescript on file with authors).

105. See Myers and Wolch, "Polarization of Housing Status," 317.

106. Timothy S. Grall, *Our Nation's Housing in 1991,* Bureau of the Census, Current Housing Reports, Ser. H121/93-2 (Washington, D.C., 1993).

107. See Myers and Wolch, "Polarization of Housing Status," 278.

108. Young Hispanics form a larger fraction of the American Hispanic population, with those under age 35 comprising 38% of all Hispanic householders. Bureau of the Census, "Statistical Brief: Housing Changes, 1981 to 1991." Census Bureau experts speculate that both low homeownership rates and a relatively young adult population may result from immigration of Hispanics, which is concentrated among young adults. Whether these young Hispanics will eventually become homeowners is a matter for speculation. For now, it is only clear that with a younger population and a population less able to purchase homes, Hispanic Americans showed the greatest decline in homeownership among any ethnic or racial group.

109. See Myers and Wolch, "Polarization of Housing Status," 278.

110. See ibid., 297, table 2.

111. Oliver and Shapiro, *Black Wealth, White Wealth,* 18–22.

112. Other practices may also drive up the costs of home mortgages for African American and Hispanic American homeowners. A study by the Chicago Fair Housing Alliance, e.g., identified practices by which real estate agents steered minority buyers to minority neighborhoods and to buyers that specialized in higher-priced FHA loans. Bill Dedman, "Home Loans Discriminate, Study Shows," *New York Times,* May 13, 1998. There is some suggestion that insurance companies also redline, driving up the cost of homeowners' insurance for purchasers in some neighborhoods.

113. Bureau of the Census, "Statistical Brief: Household Wealth and Asset Ownership, 1991." The difference between black and Hispanic net worth nationally is not statistically significant.

114. Ibid. The Census Bureau makes this report only for households they

357

identify as white and as black; they do not give an equivalent report for Hispanic or Asian households. The most likely reason for the omission is that the data base may not have enough Hispanics and Asians for reliable inference. These data come from sample surveys, not from the whole census.

115. Ibid.

116. See Myers and Wolch, "Polarization of Housing Status," 287.

117. See ibid., 288. The relationship between black and Hispanic homeowners and white homeowners who suffer excessive payment burdens outside of bankruptcy is nearly identical to the relationship between black and Hispanic and white homeowners who identify problems with their homes as a reason for filing bankruptcy, with black and Hispanic homeowners listing such problems at about twice the rate of the remaining homeowners.

118. Reports calculated by indirect standardization using Grall, *Our Nation's Housing in 1991,* and data from the Consumer Bankruptcy Project Phase II.

119. With regard to the frequency of mentioning homeownership problems, there is no statistically significant difference in the bankruptcy sample for black households versus nonblack households or for Hispanic households versus non-Hispanic households, or for either group compared only with white households. Only when black and Hispanic debtors are combined and compared with non-black and non-Hispanic debtors do differences become statistically significant. Again, this may be a statistical quirk resulting from the relatively low number of debtors in each home-owning subgroup. When the two subgroups are combined and the number rises, it becomes somewhat easier to discern statistical significance.

120. As we noted earlier, there is no incentive for most homeowners to minimize the value of the home in California. State exemptions permit homeowners to shield $200,000 from their creditors in or out of bankruptcy. They would have lost nothing by valuing their home at any amount up to $315,254. It is impossible to know the value of the home without selling it, but the legal protection available increases the likelihood that the parties are giving their best assessment of the value of the homestead.

121. The number of homeowners in bankruptcy went from an estimated 165,000 in 1981 to an estimated 650,000 in 1996, an increase of 394%. Calculated from 1981 Consumer Bankruptcy Project and 1991 Consumer Bankruptcy Project and bankruptcy filing data from the Department of Justice, Administrative Office of the U.S. Courts.

### Chapter 8: The Middle Class in Debt

1. As of 1996, the Census Bureau reported 99.6 million households in the United States. Bureau of the Census, *Statistical Abstract of the United States: 1997* (Washington, D.C., 1997), 59, table 66.

2. See, e.g., Senate Judiciary Committee, *Personal Bankruptcy Credit Crisis,* Testimony of Sen. Chuck Grassley, Senate Judiciary Committee, Subcommittee on Administrative Oversight and the Courts, Apr. 11, 1997.

3. A comparison of our 1981 and 1991 data has shown that there is no statistically significant difference between the nonmortgage debt-income ratios of the two groups of debtors. Teresa A. Sullivan, Elizabeth Warren, and Jay Lawrence

Westbrook, "Consumer Debtors Ten Years Later: A Financial Comparison of Consumer Bankrupts, 1981–1991," *American Bankruptcy Law Journal* 68 (Spring 1994): 121, 136, table 2, and 138, table 3. This article reported on the three districts in the 1991 study that were also included in the 1981 study.

4. The *Wall Street Journal* estimated that one out of eight jobs lost in the United States between April and July 1998 was lost because of a merger. Business Bulletin, *Wall Street Journal*, Aug. 13, 1998, 1. That sort of job loss is particularly unexpected.

5. The job-loss aspect of this problem must importantly include the failure of small businesses. As we noted in Chapter 2, many small business people are in the bankruptcy sample, although relatively few of them cite the failures of their businesses as the cause of their bankruptcies. An employee may be fired or an owner-operated business may collapse. In either case, the family's income has disappeared while its debts continue to grow.

6. There were 341,189 nonbusiness bankruptcy filings in 1985, compared with 1,350,118 nonbusiness filings in 1997. Department of Justice, Administrative Office of the U.S. Courts.

7. William P. Kreml, *America's Middle Class: From Subsidy to Abandonment* (Durham, N.C.: Carolina Academic Press, 1997), 153–55; John E. Schwartz, *Illusions of Opportunity: The American Dream in Question* (New York: W. W. Norton, 1997), 145; Louis Uchitelle, "The Middle Class: Winning in Politics, Losing in Life," *New York Times,* July 19, 1998.

8. See Diane Ellis, "The Effect of Consumer Interest Rate Deregulation on Credit Card Volumes, Charge-offs, and the Personal Bankruptcy Rate," *Bank Trends* 98-05 (FDIC, Division of Insurance, March 1998); Juliet B. Schor, *The Overspent American: Upscaling, Downshifting, and the New Consumer* (New York: Basic Books, 1998), 83.

9. See data reported in figure 4.1.

10. See Schor, *Overspent American,* 72–73. This interesting study must be read with the understanding that her "Telecom" sample represents a slice of the middle class distinctly above average. Ibid., 200, table B.1.

11. George M. Salem and Aaron C. Clark, *Bank Credit Cards: Loan Loss Risks Are Growing,* GKM Banking Industry Report, June 11, 1996, 25.

12. See Ellis, "Effect of Consumer Interest Rate Deregulation."

13. Ibid.

14. Leading National Advertisers, Inc. (Arbitron), "Ad $ Summary," January–December 1991, 4. These are gross figures and no doubt include some commercial-loan advertisements and institutional ads as well. On the other hand, they probably do not include all the various sorts of money advertising. They likely give a reasonable approximation of the amount of money spent advertising money. More recent figures are hard to get because the information is now distributed only to customers who pay very large sums for them.

15. Website advertising in consumer shopping guides now includes click-on sites for more credit, enticing "Bad Credit, No Credit, Bankruptcy?" See <http://www.austin360.com/ogl-bin/eats/search.agi>.

16. The amount of consumer debt outstanding for October 1998 was $1,297.2 billion. <http:www.bog.frb.fed.us/Releases/G19/Current/> (Jan. 20, 1999).

17. These people were lumped into "general reasons" in our initial coding,

but we were struck by the force of their embarrassment. We went back through and counted. We found fewer than we had estimated, realizing that their candor and vivid language had made them seem more numerous than they were. In the end, 147 of our debtors blamed their own bad credit decisions for their bankruptcies. Perhaps 50% more made comments consistent with that focus, though not clearly enough to be included.

18. There are no national statistics on "irresponsible charging" to which we could compare our bankrupt debtors, as we compared them on divorce or job interruptions. The closest example is the Panel Study of Income Dynamics. See Chapter 3, note 66. But that study illustrates a recurring problem. The coded response stated: "Debts too high, [bills], credit card misuse." We feel quite sure that debts were too high for around 100% of the bankrupt debtors, so the inclusion of that phrase leaves the finding virtually useless. Bills may arise from wild dissipation or leukemia. To some extent, this sort of categorization, like the findings in a 1994 Canadian study may reflect the viewpoints of comfortably middle-class observers (like us). See note 19, below.

19. Iain Ramsay, "Individual Bankruptcy: Preliminary Findings of a Socio-Legal Analysis," *Osgoode Hall Law Journal* 37 (1999): 15. Canadian insolvency practitioners combine some of the functions performed by debtors' lawyers and by bankruptcy trustees in the United States. A survey of bankruptcy trustees in the United States would be similar, but the different roles might produce different biases, either way. In both cases, the judgments of these persons may or may not be too harsh or too lenient.

20. This phenomenon is the subject of Schor's book, in which she attributes the problem primarily to competitive spending but recognizes the enormous impact of advertising. See especially Schor, *Overspent American,* chap. 5.

21. The cost of salaries and other inputs to higher education institutions increased by almost 75 percent between 1985 and 1994. Bureau of the Census, *Statistical Abstract of the United States: 1996* (Washington, D.C., 1996), 185, table 286.

22. Ibid., 187, table 290.

23. Ibid., 186, table 288. Allen B. Crenshaw, "Meeting the Obligation of Rising Student Debt," *Washington Post,* May 17, 1998, reports that half of all students borrow, accumulating an average debt of $12,000 from public institutions and $14,000 from private institutions. Annual loan volume in 1996 was $32.4 billion (constant 1996 dollars). Delinquent student debt in the government portfolio amounts to $20.8 billion. Stephen Barr, "Treasury Takes Stock of Delinquent Debts," *Washington Post,* May 19, 1998.

24. H.R. 3150 proposes this solution, applied to anyone who makes at least 75% of the median family income in the United States. In 1995, that standard would have been applied to 65% of American families making $30,500 or more per year. Calculated from *Statistical Abstract: 1997,* 469, table 723.

25. Credit card banks have a return on assets that is double the return on assets of commercial banks. Federal Reserve Board, "The Profitability of Credit Card Operations of Depository Institutions" (August 1997); Lawrence M. Ausubel, "Credit Card Defaults, Credit Card Profits, and Bankruptcy," *American Bankruptcy Law Journal* 71 (Spring 1997): 249.

26. See, e.g., Lawrence M. Ausubel, "The Failure of Competition in the Credit Card Market," *American Economic Review* 81 (March 1991): 50.

27. Timothy J. O'Brien, "Lowering the Credit Fence: Big Players Are Jumping into the Risky Loan Business," *New York Times,* Dec. 13, 1997. There have been claims of nascent competition recently, which would greatly benefit the consumer and might even affect the bankruptcy rate. Some creditors are decrying this development. Jeff Bailey and Scott Kilman, "Marketplace: More Borrowers Appear to Be Wising Up About Credit," *Wall Street Journal,* Mar. 1, 1998.

28. James Medoff and Andrew Harless, *The Indebted Society: Anatomy of an Ongoing Disaster* (Boston: Little, Brown, 1996), 12.

29. Marianne B. Culhane and Michaela M. White, *Means-Testing for Chapter 7 Debtors: Repayment Capacity Untapped?* (Washington, D.C.: American Bankruptcy Institute, 1998), 1–8. For a more detailed discussion of this study, see Chapter 2 and Appendix II.

30. The comparative data reported here are collected from the Administrative Office of the U.S. Courts (U.S.), Federal Reserve Board (U.S.), Bureau of the Census (U.S.), Department of Trade and Industry, Statistics Directorate (England, Wales, and Scotland), Office for National Statistics (United Kingdom), Industry Canada, Office of the Superintendent of Bankruptcy (Canada); Statistics Canada (Canada); and Bank of Canada (Canada). The data reported here are collected and reported together with about 20 years of similar data from these countries as well as Finland, Australia, and New Zealand in Trent Craddock, O.S.B., "International Consumer Insolvency Statistics"(paper presented at Conference on the Contemporary Challenges of Consumer Bankruptcies in a Comparative Context, University of Toronto, Faculty of Law, Aug. 21–22, 1998).

361

31. Quoted in Charles Warren, *Bankruptcy in United States History* (Cambridge: Harvard University Press, 1935), 159.

32. Johanna Niemi-Kiesilainen, "Changing Directions in Consumer Bankruptcy Law and Practice Europe and USA," *Journal of Consumer Policies* 20, special issue (1997): 133.

33. Jacob Ziegel, "The Philosophy and Design of Contemporary Consumer Bankruptcy Systems: A Canadian-U.S. Comparison" (typescript, 8).

34. Ibid. Ziegel makes the Canadian-U.S. comparison: "Although the U.S. population is nine times greater than Canada's, our lifestyles are similar in many respects. Both countries have federal systems of government and private law rules based on common law concepts. Both have market driven economies. Both are very heavy users of consumer credit. Both have experienced an explosive growth in the number of consumer bankruptcies over the past 25 years. One difference between the two countries is that Canada has a significantly stronger social safety net than the U.S.—through the existence of a national medicare system, programmes of child support and support for single parents, paid maternity leave for new mothers, and better benefits of unemployed workers."

## Appendix 1: Data Used in This Study

1. For detailed methodology information from the earlier study, see Teresa A. Sullivan, Elizabeth Warren, and Jay Lawrence Westbrook, *As We Forgive Our Debtors: Bankruptcy and Consumer Credit in America* (New York: Oxford University Press, 1989), 342–54.

2. One bit of direct evidence about the stigma of consumer bankruptcy

comes from a study conducted by Roper Starch Worldwide for *Worth* magazine in 1993. In a survey of 2,000 adults, those who had ever declared bankruptcy (2% of the sample) were asked: "Please look over the list of feelings or reactions . . . and tell me which one best describes how you felt when you filed for personal bankruptcy." The responses "perfectly fine" and "no big deal" each drew 5% of the responses. Another 12% said they chose "a little upset." More than three-fourths — 76% — chose the response "just terrible" to describe their feelings about bankruptcy. From the electronic files for the Roper Center for Public Opinion Research. Our Business Bankruptcy Study, currently in the field, uses petition data followed by a phone call to the debtor. Even though we were able to schedule phone calls very close to the date of filing, we were still unable to locate a large number of the debtors. Moreover, even though the stigma attached to business bankruptcy is allegedly lower than that of consumer bankruptcy, many business debtors were not willing to speak with us.

3. In terms of the numbers of cases filed, Illinois ranked 19th with 42,710 bankruptcies, one for every 98 households. Texas, with 47,765 filings and one filing per 128 households, ranked 31st. And Pennsylvania, with 22,706 filings, or one for every 198 households, ranked 48th. Department of Justice, Administrative Office of the U.S. Courts, "Bankruptcy Statistical Information," March 1992, 8.

4. Philip Shuchman, "Social Science Research on Bankruptcy," *Rutgers Law Review* 43 (1990): 243–44.

5. Sullivan, Warren, and Westbrook, *As We Forgive*, 353–54, n. 1.

6. Ed Flynn, "Monthly Patterns in Bankruptcy Filings," *ABI Journal* 11 (May 1992), 24.

7. Bureau of the Census, *Statistical Abstract of the United States: 1992* (Washington, D.C., 1992), 471, table 738.

8. Data from the U.S. Bureau of Labor Statistics website. <http://www.146.142.4.24/cgi-bin/surveymost>. The index value for 1998 was 163.0.

9. Bureau of the Census, *Statistical Abstract: 1992,* 472, table 741.

10. Ibid., 472, table 742; 474–475, table 745.

11. Ibid., 473, table 743.

12. We used data from the Department of Justice, Administrative Office of the U.S. Courts, for counts of nonbusiness filings by district.

13. Sullivan, Warren, and Westbrook, *As We Forgive*, 345.

14. The standard deviation for the nonrespondents is 2.712, and for the respondents it is 4.197. The value of the t-test is −0.18, which has a significance probability of 0.854. We use a probability level of 0.05 or less as our criterion for significance.

15. For Texas and Illinois respondents, the total debt-income ratio was 2.324 with a standard deviation of 2.118. The equivalent data for the nonrespondents are a ratio of 2.906 with a standard deviation of 2.712; the t-value is 1.69. For the nonmortgage debt-income ratio, the Texas and Illinois respondents had a ratio of 1.522 with a standard deviation of 1.963, compared with a ratio of 1.292 and a standard deviation of 1.519 for the nonrespondents. The t-value is −1.07.

16. Teresa A. Sullivan, Elizabeth Warren, and Jay Lawrence Westbrook, "Consumer Debtors Ten Years Later: A Financial Comparison of Consumer Bankrupts, 1981–1991," *American Bankruptcy Law Journal* 68 (Spring 1994): 121–54.

17. Sullivan, Warren, and Westbrook, *As We Forgive*, 77, n. 77. The 17 debtors eliminated as outliers because of their debt levels would have raised the mean debt for all debtors by $12,100 per debtor. Ibid., 78.

18. "When we look at some batches of values, we see certain values as apparently straying out far beyond the others. In other batches straying is not so obvious, but our suspicions are aroused. It is convenient to have a rule of thumb that picks out certain values as 'outside' or 'far out.'" John W. Tukey, *Exploratory Data Analysis* (Reading, Mass.: Addison-Wesley, 1977), 43–44. The computer package, SPSS for the Macintosh, permitted us to identify both "outside" and "far out" cases. The set of "far out" cases was virtually identical with the cases identified by using our earlier 1981 data.

19. Statement of Randall J. Newsome, House Judiciary Subcommittee on Commercial and Administrative Law, Mar. 17, 1999.

20. Michelle J. White, "Why It Pays to File for Bankruptcy: A Critical Look at the Incentives Under U.S. Personal Bankruptcy Law and a Proposal for Change," *University of Chicago Law Review,* 65 (Summer 1998): 685–732.

## Appendix 2: Other Published Studies

1. General Accounting Office, "Personal Bankruptcy: Analysis of Four Reports on Chapter 7 Debtors' Ability to Pay" GAO/GGD-99-103 (June 1999). The authors of the reviewed studies also had the opportunity to place responses in this document, and the GAO rejoined.

2. Gordon Bermant and Ed Flynn, Executive Office of U.S. Trustees, *Incomes, Debts, and Repayment Capacities of Recently Discharged Chapter 7 Debtors* (Washington, D.C., January 1999).

3. John M. Barron and Michael E. Staten, *Personal Bankruptcy: A Report on Petitioners' Ability to Pay* (Washington, D.C.: Credit Research Center, Georgetown University, Oct. 7, 1997). Additional statements are Michael E. Staten, "A Profile of Debt, Income and Expenses of Consumers in Bankruptcy," Testimony before the National Bankruptcy Review Commission, Washington, D.C., Dec. 17, 1996 (reporting on 2,252 Chapter 7 and 1,115 Chapter 13 debtors); Michael Staten, "Repayment Capacity of Consumers in Bankruptcy," Testimony before the National Bankruptcy Review Commission, Jan. 23, 1997 (reporting on 2,207 Chapter 7 debtors); Michael Staten, "Repayment Capacity of Consumers Who Seek Bankruptcy Relief," Senate Judiciary Subcommittee on Administrative Oversight and the Courts, Apr. 11, 1997 (reporting on 2,380 Chapter 7 debtors). These additional statements appear to be based upon the same database, but the reason for the changing number of cases is not clear.

4. General Accounting Office, *Personal Bankruptcy: The Credit Research Center Report on Debtors' Ability to Pay,* GAO/GGD-98-47 (Washington, D.C., Feb. 9, 1998). This publication also contains a response from the study's authors, Michael Staten and John Barron.

5. Purdue University, Credit Research Center, Krannert Graduate School of Management, *Consumer Bankruptcy Study,* 2 vols. (1982).

6. Teresa A. Sullivan, Elizabeth Warren, and Jay Lawrence Westbrook, "Limiting Access to Bankruptcy Discharge: An Analysis of the Creditors' Data," *Wisconsin Law Review* 1983 (October 1983): 1091–1146.

7. Ernst & Young, "Chapter 7 Bankruptcy Petitioners' Ability to Repay: The National Perspective, 1997," Ernst & Young, May 11, 1998; Ernst & Young, "Chapter 7 Bankruptcy Petitioners' Repayment Ability Under H.R. 853: The National Perspective," Ernst & Young, March 1999. We also read Tom Neubig and Fritz Scheuren with Gautam Jaggi and Robin Lee, "Chapter 7 Bankruptcy Petitioner's Ability to Repay: Additional Evidence from Bankruptcy Petition Files," Policy Economics and Quantitative Analysis Group, Ernest & Young LLP, February 1998. This study is based on 5,722 Chapter 7 petitions filed in 1992 and 1993 in four cities: Boston, Chicago, Los Angeles, and Nashville.

8. General Accounting Office, *Personal Bankruptcy: The Credit Research Center and Ernst & Young Reports on Debtors' Ability to Pay,* GAO/T-GGD-98-79 (Washington, D.C., Mar. 12, 1998). The GAO report commented on two of the studies as follows: "The assumptions, data, and sampling procedures used in the [Credit Research] Center report and February 1998 Ernst & Young report raise questions concerning the accuracy of the reports' estimates and require the reader to use caution in interpreting the types of firm conclusions stated therein. Neither report provides reliable answers to the questions of how many debtors could make some repayment and how much debt they could repay." See also GAO/T-GGD-98-76 (testimony of Richard Stana before the Senate Judicuary Committee, Subcommittee on Administrative Oversight and the Courts, Mar. 11, 1997).

9. Tom Neubig, Gautan Jaggi, and Robin Lee, "Ernst & Young: Chapter 7 Bankruptcy Petitioners' Repayment Ability Under H.R. 833: The National Perspective" *American Bankruptcy Institute Law Review* 7 (Spring 1999): 79–117.

10. Marianne B. Culhane and Michaela M. White, "Taking the New Consumer Bankruptcy Model for a Test Drive: Means-Testing Real Chapter 7 Debtors" *American Bankruptcy Institute Law Review* 7 (Spring 1999): 27–28. A critique of this study was issued by the National Association of Federal Credit Unions: Lisa Ryu, "American Bankruptcy Institute's Study Flawed, NAFCU Analysts Revealed," NAFCU press release, Jan. 15, 1999. The critique alleges, among other flaws, that there was a selection bias in the districts studied. A response by White was summarized in "Between the Lines: Advantage, ABI," *Credit Union Regulatory Insider,* Jan. 18, 1999, 1–2.

11. General Accounting Office, *Personal Bankruptcy: Methodological Similarities and Differences in Three Reports on Debtors' Ability to Pay,* GAO/T-GGD-99–58 (Washington, D.C., Mar. 17, 1999).

12. SMR Research Corporation, *The Personal Bankruptcy Crisis, 1997: Demographics, Causes, Implications, and Solutions* (Hackettstown, N.J.: SMR Research Corporation, 1997). Related studies by SMR include *Credit Cards, 1996: Managing Through the Growth Paradigm* (Budd Lake, N.J.: SMR Research, 1996), and *The Personal Bankruptcy Crisis: A 2 1/2 Year Study* (Budd Lake, N.J.: SMR Research, 1992).

13. Visa USA, "Consumer Bankruptcy: Causes and Implications" (July 1996).

14. George M. Salem and Aaron C. Clark, "Bank Credit Cards: Loan Loss Risks Are Growing, Personal Bankruptcies a Major Catalyst," Gerard Klauer Mattison and Co., June 11, 1996, 30.

15. Susan D. Kovac, "Judgment-Proof Debtors in Bankruptcy," *American Bankruptcy Law Journal* 65 (1991): 675–767.

16. Gary Klein and Maggie Spade, "Self-Representation in the Bankruptcy

Court: The Massachusetts Experience" (typescript, Boston: National Consumer Law Center).

17. Ibid., table 3.

18. Ibid., table 1.

19. Ian Domowitz and Robert L. Sartain, "Determinants of the Consumer Bankruptcy Decision" (typescript, January 1997). The sample is described further in General Accounting Office, "Bankruptcy Reform Act of 1978: A Before and After Look," GAO/GGD-83-54 (Washington, D.C., 1983). Some other papers include Ian Domowitz and Elie Tamer, "Two Hundred Years of Bankruptcy: A Tale of Legislation and Economic Fluctuations" (typescript, May 1997); and Ian Domowitz, "Statement," to the Senate Judiciary Committee Subcommittee on Administrative Oversight and the Courts, Apr. 11, 1997 (arguing no statistical role for the impact of 1978 legal changes on the filing rate and arguing that claims that the filing rate is no longer affected by the business cycle are unwarranted).

20. Michael J. Herbert and Domenic E. Pacitti, "Down and Out in Richmond, Virginia: The Distribution of Assets in Chapter 7 Bankruptcy Proceedings Closed During 1984–1987," *University of Richmond Law Review* 22 (1988): 303–23.

21. Oliver B. Pollak, "Gender and Bankruptcy: An Empirical Analysis of Evolving Trends in Chapter 7 and Chapter 13 Bankruptcy Filings, 1967–1997," *Commercial Law Journal* 102 (Fall 1997): 333–38.

22. Philip Shuchman, "New Jersey Debtors, 1982–83: An Empirical Study," *Seton Hall Law Review* 15 (Summer 1985): 542–892; Philip Shuchman, "The Average Bankrupt: A Description and Analysis of 753 Personal Bankruptcy Filings in Nine States," *Commercial Law Journal* 88 (June–July 1983): 288–307; Philip Shuchman and Thomas L. Rhorer, "Personal Bankruptcy Data for Opt-Out Hearings and Other Purposes," *American Bankruptcy Law Journal* 56 (Winter 1982): 1–28.

23. David T. Stanley and Marjorie Girth, *Bankruptcy: Problem, Process, Reform* (Washington, D.C.: Brookings Institution, 1971).

24. For a review of these studies, see Ramona K. Z. Heck, "Identifying Insolvent Households," *Journal of Home Economics* 72, no. 4 (1980): 14–17; and Teresa A. Sullivan, Elizabeth Warren, and Jay L. Westbrook, "Bankruptcy and the Family," *Marriage and Family Review* 21, nos. 3–4 (1995): 194–215.

# Index

References to illustrations and tables are in italics

368

Craddock, Trent, 360n30
Credit: availability postbankruptcy, 322n47; democratization of, 136; difficult to estimate, 319n20. *See also* Consumer credit
*Credit Card Crunch,* 300n25
Credit card debt: as absorbing all consumer credit, 245; availability, 130, 134, 136–37; in bankruptcy, 321n45, 323n53; compared with debt-income ratios, Visa estimates, 325n66; credit solicitations, 324n61, 329n106; debt-income ratios, 319n19; different from other consumer lending, 245; families with defaults, 137; as fraction of income, 124; growth *1980–95,* 123, 324n60; growth among low-income families, 136–37; increase as cause of bankruptcy, 245; market saturation, 134; median balance, 123; minimum payment, 247; per household, 135; profitability, 135–36, 329n98; reaffirmation estimates, 322n48; revenue from interest, 135; small businesses, 320nn25,37; students, 329n110; subprime lending, 329n100; substitution for other debt, 130; understated, 318n14, 323n55
Credit card debt in bankruptcy: amount listed, 119–20; compared with credit card debt generally, 122; comparisons *1981–97,* 121–22; correlations with reasons for filing bankruptcy, 120; effects of high interest, 127; effects of unemployment, 140; estimated total, 323n51; as fraction of income, 125; growth *1981–97,* 122, 124, 131, 326n75; growth in debt-to-income ratio *1981–97,* 126; interest payments, 325n71, 326n72; *1997* California data, 120; number of debtors owing, 122–23; payment obligations, 325n70, 326n71; as proportion of debt, 131; proportion of debtors with debt over $20,000, 123; rate of increase, 121–22; rise related to consumer debt in Canada, 327n82; underreporting, 120–21; understated, 321n40, 324n63; Visa estimates, 322n49, 323n52; vulnerability to employment problems, 140
*Credit Card Defaults, Credit Card Profits, and Bankruptcy,* 327nn80,83, 329n98, 360n25
*Credit Card Industry Outlook Growing More Gloomy,* 328n94
Credit cards, 18–19, 108–40, 294, 300n25;

access for low-income families, 111; amortization of debt, 112; average interest rate, 319n15; continuing growth, 136; cost to acquire new accounts, 328n94; debt by income levels, 110; debt per household, 110; extension of new credit after warning signs, 115; history of development, 109–10; marketing, entrepreneurs, 117; number in circulation, 135; purchases exceed $1 trillion, 108; small business use, 115; solicitation, cost, 135; solicitation, number, 135; spending outstrips cash, 108; subprime lending, 320n25; 34 years to pay off, 112; time to pay off debt, 112; use among Hispanic Americans, 318n11; use by entrepreneurs, 117
*Credit Cards Bankrolling Small Firms,* 320n30
*Credit Cards, 1996: Managing Through the Growth Paradigm,* 364n12
Credit industry: lack of competitive interest rates, 254; prosperity, 254; relation between costs and rates, 255
Credit Research Center, 289, 363n65
Credit scoring, effect of homeownership, 355n89
Credit solicitations: cost to acquire new accounts, 328n94; growth, 324n61; students, 329n110; targeting low-income families, 325n64
Credit standards: lowering, 135
Credit systems and safety nets, 257; dependents in divorce, 344n61; divorce, 342n40; rise in bankruptcy filings correlates with rise in consumer debt, 327n82; single-parent families, 340n27; studies, 184
Creditors, 9, 11, 12, 68
Crenshaw, Allen B., 359n23
Culhane, Marianne, 67, 289, 310, 360n29, 364n10
*Current Issues in Economics and Finance,* 327n80
Current population survey, 282

Danko, William D., 301n8
Data collection, 263–64, 273
Davis, Nancy J., 301n3
*Day the Credit Card Was Born, The,* 318n8
Debt, 11, 66–67, 69–70; availability, 130, 134, 136–37; and bankruptcy, Congressional Budget Office findings, 129–30;

371

372

373

375

377

378

379

380